ADDICTION

...One Man's...
ROAD TO RECOVERY

~~~~~~

GETTING CLEAN & STAYING CLEAN

STORMY LEE MONDAY

FINDING THE WAY

The Library of Congress has cataloged the soft cover edition as follows:
Title; ADDICTION One Man's Road to Recovery ©
The text of this book is set in Calibri light font, 11 pica
Content 428 pages... 2015

Summary: One man's incredible journey through chaos and self-destruction.
Struggling through a near life-long battle to overcome the deadly disease of addiction.
Finally, finding the way and learning to help the next suffering addicts.
If you're suffering... this book is for you.

Monday, Stormy Lee
ADDICTION... One Man's Road to Recovery, Stormy Monday
ISBN- 978- 0- 578- 51888- 6   paperback- 2020

MANUFACTURED IN THE UNITED STATES OF AMERICA

BookBaby

TABLE OF CONTENTS

ADDICTION
"One Man's Road to Recovery"
Stormy Lee Monday

Remarkable, Stormy! This book is as REAL as it gets! It's so hard to put down! It keeps you wanting to read more and more throughout the entire book. Everyone needs to read this, whether you're affected by addiction or not. After losing my son, Alan Vaughn, at age 24, to an overdose, reading this, for me was an emotional, eye-opening experience. It actually put me in his shoes. Recovering addicts are warriors... keep fighting the Fight!

Wendy McCready, Co-founder
Fight the Fight against Addiction

CALM BEFORE THE STORM BY STORMY MONDAY

~<>~

INTRODUCTION

Enter with me a world unlike any other. Completely real and shocking. This is the world of active addiction. Cold, ruthless, brutal and unforgiving. The chaos, self-destruction, pain and misery it inflicts on families are devastating. Addiction's not a game. It may start out as an innocent, fun, good time with friends, but, for way too many, this nightmare slips in unannounced and flips lives upside down. People die every day because of addiction. Many deny there's even a problem, right up to the moment of their death.

This is a story of hope. Much of the underlying message of recovery in the latter pages are the collective wisdom of, not only my life mistakes, but, also, the wisdom of all the members of Narcotics Anonymous, past and present. Narcotics Anonymous is a 12-step program that's saved and continues to save, countless, hundreds of thousands, if not, millions of lives all over the world in many languages. The disease of addiction is both cunning and baffling. Many, many decades of life experiences have taught me that every person is different. We really are. But, when an addict is willing to go to any length necessary to find recovery, NA works. I know this first-hand, because, N A works for me. I accept the reality that what works for some may not work for others. For example, A A, although it works for many, many alcoholics, it doesn't work for me. I'm an addict. If I've learned anything, I've learned this, judging heals no one. So, for the sake of being open-minded and understanding, please embrace all who are trying to reach their full potential, no matter their particular path to get there. This story must be told to help as many addicts as possible find a new and better way to live without drugs, including alcohol. It's important to show how clever addiction can slip in and without warning or remorse, turn an otherwise normal life completely upside down. It wove itself into the fabric of my being and changed my path, my psyche, my behavior and my future. I did not share all the insanity in my past. I did, however, skim across enough to show my spiral downward and the long journey through hell, to get back to a purpose-filled life worth living. My objective is to help all affected by addiction to understand better the inner-workings of the mind of an addict in active addiction.

It's been said many times, a grateful addict will not use. I've grown to believe that. If you believe there's no hope for you anymore and your life is so destroyed, you don't see any way out, I dedicate the information inside these pages to YOU.

Stormy Lee Monday
Author/ artist/ hope dealer

Trust me, you'll lose everything …
and your soul will die.
Sincerely,
Heroin, cocaine, meth, booze, pills, etc....

STORIES FROM THE STREETS

Mingo Agin & Stormy Monday
If nothing changes...nothing changes.

~<>~

This book is for suffering addicts, their families & friends.
All over the world.
In loving memory of those now gone.

Chapter 1

Here's my story...

THE PREACHER'S SON

Summer 1963... Middle Tennessee...

HELP ME!!! Please, help me! Help me! Help me! I could hear myself scream it inside my head, but, the sound wouldn't come out of my mouth. I couldn't move. Deep sleep had devoured me and fear was squeezing the constraints of my brain, choking out my ability for conscious sound. Panic had taken over. I was frozen in terror. Another paralysis dream had consumed me, on the couch, in the back room of our home. That's where I slept.

We lived under an old viaduct, just down a short alley to Ike Brown's junk yard. It was next to some train tracks. This happened around 3 in the morning on another hot and sweaty night. An evil entity with cold black eyes was hovering over me, pressing down on my chest like concrete, with big, ugly crushing hands. His long fingernails were digging into my shoulders so hard, it felt like sharp knives stabbing into my 11 year old body. Huge demon eyes were inches from my face and piercing through every inch of me, holding me in place, frozen in fear. I couldn't move or scream for what seemed like an eternity. I couldn't even take a breath. PANICKED and trying desperately to fill my lungs with any semblance of air, trying desperately to make any part of my body move, I was literally about to explode from this invasion of my unconscious thought. Inside my mind, manic shock raced through me and finally, after what seemed like forever, my body broke free. My eyes popped opened and I screamed as loud as I could. My heart was beating out of my chest and I was covered in sweat. Quicker than jumping Jack Flash, I sprang from the couch to my feet, into pitch darkness. As I felt blood trickling from the new scratches on my shoulders, I was speechless.

Next door to this home was a dilapidated structure, grown-over by shrubs and bush. Inside lived an elderly black lady named Jessie, who hardly ever left her home. A mysterious black man would set a brown paper bag filled with food on what was left of her porch, usually, about once a week. One day I was playing under the viaduct and I saw her outside. That was a rare sight, so, I said hi to her. She nodded and seemed friendly enough, so, I asked her why she rarely came outside. She said she'd lived in that home over 60 years and got used to staying inside. I asked her why she'd do that. It didn't make any sense to me. She said, "You being young, my neighbor and all, I probably shouldn't tell you this story, but, I think I've been holding it inside for a long time. I don't talk to very many people at all. But, since you asked me, if you've got a few minutes, I'll just go ahead. I nodded my head to say, sure, go ahead. "Well, in the late 1800's, when I was just a little girl, before this viaduct was even here, something terrible happened back there in the woods, and I was scared about it for years. It keeps running through my head just about every day. Even now. Some nights I still have bad dreams about it. I was always afraid somebody would find out that I'd saw it happen. Lord, I didn't want that. Well, one night, the sun was just going down and I was playing in the woods, behind the houses. My momma and I would pick blackberries over there a lot. I was in the bushes when I saw two white men ride up on a wagon pulled by a big black horse. They stopped, jumped off and pulled this black man out of the back of the wagon. They drug him over to that big tree, kicking and beating him the whole way. I laid there in the bushes by myself, real quiet, and watched. I didn't move an inch. Let me tell you, I was scared to death. They were beating on him something terrible. I almost screamed when I saw them take a rope out of that wagon. I watched them hang that black man from that big tree. He was begging them not to hang him, saying he was innocent. He had chains locked around his hands and legs, so, he couldn't get away. Those men were screaming that he'd raped some white girl and now, he had to pay. They left and he shook for a minute, then, he was just hanging there. I screamed after they left and my momma came out and seen him. She got some friends to cut him down. I told them I didn't see nothing. I didn't want them to come and hang me, too". My mouth dropped open and I couldn't say a word. I was dumbfounded. I'd never heard anything like this before.

8

The huge tree she was talking about, sat out by the woods behind our home, near our outhouse. She said after that she stayed in the house to keep from being hurt by those men. Then, as she grew older, being inside made her feel safer. So, she'd gotten used to staying in the house.

Jessie asked me if I'd ever heard anybody in chains going up and down our stairs to the attic. The question surprised me because my mother, father, sisters and I, did hear that often. We had even watched those stairs and heard the chains being pulled up, and no one would be there. One night my mother was awakened by a dark entity choking her in the bed. She then showed us the actual scratches on her neck. Maybe the unhappy spirit of a murdered black man haunted our home. We lived there for many years. The sound of chains being pulled up the stairs never stopped.

Sunday morning, a year or so later...
Middle Tennessee...

Mt. Olive Southern Baptist was an old country church off Rock Creek Road. Nestled on a Tennessee hillside, it was surrounded by tall sprawling oaks and gorgeous red maples. A century-old cemetery wrapped almost all the way around the property to the left of the church. It even had soldiers from the Civil War buried in it. Honeysuckle laid like flowering blankets over the fence-lines around the newly mowed graveyard. You could smell the fresh cut grass as it lingered in the warm breeze.

Mt. Olive held about eighty church-goers. There was nothing architecturally fancy about the old church. The outside had a coat of aged white paint and a tall steeple. Inside, it was a big open room with stain-glass windows, usually full of worshippers. There was an old-time pulpit and an old black piano up in the front on the right. Jesse, an elderly, disabled man with a hump-back and a dedicated Christian, drove his 1960 Station wagon up the winding dirt road and parked by the fence, near the graveyard. As he slowly made his way inside, through the beautiful purple Iris flowers blooming around the front door, he noticed it was packed inside, like it always was. Most of those 'country folk' he knew, for one reason or another. They'd been there many times before. It was a church full of Tennessee Christians praising God. Except for a few of the more crippled elders,

9

they were all standing and singing the last verse of "The Old Rugged Cross" as the old man with the broken posture looked for a seat.

He finally found the last empty seat in the back row and sat down as the song ended. Jesse tried not to miss church when Brother Monday was preaching. This well-dressed young preacher everyone called Brother Monday, began the service, like all his sermons, with a song and a prayer. He was a small-framed man, but, the wages of sin, fire and brimstone, mixed with the word of God erupted from his mighty soul when he preached. Holding the King James Version of the Holy Bible in his right hand high in the air, he ran from behind the pulpit all the way to the back of the church, preaching the word of God all the way. Brother Monday was usually a soft-spoken man, but, he could just about scare the sin out of you when he was filled with the Holy Spirit.

On the front row sat his beautiful wife, Barbara, and their six children, one ten year old boy and five younger sisters. As brother Monday, a very strict disciplinarian and Korean War combat veteran turned preacher, made his way back to the pulpit, he stopped in front of his family, turned and gazed deeply into his son's eyes... those were my eyes. He pointed to the long bench in front of the pulpit like it was the resurrection. "You better go up there and get on your knees. You ask God to forgive you for your sins, or, you will burn in a lake of fire for eternity! Those are not my words, brothers and sisters." He paused and looked around at the entire church congregation and continued, "In the book of Revelations, Chapter 20 and verse 15... And whosoever was not found written in the book of life was cast into the lake of fire." he screamed it out wiping the sweat from his brow with a white handkerchief. His piercing eyes turned back to me and I felt the gaze of the whole church on me. Brother Monday waved the Bible in the air as the church filled with "Hallelujah! Amen brother Monday, amen." My dad, filled with conviction, made his way back to the pulpit. He was filled with the Holy Spirit as he opened the bible and not missing a beat, shouted, "Now, on down to Chapter 21, verse 6 in Revelations... "I am Alpha and Omega. The beginning and the end." The congregation hung on brother Monday's fury in every single word. I was terrified.

After church, 1963- front row, L- Sisters, Barb, Jackie, Susie, June and Markie

Back row- son Stormy Lee and dad- Southern baptist preacher- Brother Virgil Monday

20 years later... April 7th, 1983...
Peoria, Illinois...

EMPTY VESSEL

"Dammit!!! I blacked out again."
When I finally came to, my tangled hair was pressed against a toilet bowl. Through the narrow slits in my eyes, my vision was struggling for any sense of clarity.

Confusion choked me like an enemy in the night. I felt disoriented and nasty. Nausea swept through me, strangling my urge to breathe. The darkness had left and in its place were tiny streaks of light trying desperately to seep in. With that light came bits and pieces of reality. "Noooo..." I gasped. "Let me go. Just let me go, man. Sick of this shit."

Then, just as quickly, I passed out again. Nodded out. I was unconscious to the world around me. Surrounded by a black space of nothingness. It was unforgiving, like deadly fog in the early morn. I was lost in total darkness. Caught between a world of constant turmoil and a blatant hollow emptiness that consumed me without mercy.

11

Being so wasted is unforgiving! It's hard on the body and it tortures the mind with some sick, twisted level of psychosis that chokes the sanity out of an otherwise normal human being.

The soul, well, the soul, eventually, it all becomes too much and the soul dies. Gone. It's no longer there. In its place is a dark and empty hole.

I was hot, sick and empty. My skin was pale, cold and clammy. "Smells like vomit in here." I thought to myself. That was the muggy stench that lingered around me, turning the stale air into a nasty musk.

I looked around and realized I was in my own bathroom at home, but, right then, I didn't care where I was. I was miserable. "Way too high. Damn! So, I blacked out again." I thought.

For how long, I didn't know. "How many days and nights has it been?" I wondered. My hair was streaked with nasty, dried sweat and my beard felt stuck to my face. Like it had some off-brand sticky glue in it. I felt bad, really bad, like I was used-up and greasy. Inside me was a soul with no hope left. I'd forgotten how to care. There was dry vomit on my pants and down the front of my worn-out Harley shirt. The one with burns all over it, from me, existing in a constant dead nod. See, I was shooting heroin every day. The fact that I had heroin to shoot right now was all that mattered. Heroin, the rigs and the cocaine. Because of my addiction, that's all I cared about. The foul stench in the air emanated. On the edge of the sink was a bent-up spoon, part of a ball of cotton and a syringe. There was dry blood in that syringe. "Now, it's coming to me." I sat down on the stool and my head slowly fell into a nod. I started thinking to myself.

"That's my blood in the rig. Damn." I fell into a deep nod. My mind drifted into lingering thoughts. "This is a long way from Hawaii. Man, where'd the time go, back when I was a kid... in Tennessee." I was in a deep nod, so, my mind kept drifting through past memories. "Seems like yesterday I was playing in Ike Brown's junk yard. Wow. Sitting in church watching dad preach from that old leather-bound Bible, seems like he was preaching all the time. He could sure thump that Bible, though... ol' dad. Damn, I'm high. Ta fuck is wrong with me? My life's a damn mess."

Well, it was. I mean, here's the truth of it. In this time of my life, had there been a way to walk inside my head, had there been a way to take an elevator down into the reservoirs of where my soul once was... you'd be standing in a deep and miserable spot, alone in a long, dark hallway leading to nowhere. Simply put, that's where I was. I was lost. I existed with a complete absence of self. There was a great big hole in my soul and my ability to love anyone, including myself, had taken the last train to Georgia and hey, I'm not from Georgia. I was empty.

Ten years of active addiction had beat the hell out of me. Ever since I'd shot that first hit of China White heroin, back in Hawaii. That was ten years ago! Wow! It slipped in on me, somehow, it crept up. "How the hell did this happen?" Finally coming out of the nod, I shook my head in dismay and frustration. Time for another hit.

(Here's how it unfolds... so cunning. Everything starts out as fun and good times for almost everybody. We don't know that some of us are, most assuredly, addicts on a path to pain and misery. That never enters our thinking. I mean it's just good innocent fun, right? You get caught in the flow and the vibe of it all. The days and nights seem to run together. You don't notice at first. The party lifestyle kicks it up a notch. Things and people along the way, all somehow, magically merge together and begin to flow into a stream of effortless laughter and good times. Then, a circle of supposed friends are formed. The party clan. As time passes, most of those will, one by one, fall by the wayside. The few that are left are true friends. It may only be one. It's literally baffling. Almost everybody you surround yourself with are cool as hell and full of fun, with good intentions. Right? I mean, birds of a feather do flock together. Well, while all this is happening, not one single soul among the group are thinking for a second about anything becoming sinister. No one has the foresight to imagine something swooping in from the darkness and snatching them from an otherwise normal and fun-filled life. Realize, this doesn't happen to everyone that parties. Fun is fun, after all.
Be cognizant of this fact... Not everyone is an addict, or, will be an addict.

But, for way too many, like a deadly shadow in the night, the relentless clutches of addiction sneak up and slip inside all that is good in the potentially amazing world you've been creating. Be aware! Addiction will leave you destroyed, with less than nothing, without remorse, kill everybody in its wake and leave total destruction, misery and chaos all along the way. There are signs to be aware of and we'll discuss those.)

Like me, I'd sunk so far beyond despair, I didn't see any way back. The drugs had taken me over. The black hole was too dark and somehow, somewhere, along the way, it had crept up on me again. You'd think I'd learn by now. I'd be more cued in, more street smart. But, no. This demon called active addiction, or, now in 2020 the current trending term is, substance use disorder, well, call it what you want, it's very cunning and it's down-right clever. Now, here I am, 1983, in too deep all over again. Even worse, inside my weary soul, there was less than nothing, just like before. I promised myself I'd never come here again. But, I couldn't make myself stop. I wasn't even a person anymore. Not inside this empty shell.

Think about that. I wasn't living in my own life anymore. I don't remember how, or, when that happened. It slipped up on me like a cunning thief and, literally, stole me away from myself. I didn't know where to find me. I didn't even know where to look. My wife had checked out of our marriage a few years back. I was so focused on the dope, I hadn't even processed that yet. I didn't even feel the slap across my face. In the midst of losing myself, I'd lost a good woman and worst of all, I'd lost my precious children, too. My two incredibly talented children, Misty and Jesse, didn't know me anymore. Daddy had smothered them with pure love the first few years of their lives. So, this had to be horrible for them. They needed their daddy. The one they'd grown to love so much. They didn't even realize how much their daddy needed them, too.

But, I'd left myself and in doing so, I'd left them, too, in the carnage and the chaos.

They were children. This was on me. They didn't do anything wrong. Not one thing. My friends were disappearing, one by one, and were all but gone. Even most of the addicts I was shooting dope with were all overdosing, dying, in jail, gone to prison, or, just gone. My life was far too complicated for any of them. Hell, it was too complicated for me. I was an emotionally wreck. I felt helpless and hopeless. Hope, for me, had left long go.

I didn't understand it. Here I was, captured by a powerful, dark and deadly demon. Maybe it was that same demon that used to haunt me in my dreams as a child. The one that used to hold me down in my sleep and choke the hell out of me. The one that wouldn't let me move and I'd panic, freak out and finally scream when I woke up. Who knows? All I know for sure is this. This unforgiving beast was trapped inside my soul and it was choking the life out of me. No matter where I went, there it was. The self-destructive clutches of this suicidal evil had gripped me like a vice and it refused to let me go. I still had those horrible dreams, too. Have you ever had a paralysis dream? You'd know. They are by far the worst tormenting nightmares forced inside the human mind that I've ever experienced. These dark forces guided me into an endless black hole and for the life of me, I didn't know how to dig out. I didn't know why I couldn't stop using. That's really it right there. That's the thing. There's a secret insanity that grabs us in the midst of it all and we don't want to admit it to anybody. We don't want to look weak. We don't want anyone to think we're so caught up in it that we can't handle it. Inside, we're freaking out, but, no way would we say anything. That's why we go away, we disappear, we isolate. The shame of it all consumes us. We've lost the grip on our sense of reason. This is the unfortunate reality of the situation. It's a harsh and brutal truth that, many times, leads to an overdose and for way too many, death. Somewhere, along the way, that deep, black hole got deeper and deeper for me and now, here I am. Alone in hell. I just didn't see any way out of this. Not this time for sure. Not with all this dope I had. Not with these bags filled with pure Colombian coke (in the streets we called it girl) and brown Mexican heroin (boy) laying here in front of me. I knew deep down this was probably it. This time it was going to do me in. It didn't seem to matter to me, though. Not really. I was way too caught up in it. Dying would've been easier. "At least I have a new bag of rigs." I thought.

Even knowing death was at the door didn't stop me.

"Yep, this shit's pure. It's going to do me in." That thought poured from my head like blood gushing from an open wound. Active addiction was choking the life out of me. I felt empty and alone. Just a mere shell of who I thought I'd someday be. This ain't that guy.

That's for sure. But, I didn't care about any of that. Not right now. My soul was an empty vestibule. I walked across the hall to the bedroom in front of me. On the bed were more used, bloody rigs, scattered everywhere. All I could do was shake my head as my memory poured over the last few days through this dirty shot-glass of empty despair.

"Damn man!"

But, on the other hand, on the flip side, and at the same time, I had this other voice in me, eerily excited. "Look at all that dope you've got! That next shot's going to feel good. Cook up another hit, man, don't worry about it. Do another hit. Come on now... you'll feel a lot better. Fuck everybody else. Think about the rush! Do it now. Just do it! Make a big hit. Drop a big rock of coke in the spoon after you cook up that *boy*. Ear ringer. Edge of death! Go for it! You'll feel that for sure!"

Part of my committee...

This dark crew of voices inside my head, inside my thinking, were relentless. One telling me, "do it, do it," over and over, "do it, do it, man," and the other just as persistent, telling me, "no don't, no, no, no, don't, stop this shit, stop it, man. You're smarter than this. Come on, don't do this." All the time. These crazy thoughts inside my head were constantly in a never-ending battle with one another. One is a miserable victim of circumstances, crying all the why bullshit, constantly, trying to shove reason down my throat and the other one is an evil, very cunning, always plotting, very convincing master of manipulation, controlling the unsavory decisions within, no matter how insane they are. I'm serious when I say this. It's like I have an endless mixed martial arts fight going on inside my head. What's most messed up about that is the fact that there's no winner, ever. Nobody inside my thought-splitter ever wins. Here's the thing, even if I somehow figure out a way to stay clean for a little while, the thoughts are still there. Still there. Sitting there quietly in some dark closet in my head, just waiting to pounce, just waiting for me to have one inkling of a weak moment, just one sliver of some shallow distraction and BAM, this familiar voice appears out of the darkness with all these seemingly perfect reasons why I should go ahead and get high again, just one time. Like spitting this crap right in my face!

16

No harm there. It's only one time. I can do this, right? Why not? Just one time. Sound familiar? But, hey, slap my bone-headed noggin across my weary skull. Why don't I get it? Why don't I wake the hell up! There's no such thing as *just once*! I'm telling you, this never-ending battle that goes on inside an addict is beyond reasonable understanding and if you're not an addict, there's an incredibly high probability that you'll never possibly understand the depth of this. Even if you love someone with all your heart and would die for them to stop this behavior, you still, most likely, will never understand how the mind of this addict you love so much, works. I know, deep down, you want to understand this and I promise I'll try my best to help you grasp this insanity inside these pages, but, just know, our brains never stop and in active addiction, we have minimal, if any, coping skills. Let's begin there. I hate that, but, it's real. That's real life addiction, well, actually, that's existing in deep at an animal level and, believe me, it gets much worse, given the time to do more damage.

Here's a few symptoms of substance use disorder, (active addiction) from my experience. If you love someone caught in the hell of this disease and they're in active addiction, (meaning they're actively seeking and abusing drugs, sex, food, gambling or whatever their addiction happens to be) there's a good chance you're completely baffled by their alarming and even shocking behavior. You may not understand why they do a lot of the things they do. If that's the case, here's some things to pay attention to.

Look for the following...

In active addiction, in the beginning, the addict will disappear from friends and family overnight, then, a few excuses later, maybe, for a few days. Pay attention to these signs. More than likely, the addiction has already gotten a foot-hold and, if so, that'll quickly turn into days on end. They'll always appear at some time with a seemingly excellent reason why they need to borrow some cash. Don't let your love for the addict remove your sense of reason. 99.9% of the time it's a lie. You won't get that money back, even with your best of intentions. You're, most likely, buying their dope, but, they'd never tell you that. Addicts will lie to their own sweet, sweet mother to get cash. They'll always have a believable excuse

17

and the excuses will work for a while. Then, there comes a time when the person in question will disappear with no excuses. Just start not showing up for things planned or scheduled. This is because the addiction has taken root and has a firm hold on the body, mind and spirit. Don't take that personal. Most of the important things in life have been pushed way down on the priority list, at this point. A beautiful soul is dying. The drugs are winning. The drugs are taking over the ability to reason and make good sense of things. The once clear thinking is getting cloudy. Now, nothing matters except TWO THINGS. Those two things are getting high and staying high. Personal hygiene becomes less and less important.

I remember developing a real bad case of the fuck-its. I didn't know how to make it stop. The need to get high filled my head with fuck-it! That's messed up, I know. But, it happens. Then, afterwards, when the dopes running low, or, the moneys about gone, here comes the next phase. "I should've bought food, I should've paid rent, or, I should've got the car fixed. I should've stopped using while I still had some money." Too late. But, self-pity slips in about here. "I shouldn't have copped that last bag of dope, or, I shouldn't have spent that rent money." Even knowing these things, I still didn't care. By now, the cravings have taken over. I was already out trying to figure out how to get more dope or money for dope. Of course, not too much later comes the must-abating. "I must've done something wrong, or, I must've lost my mind."

Rationalizing, justifying and even intellectualizing the bad behavior like that'll somehow make it make some kind of sense, inside the sick thinking of a using addict.

Thinking is a behavior and for an addict, thinking is a very sick behavior.

Sometimes, as we all know, life sucks and people don't act right. That's life on life's terms. Well, multiply the chaos of that ten-fold or even more and try, inside your head, to feel that level of hopelessness.

That's what an addict in active addiction feels. These are people that exist in never-ending and complete chaos. Unfortunately, this chaos has become their norm.

(WARNING... I apologize for any triggers within these pages. However, these experience must be shared to help people understand the self-destructive thinking of an addict while using. Just to be safe, if you're in recovery, especially, new in recovery, you may want to skip ahead past the stories about my active addiction to page 301- Chapter 19- The Last Flicker of Hope.)

Back to my story...

On the bed was a tray with almost two ounces of pure coke and almost two ounces of brown Mexican heroin next to a bag of fifty or sixty new syringes. The bag was half-full of rigs and the rest of them were piled on the bed. The used ones... The heroin and the coke had been dipped into pretty good. I'd made that dope run to Chicago with a pocket full of cash. Now I remember. I'm deep in this shit. My reality is dismal. I'm a heavy drug-dealer and I've lost all control.
"Hmmm, I'd been busy." I thought. "Shit, look at all that dope I have. To hell with everything!"
I scooped up a big hit of the brown Mexican mud (the heroin) into an already used, bent-up spoon. Then, I grabbed one of the new rigs out of the bag. I pulled up about 20cc's of water, from a nearly-full glass, sitting on the dresser nearby. I shot that over the dark coffee brown powder laying quietly like the devil, in the spoon. Striking a nearby match, I carefully and strategically placed the lit wooden stick under the spoon to cook away the garbage. There wasn't any. After I had the dope cooked up nice, I let it cool for a few moments. Then, I put a 30 or so dollar rock of the cola in that. Stirring it up real nice, I pulled the new rig full of the fresh mix of dope. The syringe barrel felt hot in my hand.
As I popped it into the ugly, scarred track inside my left arm, the cocaine hit me first in the back of my throat. That *girl* was climbing on me. My ears started ringing. I slid it in ever so slowly, drawing it back once to see blood like a well-rehearsed ritual. Then, I pushed it in, pulled it out of my arm and threw the empty rig on the bed. Euphoria started at the top of my head. The feeling, felt like a woman running her fingers around my head. Then, the brown mud hit me. That damn *boy*. I could feel the steady warmth going down my body. It felt like a woman's hands sliding down my skin... like some hypnotic satanic ritual.
The euphoria was overwhelming. I was feeling it when BAM, that blast of cocaine hit me again in the back of the throat and rushed

through my body like a bomb. The blast knocked me down on one knee, against the bed, while the coke euphoria rushed through me. My ears were ringing. I felt like puking and I thought I might pass out. Mm mm mm... went through my body. That lasted a good twenty minutes. Sweat poured out of me and I realized, once again, I was standing on the edge. Death was in my face and that's where the high felt the best. I know that's sick! The thought of that's sick. But, it's real shit. The consequences of that have proven deadly, time and time, again. A great many of my friends have left this world right here in this mad, sick, twisted and dangerous place. Like a madman, fully aware of the insanity of that, I closed my eyes to feel the rush of near-death once again. As I felt myself coming back to the world, I didn't hesitate, I repeated the entire process all over again....and again...and again...and again. Over and over I continued for several days and just as many nights. I lost track. I lost time, places, people and most of all, I lost myself. Nothing else mattered. I became so weak that the rig filling with the almost pure dope, actually felt heavy in my hand. My arms grew heavy. My head grew heavy. Once again, I'd been taken over by a dark force.

My soul was gone. But, like a child left to play in a room filled with toys, I continued...

Then, it happened!

I don't know the exact moment it happened. All I remember is, I kept mixing the hits bigger and bigger. It was almost like an act of desperation. It took more and more for me to get high. I was covered in sweat, clammy and pale. All the color in my face was gone. I was a mess. My days were running together and the nights were lost somewhere in the haze of blacking out, my ears ringing and me constantly running to the john to vomit. I was constantly chasing the high I felt when I first started shooting the dope so many days and nights ago. Let me try to help you understand that.

It's like running full speed up a hill to get to the top of a hill for some sense of major achievement, or, some unattainable fulfillment, but, here's the deal, the top of the hill never comes. The sense of achievement never happens. There's never any fulfillment. It seems attainable, at least in the addict's mind-set of possibilities... So, you keep on running, or, in my case, I kept on shooting more and more

20

of this dope trying to get that feeling of momentary fulfillment, that certain euphoria, until it finally happened....

I overdosed. I stopped breathing. Hey, I've overdosed a dozen times or more through the years. It's a miracle I didn't die many, many moons ago. When I was in Hawaii, as you're about to read, I was deep in a heroin addiction, I find it nothing short of a miracle that I'm even here to tell you about it. When we're younger, we think nothing will harm us. We think more reckless and as youngsters, we're masters at not thinking anything through. We just dive in head first. So, here I am, trying to shoot enough heroin and cocaine to sink the Titanic... From past experience, when I would overdose, I've been pulled by friends to an ice cold shower to revive me, so, I can continue my insanity. All is well, in my sick mind. We didn't have that shot to revive us. We usually died, or, woke up freezing in a cold shower.

But, this time, this overdose...

Well, before we talk anymore about this overdose...
Let's go on a journey...
Travel with me, back eleven years. It's the summer of 1972...

The Vietnam War was the top story on Walter Cronkite's actual unbiased news. It was the last year of the draft-lottery. That was a dreaded reality for most of the 18 year young men in the country. If they drew your birthday on the news, you were, most-likely, classified 1A and drafted into the military for two years. The hippies with their patched bell-bottom jeans, shades and long hair were high on the sexual revolution, the psychedelic drugs and the exploding rock & roll. Rednecks everywhere were imploding from all the changes in the fore-front of everyday life. Haight-Ashbury district in San Francisco was now famous for pioneering the peace and love movement. This was complete with the newly created peace sign. It was spreading like a brush-fire across America. Just by flashing the first two fingers in the air and WALA, PEACE, my brother! David Osley and Timothy Leary acid came in a rainbow of flavors for a buck a hit and it seemed everybody was tripping the light fantastic. That, coupled with a far-out vibe unleashed straight out of Berkley with

21

that Pink Floyd ambience, the times, they were a changin'. Like a spin-off from Woodstock a few years prior, Hendrix, Aerosmith, Kiss and Zeppelin were on every turntable. Electric spools for tables to sit around and smoke Jamaican or primo Colombian weed at 15 bucks an ounce, sat in every living room. Nixon was President and colleges across the country were filled with protesters against the Vietnam War. On May 4th, 1970, four college students were killed by the cops during one of those protests at Kent University in Ohio. The country was still reeling from the tragedy when Crosby, Stills, Nash and Young immortalized the traumatic events in the song, "Ohio".

In June of 1972, I joined the U S Army.

Stormy Monday, younger years...

LOST AT SEA

It was a bright, sunny, Saturday afternoon on Waikiki Beach. The swaying, flowing rhythm of paradise was all around me. I surrounded by tropical beauty. You can even smell it in the air. The mango, papaya, pineapples and exotic, tropical flower smell, lingers in the air. It's everywhere.

I don't think a soul on the planet doesn't know where the white sandy beaches of Waikiki Beach are. Full, vibrant, well-cared for palm trees line the swank hotels along the main walk next to Waikiki beach. Hot, sexy, damn-near naked and dark women had all their sun-drenched favorite spots, tanning their hot-oiled covered bodies, all along the white sand. The steady crest of blue water and bright turquoise waves, languished onto the shore. One after the other, the white caps of the waves slid onto the white sand and lingered for a few moments, then, made their way slowly back into the calm, beautiful Pacific.

The smell in the air is so tropical, it makes you want to bottle it. As a matter of fact, I think they do bottle it. The whole experience is hypnotic and down deep in the clutches of my soul, it felt spiritual. It moved me and I loved how it lingered. I was an eighteen year old country boy and I felt like a kid in a candy store. Right now, my life was awesome. I think I was really happy inside.

I'd just completed Basic Training in Ft. Polk, Louisiana. Talk about being in tip-top shape. When I think back to Ft. Polk, I automatically think about how tough they were on all of us, whipping us into shape. 106 degrees at midnight every night. June, July and August, 1972 in Louisiana. Miserably hot! It was war-time and we had to be ready for combat in the scorching jungles of Vietnam. I was into it, except for the heat. I hated the heat. About 4 grueling weeks into the 12 weeks of Basic, we finally got a weekend pass. I'd already been restricted to base for the past three weekends for disciplinarian crap. One weekend, I had to clean the grease pit in the kitchen, it took me 12 hours, because they kept checking it and finding something wrong. But, of course they did. Then, on another weekend, I had to peel potatoes for 8 hours, until my fingers were bleeding into the taters. Big fun. Then, the last weekend, I had to scrub the latrine for several hours with a toothbrush. Never again! I guess I had a problem with authority. Anyway, finally free for a few days, my brother Ed and I went to Lake Charles for the weekend. As soon as we get off the bus, this smooth-looking black dude approaches us with what he described as a great deal. Give him a hundred dollars and he'll walk up to the front door of this home, just a few doors down from where we were standing and he'd cop the best dope ever, just for us. I think it was some killer weed and some orange sunshine acid. What a deal, right? In my head, I'm thinking, I don't know this dude, so, common sense tells me I'm not fronting this dude shit. But, we were young and my friend, Ed, was a bit more trusting and points out how perfect it'd be if we had some dope to party on. I'm thinking, yeah, that's true. Yeah. True. He hands the dude the hundred dollar bill and he immediately turns toward the houses and says he'll be right back. It smelled bad to me right away. Didn't feel right. So, my red flags went up. I'm watching this dude like a hawk. He proceeded to walk down the sidewalk to the second house and turned to go up to their door. Just as I felt his energy shift, he was gone like a beam of light... zipped away from us in a full sprint like a track star. There was one minor little technical part of this equation that Mr. Smooth hadn't figured into his conniving and trifling plot. Me. He hadn't figured on this young white dude's evolving phenomenal athletic finesse being an important integral factor in this potentially criminal encounter. He didn't know this particular same white dude was, at this very moment, in the best condition of his life. See, I'd been in extremely tough and bad-ass Infantry training for nasty jungle warfare, so, I took off after this thief like a silver streak on injected crystal meth. Mind you, he had at least a two hundred feet head start on me. In my head, however, this was, at this particular moment and at this particularly unique juncture, an unimportant variable, because, you see, I'd decided in the blink of an eye, (that's the iota of a mini-second, by the way,) that no matter what anyone on this earth had to possibly throw at me, I was getting Ed's money back. This dude was not getting my brother's C-note.

I chased that thieving son of a bitch for well over 3 miles. Maybe even further. We went down tracks, across big wide-open fields, down some highways, through a bunch of yards and down a long-ass dirt-road, back across a huge field and finally, across several good-size parking lots and, at last, into a big super market and then, I knew his ass was mine. Through the aisle he ran as fast as he could. But, my perseverance paid off. I was on him like stink on shit. I ran right up to him and screamed like a mentally deranged psychopath, "Oh, hell no! Give me the hundred-dollar bill back, motherfucker! Do it now! Give it to me!" I was screaming. Everybody in the store stood still. Time froze. I could see the shock in his eyes that this white dude just chased him for several miles and actually caught him. Shock & awe! I wasn't even breathing hard and I was being loud on purpose. I could tell he couldn't believe I caught him. He didn't know I'd been training like a savage for this day, for this moment, for some bullshit just like this. He didn't know that. After I watched his mind jiggle, zig, zag and shift through indecision and possible manic overdrive, he started shaking his head and finally submitted to reality. He gave it up. He reached in his pocket, tossed the wadded hundred dollar bill into the canned green beans and took off running. I grabbed the money and let him go on his way. Took care of business. Not today asshole and I don't need any damn green beans either. "Not going to burn us, man!" I thought to myself. I jogged back to where Ed was and handed him his money. "Brother Ed hadn't moved ten feet. Just stood there all that time." I thought. I smiled about that. Kind 'a cracked me up. "Here you go, brother. I can't let a thieving dick-weed rob us. Nope."

To this day, we still laugh about that. Here's the thing... In high school, we were druggies and we were in horrible shape. We'd both been acid freaks, wasted and drunk just about all the time. So, this was awesome for me, knowing I succeeded in getting that money back. It was one of my first little successes in life. It felt good. Another thing for me, I can only speak for myself here, but, Basic was also an amazing change and accomplishment in my life. I'd completed combat training and the confidence course in Ft. Polk with a perfect 800 score. I was also classified expert marksman with an M-16, trained with a 45, I could hit the belly of a tank with an M79 Law or an M-72 grenade launcher from a hundred yards and I was a pure savage with an M-60 machine gun. I fired ball, tracer and armor-piercing rounds in training. At this time of my military life, I was gung-ho and loving it in the Army. My capabilities were coming into fruition. I had no idea. They assigned me 11 Bravo. That's an infantry grunt in the MOS world. That means we lived in fox-holes, ate k-rations and walked everywhere all the time like we loved it. We didn't love it, but, we were proud to serve.

My friend, Ed, had joined with 6 other guys. They were scheduled to leave the day after graduation. I jumped on board and all 8 of us joined on the buddy plan. We shipped out of Chicago to Ft. Polk, Louisiana for Basic Training, and then, on to Schofield Barracks in Hawaii. We began our Advanced Infantry Training at Schofield Barracks, out toward the North Shore in Oahu. After extensive testing, one of the guys, Dave B and I were assigned to Infantry. The rest were artillery and one became an office clerk. We're being trained on the big island to go to Vietnam. I was okay with that. Fight for my country. Hell yeah! They'd shipped us to the middle of the Pacific Ocean for advanced jungle training. Imagine that! So, here's the deal. All this Island stuff was new to me. I hadn't been on the Island for more than a couple months. It'd been another rough week, after doing a three-day bivouac on the Big Island. I'd actually shot at a big-ass wild-boar on that Island with my M-60. The M-60 in Nam, I was told, was better known as "The Pig".

Actually, the boar was running toward us about a football field away. This was a first for me. Do I shoot him? Do I not shoot him? Hell, I don't know. I'm an E-2 green horn. I'll tell you this. I damn sure shot at him. He scared the shit out of me, so, I tried to scare him back. I swear I had piss running down my leg. Imagine this in your mind. I had an 80-round clip in that M-60 and had it mounted on a tripod. Three round bursts, my ass! I know I saw 4 or 5 tracer rounds zipping all around his big head. Thank God, he turned off about fifty yards away and disappeared into the jungle. Man, I never quit hearing about that shit. I found out if I'd have shot or killed him, I would've been charged with an article 15, probably lost some pay, restricted to base, work CQ for a few weekends. Hell, they'd give us an article 15 for having a sunburn. Destroying Government property. Anyway, every time I went out with my brothers on the base, or, out in the field, I heard about it. It was some funny shit, thinking back. See, I'd never been to Hawaii, so, this entire experience was already the adventure of my life.

I didn't know what to expect and all I really knew was, we were training to replace wiped-out platoons in Viet Nam, for my Division, the 25th Infantry. We were "Tropic Lightning." There was a big, golden Dragon that sat at the corner of our quad at Schofield Barracks. We were a block down from the main entrance, so, if you've been there, you know exactly where I was stationed.

Hell, I was a kid just trying to figure shit out. I was still wet behind the ears. But, I was willing to try just about anything. Full-blown addiction hadn't grabbed me by the ass just yet. I don't think. Maybe it had and I was in denial. Could be. After all, I'd partied some in high school, I literally ate hundreds of hits of acid my junior and senior years with my good friend Ed M and some girlfriends we knew. We tried massive amounts of mushrooms and then I dove into the deep side. I popped all the pills I could find, drank way too much beer & whiskey on Friday and Saturday nights and I admit I smoked literally pounds of weed with my buddies. Innocent enough, right? I was a teenager doing all this shit. Maybe I was in denial. If I was in denial, I sure wouldn't admit it, because, well, hell, I WAS IN DENIAL. Sadly, at this time in my life, I didn't realize I had other options. I thought everybody was partying and getting high.

Now, here I am, 18 years young, out on my own in the South Pacific, several thousand miles away from my family, in the Army and curious about everything. Plus, I had the weekend in front of me and Monday off, too, for some reason. So, when I came upon this somewhat secluded part of the beach filled with all these sexy women sprawled everywhere, dressed in damn-near nothing, I figured this might be a good place to cop a squat on a nearby retaining wall, in the shade of some tropical bushes and a big palm tree. So, that's what I did.

It was time to think all this through. So I put on my thinking cap. I realized most of these women were on vacation and, maybe, looking for a guy to hang with. I sat there about 20 minutes thinking about all those possibilities, enjoying the calming effect from the waves rolling slowly in to the white sandy shore. This doobie I was smoking was tasty, the view was like a fantasy unfolding and the fact that I was in Hawaii just blew me away.

Out of nowhere, this dude about 35 or so, walked up and copped a squat on the wall, just a few feet away from me. He struck up a conversation, small talk, and all. He said his name was Art. The dude was Hawaiian, a biker, and helped me finish my joint as we talked. I told him I'd been on the island about 2 or 3 months and didn't really know anybody. After we'd sat there about a half-hour talking about which sexy-ass we'd like to be with on the beach and just bullshit, Art tells me he knows a cool bar out on Kalakaua Avenue. That's the main Street that runs down Waikiki.

"It's 'The Lemon Tree'," he tells me. "Live music all the time." "It's where all the bikers and fine-looking female tourists go." "Well, hell yeah!" So, off we go.

We're stoned on the weed and laughing about everything for no good reason. It felt good, too. So, we take off down the beach and I follow along to check out this bar he's talking about. Hey, I'm ready to get in to just about anything. We cut through a fancy Hotel to get out on Kalakaua. Now, we stroll down to this bar called "The Lemon Tree".

"Ahhhh, the Lemon Tree." I say under my breath. As we walk in the place, I'm digging it. This place was about half-full of party people. Fine-looking females, too! There were some local bikers sitting down the bar. Plus, I saw a few long-haired Hawaiian dudes at the bar.

Here to pick up the hot tourists, no doubt.

"Come on, I'll introduce you to some people." Art says.

(You know what they always say... hindsight is 20/20. If I knew then what I know now, this is that place where I'd jump off that wall, and run out 'a there as fast as I could. Just disappear into the palm trees, go back to the base, back to Schofield Barracks. I'd be a good soldier and never look back. So, is that what I did? Hell NO! Like I said, I'm young, green and still a boy inside my brain. At this time in my young life, I didn't know jack shit. Hell, I knew less than that.)

The Lemon Tree...

The band's got the dance floor full and everybody's having fun. The next thing I notice is lots of locals in the place, mixed with some tourist women of every shape and size. I'm digging that. So, we grab a stool and order up some drinks. Art begins to introduce me to a few different locals. I couldn't help but notice there was a lot of people sliding up next to Art and whispering shit to him. That has me wondering what the fuck he's into. It seemed everyone gave him a lot of respect. The dude singing in the band, I found out was Max. He

28

was another friend of Arts. Max and his crew were all bikers. Badass band, too! "I bet those Harleys parked outside belonged to the band." I thought.

In no time, I met those dudes. Yep, after we talked for a bit, I realized all those steel horses did belong to the band. Then, I was meeting locals. "That's a good thing," I'm thinking. "It'll be easier for me to move around on the Island. It's all working out."

In my head, I thought I was getting an 'in' to the Island. I felt so lucky I'd met this dude, Art. Everybody was showing the dude mad props and since I was hanging with him, I felt good about being there. We partied hard into the night. I had nowhere to stay unless I went back to the base. That was on the other side of the island. So far away! Of course, at the time, I didn't give a shit about any of that. I hooked up with some chick named Ginny from Ohio, I think. She said she was going back to Ohio in 3 days. Sounds good to me! We got drunk as hell together, dancing and boogying all over the bar. It didn't close till 4 am. By then, we were a mess. The place had filled up with partying tourists and Ginny and I were all over each other. I barely remember seeing Art after we got drunk, but, he was still sitting at the bar when she and I headed to her hotel room. To be honest, I don't even remember having sex with the girl. We were wasted. We might've hit the room, hit the bed and passed out. I'm not really sure and that does kind 'a suck, now that I'm flashing back. She was a scorcher! Straight up sexy as hell. I know when I woke up the next morning in the middle of the day, Ginny was in the shower. I laid there a while. "Damn man." I felt like shit, so, after a while, I yelled to Ginny that I'd see her at the bar later. I needed to eat. I dressed and went downstairs to see if there was a food buffet or anything. There was, and guess who was sitting there chowing down? None other than my new friend Art. So, I grabbed some food from the buffet and pulled up a chair at his table. We ate and he was telling me some things. We talked about how Hawaii's tourist were constantly changing. Art explained that meant there were always new and different hot women on the island. "Hmmm, wow!" Things you never think of! All in all, everything is good. As we finished up, I was feeling a little bit better. I needed that food in me. I felt like a new man ready for another day in Hawaii. I sat back for a minute and started thinking, "I'm thinking a day on the beach would be good. Just lay there in the shade and chill. I'll go see if this Ginny really wants to hook up tonight and have some more fun. Yeah, this was going to be a fun military tour." Art mentioned he lived nearby on Seaside Blvd., just a few blocks down. I'm like, "yeah, cool, let's go smoke a doobie."

"No problem." Off we head to his crib to smoke a doobie.

This dude tells me he lives in a place that's right behind the 'International Marketplace'. That's a spot on Kalakaua Avenue, the main drag. It's filled with cool-ass tourist traps, restaurants, Polynesian dancers and the like. We walk through that, go out the back, and up some stairs at a place called, 'The Hippie Hilton'. I'd find out later, this was where all the drug-dealers on the Island lived and worked, selling their goods. Art lived on the second floor and had a cool, tropical setting, with a lanai. His crib was laid out. It was obvious he had no shortage of money.

"That's an outside deck", he points to the deck. "We call those lanais on the islands."

"Oh, okay, cool." I reply. We sit back and he's playing some cool ass tunes and says,

"Hey, my friend, I've got something you might want to try."

I'm like, "What you got?"

He says, "Tell you what, I'll turn you on to a hit and you can tell me what you think. If you don't like it, you don't have to do it again. Hell, you don't have to do it all if you don't want to. It's up to you." I was young and naive. I didn't have a clue about shit, but, I was just about willing to try anything as long as it wasn't gay. I'm into women, so, I'm not going to be with a dude.

So, I said, "hell yeah, let's do it, man! I'll check it out. Sounds good to me."

I watch him put 2 little white rocks in a spoon. He pulls out a syringe and draws up some water. He puts that over the rocks. I had no idea what he was doing. No clue. I was even scared of that syringe.

He put a lit lighter under it and started cooking the wet rocks.

"Hey, I don't know about using that needle, man. I've never done that. It kind 'a freaks me out. I don't know. I'll have to think about that. I don't know."

Art is holding the rig with dope in his hand. If you don't want it, no problem, I'll do it. But, let me know. One of us has to do it. I don't want to waste it."

I look at him and say, "Are you going to do one after me?"

"Oh, hell yeah I am."

"Okay, then, I'm going to turn my head. That needle freaks me out."

"Alright cool. You won't even feel it." Art says.

I stepped to the door leading outside and turned my head away from my arm.

All I heard him say was, "Take a breath and just go with it. This is China White! Dis "da boy."

"Hmmmm." (Native street talk.)

I didn't want to see it. I didn't know anything about addiction, overdosing, or, any of that shit. I was new to the game. I'd just fell off a truck. All I knew about partying was what I mentioned before... with friends back home, kids drinking booze, smoking weed, eating acid, orange sunshine and shit like that.

But, this? I didn't know about this.

I had no idea how deep I was about to jump. He was right, I didn't feel the needle go in at all. The next thing I did feel was like nothing I'd ever known. I remember getting nauseous all of a sudden, and I started sweating really bad. I ran to the lanai rail and vomited in a bush below.

After that, I stood up and the euphoria hit me. The nausea and sweating went away. It started at my head and moved down my body, the feeling was like the hands of a woman. "Wow, wow, wow, wow..." I said it over and over.

The feeling was overwhelming to my youth and innocence. It was indescribable. In my whole life, I'd never felt like this. Not for one moment in time, anywhere or anything I'd ever known made me feel this way. I sat down in a chair and drifted away. I nodded. I nodded for the longest time.   Then, I fell into the abyss...

I'd just kissed the most deceptive, cold and evil killer known to man. Da boy.

I'd just kissed the devil. "Heroin. China White Heroin." Death was knocking at my door and I didn't even know it.

(What I'd learn and none too easy is this... you can dress death up really pretty, nice and sharp, with a cool name and everything, but, when it's all said and done and when you least expect it, it's still death. After that night, my life, for many, many years, with literally everything in it that I knew and loved, became lost at Sea.)

~<>~

Every time you judge someone...
You reveal a part of yourself...
That still needs healing.

Waikiki Beach, Hawaii, 1972-73

TROPIC LIGHTNING

In the Army, 1972-73

My division, the 25th Infantry Division had a heavy presence in Vietnam. We were either boots on the ground or training to be there. It was war-time. Somehow, by the grace of God, I didn't make it in country, while others all around us, got orders and went. There

32

was literally a 95% chance we were going to do a tour of duty in Vietnam. Maybe 2 or 3 tours. I think God stepped in and kept me from certain death, maybe. I don't know. I fully expected to do a tour in Nam. I will say this. While I was in the military, I made some friends I'd never forget.

Like Butch R, from Tazewell, Virginia. Talk about some hell-raising soldiers all in the same squad in Alpha Company. We met at Schofield Barracks and were like brothers. Butch was built like a Pitbull and twice as tough. I swear he was just as wild as me. Just a true back-woods country boy that wasn't scared of anything. We had some times for a while. Then, there was Skeeter, Rodney Mc. You want to talk about a crazy-ass southern boy from Lexington, Kentucky. Overseas, this dude and I became tight as brothers, too.

Let me tell you a little about Skeeter. He looked like a lumberjack. He was a big, farm-fed country boy. We clicked like blood! The man was a maniac.

There was this one time, we were in Wahiawa, Hawaii, this little town outside the gate at Schofield Barracks. Skeeter and I were doing shots of Tequila and smoking Hawaiian Elephant weed. I lost count at about 14 shots. No shit. I vaguely remember shooting pool for money with some Filipino dude who had about six or so Filipino friends with him. I was so drunk I was seeing double and probably triple, but, I'm almost sure he had at least 6 dudes with him. We were wasted. We got in a fight and I vaguely remember Skeeter throwing these dudes all over the place, like ragdolls. He beat all their asses. It's a good thing. Call me drunk as hell. I was in no shape to beat my own ass. I mean I'm no punk, but, tequila whipped my ass on this night. So Skeeter, after he cleaned out the whole bar, I vaguely recall, he scooped my drunk ass up and carried me over his shoulder out of the bar and down the street to a cab that did regular runs to the base. Now, that's a real brother.

I woke up the next morning on the Lanai with my head-pounding and the squad leader trying to get me up for 5 am formation.

"Oh HELL NO! ARE YOU OUT OF YOUR DAMN MIND? Write me up. Now, leave me alone! " I was sick as a dog, puking everywhere. I had the worst hangover ever. A few weeks later, I sold this black dude, Daquan that was in our squad some acid. I didn't even want to sell it to him. But, he kept bugging me about it and I finally caved. I went ahead and sold him a few hits. He was from Harlem, New York. The reason I know this is because he told us about every single day. So, I go over to the Artillery quad on the other side of the base, to party with some of my homeboys. We got wasted in the barracks of their quad. Somebody had a great idea. Let's go see Frank Zappa in Honolulu. We smoked a stick of that Hawaiian elephant weed rolled in a Cheech & Chong paper, from the album. While Zappa and the band were going on stage, we lit it up. After we got about half way through that fat joint, I started getting sick as hell from too much weed. I was miserable.

So, I go outside and I'm literally puking against a palm tree. After a couple times, I sat down to get some air. That helped. What a night. We had a blast. Cecil M, Ed M, Dave B and a few more Illinois boys and I did it up. Way in the night, I started coming down off all the whiskey, dope and everything, so, I go back to my quad. This black dude from New York, Daquan, jumps in my face with a couple of his black buddies, when I walked on the lanai. I have buddies, too, and out on the lanai they came to back me up. Get this, this dude is pissed because he's too high on the acid. All I could do was laugh in his face. I was still somewhat high, too. So what, right! "Let me get this straight. You're mad at me because the acid was so good, you got too high on it? Really? Tafuckoutahere!" We swung at the same time. Everybody made a circle around us as we slugged it out. Yeah, we fought like savages. This country boy whipped his New York ass all over that big, long balcony. Everybody else was watching everybody else to make sure nobody jumped in. It was over in a few minutes

. I left him lying on the lanai, knocked out and his buddies trying to wake him up. Thing about it is this. After that fight, we showed more respect toward one another. Daquan and I became friends. Well, at least we felt we had each other's back. That might be a life-saver in our future.

Now, about 3 weeks after that, we're all out training in the field on the big island. It was a live ammo operation to depict Vietnam, because for all intents and purposes, that was our destination. M60's were set up and firing around us in the fire-fight. It was early evening in this huge, spread-out jungle environment. Grenade launchers (M-79's) were being used as well. Our four man fire-team was working our way around the perimeter to flank the enemy and we came up on some cliffs. We were all going down those cliffs, rappelling. The plan was to set up a rendezvous point with our squad leader, 1 kilometer from the base of the cliffs. Three days and nights later, worn the hell out from these military war-games, we finally made it back to Schofield Barracks. But, no rest for the wicked. Five a.m. the next morning, we're right back in formation for exciting morning P T and a brisk 3 or 4 mile run. The infantry will kick your ass if you're not mentally and physically prepared for it.

Anyway, we didn't have a lot of free time during training, so, we took advantage of it when we could. One night, a bunch of us in Alpha Company and some of my homeboys went skating at the skating rink, on the base at Schofield Barracks. What most of them didn't know was that I grew up on roller skates. I was actually very good on skates from a very young age. In Tennessee, it was my escape from dire poverty for a few hours on Friday nights. There happened to be a group of hot females our age, also at this skating rink on the base. Since, unbeknownst to my friends, I was a damn good speed-skater, I had the bright idea to speed skate. So, we all started racing on the skates. We were a bunch of young and horny alpha males showing off for the girls. My intention was two-pronged. I wanted to look cool for the ladies and I wanted to beat all my buddie's asses racing at the same time. We were all zipping full speed and somewhere along the race, I crashed really badly. I mean bad. I don't even know to this day if anybody else was involved in the accident. It literally knocked me out. I was rushed to Tripler Hospital in Honolulu, completely unconscious. I had a small skull fracture, plus, the doctors took x-rays, shot dye in my knee and did an MRI after they admitted me. A few days later they put my leg in traction to straighten it out. I woke up in the hospital room about two days after I was admitted. I didn't even know what happened until one of my buddies told me. All I can remember is seeing all the hot females and us all taking off to race. I don't remember anything else to this day. I was in that hospital bed in traction for well over 10 weeks.   Anyway, while I was in the hospital, I met a girl named Sandy Leomi Yashida, or, as I called her, Sly. She was there to visit a friend who was in the bed next to my bed. His name was Lee Simone. Sandy would come visit Lee because she was best friends with Lee's sister. We'd become friends from being in the same room for so long. He was cool. I was 18 and Sandy was 17. We clicked right away. She started coming with Lee's sister and while his sister visited him, Sandy would visit me. She was Hawaiian, Japanese and honestly, one of the most beautiful women I've ever known for the whole of my life, to this day.

Once I got out of the hospital, I started living with Sandy, her mom and dad. They had a beautiful home in Aiea, above Pearl Harbor, up in the hills. Sandy and I grew really, really close. Young, passionate and deeply in love. That was us. We had a lot of unforgettable times together. We double dated with her mom and dad several times. Once, they took us out to dinner at Pearl Harbor, and then, they surprised us with great seats to see Elvis Presley. It was a great concert, recorded for the "Live via Satellite, Elvis in Hawaii", album. It was 1973. We were there at the HIC, Honolulu International Center, for that. It's a forever memory.

Sandy and I lasted a few months and I realized I was too wild to be hanging with her. We'd fell deeply in love and I didn't want to hurt her in any way. When I decided I should go, I left her a love note and I let her keep my High School class ring. I often wonder if she still has that ring somewhere. I fell in love with her, too, and it scared me. Who knows? She wrote my sisters for quite some time. I've never forgotten her. But, it was better for me to go. So, being young and wild, one day I left and I never went back. This is when I met Art, the dope smuggler. I told you about meeting Art earlier.

Like I'd said before, this dude, Art, was a big-time drug-dealer. I didn't realize it at the time, but, Art was about the worst person I could've met at this time in my life. He taught me a lot about street life. A whole lot more than I needed to know at that time, based on where I was in my path of life!

He had the connect bringing the heroin in from Canada. Art was a dope smuggler, far more in the game and far more involved than I even knew. He'd just finished 7 years in prison for drug-related crimes, smuggling heroin from Canada into California and Hawaii, etc., so, he had to watch for the heat. He had to be cool, but, he was cued in. At the same time, wild man that he was, he was very cunning with a lot of street-power on those islands. I found out he controlled the heroin market on the entire Island of Oahu and Maui. He also had runners taking large amounts of heroin to San Diego and LA. The dude had two Canadians bringing in a shit-load of this dope every couple of weeks.

My job was clear. All I had to do was bag the quarter-pound or whatever he gave me into quarters and hundred-dollar packs. Then, I had to do the deals, meaning, hand the packets off to the junkies through the door of the dope-house and collect the money. The rest of the time, as long as I kept shit straight, myself and a few choice shooting partners, and sometimes Art, could sit around, shoot dope, nod and burn our t-shirts with our cigarettes and Hawaiian weed. We lived in a nod. I burned every shirt I wore. Of course, shooting an unending supply of da boy has its cost and draw-backs. I over-dosed at least a dozen times. It was bad every time.

In no time at all, I was shooting myself up. I had my own rigs and no concept of limitations and boundaries. Art was in and out doing business. God only knows all the shit he actually had going on. I didn't want to know. Just give me my quarter-pound of China white and leave me alone to do my shit. I was reckless. How I lived through that I'll never know. How I didn't go to prison I'll never know. I do know, actually. I survived it by the grace of God. Think about it, I'd constantly cook up too much dope and shoot it. There were so many times I'd hit the floor before the rig left my arm. Art or somebody would drag me to the shower and hit me in the face with ice cold-water to bring me back. Every time, they'd tell me in great detail how blue and purple I was before I was pulled in to the shower.

Here's the sick part of that shit. Remember, I'm only 18. I overdosed so often that I honestly thought the overdosing and waking up, then, freezing my ass off in the ice-cold shower, was a natural part of shooting dope. Imagine my surprise when I woke up one day after overdosing for the eleventh or twelfth time and Art and another buddy were sitting there on the floor next to me. They were staring at me and they both looked worried. Hell, they looked scared to death. I hadn't seen that before.

Art says, "Stormy, you're shooting too much dope in one hit, man. It'll kill you. You have to stop OD'ing, just do a little bit less in your hits."

I'm like, "Really? OD'ing? What'd you mean? A little less? Okay." Like I had a choice in the matter. He explained I needed to do a little less when I shot it, so, I didn't die. He said that so matter of fact, that I actually took it to heart. For a while. When you're strung out, getting high is the only thing that matters.

Three or four months later, amazingly, I'm still alive. But, I was very strung out. I had quite a hustle going, too. Regulars stopping by all the time for their dope. A room full of junkies nodding out, most of the time. Soon enough, I met this Hawaiian dude named Big Tony. He'd cop a nice stash from us, weekly, and sell it to the locals he grew up with. Plus, his brother over on Maui would cop from him. We also had a junkie named Merck from San Diego that stopped by a lot. This dude always had some hustle working. He was always ripping off tourists, grabbing purses, stealing shit from people, whatever he had to do to get high, he'd do it. He stayed wasted on our dope, too. I didn't care much for Merck. He was a bully to a lot of people and I don't like bullies. Then, there was Big John. He was from San Diego, too. One day John stops by our crib dope-sick as hell. He was hurting and desperate. The cravings had took him over. He'd ripped off two ounces of coke from a dealer out on the North Shore.

Crazy, I swear. He wanted to do some trading. He needed to get high bad. Like I said, he was dope-sick. None of us gave a shit about any coke. We were all junkies. But, what the hell. Art traded him for, 4 or 5 hundred dollar bags of the china white for one of the oz.'s. 5 one hundred dollar bags for an ounce of coke we didn't even want. We sat there and watched John shoot a hundred dollar bag of that China white in one hit. I thought he was going to drop dead. But, instead, it took his sick away and he fell back in a deep nod. He checked out for a long-ass time. Damn. Well, he was happy now.

This dope was so important that I barely ate. There was a little cart that sat on the Hippy Hilton property every day. The dude sold 2 specific things every single day for a dollar each. One was a bowl of ramen with meat. That's like ramen noodles, but, better. He cooked it with teriyaki meat in it. It was the best deal going for a dollar. So, I ate a bowl of that every day. Then, later in the day I'd buy the other thing from him for a dollar. I loved it, too. It was a peanut butter sandwich with honey, sliced banana and cinnamon on it. It was delicious. Those two things kept me and many other druggies alive.

Then, there was this sexy German chick named Kyra. I met her one day at that cart buying food. We became friends and then, I found out she was a junkie and she said she'd found her perfect connect for her dope every day. Me. She was about 20, blonde hair flowing around her shoulders. She had a nice body and really good-looking.

Kyra would come by at least once a week and try to give me a blow job for a quarter-bag. I never did take her up on it. I was a junkie, too. I didn't even think about sex and she was hot. She started stopping by at least once a day with cash for her bags, but, every now and then, she wanted to do me. Hey, I was strung out heavy, so, I didn't give a shit about anything to do with inter-acting. I just wanted to shoot dope. The dope was my sex.

I remember one time, we'd just copped. The Canadians had dropped off a huge quantity of *da'boy*. (China white) to Art. He hooked me up with the dope I was going to sell. First things first, I got wasted and then I had to work. I spent about 4 hours bagging up the quarters and hundred dollar packs. What I'd do is put 3 or 4 quarters in a cereal bowl next to a cigar box on the table near my seat. Then, I'd put with that, maybe, a one-hundred dollar pack in the bowl, sometimes. Not always, but, sometimes. That way when the dopers would come cop, I could pull it from the bowl like that's all there was. I'd keep about 30 or 40 dollars in the cigar box. The big money and dope I'd keep in a desk drawer under a clip board. Two cigar boxes full of dope and money, with a clip board laying on them. No one ever saw that except for Art. Then, at the end of the day, I'd get square with him, or, at least pay him as much as possible for the day's work. Anyway, on this day, I spent all that time bagging up the dope for sale and I was steady selling the quarters through the door. I knew I'd be busy. The word spreads quickly when a dealer cops new dope. I had well over 200 quarter bags to sell and I had about 30, or, so, hundred dollar bags. Then, I'd get a tap on the door and I'd slide down the wire window to see what they wanted. They push me the money and then, I pass the dope through the window. Poof... they're gone. But, this time, as soon as I slide it down, a huge Samoan kicks the door open and puts a 357 right in my face. WHOA! That happened fast! I'd been selling a lot of quarters through the door. The sliding wired window was there so I didn't even have to open the door, unless I wanted them to come in for a bit. Two of my shooting partners had just copped from me and were sitting on my floor nodding. Here's what happened next. The Samoan dude was a good 6 foot 5 and about 300 pounds of ugly, long-haired, crazy looking drug-addict. So, I see the door fly open and a 357 comes right into my face. In the blink of an eye, I'm staring down the barrel of a cannon. All he said was, "Dope and money, all of it!" He had an empty pillow case in his other hand. My adrenalin shot straight out the top of my head. I thought, if you're going to shoot me, it'll be in my ass or elbows, because I'm not sticking around for this shit. In the blink of another eye, I dove from the door all the way through the bamboo curtains at the Lanai door leading to the lanai. I dove over the lanai and hit a palm tree on the way down from the 2nd floor, where we lived. I didn't even stop. Real shit. I hit the tree, hit the sidewalk and sand, jumped up and ran into the apartment under us. Pure adrenalin. Told the dude on the way in that we were being robbed. He was a coke dealer, so, I was giving him a heads-up. He grabbed his pistol and coke to stash and we both ran in his kitchen and stopped. I waited a few minutes while he was hiding his dope in a back room. After a few minutes, I went back upstairs. One of the junkies said he got all my dope and money. I was furious and pissed at the same time. The first thing I see is all the desk drawers wide open. Shit! He got me. I felt sick to my stomach. So, I sent the dudes on their way and I started checking things out. The Samoan moved quickly. He got the 2 quarters I had left in the bowl and the fifty dollars in tens, fives and ones I had in the cigar box on the table. It looked like a big stack of cash, but, it was actually only fifty bucks. Thank God for that. Then, I go to the desk drawers to really get pissed and sick. Like I said, the desk drawers are wide open, so, I know he went through them. Bummed. I'm about to explode from rage. I grab the clip board off the cigar boxes. He left the cigar boxes. "Thanks asshole". I figured he must've thrown the dope and cash in the pillow case. I opened up the cigar box that had the cash in it. WHAT? Would you look at that? There's over 3 thousand dollars and it's still in the cigar box. He never touched it.   He missed it! So, then I grabbed the cigar box with all the dope in it and I opened it. There piled full of over 200 quarters and 50 or more 100 dollar bags was my dope, untouched. I felt like a little kid in a candy store. The sonofabitch was in such a rush, he slung those desk drawers open and saw that clip board and kept moving. WOW! So damn lucky. That could've been real bad. That little shit he took, no biggie. After that day, I had a loaded 45 in the desk drawer, too. "Rob us again, jack-off". He never did. Knowing Art, he probably tracked who the dude was and took him sight-seeing, one way, into the jungle. You go in, but, you don't come out. I hear there's lots of bad stuff in the jungle. But, I don't know anything about that.

40

The ritual...

Check this out... No matter where I was in life, in time or space, or, what my situation was, I would always gravitate to the hard-core dope shooters. Why? Because they knew where the dope was and being an IV user made us some kind of sick, kindred spirits. If you're an addict, you know exactly what I'm saying here and this doesn't seem abnormal to you at all. But, if you haven't lived this, I'm sure, for you, this sounds completely insane. You'll discover inside these pages, a multitude of behaviors that fit well in that same box. These are all scenarios and situations, habits and behaviors of addicts in active addiction. I just wanted to share that with you, the reader, to give you yet another glimpse. This just happens to be one of those behaviors.

(All through my life, from that first time, when I was scared of the needle, till, in a matter of days, I was literally like a doctor shooting everybody up, and then, for the rest of my years in active addiction, I had an eerie fixation with the sinister ritual of shooting the dope into my body.)

Laying the rig kit out, breaking the dope down, cooking the hit and finally, shooting that shit. It's like a ritual. Even cleaning the rig right after I shot the dope. Old habits. We didn't have access to syringes so freely the way it is now. Maybe it stemmed from being taught the entire process, at 18, by Art. Maybe it stemmed from knowing I fixated on heroin so much, I knew I'd always need to be able to shoot myself up, like a sick survival technique. Maybe I'm just a control freak and I insisted I put the needle in my arm, every time. I think I also just wanted to make sure I wasn't following anybody else with any syringe, so, I didn't catch any weird shit. I don't know what it was, but, I do know, I was like a doctor when it came to cooking or mixing dope for injection. I was good with a needle, it was uncanny. I'm sure one would say, "Well, you had a lot of practice". True that, but, no matter, I could pop a hit in a vein in the dark. 95% of all my dope partners, throughout life wanted me to blast'em. Sick shit, I know, but, none the less true. Like I said, I'm giving you a peep inside the mind of a drug-addict. I hope it helps you understand.

Anyway, after a few months of shooting china white all day and working in the dope house, every day, with Art, I met a black dude named Dollar Bill. Dollar Bill was a slick black dude. He had a hooker ol' lady named Black. Every day, they stopped by the dope house to cop their dope. They were smooth, hard-working street hustlers from the word GO. Dollar Bill taught me how to 'quick-change hustle' store clerks, on the register. Young clerks were the best. I watched Dollar Bill walk into a drug store or a store and straight up hustle the cashier. He'd leave every time with cigarettes and money he didn't have. Usually around 14 dollars. Small potatoes, in my mind. But, it's another peep inside the mind of a street hustler creating ingenious ways to get his drug of choice every day.

I remember one time, Dollar Bill and I were outside a motel room in Ala Moana (in Waikiki) waiting a bit for Black, his hooker, to get the trick naked, (the tourist} so, he (Dollar Bill) could roll into the room and make some silence money. So, we're sitting there in this car and she comes out while the trick's in the bathroom and tells us this guy has a long case under the bed. It looked like a rifle case and we should be careful. I jumped right on that. I said, "Hey, Black, go in there and put him on his belly on the bed, naked, and give him a massage, so, his face is looking into the bed. Keep him there for about ten minutes."
Dollar Bill's like, "What's happening?"

I said, "I'll sneak in there and take that case. Who knows, it might be worth something. Leave the front door cracked when you go in the bedroom."

She looked over at Dollar Bill. I looked over at him, too, and I said, "I'll give you both a quarter bag. But, I keep the case."
He says, "Give me 3 of 'em and we got a deal."
"I will unless the case is empty. Then, I'll give you two. Deal?"
"Alright. Let's do it."

I nodded my head up and down. Black went back in and left the door cracked. We waited about 7 or 8 minutes and I crept up to the front door and slipped inside the door. I could hear them in the bedroom. I peeped in. It was just like we planned. The guy was naked on the bed and she was sitting across him, rubbing his shoulders. She looked back over her shoulder real quick and saw me. The guys face was buried into the bed. He didn't care about anything else. He was loving that massage. I got down on my knees and crept slowly from the door to the foot of the bed. I slowly slid the case out from the bed and slowly backed quietly out of the room. Slowly. No one even noticed at all. I carefully picked up the case and went back to the front door. I slowly made my way through the door and left it cracked for Dollar Bill. He was about to go in there and do his thing. We weren't that far from the dope house, so, I carried the case from Ala Moana Motel, where we were, down the side roads and back to the Hippie Hilton where Art and I lived. I went in and laid the case on the table. I couldn't wait to see what was in the case. The case was very expensive. It was black leather and about 4 feet long, with gold clasps. I popped them both open and lifted the top. Oh my God! Here, inside this black leather and gold case was a broken-down, gorgeous .300 Winchester Magnum and 2 boxes of .308 (7.8 mm) shells, a cleaning kit and a beautiful, long-range scope.   "Damn! This dude must be a hit-man." I'm thinking. "Of all the rifles in the whole damn world that I could've taken, I took a hitman's money-maker." All I could do was shake my head at my less than ingenious stroke of bad luck. "Well, would you look at that? He's going to have to buy himself another one now." I laughed. "I'm not telling a soul about this shit. No telling who he might know. Damn! No doubt he'd kill my ass if he found out I took his weapon."

Being young, I was just a wee bit worried about this dude finding out I took it. Being strung out, I didn't care. He never did find out to my knowledge. I'm still here! Well, lucky for me, I never heard from him again.

Art was out partying, taking care of business, who knew? I decided to close that case up and hide it in the closet for a while. At least until that guy left the Island. So, I hid it in the closet. Just as I was hitting a hit of dope, Black and Dollar bill came to the door. He'd pinched the guy for two hundred and forty bucks to keep quiet about him being with Black. We laughed. Dollar Bill copped 2 hundred dollar bags, plus, the three bags I gave them for the case, and left. I sat back into my nod. Just another day in the streets. Every day it was another hustle. Fast money meant fast dope to a junkie.

Thing is, I stayed wasted on this dope. It was pure china white. It had a tight grip on me and I didn't know how to stop and at the time, I didn't even want to. Not at first.

I wasn't the only one strung out on the Island. That's for damn sure. Most of the junkies had the same hustle going. Snatching purses from the tourists and they'd hit their rooms and steal cash, cameras, whatever they could get their hands on, while the people would be out sight-seeing, eating, partying, or, on the beach. They'd trade their vacation shit for a hit, or, a bag. If we didn't want it, they'd sell it to this local fence named Blonde Bobby. Blonde Bobby was a coke dealer, but, he'd buy their cameras and the like, all the time and resell them, several days later, on the beach. All I know is, there was a steady path to our door for the China White. 24-7.

My world changed.

It wasn't for the better, either. I spiraled straight downward. I had a dealer's habit. What the hell, we had an endless supply. I did dope all day, every day, too. Soon enough, I lost my soul and everything with it.

One day, I got high as hell and left for a quick dope-run down the beach. I didn't usually leave the crib. Not too often. But, this Hawaiian dude, Keno, was a local friend of mine. He kept it cool for me, with the other locals, so, I went to help him out. I knew he was dope sick and since he only lived a few blocks down, I figured I'd go hook him up. I knew he'd get flush, soon enough, and come hook me up. He was a good dude for a junkie. Well, while I was stumbling down Waikiki beach, headed to Keno's, wouldn't you know it? I was caught by two Marine M P's. They swooped on my ass. It's like they were waiting for me.

Like they'd gotten tipped off or something. I know they caught me off guard. Man, I was bummed. They handcuffed me and off we went to Kaneohe Marine Base. That's out toward the North Shore. I couldn't believe it. How did this shit happen? Damn! They held me there for ten days or so, waiting on the Army M P's to come get me from the stockade. Talk about a wake-up call! Damn. They were in no hurry. I'm sure they were told to let me lie in the cell for a week or so and suffer. I did. I almost died that week. The Marine MP's did not give a shit about my heroin habit.

They treated me like I was a low-life drug-addict.

I laid in that nasty-ass cell and I suffered, intensely. I ached all over my body, my stomach cramped, I screamed, I cried, I wanted to die, I begged, I pleaded, I cursed and God knows, I lost my mind. I vomited till I had nothing left. Then, I dry heaved for days. My eyes started

44

watering and they wouldn't stop. They stayed wet and burned my eyes bad. Then, my nose started running nonstop. I was so miserable. I ached deeply all over. I was so alone. I wanted to die. I really don't know how I survived that. They'd check to make sure I hadn't died and then, they'd leave. Maybe set me a glass of water by the cell door and a plate of food. I didn't eat much and I didn't drink much water, either, for about 3 or 4 days. For the rest of my life, no matter what bullshit I've survived or dealt with, when I hear the word, suffer,   I think about that time. That time I kicked heroin cold-turkey in a nasty jail cell, in Hawaii.

I'll never, ever forget that. Never.

The Allure...

The following pages I've written to show the allure of addiction. How it quickly becomes the over-bearing enemy complete with deadly consequences. Just know, what you're about to read happens and it happened to me the way I've written it. Notice at times, I sound like I'm proud of the behavior and the events that unfold, but, don't misinterpret the actual purpose of that. There's far more actually happening beneath the surface. I want you to think about how alluring some things would be to a 19 year old boy, or, for that matter, to just about every young person with an eye for new adventure. Seriously. I'd already been an acid freak in high school, a junkie in the Army and I still didn't realize the fragile ground I was standing on. Let me be clear, this doesn't mean everyone that parties will be an addict. It just means, be aware of the danger signs and pay attention to your written priority list along your journey. Are your goals and priorities changing? Are you justifying that right now? Well? Are you?

Chapter 2

~LIFE ON THE ROAD~

ETS – Last day in the Army...
Late fall, 1973...

   This will always be planted in my favorite garden of thought. It all started on a beautiful sunny afternoon. I walked outside that big, guarded front gate in Oakland, California and stopped to look around for the last time. I can remember it so well, like it was yesterday. Seagulls filled a wide-open, clear, blue sky and I breathed in a deep, long breath. I took that last good look around. I'd just flown in a few days prior from Schofield Barracks, in Hawaii and processed out in Oakland, California. It'd been quite a journey. Little did I know, the real journey was about to begin. For me, I'd never forget what happened next.

   I was out! I was finally out! Free! I was free at last! End of Term of Service, or, in Military lingo, ETS. "No more of that shit!" I thought as I let that big breath of air out! "No more of that!" I did keep my green army cap. It had the patch on the front of it with the lightning bolt. It read '25th Infantry Division'. I had broken it in good, so, I kept it. Might do me good in the desert, I thought.

   So, I slid the cap down over my eyes and put my thumb in the air as I stepped off the base. About 5 minutes later, no shit, five minutes later, as I tried to look into the sun, they appeared. "Thank God for this cap." I thought to myself. "It was bright out. Really sunny!"
The driver's old van was covered in Eagles and a mystical space scene. As I climbed in, the smell of Mary-jane filled the air. It was a thick, beautifully carpeted room inside, a very nice room. It looked like the inside of a native room that had been well-thought out. Right down to the big bed on the floor with the brightly colored blankets. But, what really grabbed my attention was the two beautiful Native American women sitting on the blankets. They were drinking from a gallon jug. Whatever was in the jug looked bright red.

   They were also smoking from a big pipe with Eagle feathers hanging from it and eating what they called peyote buttons. The whole scene had me transfixed. The old Indian driving had spirits dancing in his eyes. "I'm thinking, WOW! What have I stepped into?" He wore a big hat with an Eagle feather. Turquoise and silver rings covered his fingers and around his neck was the coolest Turquoise piece I'd ever seen. "I'm Sky Eagle," was all he said. The music playing was Native American. It was a mixture of harps and drums, like nothing I'd ever heard. I settled in for the journey. He said, "My friends and I are headed toward Arizona". That was fine with me. "Let's do it. I'm up for an adventure." "Adventure it will be, my new friend." Then, he hands me the jug of rainbow juice and a couple of those peyote buttons. They gagged me, but, I still ate them.   I drank a few drinks to wash them down and I sat back. The Native American music carried me away, into some mystical trance. I started hallucinating. What a trip! I drank some more of that rainbow juice. Shit started getting heavy. Everything was turning different colors. The dash board was melting and sliding down into the floor of the van. The cars outside the window were like trails of light zipping by. There were voices all around me and I couldn't make out what they were saying. I'm telling you, this is where the sky opened up and the van lifted up like it had wings. We drove right into the sky. Out of the clouds they came. There were Harleys in front of us and there were Harleys behind us. All the Harley riders had angel wings, and the riders were smiling, as they flew all around us. I looked around in the van to check out the two Indian Princess's. One was stroking Sky Eagles long hair, as we flew across the big open sky. She smiled and said, "I'm Whispering Wind, it's nice to meet you.   Welcome into our world. Just take a deep breath and enjoy the visions."

The other woman moved closer to me and with her big, brown eyes, looked inside me. I felt like she could actually see into my person. That tripped me out.

"Hey you. What's your name? I'm glad to meet you."

"Hi. My name's "Morning Star."

I drank her in like a parched, thirsty man. "I'm Stormy. Stormy Monday." Her big brown eyes captured me. I believe I felt what she felt. There was some spiritual shit going on far beyond my understanding. That's for sure. I could feel it moving around inside me. It was deep. I don't want to be corny, but, it was deep like the deepest ocean. Hey, I was 19 and this was some cool shit I'd just

48

walked into. The whole thing was a trip. Maybe it was a vision, maybe, I was tripping my brains out. I think it was both. Anyway, I moved to the back of the van to be with this hot and sweet Native woman named Morning Star. Everything felt good. Not too long after that, she and I were sitting close. We were laughing, joking and having fun like we'd been together forever. It was like that.

Whispering Wind climbed into the front seat next to Sky Eagle and closed the curtain between us. Morning Star and I were having fun just talking and it felt so good to be alive. Like everything about life, love and what's right or what might be wrong, all that shit, it didn't matter right now. What mattered was right now. Like we were riding on the same wave, holding each other up. We were cuddling in no time. The back of the van was our private oasis. I felt starved for every word she spoke and every touch from her fingers. Nightfall fell around us. It covered us and warmed us. The beautiful native music played inside our souls and our hearts shared the song. No one else heard it. It was just for us. The sky was filled with the thunder of a hundred Harleys as the Native music filled our beings. Morning star caressed my spirit with the poetry of her words and the warmth of her touch. A thousand bright and vivid colors surrounded and enveloped all that we were. We became one in flight and all that we were, was everything there was.

Somewhere, much later, deep in the desert, Sky Eagle pulled to a stop on a long desert road. The Harleys continued on in the night. Their thunder filled the sky as they disappeared across the horizon. I was transfixed by everything that was happening around me and I was mesmerized by everything happening within me. Together, the four of us walked across the sand and around the cactus in the desert. We continued on as the colors of the desert filled the night. Seven large Eagles flew just above us as we climbed the mesa to a higher ground. In their mystical flight, they were guides in the night showing us the way to our vision-quest. On the highest part, we stopped and built a fire, large and bright. We sat on large, red rocks, around the blaze. The seven large Eagles soared just above our heads and landed on the huge rocks all around us.

As we stared into the flames and watched the billowing grey smoke float lackadaisically into the night, Sky Eagle told us a story. Mysterious spirit shadows in the night desert wind danced slowly across the huge wall of rocks around us.

He said wolves would come someday and take all that we had. They would be led by a large white wolf. Our work would be much and all that we had, would be much in the ways of the world. The loss would be overwhelming and we'd feel great pain and suffering. We'd come to understand that without this great loss, our strength would never grow. Some of us would lie down and never get up. We would give in to the ways of the white wolves. These great wolves would take the soul of our beings, never to return them. Some of us would fight, but, we'd lose. But, from this loss we would win. From this loss we'd grow with humility. This humility would give us a strength and wisdom like we'd never known before. A few of us would learn from this suffering and we go back to face these wolves. But, we would bring with us the strength of ten men in each of us. The wolves would fight, lose and go away, but, like us, they would return again to fight us some other day. In this time, with wisdom growing inside our souls, we'd be ready for that majestic day of war. A war that had to be, for us to be reborn. One among us would be given a gift from the Creator and the blessings from this gift would grow with many colors, like the seeds planted in the garden of life. Our gardens would be full of life, our land filled with the meat of many animals and we'd all be as one for a great many moons. We'd eat, live and love well. Our children would grow in the ways of who we are and their children would, too.

As Sky Eagle talked, I saw, over his shoulder a large white Wolf run up to him from the darkness. The white Wolf walked into Sky Eagle as he spoke and became him. We all jumped up, startled, and the fire grew larger in the circle. We could feel its flame within us. We began to dance, under the moonlight for many hours. It was written in the stars before I even met them, but, now I understood. Sky Eagle was an elder to his tribe. He had the spirit of the white wolf, already within him. This wolf had not walked into Sky Eagle.

Many moons ago, before my time among them, Sky Eagle had walked into the wolf. He had taken the life of the wolf in that war he spoke of, so, that he could become the wolf, just as he became the elder. The white Wolf was Sky Eagle. His stories were for the children of his people. His stories were for those that he met on his winding path, through time, like me. He was surely the elder to his tribe and all the tribes of his people. This enlightenment washed through me and covered me like a warm and carefully stitched Native blanket. I

50

was forever changed. Morning Star and I embraced because she knew I knew and together, we slowly danced to some large, red rocks, away from the fire, behind the red rock wall. We lay down under the stars with the shadows of the Desert Mountains moving all around us. Her dark skin became my skin and our touch become one in the same. Her brown eyes found my soul and together we walked through the path of many red rocks. The rhythm of the universe was the music we shared within our hearts. Together we melted into one flaming soul. We made love way into the wee hours of the morning. Seven large Eagles soared in flight above us as we exploded together into multiple orgasms. It felt far better than any dream in all the dreams I've ever known to this day. Embraced into one soul, one body and one mind, we fell asleep under the light of a million stars. A few hours later,

the warmth of the desert sun opened my eyes... The vibration of the night echoed through me. My eyes slowly opened to the crest of the morning. The peyote buttons were still affecting me. My body was humming from the body high. I slowly sat up. As I looked around, I realized I was all alone in the desert. Next to me was a canteen filled with water. "I'm glad they left that." I thought. I grabbed it and took a big drink. The water felt good against my lips. I tightened the cap on the canteen and put the strap around my neck. Water for the road. Rubbing my eyes and stretching, I looked around to see nothing but empty freeway in both directions. I shook the echoing vibrations of the night off my skin. The memory of last night will never leave me. "Was that a vision? If it was, let's do that again." I said to myself and smiled.

In the distance, I could still hear Native music playing. Maybe it was my imagination. Maybe not. Whether it was real or not, it sounded far away and it was beautiful.

My soul smiled inside, as I stuck my thumb up to the one car that drove by. Above my head, I saw seven large Eagles soaring toward the Heavens, only to disappear. "How can this be? I mean come on really?" I thought. "Did that happen? Was that a dream? Was that real? Wow." I scratched my head thinking about it. "It seemed real. It had to be real. Yeah. I know that happened."

I continued walking down that empty freeway for what seemed like forever. The memory of the night before wouldn't let go.

~ Something will grow from all you've been going through and it'll be you. ~

HITCH HIKER

Back to my story...

The desert sun was starting to get hot. I could feel the heat on the highway coming through my boot soles. The blacktop was sizzling and it was, at least, a hundred degrees. On that freeway, alone, taking in the view around me, I couldn't help but notice how open everything was. Big, tall Saguaro cactus were standing all across the desert. Their beautiful, flowering blossoms were pointed to the open sky, like they were bathing in the sunlight. Tumbleweed were lying near the cactus, waiting for the hot summer breeze to move them along. Red boulders, large and small, were scattered around of every size and shape, almost, like the master landscaper carefully placed each one exactly where it was supposed to be. It was quite a view to take in all at once. There wasn't a car, a truck or anything coming from either way on that freeway.

"Where the hell did they go? Why did they leave me out here? Some survival test? I'm sweating those drugs out of my system. But, I still had a body high from the peyote. I don't get it. That's what I want to know. I mean, I'm out here ready for whatever, for just about anything. But, man, shit! Last night. Now, look at me. Walking down this damn freeway and it's hot out here. Shit, I could die out here. That van... Morning Star, so sexy. I wonder if I'll ever see her again. God, I hope so. Damn, she felt good. Those wolves, the eagles, hell, all those bikers on the Harleys riding through the sky. Come on now. Heavy shit. I know, I know, I ate some peyote. I did drink some of that rainbow Kool-Aid. I mean, I was tripping, but, still... there's got to be a reason for all that, right? That's heavy shit, man. Damn..."

I'm walking down the Interstate, like I'm in a fog, still tripping on the night before.

"Wow!" My mind was moving full-force thinking about the last 12 hours.

Here I am... nineteen years old and I'm trying to figure out what my next move was. I knew I didn't want to go home, yet. Not back to Illinois. That didn't sound good. Not right now, anyway. So, I walked up to this underpass and found a shady spot to sit down on the concrete.

"This'll work." I thought. "I'll chill here for a few minutes." With nothing else happening, I started thinking some more. I realized I still had a body high from the peyote and the juice.

After spacing out for a few minutes, I started looking around and noticing the desert again.

"Wow, man, I love it out here." I thought to myself.

All this open desert looked so beautiful. The cactus, tumbleweed, distant mountains and the big blue sky. It was all so beautiful. Like a gorgeous painting created by God himself. This felt good. Sitting out here all alone. "Nobody telling me what to do. Now that I think about it, this felt so peaceful." For the first time since Hawaii, I felt good inside. "No more of that fucking heroin. No more of that chain of command barking orders. " I thought. It felt good not being strung out on china white, for a change. It felt damn good and no more cleaning the latrine, or, ten-mile, double-time at 5 am. I was starting to feel like a person.

"I really need to wash my hands of that shit." I told myself. "I don't want to do any of that shit ever again." I really meant that. I just didn't know how persistent my addiction was going to be. Not really. I found out while I'm traveling that staying away from that damn dope is about the last thing on my mind. It's the roughest thing I've ever been through. I had no idea how much rougher it would get.

"Last night. Wow!" I couldn't stop thinking about it.

"Morning Star blew my mind out there, all of it. What a night! Peyote. That's some good shit, man. Damn. Damn... she was hot. I'll never forget last night."

Finally, I hear a truck coming...

I run over to the side of the road and stick my thumb out. Rides were scarce, so, I wasn't taking any chances. He pulled over. So glad he did. It was a big semi. I walked up quickly and as I stepped up to get in, I noticed the logo on the side of the truck.

"White Wolf Trucking".

"Really? Seriously? No shit? Wow." I couldn't help but think it. "I swear, if those Natives were in this truck, I'd be deep in the twilight zone." I chuckled to myself.

But, they weren't. It was an old redneck. He had a big cowboy hat on and George Jones playing on his cassette. There were several other cassettes lying loosely in the seat. They were all country. Cassettes were a new thing to me. When I went in the Army, we had eight-tracks. "Cassette player, huh? How about that?" We really didn't talk much. We just listened to George Jones sing for a long time. Then, he popped in some Merle Haggard. He told me his name was Bob. Said his handle was 'Cowboy'. Cowboy Bob. About 80 or so miles down the road, he dropped me at a 24 Hour truck stop and said he had to eat and had work to catch up on. "Cool with me." He said he had to call for a load or something. Cowboy Bob told me good luck, parked and we both went inside. I went in the bathroom, used it and then, I freshened up. I don't know where he went. I never saw him again.

After that, I went in to the restaurant part and sat there in the air conditioning for a while. I soaked that up. It felt good to just sit there in the cool air. I thought a cheeseburger sounded good. I was hungry. Starved actually. It was time for this fella to get some grub. While I ate my big juicy cheeseburger, I just sat there and chilled for a bit. Then, all of a sudden, a Mexican lady that worked in the restaurant walked up to my table. She spoke really softly and she was a bit older. "May I sit here and take my break, please?" "Of course. " I answered. So, she sat down and I continued to finish the rest of my burger. It was tasty, so, I ate every bite. "I don't mean to bother you." she said. "Hey, you're not bothering me." "Oh good." She smiled at me. She was a nice lady, but, I was starting to wonder what she was up to. She just sat there and sipped her glass of soda. "May I ask you a question?" she smiled and ask me. I said, "Sure. You can ask me anything." "Oh good. I notice your cap. Were you in the Army?" "Yes, I was." "Is your name Stormy?" "Oh shit!

What's going on here?" I'm thinking to myself. "Why would you ask me that?" I asked. "Because if your name is Stormy Monday, I have a note for you from someone." "Wow. Really? From who?" "I don't know who she was. She was Native American and she said if a young man wearing that cap you're wearing comes in here, to give you a note from her. Are you Stormy Monday?" "I am. That was Morning

Star. Yes!" This nice lady reaches in her pocket, pulls out a piece of paper and hands it to me. "Okay, I'm going to go now. I have to go back to work. I'm glad you came in here. I think that beautiful woman that gave me the note really likes you." "Thank you so much. I like her, too." She smiled and walked away. I opened the note and read it.

It said, *"Stormy, I don't know if you'll get this message, but, I hope you do. Thank you for one of the best nights of my life. I know you're wondering why we left you there asleep. I didn't want to, but, Sky Eagle is my big brother. He thought it would be best. He said the journey would be good for you and you have a good, strong spirit. I have to be honest. I'm headed to Phoenix to end it with my ex-boyfriend. He's abusive and I didn't want you to be in the middle of that crazy mess. I'm trying to get away from him forever. He scares me and Sky Eagle says he's bad medicine. I want to get away from him and never see him again. I hope someday you find me. You made me feel so special. Thank you for that. I'll be living in Phoenix for a while, but, if he hassles me and he will, I'll go back to my mother's home in San Diego. She lives near Ocean Beach. I go to Ocean beach a lot. You can find me there. I'll never forget you. Peace and love. I hope the water helped and I hope I see you again. Morning Star."*

"So, now I know. I'm so glad she left me this note." I thought to myself. I just sat there for a long time deep in thought. Thinking about all the things we did last night. "Ummm. Let this food settle." I thought. "Well, at least, now I know. Yep, that water did help. So glad you left it. God, I hope I see her again someday. Her big brother. Wow! How about that? San Diego huh, Ocean beach... I'll be checking that out."

I got up to buy a candy bar and a cream soda for the road. Heading out the door, I saw another trucker gassing up his truck. "What the hell. Why not? I might as well give it a shot." I said to myself. "Another ride would be good right now."

So, I mosey over to this dude. He's a big redneck looking guy, big cowboy hat on his head and worn out boots on his feet. He had a long scar running across his face, right over his nose. "Damn." I thought. "Looks like somebody slashed him all the way across the face. Bet that bled." I said to myself. I walked up to him. "Excuse me, sir, I was wondering which way you're going?"

He looked over his shoulder and kept pumping his gas. "I'm headed south. Going over to Jacksonville, Florida. How about you, young fella?"

"South sounds good. I'm just out hitch-hiking around. Just got out of the Army. Need to..."

"Oh, I know, I know. You ain't got to say another word. I'm a veteran, too. I have to pay for the gas and use the john. Give me about a half-hour. You can catch a ride with me. Now, Listen, I might be a while. I'm just letting you know. If you find another ride, No biggie."

"Thanks man. I'll go sit over there and wait. I'll be right here." I pointed at the slope of grass by his truck.

He nodded and went inside.

I love to watch people. Especially with a body high off that peyote, still lingering. I've always been a people-watcher for as long as I can remember, anyway. So, I start watching the trucks pull in and out. Then, the gas pumps were full of cars, too. In and out, in and out. I start watching them to check out the good looking women. After about ten minutes, this big Buick pulls up to a pump. Some guy in a greyish suit gets out and starts pumping gas in the car. There's a hot chick in the car, but, she's not getting out.

"Dammit!" I say out loud to no one, really. "Get out of the car!" I blurt out.

I could tell she was a good-looking chick, maybe 25 or so. "Hmmm, I'd love to get some of that." I thought. "She's probably a serial killer." I chuckled to myself.

The guy went in and in about ten more minutes, he came back out with a couple of sodas in his hands. This trucker I was waiting on was still in there. I keep watching this couple. He gets in the car and pulls the car over by this slope I'm sitting on, so, they could get in the shade of the big tree that was there, I guess.

"Smart move. Hmm, maybe they're going to talk or something." I thought. "I wonder what they're doing." I tried to catch her eye when he first pulled up, but, she doesn't even look around at me. I'm trying to be cool, but, damn, she looked good up close. Even better than I thought. So, I keep looking at her and I tried to not get caught by the man she's with. He's a lot older than her, but, it was obvious he had money. Money talks, I'm learning. They keep talking for a few minutes, then, she starts getting louder. They're arguing

56

and now they're both getting louder. I can almost hear them through the car. Even with their windows up, they're getting louder.

"I can't believe this shit. Right here next to me. Damn, I better keep an eye out here, in case somebody starts shooting." I was kind of joking with myself, but, who knows what might happen. People can get crazy quick.

It's getting interesting as hell here. I'm young. I know I am, but, I can't help it, here I am being nosey as hell. I'm watching them now to see what happens.

About five minutes later, she opens her door and looks in the car at him and says, "Hey, go to hell, you bastard. Stay away from me!" Then, she slammed the door really hard and turned and looked right at me. She just stood there and stared at me, but, not really seeing me. She was so pissed, she was glaring into space, I think. It's like she didn't even see me and I was right in front of her. Bout that time, he put the car in DRIVE and burned rubber out of the big truck-stop parking lot.

She threw both her arms in the air with 'screw you fingers' sticking in the air, on both hands as she screamed at him, as he was screeching out of there.

Big, firm tits busting out of a skin-tight, hot pink halter-top, nipples hard and those tanned, sexy, hard-body legs, pouring out of these skin- tight, little blue jean short, short cut-offs. Plus, even better, going down her thigh, a sexy tattoo of a mermaid sitting on a rock by the water on a beach. Palm trees, sunset and all in full-blown color. It flowed around and down her leg perfectly. This is what I'm looking at. "Oh man!" quickly came to mind. Then, I started looking around real quick for other guys nearby. I'm thinking this has to be a set-up. "Somebody's trying to rob me," was running through my head. "They got to be. How'd she end up here with me? Damn. I can't believe this shit."

But, nobody else was around. I smiled at her real quick because of her sending the guy the two "go to hells" with her fingers!" She just looked at me for a minute or so and then,
"Hi, I'm Angel," she was furious. I mean, I'll kill your ass kind of pissed. "Hi Angel. I'm Stormy. Well, I couldn't help but notice, that didn't go well." I was shaking my head. "Was that your old man?"
"HELL NO!"
"He didn't really leave you, did he?"

"Hell NO! He's not my old man and he can go to hell. He'd better not come back here, either. I'll tell you this, though. My ex old man, Bobby, I better never see his ass again either." she slung back at me. "I just met that guy."

Hmmm, it made no sense to me.

She looked at me and started shaking her head back and forth. "I don't know what I'm going to do now. Damn! Where'd you come from?" she asked. She's looking at me suspiciously, like I'd been watching her or some shit. Like she's wondering what I'm up to here?

"Hey, don't worry about me, really. I just got out of the Army. I'm just out getting the cobwebs out of my hair." I answered.

She took a breath and relaxed a little bit.

"I'm waiting on this truck driver." I pointed at the truck. "He said he was giving me a ride about a half an hour ago. Hey, where are you going? Maybe he'll give you a ride, too."

"Really?"

"Where you going?"

"Phoenix, where my sister is."

"Hey, what'd you mean about your ex, if you don't mind me asking? What happened?

"Oh. Well, ok, Bobby's my ex's name. We were living in L A for like, 4 years now. I hate it there. Bobby for some reason likes it. Anyway, I've been wanting to move back to Phoenix near my sister ever since we've been there, really. He knew that, too."

"So, what happened to him?"

"That bastard left me at that motel about fifteen miles back. We got in a big fight. He didn't want to leave L A. Said he was going back." She sighed. "So, I guess he went back."

"Really?" I was startled by that. "So, let me get this straight." She sat down on the curb next to me.

"Ok, you're saying you got in a fight with a guy who's now your ex and he left you. He really went back to LA?"

"That's it. Yep."

"I don't know him, but, I think he's crazy."

"He is crazy and now, he's lost me, too."

"That man's nuts. He left you at a motel? I can't believe it."

"I think he actually went back to LA. I'm so pissed at him. He took my clothes, too. The bastard took my clothes. Look what I'm wearing out here. This isn't good for out here."

"Well, that's true, but, hey..."

After about an hour of us sitting there talking, I realized this trucker was in no hurry, but, he did say that. So, I had another idea. I suggested we walk up to the front of the parking lot where the cars and trucks drive in and out. Somebody will give us a ride from there. So, we start walking to the front of the lot. She got quiet and a little distant. I could feel it. Plus, I could tell she was cussing out this Bobby dude in her head and hoping I wasn't some dick like the last guy. I left her alone to her thoughts while we walked across the lot.

"How's this happening to me out here? Damn!" I'm thinking. This chick looks good and she's furious all at the same time, walking next to me.

"How she could juggle both those things at the same time was a marvel in itself." I said to myself. But, she was doing it well. She made it clear she was done with this Bobby dude. Oh, she was pissed. Then, she started telling me about that traveling salesman, Raymond, or some shit like that. He'd picked her up from the weekly and she said at first, he seemed nice enough. He told her he'd give her a ride to Phoenix, where her sister was, but, then, wouldn't you know it, he tried to have sex with her after they'd left the Truck Stop. He pulled over by the road after they took off. He wanted to trade the ride for a piece of ass.

She wasn't having it.

"She's lucky he didn't rape her." I'm thinking.

They were fighting ever since. That made sense. She was hot. Hell, I wanted to have sex with her, too, but, of course I did. I was a young buck.

She said when she jumped out of his car, he was still trying to trade the ride for sex. Sounds like he had big plans.

"Wow. This dude." I'm thinking. Call me crazy, but, I could see his side of it, too.

"Wow! Damn." ran through my mind as she's telling me all this shit. While she's talking, I'm thinking, "How's this happening to me? Damn, I can't believe this shit. Someday, I should write a book about this shit." I laughed. The irony.

She said, "Hey, I'm sorry. I don't mean to dump all my drama and bullshit on you." We were at the entrance to the place now, just standing there.

"My EX!!! To hell with him! I'm really done with his ass. That bastard actually left me! I can't believe he left me. That's not love." she kept saying that to herself, almost in a whisper.

Some lady finally picked us both up in a big, blue, new looking Cadillac. That's good, because my thumb was getting tired of sticking up in the air. She was nice enough. Angel got up front with her, so, they talked while I closed my eyes and rested. After what felt like an hour or two, she stopped in for gas a hundred or so miles down the road. The place had big American flags flying on several poles, lined up across the front of the building. Then, over the front entrance to the place, there was a big USMC flag flying proud. I thought that was some cool shit. We all went in and ate some tacos and drank a coke. Afterward, Betty, I found out was her name, well, she filled up her car. I went ahead and pumped the gas for her. We all went in together, so, she could pay and we figured we'd stretch our legs some more before we hit the road.

Flash Cadillac...

We all walked in and Angel and I grabbed some cold soda out of the cooler. Betty was paying for the gas. We're standing in line behind her to pay for the drinks, talking about nothing, really. There wasn't anybody else in the store, except these two strange-looking dudes browsing around. They looked like they were just walking around buying food and whatever. We hadn't thought too much about them. No biggie. Well, I was watching their reflection in a mirror. All of a sudden, ALL HELL BROKE LOOSE! Those two guys were robbing the damn place. They both pulled out pistols and started waving them around, screaming real loud. We all about shit on ourselves! Well, those guys met head-on with an old man with a long white, scraggly beard and a real bad attitude. He was running the joint.

Now, this cranky old man took his job real damn serious. He wasn't giving up a wrinkled dollar to no stinking speed freaks. Time to kill 'em all. Let God sort 'em out! He had an old USMC cap sitting forward on his head, just about covering his beady, wrinkled and grey eyes. I could see the long white hairs sticking out of his ear and nose, from the side I was standing on. "Damn!" I thought. The old man wasn't bullshitting. "Now I know who hung that USMC flag." I thought. He started unloading a sawed-off 12 gauge shotgun all over the damn store. He must've owned the place. He wasn't giving up shit! I couldn't believe I was seeing this go down.

The dope-heads went down fast. The force of the blast threw them both back into a shelf of canned goods, blood flying everywhere. Plus, there were 12 packs of beers flying everywhere. They'd been stacked in the aisle. HAVE NO FEAR, UNDERDOG IS HERE! BULLSHIT!!! All you could see from us were assholes and elbows. I caught all that chaos out of my peripheral vision, because, no shit, we were already out the door and diving into Betty's car. Angel and I both jumped in the back seat, and fast. Like two Olympic swimmers, flash and gone!   Betty burned rubber all the way out of there. With lead flying and highly explosive gas pumps around, we hit the blacktop burning rubber all the way to the street. Betty went from zero to ninety in a blink. Her new Cadillac took off like a low-flying jet. Impressed the shit out of me. I named it right then, while we were cruising a hundred and ten. "FLASH CADILLAC!" Betty loved it. She said when she got back home, she was going to have that written on the car somewhere. I bet she did, too.

When we got down the road a ways, she took it back down to seventy, I could feel the senses start to relax through my insides. We all finally took a breath.

"What the hell?" I yelled out of the thick air.

"Lord God!" Betty screamed out. Our adrenalin was sky high. We all laughed for a minute, not knowing what else to do.

"WOW!" said Angel. "I can't believe that just happened. I've never seen anything like that before. Shit!! Have you?" "Hmm... NO, no, no." I just smiled at her.

We were sitting close. I didn't expect that. But, it was fine with me. Betty was classy and friendly, actually a sweet lady. She was quite a bit older than Angel and I. I'm guessing she was at least forty. For a few more hours, we rode in the back seat. Angel and I just sat close and talked for a long time while Betty drove. We finally both closed our eyes and drifted off for a while. Resting was just what we both needed. We cuddled most of the way. She felt good. I'm still young, but I could tell this chick was still into her boyfriend. I could tell. No doubt she was too old for me, but, she looked much younger and very sexy. Inside my mind, I'm thinking, there's no way this dude's going to let this chick just go her own way. They had a stupid fight. They had a stupid fight and he got pissed and split. She's got roses and dinner coming soon. Guaranteed. I knew they'd most likely make up and have the best make-up sex ever. I smiled at the thought of the make-up sex. I only knew having her with me, right now, felt pretty damn good, no matter where this might or might not lead.   A couple of hours later, Betty pulled into a bar-b-que place in Happy Valley, Arizona, so, we can knock down something cold and see what's going on. Happy Valley bar-b-que, we found out, was a blues and brews spot in the desert, 15 or so miles north of Phoenix.   The parking lot was full of Harley's and the grub smelled pretty good. As we sat at one of the outside beat-up tables, I noticed an old biker passed out over by some rocks. He was all inked up. I noticed he had some cool tattoos all over his neck and arms as I walked up on him. He wasn't moving, so, I told Angel and Betty to sit tight. I thought I'd check this dude out. I'd never owned a Harley, but, I sure wanted to. It looked like somebody needed to help this fella out. There was a shit load of other bikers drinking and partying, bullshitting and the like, but, everybody was doing their own thing, just having fun. I'm glad I noticed him. He looked sick, maybe, real drunk?

Maybe just partied out. Who knows?

"Hey, brother, you okay? Damn, nice ink, man."

"Oh, thanks... yeah, yeah, well, I think I'm okay. I had a rough night."

He kind 'a smirked at me with a lost look in his glazed, wrinkled eyes. "You going to make it?" I helped sit him up. He paused for a minute. As he got his breath, he started to talk. "Wow, I blacked out. I don't know what happened. Damn, I must've fell out, man. That whiskey, Oh yeah. My back was hurting, too. I took some pain pills, too many, maybe. Damn! I have a bad liver, so, I'm always hurting.

Hey, brother, what's your name? Thanks for helping."

"I'm Storm. Just call me Storm. I think you're going to be okay now, man."

He nodded in agreement as we shook hands. He smiled at me with thankful eyes. I think he was just glad somebody stepped up. "Hey, I'll be right back." I went into the bar and got the guy a big mug of ice water and took it over to him. He was happy to see that. I could tell he needed a big drink of water. "Okay, bro, you take care now, man." He was getting color back in his face, so, I bid him farewell. Angel and Betty were both smiling as I walked back to the table.

"You always like that? So helpful, I mean." Angel asked me. "Sure. Why not? It's the right thing to do. He had no color when I walked up. He was sick. I think that water helped him. I was just trying to be a good person, do the right thing!" We both nodded and grabbed a menu. "Dude has some nice ink. I'm going to sleeve out my shit one of these days. Both arms."

"Really? Hmmm. Yeah, tattoos look good if they're done right. Hey, the food here looks good?"

"It does look good. I might draw my own tattoos and put them on myself." "Really? You can draw?

"Yeah, I think I can."

We kept talking about how nice it was out there in the desert. How good the bar-b-que smelled. How she never wanted to see her ex again. She cussed him some more, too. They were playing some great music.

"Hey, Stormy, I really do appreciate your help." Angel said out of nowhere. She scooted closer to me. "Thank you for saving the day for me back there. I'm so pissed at my ex. I need to get that bastard out of my head."

I thought about that. "Yeah, she does. She's really sweet. I like her." I thought to myself. "But, I did get to meet the bitch side of her, too. I'd love to see her run into her ex." I thought. "Well, maybe not." I smiled.

The place had great atmosphere. I could tell Angel was thinking about the shit that went down with her ex. After a few minutes of silence, I spoke up.

"Alright then, hey, Angel, you can't let that shit control you. I'm sure you already know that. Your ex, that Bobby, I don't know how he could just leave you, though. I mean, he's supposedly loves you, right? That's crazy shit to me. I could never do that. I could just never leave a woman like that."

"Oh, I'll be okay. Hey, you know what, I bet my sister will like you, too. " She whispered in my ear.

We both looked around at Betty. She was smiling, drinking a beer, sitting in a big stuffed chair near our table, getting into the music. She was fine. I could tell she really liked this place.

"I bet she checks this spot out again. Hey, Betty, let's get some barbeque."

"Great idea. I'm starving. I don't have to be down in the Valley till in the morning." She said. "I have a conference. Relaxing here for a little while sounds good to me."

"Cool." We all ordered a plate of that bar-b-que and an ice cold bottle of beer.

Angel left while we waited. She said she wanted to walk out in the desert for a little ways and check out the view. In that moment, when I was sitting there, listening to the music playing, looking up at the big sky with all the stars coming out, I felt really good. For the most part, I'd gotten rid of most of my heroin cravings. I wasn't thinking of it all the time now and damn, that, in itself, felt good. But, I still thought about it every now and then. It looked like good things were really happening.

About that time, I could hear several Harley's all fire up at about the same time. "Man, I love that sound." I thought. "One of these days I'll have me a Harley. I swear I will."

I got up and took a short walk looking for Angel. I stopped and took in the lights spread across the whole desert, all across Phoenix. I stopped and took in a long, deep breath and breathed the clean, desert air into my lungs. With my peripheral vision, I could see some really pretty eyes staring at me, with some beautiful cactus flowers in her hand. It was Angel.

I told Betty I'd be right back. I walked over to Angel. "Hey, let's take a walk." I said.

We walked out in the desert away from everybody. Side by side, we sat on a big, flat rock just talking and enjoying the beauty of the desert. We watched the sunset go down over the horizon. It was breath-taking. Nature's bed felt great as we laid back and she actually kissed me. It surprised me since I knew she had a boyfriend. Then, she caught herself and jumped up. I stood up, too.

"We better get back. I bet our foods there." She said as our eyes poured into one another. We stopped right there and hugged. Warm and snug...

"Well, now, that was a nice surprise. Thank you for that." She put her finger over her lips and whispered in my ear, "Mums the word, okay? I'm mad at the asshole, but, he's still my boyfriend." "Not a word from me." I replied. We walked together, back to the table. Betty was into her food. She just looked at us and kept eating.

"Ooooh, this bar-b-que is good. That's some good sauce in that bottle right there." She set a bottle of sauce in front of me as I sat down at the table.

I believe both of us almost felt a tinge of guilt for leaving and having such a nice moment together. A moment that felt unforgettable to me and that feeling of guilt, it left fast. At least, for me it did.

After the barbeque and drinks with some music and conversation, we paid and headed out. "The food here's really good" I said while walking to Betty's big Cadillac.

"It sure was."

The rest of the ride into Phoenix was peaceful. As the food settled, we sat back quietly for the ride. It looked like we could reach out and touch the stars. As we rode into the Valley from the north, all of Phoenix was lit up. We said our goodbyes to Betty on Bell Road at the northern edge of the city. We both thanked her for the ride and the good company, then, got out of the car. Before I closed the door, I told her she should have FLASH CADILLAC written on the car somewhere. We both smiled, briefly, thinking back to what we'd all went through together. I mean, we actually saw two guys get killed during an attempted robbery. That's heavy shit. Anyway, she loved the idea and said she was going to do just that. Just like that, there we were, standing on a corner in Phoenix, late evening. Angel said she had a sister who lived nearby. "Ginny and I are really close." Then, she said that's where she'd be staying for a while. "My sister won't mind if you crash there for a night or two."

That sounded good to me. I was tired.

About a half-hour later, Ginny picked us up at a gas station near her house. She seemed cool. She was part-Spanish, part-white and had an exotic look about her. With her crazy long, dark and blonde hair with bright blue on the tips, she looked wicked as hell. Plus, something I dug, she was also covered in ink. Think about it. This was the early 70's. It was unheard of for a woman to be covered in ink in the 70's. That made it even better. To this day, I love a woman with really good, well-placed ink all over her body. Her wild hair framed her big smile and pretty face. I think Ginny was about fifty years ahead of her time. She was a true turn-on for any red-blooded man. I bet a lot of women liked her, too. She could've quite possible, traveled back in time. I mean, think about it, I'd never seen a woman with colored hair, covered in ink. Not in the seventies. I loved it, though.

Anyway, they hugged and we jumped in her car. Right away, she tells Angel that her ex, Bobby's been calling to talk to her. He said he was in New Mexico for the night, but, first thing in the morning, he was coming here to see her. Well, I knew right there, they'd probably be getting back together. But, who knows, right? We told Ginny about seeing the two dudes shot and killed, about Flash Cadillac and zipping down the highway at a hundred and ten. Crazy shit.

Anyway, Ginny had a cool condo. She lived at Bell and 19th Avenue, in a badass setting. There was a big pool and a hot tub right outside her front door. "I could sit right there on her walk out balcony and watch the fine women tan and lay by the pool." I thought to myself. "I'm loving that." She also had cactus and Aloe Vera plants everywhere and a great view of open desert, out of her front window. It was cozy. Angel showered while I chilled in the living room with Ginny. "Damn, she's exotic." I thought. Angel walked out in a robe and then, I showered. Ginny said Angel could sleep in her other bedroom and I could sleep on the couch. Cool. I was tired.
Ginny handed me a blanket and a pillow and we all went right to bed.
Sleep came quickly.

The next morning Ginny and Angel both cooked us some breakfast. We sat around the table talking and Angel was pre-occupied. She was tripping out about this dude she'd been living with. So, I kept it friendly, because, I think she wanted me to. That was the vibe. It was obvious she still had feelings for this Bobby dude. Hey, no matter, I'm a gypsy in the wind, anyway and I don't know how it happened, but, somehow, Angel and I had a moment at the bar-b-que spot. It was one of those kind of things a man never forgets. I know I never did and I don't think I ever will either. .

After breakfast, I helped wash the dishes, dried them and put them away. Then, I brushed my teeth, shaved and washed my face to feel fresh. Before I left, I gave Angel and Ginny a long, warm hug. I asked them both if they'd give me their phone numbers, so, I could get in touch if I were ever in Phoenix again. They did and they both smiled at me. I thanked Ginny for letting me crash there. Then, I gave Angel one last, good long hug and out the door I went.

Time for some more adventure...

I walked out to the side of the road and found a good spot to stand. It was time to stick my thumb in the air, again.

~<>~

Chapter 3

Sometimes a person has to be big enough...to see how small they really are.

WILD AND FREE...

I stopped and took a final look back as I I left Ginny's place. "Sexy sisters! Cool as hell, too!" I thought. Then, I put my thumb in the air as I walked out on Bell Road. I was trying to get to the freeway to head toward Albuquerque. But, I ended up hitch-hiking, east, down Bell Road toward Scottsdale. I don't even know how that happened. I was just moving with the flow, I guess. The feel of the desert was in the air. It seemed like one of those days when anything could happen. "This city's got a good energy to it." I thought. "Lots of nice rides around these parts. Seems like everybody's got a convertible. " The sun was climbing in the bright blue morning sky. There wasn't a cloud anywhere. It was going to be a hot, but, gorgeous day. Looking down in the valley, the cityscape was breath taking. Some dude pulled over in a really clean black and chrome Mercedes and snagged me up. He seemed like a cool dude, said his name was Brad. We started talking about all the fun things there were to do in Phoenix, women he dated and other shit like that. He said he was headed to the Salt River and he and some friends were going tubing. They were meeting at the Blue Point Bridge and there's a beach there. He smiles and says, "Lots of sexy women all the time." "Well, hell, Brad, that's all you had to say. Wow. A beach full of prime filet mignon! Oh, hell yeah! I'm all in!" That sounded fun to me. Like I always say, life changes on a dime.

I mean, I've never heard of any of these places, but, they sounded like a good time. Like, maybe, another good party might be popping out of nowhere. I love it when that shit happens. "Sure, man, I'm game. Let's do it!" We're cruising along in his badass Mercedes,

68

checking everything out and it felt good as hell. Brad kicks up some Led Zeppelin and hands me a joint. Life is good. A few miles down the road, we see a bar on the right. He passes me the doobie, pulls in and says, "Hey, man, let's check this place out, have us a quick drink. We'll grab some brew for the beach, too."

"Hell yeah!" 'Stagger Inn' was sitting just off Scottsdale Road, so, we wandered on in. There was a half-dozen or so people sitting round drinking. The juke box was playing Pink Floyd, so, I was digging that. I saw a sign on the wall that said, 'Old Scottsdale'.   We sat on the end barstools and I ordered a glass of ice water to cool down. The desert was getting hot out there, and fast, so, the ice water and the A C felt like a pool of cool water on a hot, summer day. Brad ordered him a shot of Crown and a bottle of ice-cold Bud. Then, he ordered me the same. Shit happens, right! Here we go. Anyway, I drank down my glass of ice water, thanked the dude for the drinks and did the shot of whiskey. He ordered another round and went to the john. Sitting there alone, I started thinking and planning my moves. "Well, I'll do this beach thing and we'll see what that turns into. After that, Albuquerque sounded good. I've never been there, so, what the hell. We'll drink these drinks, go out to this Salt River, I think he called it, check out this tubing thang, meet some women there, hopefully, get lucky, and then, I'll figure it out, maybe, head to Albuquerque."

My new friend got back and we did a few more shots. He headed toward the pool table and racked up the balls and started shooting with himself. I was thirsty. I sat there drinking. "It's hot out there." I said to the bartender as she washed the bar in front of me.

She was an older lady and probably owned the place. She had that look about her. "Oh yeah, it's hot here every day, honey. This is the desert. By the way, I'm Joyce, if you need anything." "Oh, okay. Thanks Joyce." I couldn't help but notice this one chick down the bar a ways. I started watching her. Hell with it. Why not? She was short and I could tell she had a small frame. Short, petite women automatically turn me on. I don't know why that is, but, it is, so, I was checking her out. "Maggie," Joyce said to me under her breath, and nodded toward the chick. "Thanks." I nodded back. This Maggie didn't look too bad. At least, she wasn't ugly. What I first noticed was she was hanging on a bar-stool and half-drunk. "Yeah, she's at least half-drunk." I smiled at my own thinking. So, what the hell, I sized her up for general principles, her being petite and all. I stood up to get a better look. "I'm a little oozy, too." I thought.

"Well," I'm talking to myself, "Not a bad body, about 5'3', I love that, not too bad in the face, listen to me." I chuckled at myself. "Too damn hot outside. I'm getting silly, sitting here and checking this chick out like I'm hooking up with her, or, some shit. I'm a funny man.

I'm going tubing damn it."

I ordered another round for Brad and I sent them over to the pool table. Now he's shooting pool with some big, biker-looking dude. It looked like they were involved. "Probably playing for money." I thought. To hell with it, after a few more drinks, I slid down the bar and put on my happy face. I introduced myself to this Maggie chick. She seemed to be alright. Maybe a little drunk, but, so what. So was I. We sat there drinking for a couple of hours. We did some shots together and talked for quite a while. She was friendly enough as we got sillier and sillier with every shot.

Somewhere in there, I bought Maggie and me another drink with those shots. I did that several times in a row and started shooting pool with Brad and this biker dude. We were playing nine-ball. The big dude said his name was Thumper. "Thumper huh?" I watched them both play for a while, more focused than I made it seem. I knew I could beat them both. Growing up on a table did help from time to time. I still had about 200 bucks stashed from my military severance pay. I was drunk as hell on whiskey, so, I said, "Let's do it!" I found the cued-in third eye zone when I was drunk on whiskey, most of the time. The bar got smoky as hell and hazy, too, when we were shooting, sometime later. That would be ten or more whiskeys later, I think. Maybe I just thought it did. I do remember we started off, playing for five bucks a game. We were all laughing and carrying on, having a good time. We were taking turns buying rounds. It was just a fun day going down at the Stagger Inn.

Then, we started playing for 20 bucks a game. Brad lost a few hundred and bailed on the game. That left me playing this Thumper dude. Brad said he'd lost enough, a couple of hundred bucks, at least. He did lose quite a bit. I noticed Brad was, probably, as drunk as I was. He sat down at the bar and literally turned into a zombie. Man, he was wasted. "He's too drunk to drive." I thought to myself. This Thumper guy started losing his ass to me and shit started getting serious. Well, I'm drunk on whiskey and I'm stroking that stick, so, shit got real, real quick and that was cool with me. I was drunk as hell, too. Plus, we were smoking weed out the back door.

Somewhere, in there, I remember we started playing for a few hundred dollars, no shit, how the hell did this happen? Hell, I only came in here with 200 and something dollars. Now, my pocket's getting full. This game getting so serious slipped up on me. So, he thought. His confidence started spiking after I lost a couple games in a row. He just knew he had me on the wall. He just knew. But, he was wrong. I was on a roll.

I went to the bar to get a glass of water to keep my head straight. I was wasted at the perfect place to be cued in and I didn't want to go over the edge and get too high. So, I downed a few glasses of water real quick. Then, I look around for Brad, the dude I came in with. I was going to ask him if he was about ready to go. My pocket was full of cash. I wasn't going to count it here in the bar, but, I knew I was up big time. I was ready to head to the Blue Point Bridge and party on. Looking around, I don't see Brad. I'm like, "What the hell?" I walk over to the door and look out at the parking spot where we parked. That sweet, classy Mercedes was gone. He'd staggered out while I was shooting. This drunken fool has done left my ass at this bar. "What the hell? Oh well, he was wasted. I hope he doesn't wreck that nice car. Hell, I was hitch-hiking before he picked me up, so, no loss.

It's all part of the adventure, right." I shrugged and went back to the pool table. We played double or nothing a few times. I'm thinking, "Damn, this shits getting serious." I drink down a few more waters to get a little less drunk. I mean, damn, we're playing for some real cash.

(The bets kept getting higher. He kept losing. The more he lost, the more he'd get pissed, the more he'd get pissed, the more he'd get stressed. The more he'd get stressed, the more he'd lose, the more he'd lose, the more he'd get pissed... and the wheel of misfortune keeps rolling on down that painful losing that ass, highway!)

Simple shit to figure out, when you're winning fat money from some dude completely oblivious to the fact that you grew up stroking that 21 ounce Jimmy Rempe stick from 1977. Hell, I was hustling old men at 12, on 8 foot Brunswick's before tables had coin slots. They had nice leather pockets. Anyway, then, it got really real. On the serious level. We played a game for 400 bucks. No shit. That's a lot of money. It was for me. I was only 20. That's eight hundred dollars to the winner, in case you're math illiterate. I was drunk as hell and get this. I won. I don't even know how. He won the break, broke them and ran it down to the nine ball and in a stroke of bad luck, for him, he missed it. All I had to do was stroke that nine in the corner and game over. Done. I was drunk as hell and so was he, by then. Now, I have eight hundred dollars in my pocket and when we pulled in the parking lot, we just wanted to have a quick drink. "Wow! Love it!" My pocket was on fire with all that cash.

So, this dude, Thumper is shitting all over himself. Talk about bummed out. Then, he says, "Okay, let's play one game for 800 bucks. That means the pot is now 1,600 bucks to the winner. I said, "Okay, but, this is the last game." He looks at me and says. "Sure. That works for me." I had to win this. This was the last game for the whole shebang, the last enchilada, all the pesos, the final finale! "Sixteen hundred bucks would be a good stash for the road." I'm thinking. So, he won the break. "How did I just let him win that break?" This is not good. "Oh shit. I'm not even going to get a shot." I said to myself under my breath. He breaks the balls and the 2, 5, 7 and 8 drop. "Wow. Dammit" I mumbled under my breath. So, he's got a shot on the one. It's sitting in the middle of the table and the cue ball is sitting tight on the side rail.

With polished precision, he slowly chalks the stick and carefully strokes the stick into the cue ball and sends it slowly toward the one. "It looks good. It looks good." My mind is sitting on the edge of my seat, while my body language was trying my best to be cool. The white ball taps the yellow ball, perfectly. The one slowly rolls straight to the corner pocket. "Perfect shot." I'm thinking. The yellow ball slowly rolls down the table. "It's too slow. It's too slow. It's not going to make it." I'm talking to myself. I could feel my asshole muscles clench, pucker and tighten up. In my mind I was trying to puff up the green fibers of the table cloth custom-fitted over the slate. Anything to make that damn ball stop rolling. The one's barely moving now. I think its stopping. Yes, yes, yes, please... My minds in overdrive. "It's a foot from the pocket. Ten inches from the pocket. Six inches from the pocket. It's not going to make it. Not going to make it."

I'm choking on my own words, almost praying for the damn one ball to stop rolling. It's 2 inches from the pocket and it's almost at a complete stop. I can barely see the ball rolling. Now it's like slow motion. Even surreal. "Yes, yes, yes, it's going to stop. He shot too light. Alllll righhht!" The yellow one-ball rolled right up to the edge of the corner pocket and stopped.

"It stopped! It actually stopped. It's not moving. It's not dropping! Now, it's my shot!" In my mind, I clicked and breathed out a big sigh of relief. My ass muscles started to unclench. I fought off the feisty, inner-eagerness to explode on the table and win this damn game! I started my deliberately slow walk to the table and what do you think happened? What do you think just happened right here on this table? Oh no, it didn't! Oh yes, it did! It was slow, horrible and surreal, like slow-motion. That damn yellow-belly one ball fell into the damn corner pocket. "Sonofabitch!" He didn't even react. He was focused on beating my ass in this game. There sat the 3 ball and the 4 ball right in front of the side pocket like ducks. "Shit." He makes the 3 effortlessly and pulls the cue ball over for the 4.

He lined it up like a champ. "Beautiful." I think to myself. "Well, there went all that cash." He checks out the table for his next shot, after the 4. That's the six and it's sitting right on the break spot. Worst yet, the out ball, the 9, is a duck in the pond in front of the other side pocket. So, I noticed he hesitated, but, then, he taps the 4 in and applies enough side English to pull the cue ball down for a quick short shot on the 6 in the corner, and then, of course, a win with the 9 in the side. Oh, I was bummed seeing all that play out in my head. So simple. Sure enough, the English he put on the cue ball pulls the cue ball down the table as the 4 drops in the pocket. But, because he hesitated, that moment of nerves some get when the stakes are really high, kicked in and he used a wee touch too much English and pulled that beautiful white cue ball into the corner pocket. He scratched. I can't believe this shit! "Oh, shit, hell yeah!" I pounced like a jackal in heat. Pure savage! No hesitation!

I made quick work of that mistake. Before I could even think about how much cash was involved. I ran them out in the blink of an eye, grabbed those 8 hundred dollar bills from his shirt pocket and put the money in my shirt pocket with my other 800 bucks. Then, I buttoned the pocket. Game over! He lost all his money! Yes! He lost his stash. His kitty. His roll. His funds. His playtime. He's lost it all it seems. That sobered his ass up and quick. I thought he was going to have a stroke. Then, just when I think it's time to roll the hell out of this place, flush this toilet, skedaddle, blow this popsicle stand, disappear, be gone, hit the freeway flush with cash and hmmm, head to Albuquerque since that Brad dude flew the coop on me, Thumper walks up to me. He had the ultimate idea of the day! Now, he wants to play me one big-time game. "One final game, winner takes all, and it's over."

"Really? Hmmm...one game and it's over. Didn't we just do that, man? Huh?" "No, no, no, listen to me..." "Okay. Go ahead." He says to me, "I'll play you for that sixteen hundred bucks in your pocket, if you're game." "Well, obviously, I'm game. You got 1,600 more dollars to put up against this 1,600?"

"No, I got something a lot better than that." "Really? Like what?" I'm curious now. "I'll put my sweet ride worth 10 times that in the bet. I have a 67 Lincoln Continental outside. It's baby blue with black leather interior. Runs great, too, man. One game, winner takes all. I need that money back."

"Yeah, no shit. I need it, too."

"Are you serious?" "Yes, I am. Go look." I go outside to check this Lincoln out. Oh my god! I'm trying to be calm. I knew I had to be cool and not let my adrenalin shoot out of my head, but, man, this was gorgeous, just like he said. It looked gangster as hell. Even had the gangster doors, tinted glass and nice rubber. It was badass... and I don't' have a car!

I say to him, "So, it runs good?"

Thumper looks at me and says, "Go ahead, man, drive it around the block. It runs great!"

"Cool." Damn, I was drunk, I realized.

So, I get in and look it over closely. "Wow. It looks like a new car." Then, I start it. Smooth as silk. Clean. Sounds strong and purrs. Sound system's off the charts. This almost sobered me up. Now, I have to get very serious. Playtime is over. This is the shit!

"I can't believe this dude is going to play me for this. This'll sure beat the hell out of hitch-hiking. Damn, I have to win this." I was in love with this ride. Who wouldn't be? So, I have to be cool. Not sound too excited, so, he doesn't change his mind.

"Hey man, you sure you want to do this? You can change your mind. It's not too late. " I said as I rolled back in the parking lot. "Yes,

I want to do it. I need that money back. I beat myself that last game. I had you beat." "Okay. Okay, yeah, you should've won that one. I'm just making sure. If you really want to do this, let's do it. My $1,600 against this car, title and all. He looked at me and nodded.

So, back inside we go. He racks the table and we lagged for the break. I won the break this time, and then, things went a whole lot different. It was down-right surreal. I took in a deep breath and I ran that table in about four minutes and 15 seconds. He didn't even get a shot and I did make that nine ball when I ran the table. I called it 3 around the table in the corner and knocked the back of the pocket off as that 9 found home. "Well, would you look at that!" was all I could say. The dude puked right there, in the floor, by the pool table. He pulled the key to that badass Lincoln back out of his pocket, and with his hand shaking from anxiety, he handed it to me! I think he might've been crying. "Wow! Thanks. Hey, let me get that title, too." He signed the title over to me, said, "I just filled it up before I came here, too." He was cursing the whole time, and now, I own a sweeeeet Lincoln Continental. I turned and asked Maggie if she needed a ride home, and she headed to the door with me. We got in my Lincoln. I let Thumper clean his shit out of the car and put it in a bag. Then, we went to her apartment. Damn, the car ran smooth as hell. I couldn't believe I'd just won this car. "Wow."

Plus, now, I got over 1,600 bucks in cash, in my pocket, too. "Wow! What a day!" Life can change on a dime! Would you look at that! Well, Maggie and I were both drunk as hell. But, I wasn't too drunk to go in the bathroom and stash all my money in my sock. After that, we started tearing each other's clothes off as soon as I walked out of her bathroom. Then, like two wasted wild dogs, we did naughty things to each other in drunken oblivion. Somewhere in there, we passed out.

God knows how many hours later, we both woke up, at about the same time. Then, here comes a passage straight out the pages of the Twilight Zone. This shit blew me away. It came right out of left field. I didn't know whether to laugh or cry. This woman, Maggie, as she was standing there in her front room putting her top on backwards, with her hair all crazy and messed up, and I have to be honest, she was looking about half as good as she did when I was twice as drunk. She was serious as a heart attack, too. She said from the moment we met, she knew. She knew I was the one. She said she's been soul-searching from that first moment, when I looked in her eyes. She just knew she wanted to spend her life with me. This woman was dumping it all out there. She was laying it all out on the floor. Hey, I'm 19, maybe 20.

I was tripping out. She said she had all these plans for us after a shit-load of serious thought, she figured it all out. She wanted to do this with me, then, she wanted to do that with me and then, she wanted to go here with me and after that she wanted to go there with me, because, her words "We're like one person and her life's so much better, now, with me in it". Honestly, her words! I laid there a while and soaked all that crazy shit up the best I could. I mean, really, the truth is, I guess we all want to find that. We all want true love.

But, I believe a good sign of that, of true love, would be when the feeling goes both ways. Now, that's a beautiful thing. But, here, right now, with this Maggie, well, I didn't feel the same way she did. So, casually, nonchalantly, I thought to myself, "Chick, come on, you were a piece of ass. This was sex." Then, out loud, I said... "That sounds nice, Maggie. I appreciate your liking me like that, but, now, think about it, we just met, really!"

She wouldn't shut up about it. It was non-stop. I don't mean to sound cold, but, she drove me, literally, out of my ever-loving mind. After that good dose of sex and about fifteen minutes of la de da, I was ready to fly the coop the hell out of there. Talk about smothering a man who just wants a quick piece of ass and a good party. She made quick work of it. The psychopathic ranting drove me fruit loop, bananas. "Oh my God..."

Anyway, after one more quickie for the road, I said goodbye, went outside, got in my 1967 Lincoln and headed down the highway.

(Hey, yeah I know, I used her for sex, but, think about it, she used me for sex, too. So, when you throw all the dice on the table, it was a wash for us both. Anyway, the sex wasn't bad and I bet she'd agree.)

Now, moving forward on this journey, both on the road and into the inner-workings of my battle with addiction, I just want to say a few things about where this somewhat adventurous and seemingly innocent road is leading. The deadly allure of this madness is, once again, about to slip into my life. Before I even realize it, it's going to grab me with a death-grip again and it's not going to let me go. I want you to pay attention to how it manipulates and weaves its way into my world. This time it uses women that are also addicted to pull me in and, once again, change my path.

So, let's get back to the story...

I just got back on the road after saying my goodbyes to Maggie, the girl I met in the bar where I won the cash and badass ride, back in Scottsdale, Arizona.

I'm cruising down the highway and checking out my ride. This black leather interior was like new. Engine sounded sweet, too. The sound system was mind blowing. "I need to get this ride registered and tagged in my name," I thought. "I will when I settle in somewhere for a bit." So, I'm getting into the whole feel of my ride. I'm telling you, I didn't get more than 10 miles and this red Porsche rolled by me doing about a hundred and something. Hell, I was doing 90 and it went by like I was sitting still. "Well, would you look at that?" I pushed that gas pedal down just a little and took off like a rocket. I hit a 130 miles per hour and rolled toward that Porsche. About three or four miles down the road, I caught up to that red zipper. I pulled up next to him and we cruised side by side at 140 miles per hour. It looked like some nerdy guy in a suit. Go figure. We honestly drove 140 miles per hour for over a hundred miles.

We weren't racing. It wasn't a competition. We had an unspoken conversation. An understanding among vagabonds. Let's roll! Then, just as mysteriously, out of nowhere, he waved at me, gave me a thumbs up and exited the freeway, up a ramp at 90 miles per hour, and gone. "Well, that was fun!"

I slowed back down to 90 and cruised all the way in to Albuquerque, New Mexico. This was a sweet ride. I loved it. I didn't have one problem with it, either.

I didn't even know where I was going. So, once I got to Albuquerque, on a whim, I took the Coors Boulevard exit. I don't know anybody in this town, at all. Not a soul. I don't even know why I took that exit. I just did. Well, I pulled over, trying to figure out my next move and lo and behold, I see this hooker at a bus stop. Looked like a black and Mexican mix, she was about 30 or so, and the woman, up close, looked like life had been real hard on her. She seemed cool, but, she was definitely a cheap whore. I couldn't help but notice she was definitely dressed for the job, with her little tight skirt and pink halter top. She had a nice body, which is why I probably stopped, but, being for real, after talking to her for about 5 seconds, I knew I wouldn't touch her, because of the used-up vibe. I watched her for a while, then, I got out of my car and approached her. She thought I was going to ask her about doing a sex deal. But, instead, I asked her, "Hey, where's something happening in this town about right now? I don't know a soul here. I just rolled in from out west."

She's like, Hey, call me honey, baby. Yeah, I'm headed to a place right now. I was going to take a bus, but, you give me a ride and I'll take you there. Oh, you'll love this place." "How you know I'll love it? Are you sure?"

"I'm damn sure."

"Oh yeah. What we talkin' bout here?"

"Strip Club. Probably got 30 or more strippers there right now and that's just the day shift. That cool?"

"Oh yeah, okay!"

"Now, check this out, later tonight, when that night sift comes in, there'll be at least 50 more, coming in to work. There's usually a hundred, or so, dancers working this club."

"A hundred dancers in one club! Damn! Yeah, I can't wait to check this spot out."

"Palomino Club baby! We be going to the club!"

So, I tell Honey I'll give her a ride. She tells me we have to stop by her house so she can freshen up. "It's just a few blocks down." She said she's going to try to make some money.

I'm thinking, ok. I'm glad I stashed most of my money in the trunk of my car. Just in case I got robbed, I had to have a stash roll. So, I'm not doing anything else, let's go. She gets in and off we go. I park and we walk into her little house in the ghetto. Sitting at the dining room table is her mother. She's arguing with a voice from the back room. I sit down after she introduces me to her mother. She seemed nice enough. Honey goes into the bathroom. Her mom lifts her shirt and shows me her back. It has a big hole in it. Her back has a big hole in it, not her shirt. It's healed up and covered in scars, but, it looked bad, like a big meteorite had hit her in the back. She told me her husband had shot her with a shotgun about a year ago. She pointed

78

at a room. Then, here comes this little skinny Spanish looking dude from that same back room. This guy has a suit on, tie and all, a pistol in his hand, and he's pointing that fucker and waving it around, at me. He's drunk. It's obvious.

In this thick accent he says, "What the hell you doing in here? I'll kill your ass. I will."

Honey sticks her head out of the bathroom.

"Dad, that's my friend. I'm taking him to the Palimony Club to work. He's looking for work. He's okay."

Her dad starts speaking in Spanish. I don't understand what's he's saying. Out of the blue, he gets real loud. This dudes mental. He tells me in broken English to get out of his house. "Sure, man, I'm gone. Screw this." So, I get up to leave and just as I make it to the front door, about ten feet from him, he shoots at me with a 22 pistol. Yeah, he shot at me with one shot. He missed and out the door I went. "Oh, hell No!" I say to myself." Dudes a nut case. Must be. "He could 'a killed me inside his house and probably gotten away with it." I thought.

So, I figured out where that Palimony Club was myself and went there. It looked nice enough from the road pulling in. I parked my Lincoln right in front of the place. I'm about to walk in and I meet this dude in the parking lot, real long black hair with a big black hat on, and a feather in it. He was 100 % Native. The dude was cool. We talked a while and he told me his woman worked at the club. Right on. He was smoking a joint or doing some coke in his car. Who knows? I told him I'd see him inside. I walked in the place and right there, a black bouncer was in a fist fight in the front area with some drunk Mexican. "Seriously?"

They were going to the floor and the bouncer was on him. He took control quick. I stepped around them and went to the bar. After I got my drink, I asked the head bouncer that happened to be standing next to me, watching that fight unwind. "What times the night shift come in?" I told him I was new in town. He was cool. He told me they started showing up about 6 pm, in a couple of hours. Then, out of the blue, he says, "Hey, you just get in town? You need a job? I need another bouncer as soon as possible." "Hmmm, I hadn't thought about it. What's the pay?" "I'll give you 10 bucks an hour cash, plus, some of the dancers tip, too, and you can start at 6 pm.

Work the night shift. You up for that?" "Sure. Let's do it. Want me to work today, starting at 6?"

"Oh yeah!" he answered without another thought. "This is a rough place. Did you notice?" He pointed at the front area where the bouncer was dragging the dude out the front door.
"Yeah, I saw that."
"That's about every day, can you handle it?" "Yeah, I can handle it. Looking forward to it." He nodded in agreement.

During that shift, I found out my Native American's friend was named 'David T'. His woman that worked there was cool, too. Her name was Whispering Flower. She was a 100% Native, too. "Love that name. Some of these Natives got some cool names." I thought. He told me if

I needed a place to crash anytime, to call him. Dude gave me his number. I ask him if maybe, sometime, I could stop by his crib and smoke some weed? "Not a problem, bro. You should stop by, anytime. Just let me know up front, okay?"
"Oh yeah, for sure, man." "Here's my number." He hands me his number on a business card. "If you need weed, let me know, okay?"
"Oh yeah. Thanks man."

This dude was a master jeweler. I started going to his crib a lot and we became good friends. He'd create turquoise and silver bracelets, rings and such and we'd go down to the Art Center in Albuquerque. The stores would pay him hundreds of dollars for these pieces. Then, we'd go buy a quarter ounce of coke, or more, some booze and whatever else. We'd party all night and day. Crazy times. I'd buy dope all the time, too. That $1,600. went fast and here I was again, strung out. I didn't understand it, but, I'd shoot anything I could get my hands on to get high. Dave was cool, but, he wouldn't shoot dope at all. He did love to smoke weed and snort coke, though. He'd opened his home up to me whenever I wanted. If I needed a place to crash, I was covered. I thought that was some cool shit.   So, anyway, now, here I was at the Palimony Club in Albuquerque, New Mexico. Geno, the head bouncer, put me right to work. Ten bucks an hour, cash, plus tips from the dancers. Oh, hell yeah! I found out real quick everybody at that club got high. The cocaine flowed like wine. Here I was, nothing more than a young, ambitious broke-ass, dope-head, just hustling my way through life! I was fresh out of the military and really, I had nowhere to go, anyway, and everywhere sounded good to me.

So, I decided to check out Albuquerque closer and work in this club for a while. I noticed right away they played some bad-ass music in the place. I go see whose spinning these wicked tracks. There she was. I ran right into this short, sexy blonde with hair down past her little, tight ass. She didn't weigh a hundred pounds soaking wet. Her skin was tanned and she came off so sweet, too.

From the very first moment, I liked her a lot. Her eyes told me she liked me, too. I hung out with her before I started my shift, so, we could talk. We got along great. Laughing about everything and we were both touchy, feely, right away. Whatever we were, it had to be. Before the first shift was over, I was going home with Onya. We couldn't keep our hands off each other. I stayed with her for almost two weeks, then, one morning, the strangest thing happened. We'd not gotten to bed till about 7 o'clock in the morn. We had a long night at work, then, got into the coke and we were drinking all night. Finally crawling into bed, wasted, we were out. So, Onya gets up about 4 pm or so to get ready for work. I woke up and laid there for a minute, then, started to raise up in the bed to get dressed. I couldn't.

This was weird. It was serious. I couldn't raise up. That baffled the hell out of me. This was new. Strange. Different. What the hell's going on? She called an ambulance because I couldn't raise up without extreme pain in my head. At the hospital, they roll me in and a couple doctors and a few nurses run up to the gurney I was laying on.

The doc says, "See if you can look down and touch your chin to your chest." I couldn't.

Then, he bends down to me with a pen and a sheet of paper. He says, "You have to sign this "consent" for treatment, immediately. We believe you have spinal meningitis and we have to give you a spinal tap NOW to determine what type you have so we know how to proceed. I don't want to alarm you, but, this could be life or death, so, you need to sign this, like now." "No problem." I'm about to panic. I signed it right away and in we went for the spinal tap. After hooking me up with something to fight the spinal meningitis with, I laid there and waited in a room. Finally, they said my bloodwork was getting better, that, I did have spinal meningitis, but, it looks like I'm getting a little better. Hours later after that, they said my blood was good and I could leave. So, relieved, I tried to raise up to get dressed again. Same thing, but, worse. I couldn't raise my head up because it started pounding. The doc came in and said NOW my spinal fluid was leaking out of my spine. I had to spend the night and lay flat. He assured me it would stop leaking and I'd be fine. I just had to lay flat. "Damn!" I laid flat all night and the next morning I was fine. I left the hospital with Onya and we went to the club. That night, Onya and I had words because I was spending too much time talking with this stripper named Angel. Hey, I wasn't working because of the spinal meningitis, so, I took the night off. Angel and I sat and started talking and Onya got pissed. Damn drama! Angel was smoking ass hot, though, so, I can see why she'd get pissed. Oh well, no problem. That night, I went home with Angel and what can I say, I moved in with her. Yep, another fine looking woman. Angel and I had a great thing going on till I worked a show one night, three or four weeks later, for the Alpha Male Revue dancers. I worked security for them. They were a road show passing through from Vegas.

The place filled up with hot women and most of them were Latin. During the show, two gorgeous Latino's approached me and asked if we were hiring. "Always looking for beautiful women!" I replied. So, I went to the office and got them both applications to fill out. While they were filling them out, we started talking. The one on my left says, "I'm Maria, this is my friend, Anna." This was two fine-ass women. They were both scxy as hell, too. They watched the male dancers gyrate in their show and got horny as hell. I watched all the women so they didn't get too crazy. We flirted the whole night. I flirted with both of them.

Why not? Sometime during the night, Anna walks by me on the way to the bathroom and slips a hit of ecstasy in my hand. She leans in to me as she hands it to me, "Take this ecstasy. We both just ate a hit, too". I'm thinking these two are definitely horny as hell watching these dudes flashing their asses. A half-hour later, I felt high as hell. That ecstasy crawled all over me. Then, it was ON. We partied our asses off and I was working in the midst of all this. If you want to call it work. I had to watch a huge club full of horny women go nuts over a half dozen naked dudes. After I got off on the ecstasy, those male dancers almost had me on the stage with them.

The place was full of wild women, grabbing at me, mauling me and tipping me. I was digging it. Maria and Anna were both right there, all over me, laughing and carrying on. We were wasted. It got wild as hell and I was literally at work. What a night! Before the show was over, Anna and Maria agreed to wait for me to get off work and then the 3 of us would go out and party. By 4:45 am, we were all 3 in bed naked. This would prove to be my first threesome. It was good, too. We were all high as hell on the ecstasy and watched the sun rise through their bedroom window while we were like three savages in heat.

They lived together in a badass A-frame. I moved in with them the next day. Come to find out, another stripper lived with them, too. Her name was Teresa, She was a tall blonde with a pink flamingo tattooed up the side of her lower leg. She worked at the club, too. We had some weird attraction for each other. We couldn't help it. Teresa had an older brother named Big B. I'd been living there about 3 days and I noticed nobody was really sleeping.

They'd work all afternoon and night, then, party till it was time to get fancy again for work. So, this Big B. stops by and I meet him. He looked like a big mountain dude, long beard, shades on all the time. Long black hair and a strange guy. He asks me if I want to do a blast of ice.

"What's that?"

"Just try it. I think you'll like it." He has a black leather briefcase with him. Big B opens this briefcase and he has a bag of syringes and about 4 one ounce bags of white/yellow rocky powder.

"Grab you a spoon." I reached in the kitchen drawer and grabbed a table spoon and laid it on the table. Big B. reaches in one of the bags and lays a little rock from the bag into the spoon. Then, he takes a mirror out of the case and lays it on the table. He puts a pile of powder on that mirror and starts lining it out.

I ask him, "Do I cook this?"

"No, brother, just put a little water over it and stir it up and shoot it. Tell me what you think."

"Okay." I grab a rig, mix the dope and blast it. It blasted the top of my head off. It was like nothing I'd ever done. It was the opposite of the China White. I felt like I could run a 2 minute mile!

"Whoaaa!!!!! Mannn!!!! OHHHHHHH SHIIIITTTTTT!!!!!!!!

But, for some sick reason, I liked it, some. That's how it tricks the mind. The strippers all did their lines and Big B gave Teresa a big bag of the dope. Then, he tossed me a baggie with some rocks in it. After that, he was out the door. Right before he left, he says, "Hey, bro, I need you to try these new batches every 4 or 5 days. You up for that?"

"I'm the guy, man. Hell yes, let's do it." I'm thinking, damn, I can work some long hours now and make some money. Well, that started my crystal meth addiction. I was shooting it every day. After about two months of that, my body and my brain were fried. My head was always in overdrive. I mean fried. I never slept. I was irrational. For little or no reason, I would run drunk dudes out of the club. You could say the ice made me short tempered as hell. I started clawing holes in my arms, face and in the walls, in my bedroom at home. I stayed wasted on this shit all the time. I got worse and worse.

After a while, here I am living with three hot strippers and I just about stopped thinking about sex. Oh, Teresa would jump me sometimes. She'd come in my room and I'd lay there and close my eyes, like she asked, while she played with my body. The ice had me messed up, but, it didn't stop her. All that really mattered to me was Big B stopping by with that dope. He told me he lived up in the mountains and made this shit at his house. "Damn," I thought. I started getting paranoid as hell, shooting that shit all the time. It got bad. Nothing else mattered in my sick head. I stopped showering and wearing clean clothes. This meth had me by the ass.

For the stupidest reasons, I was tossing drunk Mexicans and Indians out of the club on the regular. Here's why I know I was messed up. I like drunk Mexicans and Indians. We partied together a lot. My brain was twisted on the meth. I was fighting all the time. Every now and then, I'd kick a truck driver out, rarely but, mostly, it was drunk Mexicans. They'd get drunk and then, they'd get ignorant. I mean, crazy as hell. I didn't let shit slide, because, I was working while I was tweaking my brains out, so, out they'd go. I had to take care of my dancers. Especially the ones taking care of me with coke, crystal, sex and cash. Then, one night at work...

I saw a table full of drunk Indians and they were getting loud. I had them on my radar already. They were red flagged in my head and I was analyzing the situation. Mostly, because the place was busy and that's a variable in a possible fight scenario. I was really high on the crystal, too, so, I was cued in to those guys tight and that's also a variable. Sure enough, later in the night, they were wasted out of their minds. I'd talked to my partner, Geno, about these dudes and we were all just about to ask them to leave. Wouldn't you know it, Angel's doing a table dance for one of the guys and he reaches around and grabs both of her breasts. That was it. She wasn't my woman now, but, she still tipped me well. So, I got her back. Geno saw it, too. We both made a bee line to the table.

The table was in a corner by a wall and these dudes were standing three thick. I push up to the table across from the guy. I leaned across the table to him while Geno was trying to push through the drunks to get to the guy.

"Hey, my friend. You know you can't touch these ladies. Time to go, buddy. Come back another night!"

He was really drunk, I could tell as I sized him up. The place was packed, but, I forcibly made it to the other side of his table. I was trying to be nice. I'm being professional. Remove the situation from the area politely, so, we could deal with whatever away from the people. I just wanted to get him outside peacefully, if that was at all possible. I would've preferred to have been right in front of him, so, I could deal with whatever, swiftly, but, there was a big crowd and Geno was headed to him. No big deal, right. I was firm, but, being nice about it. It was a simple escort out of the club, right? He could come back another night. Right?

But, NO, he had other plans, or, was just too drunk to have a rational thought. As he came up, he pulled out a 38 and pointed it directly at me and started shooting. Everybody's adrenalin shot sky high. They all panicked and ran to get away from the shooter. Thank God there was only a wall and fake trees behind me. He unloaded that weapon pointed right at me. I was standing about 7 or 8 feet away from him, just across the table.

My adrenalin spiked. I thought I was dead. I thought this was it. Adios Amigos! Gone. Goodbye. The End. I glanced down to see blood and there's no blood. I looked around at the people standing near me. Nobody got shot. WOW! "Glad your dumb ass is wasted out of your mind!" That did run through my head. With straight adrenalin exploding out the top of my head, in a blink, I grabbed the heavy end of one of the cue sticks I'd hidden behind one of those big fake trees.

They were spread around the club. My adrenalin went sky high. I lunged in fast as lightning and jumped over that table with the stick in my hand. I wore him out with it. At the same time, Geno grabbed the pistol real quick. Then, I drug his semi-conscious ass out to the front entrance, right outside the door. Geno and Butch, another bouncer, got the dudes friends out of the club, too.

"Damn! What is it with these people in this crazy-ass town? They're all nuts!"

The cops were blazing in the parking lot, fast, lights and sirens blaring, just as I let go of him when I laid him on the sidewalk. I turned around to face the cops when I knew he was unconscious. After we told them what happened with the manager present, they put him in handcuffs and put him in an ambulance. That manager ran up our asses and then, she fired me for excessive force. I beat him in the head with a stick. Fuck that! This drunk unloaded a 38 right at me and, thank God, he was wasted out of his twisted mind and missed me by inches, mind you, with every shot. Thank God there was a wall behind where I was standing, or somebody in that packed crowd would've died, for sure, no doubt about it. I can't believe I didn't die that night. Let me just say, on this night, my guardian angel was working overtime protecting me from all these maniacs.

Anyway, this was the straw that broke the camel's back for me. I might sound like a tough guy, at times, but, truth be known, this dude unloading that 38 at me just about made me shit my pants. Let's get real. This is serious shit. I'm only tough when there's no other option. It was time for me to go. She pissed me off. Let me get this straight. We contained the situation immediately, we removed the threat from the club, we saved God only knows how many people in that place from getting shot or hurt real bad and, somehow, in the midst of all this insanity, this bull dyke manager thinks I did something wrong? She's accusing me of excessive force! Oh, hell no!!! I don't think, in fact, I'm sure this wasn't the time to be polite and request they leave. Not with a 38 blasting in my face in vivid color and a whole table full of drunks. My gypsy spirit had grown tired of the nightly bullshit in this club, anyway. Military life, short relationships, stripper drama, not to mention, the crystal meth had me by the ass now. I was living on the shit. I'd lost 25 pounds. I was a border-line mental case. Just all that shit will burn a dude out

86

and it messed up everything about me. My psyche was fried, my intelligence slipping away and my self-esteem? What self-esteem? It was GONE. There's no place in this job description for positive self-efficacy.

Quite honestly, this getting shot at and almost dying was a huge catalyst for me. I had a mental breakdown. I mean, two ass-wipes in this town tried to kill me.

I left the club and went to Dave T's for some much-needed help from a friend. I knew in my soul I had to kick the dope habit. Cleaning up from shooting crystal every day for a few months was a bitch. It was hard as hell. I wanted to call Big B a hundred times and have him bring me a bag. But, Dave T was a real friend. He helped me through that. He and his wife saved me from my own insanity. I broke down a few times thinking about how seriously close I'd came to dying. That's some scary shit for a young buck. Once I finally got out and away from Big B and shooting that crystal, I started cleaning up. The human inside me finally started coming back to life.

The clarity of the shit that I'd lived through since coming to this crazy town flowed through me. It slapped me with reality. It took me about three weeks to begin to feel like a person again and then some.

Then, I realized it was time to, once again, spread my wings.

Yep, it was definitely time for me to hit the road again. I knew I was going to miss Dave and his lady. More than anyone in this crazy town, I felt close to them. Him and his gorgeous woman, "Morning Rain". They helped me kick that dope. They let me crash at their crib anytime I wanted. When I was fighting with one of those dancers, or, just needed to regroup, they made me feel at home.

David T even took me out to a Mesa to meet his "Medicine Man" son, once. I'll never forget this. They lived on a big mesa in the desert. It was surrounded by Natives with rifles, guarding all around it at the bottom of the mesa. Cool-ass spot and, "Wow"...what an experience that was. The doors to their desert-clay homes were on the roofs. You had to drop a ladder from the top to get in the home. Then, pull the ladder back on to the roof for security. I'd never seen that before or since.

So, Dave tripped me out one night as we were smoking weed, in his studio, where he made his jewelry. He had all these wicked looking stones in cloth bags, hanging along the wall. He tells me to go through them and pick out whatever stones I really loved. He had everything, apache tears, turquoise, you name it. After I picked a bunch of them out, he took them and some silver and I watched him make me one of the nicest bracelets I've ever seen.

I'd stuck around Albuquerque for a while to clean up off the crystal meth after that son of a bitch tried to kill me at The Palimony Club. After about three weeks, I decided it was time for me to move on. I was sick of fighting all the time, anyway. That shit was getting old. I was jumping from stripper to stripper like a male whore. In this town, the women were aggressive. I didn't mind that. Usually. I mean, sure, this was way before AIDS, but, the clap and the crabs were still out there. There were shots of penicillin and A22 blue lotion for those things and then, they'd go away. But, damn.

Then, there was this, too... the place was always full of drunk Indians, Mexicans and truck drivers. Drunks. I was sick of dealing with them. So, I'd saved back a little bit of cash for when I hit the road. Well, this is it. I decided the time had come to hit the road, again. I filled up my Lincoln for the long ride to who knows where. Afterward, I swing by the club to say bye to Geno, some of the strippers and sweet Onya, the sexy DJ. I have a couple of drinks and head toward the highway. This time I was a little more excited to leave.   I had a nice ride now and it ran good. Hell, it even looked good. So, I hit the ramp to get on I-35 and cruise. I hit the gas to merge in behind this old truck with a couple of Natives in it and in front of this van with tinted glass. I gassed it to slip right in between them, real cool like. Just as I hit the gas pedal to slip behind the truck, it almost hit a car that cut it off and the dude slammed on his brakes. Wouldn't you know it? I slammed on my brakes to keep from rear ending the truck. The van plowed right into my ass and I ran into the truck in front of me.

There I was smashed between them both. "Well, would you look at that?" We all got out and everybody was mad at everybody else. The front of my Lincoln was crushed. The front fender was pushed into my radiator. There wasn't as much damage to my rear end. Both the truck and the van had some damage, but, not that bad. Oh, I was pissed.

The cops came and wrote me up for hitting the truck and wrote the van up for hitting me. Man that sucked. So, I called a tow truck and had the Lincoln towed to the strippers A-frame. I told the dude to park it in front of the crib. I called Teresa, Big B's sister. She and I got close while we lived together. I told her what happened with my car. She said it was cool to park the car in front of her crib for however long.

What a cool chick she was. I told her to tell her brother if I hadn't picked the car up in three months or so to take it to his crib and keep it for me till I showed back up. She said cool. He'll love that. I was frustrated. I couldn't even believe this shit had happened on my way out of this damn town. I'd just got that car before I came to Albuquerque. I didn't even get to enjoy it that much. I believed in my heart that evil forces were trying to keep me in that town. I wasn't having it. It didn't feel right being there.

Matter of fact, now, it felt even worse. So, after they towed my car and I knew it had somewhere to be, I took off walking down the street. It was like I was new in town all over again. It was still early afternoon when I'd finally soul-searched my plan. What a trip. I'd lost my Lincoln before I really got to enjoy it. I never saw that beautiful ride again. All I knew for sure was this. There was a voice inside me, clawing at my brain, telling me to get the hell out of this town, even if I have to walk. So, I did just that. I walked to the freeway and stuck my thumb in the air.

I figured I'd head across the country. Maybe, go through Peoria, Illinois and say hi to some people and then head toward Florida for a while. Hit some sunny beaches and hang out with some fine women in bikinis. Thinking back, I wasn't really a gypsy at all. I was a lost child.   I was a young man on an endless search for nothing and everything, all rolled into one, all at the same time. It's like they say, some who wander aren't lost.

On the road I go, but, I ran into some way-out shit, along the way.... So many different kinds of people picked me up and gave me rides, fed me, helped me out and some were just assholes.

But, some I've never forgotten... Like the pig-farmer that picked me up in an old Ford pickup and got me out of the rain. It was pouring down. I was drenched. He had a wire fence around the bed of his truck, to haul pigs in, I reckon. There was shit everywhere and about fifty loaves of bread, piled back there amongst the foul doodle do. "Pig food." I thought.

We were somewhere in the middle of Kansas when he picked me up. It was late afternoon. The truck was so nasty, I almost didn't get in. "Hey, I appreciate the ride." I said as I sat down. I mean, I'd been standing on a ramp in rainy weather for a good hour, but, when I opened the door to get in that truck, dude, it about knocked me out. Everything smelled like shit. Pig shit! He was covered in it. "Take a shower, wash your ass, or, something." ran through my head. Oh, he was a nice enough old man and I could tell he had a good heart. But, I sized him up real quick. I have a keen sense of perception when it comes to those kinds of things. "This old farmer ain't never been off that pig farm." I said to myself.

I couldn't imagine living on a pig farm all my life. "Look at this guy." I'm thinking. "Wow! I'll bet he's never been out of Kansas. Backward and square as hell. What a miserable life." I deduced all this as we began talking, with my innate and keen perception. Yeah, I had him all figured out. He told me his name was Lester. Lester Seville. "What a name for a country-fed, ass-backward, square as hell, never been anywhere, pig-farmer. Damn, I wonder if he's ever even been with a woman. A Kansas pig farmer! How in the hell does that even happen?" I shook my head at the possibility of myself living such a miserable existence. "Oh, hell no!"

Lester had the old farmer-type beat-up, straw hat on his wrinkled, gray-haired head. I'm telling you, there was shit all over his cover-alls. It looked like he'd been wrestling a pig in the pig-pen, amongst the shit. Probably had been, too. He was a hot mess and he didn't give one single fuck about it. Like this might be every day for him. Every day. His modus operandi. "Damn!" I shuddered at the prospect of such dire circumstances. The ol' fella was spitting tobacco in an old coffee can. That was gross, too. He had that can sitting on the seat beside him. So, I'm thinking to myself, "He literally duct- taped the spit-can to the seat, so, it wouldn't fall over and spill that nasty chew with the spit and all in it, on the very seat that's covered in, get this, pig shit." I had to laugh, shake my head and chuckle a bit at the thought of that. "That must've happened before, so, now, he's taping it to the seat. That's some funny shit!" I had to force myself not to laugh out loud. This entire visual was a first for me.

Anyway, Old Lester had an old 410 shotgun on the rack right behind us. "Probably hung on that rack for fifty years." I thought. "Damn, this smell's about to make me puke." Hey, not everything can be sweet like sugar, right? I looked at him and almost said something about the smell, but, then, I decided, hey, he did stop and pick me up and got me out of the rain. He was giving me a ride. I should just appreciate the ride and when he lets me out, leave it at that." I decided all this while I was talking to myself and taking it all in.

Well, I rode with this old farmer for a good 2 hours. In that 2 hours of time on this earth, I learned some priceless life-lessons from Mr. Lester Seville. The story he told me crawled way down deep in my heart and it's never left me. It touched the effervescent walls of the soul within me. Actually, the story this old farmer told me literally blew my mind. I didn't expect it. It caught me off guard. It was late afternoon by now. We were cruising down the highway and there wasn't any traffic, coming or going. It was just him and me in an old truck, filled with loaves of bread, loneliness and pig shit. As I settled in a little more comfortable and got past that nasty smell, the old truck and the spittin' can, I noticed he seemed a little smarter than I'd first established. Especially, from a man who seemed from first glance to be so backward and country.

We started off with some small talk. He asked me why I was standing out in the pouring rain in the middle of nowhere. He wondered why I was out like this, hitch-hiking around with what seems like no sense of purpose. I said, "Those are fair questions."

I told him I can't change the weather. If it's raining, sunny, windy or whatever, I'm still going to be hitch-hiking. He nodded. Then, I told him a little more. How, a few months back, I'd gotten out of the army. I needed to get some of that out of my system. I was hitchhiking around trying to find my place in the world. I was restless. He looked over at me and smiled. "Yeah, I remember those days." He said. "Back when I was your age, just getting out of school, trying to figure life out." I said, "Hey, it's just you and me out here, you might as well tell me about it. He hesitated and fell into a deep thought for a minute, like he was flashing back and thinking about things from back then. "These are some things I hadn't really shared with anyone." He muttered. "I've tried, but, I couldn't get it out. I don't know, maybe I need to." I sat back real curious about what this old farmer was about to tell me.

I found out he'd grown up on his daddy's farm right there in Kansas, helping his dad with those damn pigs. He said when he was a kid, every night, he'd pray to God above that when he grew up, he'd never go near a farm again, especially, a nasty pig farm. Said his daddy worked him like a dog his whole childhood. "They were different times." he said. Lester said when he graduated from High School, his mom and dad surprised him and sent him to college. They used farm money they'd saved. They also bought him a little car, so, he could get around. His mom and dad had saved up for years, so, their only child could get a good job away from the farm. "My mom and daddy did that." He said to me with a tear in his eye. "So, I went to college for 4 years. My senior year, I met my wife, Elizabeth." "You're married?" I asked.

He looked at me, just nodded, and kept talking. "Sure am." He said almost in a whisper. I didn't say anything. I just listened. "Well, Liz and I got married right after we both graduated. I took that Bachelor's degree in Business Management and we both applied for jobs all over. Liz had a Bachelors, too. Then, when we least expected it, I got a job offer from New York." "Did you go?"

"Well, I talked to my dad and my mother and, of course, I talked to Liz about it. We all prayed about it and then, I took the job. Liz and I said goodbye to both our parents and we moved to New York. It was a happy time for us. Talk about a big city! Lord, we didn't expect it to swallow us up like it did. Everything is going on in a city that big. I mean we were in New York! We'd never been out of Kansas. Life was fun. We got us a little one room apartment a few miles from my job."

"That sounds good."

"It was. But, I didn't like that job too much. Working in a mail room with a Bachelor's Degree. That's not right. I prayed on it a lot. About 4 months of me applying at other places, I got a call one day from man at the New York Stock Exchange."

"Now, this is getting good." I thought to myself. I sat back and kept listening.

"This man asked me if I wanted to train to be a stock broker."

"Really? I didn't see that coming." I said. "Did you do it?" "Oh, yes. I did. I took him up on the offer. I loved it. It was hard work, but I was made for it. I caught on quick. He taught me to be a very successful stock broker. That same man taught me how to dress for success and I did, too. After that, money was never a problem for us."

I was speechless. "Then what?" I asked.

"Well, several months after he hired me, we were doing real well. Liz and I had a daughter and we named her Shelly. Life was perfect. Our little girl was so beautiful, like her momma. She looked just like her with the prettiest hair and the biggest, bluest eyes. Our daughter was everything! She had this infectious smile. Oh, I miss her so much." I noticed a small tear rolling down his cheek. I didn't say anything. I just sat there and let him talk.

"We were living the best life ever. We had a beautiful place off Park Avenue, of all places.

Oh, we had all the material things anybody would ever want, but, mostly, what we really had that mattered was, well, we had the best family ever. We were so close." I could see Lester's eyes welling up with more tears. He couldn't hold them back. The flood gates had opened. I didn't know what to say, so, I didn't say anything. I sat there quietly and let him cry. He was choking on the words. "We were so happy. Shelly was a smart little girl. She was so clever." Now, he had an ocean of tears flowing down his cheeks. "Hey Lester, we don't have to talk about this. It's okay."

"Well, I think I do need to keep talking about this, my friend. I've held this in a long time. A real long time. A man can only hold on to some things for so long. I do need to talk about this. I've needed to get this out of me, a long, long time."

"Okay, I understand. I'm listening."

"Well, one day, Shelly was 13. She was 2 months away from her 14th birthday. She studied dance. She could dance so well. She was also a cheerleader at school. Everybody loved her. Captain of the cheerleaders, she was so popular and that girl was so talented. Her mother was, too. I didn't tell you, Liz, her mother was an artist."

"Oh really. I'll bet she was really good."

"Oh, she was good. I still have all her paintings, and her sculptures. She did one of all of us together. Priceless to me."

"That's amazing to me. I wish I could see some of her work." "I can't believe this. This guy is far more than some simple-minded a pig-farmer. Cultured, extremely intelligent, it's unbelievable to me." I thought. "Just unbelievable."

"Liz showed in several galleries on Park Avenue, upper East side, just all over. She had work in a lot of places. My wife was becoming a very successful and known artist."

"Wow! How cool!"

"Yeah, Liz and I used to go to Shelly's recitals and of course, we'd all go to Liz's art showings. Those were my girls. That was my family." This farmer was crying his eyes out. Somewhere along the way, somehow beyond my knowing, somewhere deep inside of him, a pressure valve had been triggered in this man that had been locked-up tight for years. He'd been holding on to this unbearable pain for a very, very long time. Now, it was all flooding out. The gates had opened. He kept talking, choking on the words and the tears poured from his eyes and ran down his face.

"One day, I was at work. Shel was having a dance recital. Liz and her were going to taxi to the recital and when I got off work, I'd come and, hopefully, I'd get to see the recital, too. Then, we'd go out to dinner for some family time. Shel had talked about this recital all week. How much she wanted us to see her dance in this one. She had a great solo dance and she couldn't wait for us to see it. It was a special Friday night we'd been waiting for. I was excited to get off work and go see my little girl in that recital. So, I called our favorite restaurant near the recital hall and I made reservations. Then, I finished work, left for the recital, excited to spend the night with my family."

He'd been holding onto this pain for quite some time, I could tell. He stared straight ahead as he talked.
"You okay?" I asked. He didn't say anything for a few minutes, then, he spoke.

"Yes, I think so. I think I'm okay. So, I get to the recital and two police officers arrived just as I did." His sentence was broken. It was hard for him to talk.

But, he continued. "They asked me if I was Lester Seville. Yes, I am, I said. They asked if we could go in a room and be alone for a moment. I knew right then that something was wrong. Sure. Why not? What's wrong? Just tell me. Tell me, please. A lady working at the theater showed us to a room and we shut the door." He got quiet for a few more moments. Then, he pulled over to the side of the highway. I was fine with that. The sun was going down. His voice got lower and softer as he kept talking. The tears were pouring from his eyes. "The officer said the taxi my wife and daughter were in was robbed at gunpoint. The taxi driver resisted. They were both shot and killed in the robbery and so was the taxi driver."

"Lester. I'm sorry. I'm sorry." I was crying, too. This was horrible. Lester's tears poured from his eyes like a waterfall.

He spoke through the tears with broken words. "After we buried them, I tried to work. I tried to be okay. I tried. I couldn't do it. They were my whole world. I wanted to die. I had to come home. I thought if I came home and cleared my head, maybe, I could go back and try to live without them. I couldn't do it. I almost committed suicide." I just sat there in shock. This was a lot to hold on to.

"That was 33 years ago. After I left, I never went back to New York. I just couldn't. Not without my wife and daughter. We had too many memories there. Of us. Doing things. Everywhere." He'd pulled a handkerchief from his pocket and was trying to wipe all the tears off his face.

"Once I was here, I saw how much my mother and daddy needed me around the farm. My dad was getting old and it was hard for him to take care of that farm by himself. I knew God wanted me to stay and help them both. It was the right thing to do. So, I did. Gone was the Park Avenue lifestyle. None of that mattered without my family." All I could do was listen. We were on no schedule, so, it didn't matter anyway. I figured it was good for him to get this out.

"My mother and dad both died about 21 years ago. Three weeks apart. It's just me and those crazy pigs now. I live out there on the farm by myself. I never got remarried. I never went back to New York.

I still miss my family, every day."

We sat there for a few more minutes, quietly, and both of us wiped tears that wouldn't stop coming. I didn't know what to say. I was speechless. I was so wrong about this man. This was not a backward, square, never been anywhere fella. Wow! This was one hell of a man with a heart and soul that had both been shattered. He'd been through hell. That was just unbelievable. I was thinking, "Here he is, sitting here with pig-shit all over him. Lost his whole family. A stock broker no less. From Park Avenue! Wow!" I felt small next to him. I would've never guessed that in a million years. Now, I realized I should never, ever judge a book by its cover. "I was so wrong. So wrong." The good stuff's inside. We sat there for a good ten minutes while we both pulled it back together. Then, Lester pulled back out onto the highway. We both sat in silence for the rest of the ride. Both of us deep in thought. I had a whole new respect for this man.

He had seen far more than me. Far more than I'd realized. I didn't even know. I felt enlightened. It made me think. "When I got in this old Ford truck, I met an old corn-dog, ass-backward pig farmer. When he pulled into the truck-stop to let me out, a few hours later, I said good-bye to a very wise, old and deeply scarred man that had been through hell and high water and yet, somehow survived. At the truck stop, we both said our goodbyes. Lester was a good man. I was thankful he'd picked me up and shared his incredible story with me. He pumped some gas into his truck and then, went in to buy some things. I watched the old pig farmer walk into the truck stop, smelling like pig shit and looking country as hell. I watched as a few people coming out, were making faces and pointing at him, frowning, and saying who knows what, to one another. "If they only knew what I knew about this old man." I thought. "They wouldn't give him those looks. They'd be proud and honored to know him. I know I was." I learned one hell of a life-lesson from Lester Seville. I'm not so quick to jump to conclusions about things now. I never judge a book by its cover. These are things inside of me, even now, because I met this old farmer one day in Kansas.

I went in to the truck stop and freshened up. I bought me a burger and a coke and sat there, for a while. It must've been about forty minutes or so and this couple, who introduced themselves as Mike and Jenny, sat down in a booth next to me. It looked like they were in their thirty's. We struck up a conversation while they were eating. I was sipping on some sweet tea. While we were talking, I asked them where they were headed. Mike said they were headed to the Quad cities. Perfect. Then, he says, "Hey, man, if you need a ride, we'll give you a ride to Davenport. That's where we're headed." "Hey, thank you. I appreciate that."

A few minutes later, Lester walked by, stopped and said it was a pleasure to meet me. He said he was headed back on the road. We shook hands. Then, I can still see it now. He bent over to get closer to me and looked me right in the eyes. He said, "Thank you, my young friend. Thank you so much."

"Lester, thank you, too. I'm glad we met." I answered back. Then, he smiled at me, nodded his head in agreement, and out the door he went. I never saw that man again and I've thought about him many, many times throughout my life. It just goes to show you, we all have a story. Some of us, you'd never know it or think it, but, just when you least expect it, somebody out of nowhere might share their story with you. We all have a story.

Well, it was time for me to head on down the highway.

"Man, I just ate a big, juicy cheeseburger and drank a big glass of icy sweet tea. It was so good and tasty. I felt really good. Adventurous once again! I'm so glad I found another ride. All the way to Davenport, too. Got to love it!" After they ate, we loaded in there van and we were off. I'd crawled into the back seat and as soon as I got in, I passed out. I don't know how much time later, but, I remember, Mike saying, "Look at that sign". It woke me up. So, I look out to see what he's talking about. The sign said, 'Welcome to Iowa'. I love that. Here we are! Well, I missed the whole state of Nebraska, somehow. I must've been tired. I'm glad of that. I felt rested. Getting through Kansas was rough, but, I am glad I met that old farmer. I don't think I'll ever forget that man. Anyway, after I got out in Davenport, on 80, I put my thumb up and I headed to Peoria, Illinois.

I hung out in Peoria for a while, but, once I was there, I started shooting cocaine again and that damn voice was always in my head, constantly whispering to me and telling me, "It's okay, go ahead, do some more of that dope, shoot some coke, you'll feel better, I promise. It'll take away all your pain. Do it. Then, one night, downtown, I ran into a partner that had a shit-load of pure coke. He'd just copped it in Bogota where his parents lived. He wanted me to help him move it. Of course he did. He assured me it was ear-ringer dope. He said it was take you to your knees, dope that hit the back of your throat with a bang. We call that serious dope. Perfect. Not perfect. It was a nightmare.

I dove in head- first. In the blink of an eye, here I am, back in town, fresh, dressed to kill, hitting the downtown clubs, leaving a snowstorm everywhere I went. Before I even had a chance to stop, pause, think, and use any sense of reason whatsoever, I was knee deep in a real bad coke-habit. I had strippers hanging on me, fine women every night, everybody wanted a piece of the rock. I sunk deep, again. It's amazing how popular you are when you're holding the drugs.

Everybody loves the guy who's flush. Yeah, on the outside, I was dressed to kill. Playa, playa to the bone. I'd walk in and everybody working there and everybody partying there knew I was the snowman. I got caught up in that bullshit. The Crown Royal was always flowing like a river. I was caught up in the illusion that I'm important, that everybody wants to know me, and everybody loves me. Hey, check me out, look at me, I'm cool as hell! In the midst of that supposed popularity, it never occurred to me that all they really wanted was the dope. It was never about me at all. That was the sick shit living inside my head. It wasn't real. But, also inside my thinking, nobody knew that more than a few times, I really wanted to just die. I wanted to kill myself. No one even realized behind my smiling eyes lived a strung-out junkie who didn't even want to look in a mirror. Sometimes, I'd get so miserable. I'd be like poor me, poor me and that would turn into, pour me another one. I drank way too much whiskey all the time. It helped me come down off the coke. I know now I had self-efficacy issues, but, I didn't know it then. Hind-sight is 20-20, right?

I felt ashamed inside. I didn't know how to stop shooting the damn dope. I thought I was crazy or something. Why can't I stop doing this shit? I didn't understand. Imagine thinking like that. The suffering and emptiness is endless. I was so miserable inside and yet, here I was on full display, Mr. Cool and a smooth, smooth player, smiling on the outside. The phony facade. I didn't know how else to be, or, what I could do different to change my situation. It was beyond me and I felt lost inside. Even empty.

My sisters didn't do this shit. A lot of people I knew didn't do this shit. Why did I do this shit? I'm intelligent. I'm not stupid. I was lost and confused. I knew it was time for me to run from myself again. This addictive behavior was way too cunning and baffling for a kid like me to figure out. But, you can bet I knew all the dope heads in no time around Peoria. I had no problem figuring that out. So, you know what I did. I went to the interstate as fast as I could one day and put my thumb in the air.

I ran from myself. Looking back, it doesn't sound very intelligent to do that, but, these mistakes are part of the life lessons I had to go through to learn what doesn't work. These are the same lessons I'm sharing with you now. Maybe, after reading this, you won't have to run so far from yourself before you figure out how to change your path. At the time, I didn't know what else to do. I'd never even heard of a 12 step program and there was no book like this one, for me to read. None that I'd heard of. So, I headed south. Sometimes I'd get picked up by the coolest people. There were cool people everywhere I went. We'd party our asses off for a while and then, they'd drop me off and I'd move on to the next adventure. It was a strange trip for sure. It wasn't all fun either. Sometimes it was miserable, even horrible and just pure hell. I was a gypsy in the wind.

Belief in yourself...
is a mirror hanging deliberately before you...
Placed there, carefully, by the Great Spirit...
Waiting for your image to appear.

Chapter 4

BLUE GRASS AND REDNECKS

I hadn't had much luck hitch-hiking. It was one of those long, drawn-out days. The sun was a big, bright orange ball in a wide open sky. It was pretty outside, really. Just a little hot, but, not too bad. I'd walked for a while for the hell of it. Well, not really for the hell of it. Actually, I was trying to get the hard drugs out of my system. That crap's deadly to the body. Anyway, my thumbs in the air as I walked. Then, realizing I was tired, I had a light-bulb idea, I decided to step over the guard rail and find an over-sized shade tree to sit under, away from the freeway. I didn't really know where I was, or, where I was going, for that matter. I didn't care either as long as it was warm. All I knew was, I was somewhere in Kentucky. So, I found a shade tree growing at the edge of a large, rolling field of Kentucky bluegrass. It was about fifty-feet from the freeway. I spread the blanket out by the tree and laid out my weed and rum. I started drinking the rum and soaking up the beautiful rolling pasture. Honestly, I needed a break from it all. Think about it... I'd just came off another cocaine binge in Peoria, Illinois not that long ago. Before that, the crystal meth nightmare back in Albuquerque almost killed me, too. It takes a while for that crap to work its way out of your system. Not to mention your psyche. Well, my psyche was like a fruit loop lost in a never-ending bowl of corn flakes. These hard drugs I'm so eagerly using and getting strung out on are killing me. I was too young and too naive to realize it. The brain cells were disappearing, one by one. My lust for life was leaving, too.

Like cocaine, for example, it's a very dangerous and deadly drug. Before you go down that pathway of trying any of this shit, just research the ingredients. It's a great deterrent. Do that for all the drugs. For starters, I'll bet you didn't know, when cocaine's made, it's washed with gasoline. Wow. Gasoline. Petroleum. Damn. That's a fact. Still want to snort a line, maybe shoot a big rock? Imagine snorting or shooting gasoline. Well? Worse yet, that's just one of the toxic and horribly terrible ingredients used to make cocaine. It's actually disgusting. Google a You-tube video on making cocaine. It'll rock your socks. Scary stuff to think people actually put this crap inside their bodies. I know, I'm guilty as hell of the insanity of that. Had I only known these things when I was young? Before I started using, I may have re-evaluated putting the crap into my body. Maybe.   Now, let's talk about crystal methedrine. I'll tip you to one ingredient in it, too. Let's not even bring up the starter fluid and the other poisons used. Let's talk about Hydrochloric acid. Yes, this deadly acid is used to create crystal methedrine. Unbelievable, I know, but, very true. It's also used to clean swimming pools, among other deadly and highly poisonous uses. Now, don't do this, but, think about what would happen if someone actually did do this... pour a cup of hydrochloric acid over your hand and hold your hand out. Watch it burn into a stub on your arm. Yes, it's like that. It's like napalm. Well, in crystal meth, when you put that in your body, it's no wonder it puts lesions on your brain and they never go away. In fact, they just keep killing your brain cells and getting bigger, obviously, causing more severe damage to your brain. Finally, you turn into a celery stalk. You know what I mean. So, anyway, I had all that crap in me and I was trying to rid my system of all traces of it. Even in my youthful ignorance and lack of intellectual wisdom at this point in my life, I still somehow knew I needed to get that toxic mojo out of my body. It's not an easy road. It's horrible. Just all of it. The mental, emotional and physical ramifications are dangerous and endless. That's why I needed to sit under a tree and escape for a bit, smoke some dope, drink some rum and cop a buzz. I felt like I needed to disappear on the radar screen and, hopefully, find myself sitting somewhere in this wide open field with a few more cards in my favor, with a delicious taste in my mouth, with a sweeter and better flavor to savor... and a better life to embrace being just the right kind of high, so, I could, maybe, float away into the far and away blue sky. Did you notice how I'm sitting here romanticizing this scenario. I'm literally justifying and rationalizing the pot and rum use? Think about that. I did that on purpose because that's typical addict behavior. I wanted you to recognize how that happens. Always look for someone you love, romancing the idea of getting wasted, like it's the answer to all their problems. It's not the answer to any of their problems. It will only enhance and complicate them. Just know that thought process could be a symptom of active addiction. Birds of a feather flock together. Don't allow an addict to pull you into their mix. It's a common addict trait. Set boundaries and keep them, no matter what.

So, here I was...

That blue grass went for as far as I could see. What a sight! I noticed a big herd of cattle off a ways on the pasture. They were just grazing and standing around like nothing else mattered, except right now, eating that blue grass right there. Then, I saw a lone bull off on a hilltop watching all those cattle graze, too. I laughed because I knew what he had on his mind. Mr. Bull was picking and choosing which cow today for that roll in the hay. While I was taking all this unfolding adventure in, I was chuckling about how that bull was just going to take his sweet time and mosey down that hill. Before long, I figure he'd mount every one of those cows. He probably already had. It's like they were all just standing around waiting to see which one he'd pick today. Funny shit really. What a life for the bull, right! I decided to roll me up a big fat doobie. I lit it and smoked about half of it. Dum de dum de dum! Man, I got wasted. I started laughing for no reason at all for the longest time. You know that kind of laugh. Where there's no stopping this no matter what happens. Your sides start to hurt and tears start flowing from your eyes from laughing so hard. Imagine all this in your head. I'm lying in a big field under a shade tree by myself with nary a care in the world. Just lying there puffing away on a big fat doobie. Laughing about nothing like an acid-induced madman peaking on 8-way windowpane. I must've been a sight. High as hell and spread out there and even those cows stopped grazing and watched me for a while. I didn't give a shit. Hell that was funny, too. Well, I started thinking back to some of the crazy shit from that strip club in Albuquerque. Some of those dancers were nuts, I swear. Anyway, you know that certain high when you can't for the life of you, contain yourself. It's just uncontrollable laughter. That's where I was. I had a good buzz on the rum and I was stoned out of my mind on the weed. I'll bet those cows told their little cattle kids about me and I'll be those little cattle kids grew up and they still tell their little cattle kids about that human way back in the day that was lying under a big shade tree

102

laughing like a sick hyena. Things we think about when we're wasted. At least if felt better than the cravings from the hard dope.

This is how the younger minds gets drawn in, if they're not focused on a college education, if they're not pursuing short and long-range goals, or, working at a great job and developing a fruitful career. If they don't have a positive support system with quality time from family, etc., or, a purpose-filled journey with structure, to pursue, then, these seemingly more interesting paths seem like the way to go. Be aware of that. This is what happens when the wrong path is taken. At first and along the way so many situations, like this one, seem so mesmerizing, awesome and fun. Some of these times on the wrong paths can seem so fulfilling, so amazing, so perfectly okay, but, when you least expect it, somewhere along the way, the walls come tumbling down.

The bluegrass was thick under my blanket.

It almost felt like a bed. I laid back and finally came down off the rum and weed some. After a bit, I drifted off for a while. It felt good to close my eyes. After about an hour or so, I woke up and slowly stood up. I rolled the blanket back up, stuffed my goodies in it and made my way back to the interstate. There were cars going by about every half-hour or so. Slightly frustrated, I started walking up the interstate. Still stoned, but, even more now. I walked with my thumb out for what seemed like forever. Finally, I said, "To hell with it". The sun was just beginning to set on the distant horizon. I could see the tree shadows begin to stretch across the rolling fields. All the different branches looked a lot like a crowd of humans with their arms and legs everywhere. There was a deep orange glow to the shadows and if you paid attention to that kind of thing, it'd take your breath away. In another hour or so, it'd be dark and here I was, in the middle of Bumfuck, Egypt, well, Kentucky, anyway. It occurred to me, my 'screw it' attitude was spot on. After walking for what seemed like forever, I threw my bedroll down by the guardrail, got down next to it and laid my frazzled head on it. I propped my feet on the guardrail.

I laid there looking up at the sky for about a half an hour, daydreaming and thinking,

"To hell with y'all, I'm going to sleep here anyway".

I'd made up my mind. This didn't feel too bad. Not that bad.

"The only thing about this that sucks at all, is, there's no street lights, so, it's getting awful dark out here." I thought.

"At least I have a hunting knife with me, in case some wild animal ran up on me, like, maybe a drunk hillbilly, or, something like that." I laughed at that. "What could be worse than a drunk hillbilly?

Oh, I'm so dadgum funny in the middle of nowhere! I'm my own entertainment! Funny."

I shook my head and closed my eyes to drift off to sleep. I could hear crickets off in the woods.

About ten minutes later, a small car went zipping by me, pretty fast. I just laughed to myself. "Dodo on you, too," I said out loud. "It's time for me to crash. I've been walking too much. I don't even want a damn ride! I've done settled in."

I was stoned, half- drunk and just being coy. I closed my eyes again and tried to relax my mind. As I lay there, I couldn't believe it. I hear the sound of that same little car that just flew by me. It was actually driving backwards down the shoulder of the freeway towards me.

I'm like, "what in the actual hell is happening here? I thought.

All kinds of shit ran through my mind. "Maybe some dudes are thinking about robbing me? A serial killer? Hmmm, just what the hell? Ah, I got it, it's a redneck doing a state-wide survey, maybe the census man. " I sat up to see what was up. It was a Volkswagen, a Volkswagen with flowers painted all over it. No shit! It zipped out on the lane and stopped right next to me and the passenger door opened up. The driver had leaned across the car and opened the door.

"Hi there. Are you okay?

"Yes, I'm okay, why?"

"Damn, she's fine!" I thought to myself.

"Well, hey, you're not a psycho killer are you?

(Seriously, she was gorgeous. I mean down-right beautiful. She had long, silky blonde hair that flowed like the waves of an ocean and downward, like a cascading waterfall. Each hair was perfectly synchronized to compliment the next hair. So beautiful! It laid round her shoulders like a summer coat. On her sexy face she had the bluest eyes and the cutest nose. But, what captured me, what really

104

captured me, was her gazillion-dollar smile. I stood up real quick. I was in the presence of an angel. Well, I was in the presence of a very pretty lady.)

"No, I'm a good guy. Why? I wouldn't hurt you for the world." She just smiled the prettiest smile at me.

I just about melted right there in the road.

"Because if you're cool, I'll give you a ride to as far as I'm going"

"Oh, wow, that'd be great. I promise you, I'm a good guy!" I grabbed my bedroll, got in the car and off we went.

I forced myself not to look at her all creepy and shit. But, out of the corner of my eye, I could see her tanned legs and nice, firm boobs. She was something else and it was damn near impossible not to look at her. So, I'd grab a quick look and then I'd look back straight ahead. I couldn't help myself.

"So, where you headed?" she asked.

"It doesn't matter." I answered.

She giggled. "What do ya mean, it doesn't matter?"

"I just got out of the Army not too long ago. I'm hitch-hiking around the country. I don't even know why. I just needed to move around for a while. I think I'm trying to find myself." "Oh, okay, I see." She giggled.

We sat in silence for a few minutes, both thinking about what the other said. I continued to force myself not to look at her. She was wearing little tight blue jean short shorts and a sexy red skimpy halter top. "What a body". She was so dark and tanned, too. "You want to smoke a joint?" She asked.

"Sure." I replied. "I have some, too."

"Oh cool."

I lit her joint and we started smoking. After a few hits, we both started to relax a little bit.

She started talking. "My name's Shannon. What's yours?

"I'm Stormy."

"Oh wow, really? What a cool name."

"Yeah, I hear that every now and then." I smiled at her.

"I'm a nurse from Philadelphia, Pennsylvania. I was transferred to a hospital in Hazard, Kentucky. Have you ever heard of Hazard, Kentucky?"

"Nope, never!"

"How'd you get such a cool name? Hey, where you from?" she asked.

I think she liked me, too. It seemed like it.

"I'm from Tennessee originally, but, I grew up in Illinois. How far are we from Hazard, Kentucky" I asked.

"Well, I moved there about three weeks ago. It's a small town about an hour from us right now. I think it's really redneck. Did you know there's only one way in and one way out of Hazard? This freeway."

"No, I didn't know that. Wow, really?"

"Yes, really. So, you were actually hitch-hiking into Hazard, Kentucky and then, the Interstate dead- ends." She giggled. I nodded my head that I was doing that.

"I need to get me a map, so, I don't do some shit like this again." I thought to myself.

"Hmmm..."

We finally got comfortable and both relaxed. We talked non-stop till we got to Hazard.

It was getting dark out. We both got quiet again while we were both thinking about the same thing. Finally, she broke the ice.

"Okay, I know we just met. I know I don't know you and I know you have nowhere to sleep tonight. You seem like a nice guy. I'll let you sleep on my couch if you promise to be a good guy, a gentleman."

"Yes, of course I will. I promise. Thank you. That takes a load off my mind. Thanks again."

"It's okay." We both just sat in quiet and listened to her music till we got to her apartment.

As we walked in, I could see she'd put her touch in decorating the place. It was definitely a hippie's home. She was definitely a hippie and a creative one at that. A very cool lady, too. She had plants hanging in the windows, unique art everywhere and some very cool tapestry's on the wall. Oh wow, she had a little studio set up in the corner of her living room. There was an easel with a canvas on it and a table filled with paints and brushes. I loved it. I'd never seen anyone's home with an actual art studio in it. I thought, "What a great idea." Her apartment felt really comfortable.

"I'll bet you're starving."

"I am."

"Okay, I'll make us some grilled cheese and tomato soup. Does that sound good? Go ahead and light the bong. "Awesome. Hey, you

106

never told me you were an artist." I smiled at her. "Oh, I dabble a little bit, she replied. "Hey, in the kitchen, I have a bottle of Strawberry Hill in the fridge. Would you pour us a glass?"

"Sure will." I went in and opened the bottle and poured us both a glass. "Did you paint that one on the easel right now?" I asked her. "Yes, I did." She replied as she came in tying her long, beautiful hair back in a pony-tail. "Wow, I love it. It's beautiful." I said as I was looking at the painting. "Oh, well, hey, I appreciate that. Thank you." She had the coolest bong sitting on the floor by the couch. Since she invited me to, I grabbed it and since it had weed in it already, I lit it up. Wow! It was good. By then, Shannon was in the kitchen making the food. It was a small apartment, so, she was really close.

We ate and both sat back on the couch, talking. We talked about everything. She put "Carol King", Tapestry, on her turntable. It felt great just to be able to sit back in a warm place with a beautiful woman. We sat back listening to the music, stoned and relaxing. It was great. I didn't come at her in any way sexually at all. I wanted to be very cool and respectful. After all, she's been nice to me in so many ways. We talked till about midnight. She'd changed into her pajamas earlier just to be comfortable. I continued to be cool and not come at her in any way at all. We just sat back and enjoyed the music, stoned.

Around midnight, she said to me, "Stormy, this couch is all yours." "Cool."

Shannon went in her bedroom and returned with a couple blankets, a sheet and a pillow. I made me a bed on the couch and we both said goodnight. She mentioned she had to go to work in the morning by 8 am. And then, she disappeared into her bedroom and shut the door. I was fine. I was tired, full of good food and stoned. She left "The Doors" playing on the turntable, so, I was good for the night. I closed my eyes, grateful for the place to chill and went to sleep. "Come on baby light my fire" put me right to sleep.

An hour or so later...

"Stormy..... Stormy." I thought I was dreaming. "Stormy...... Stormy." It was like a soft and sweet whisper in my ear. After a moment or so, I opened my eyes, just a little at first to see what the sound was. Then, I opened them wide open! Shannon was standing

107

over me in a little, sexy gown. Her cleavage was in my face and I could see her nipples were hard through the skimpy top.

"Why don't you come to my bed... come sleep with me?" Her blue, piercing eyes smiled at me in the moonlight from the window. She was right there and I was looking right back into her eyes. "Are you sure?"

She nodded. She was sure.

I was in her bed before she was.

We had good sex for about a half an hour. It's like one of those things we all talk about we wish would happen, but, it never really happens. For me, it actually happened. She was clean and smelled so inviting. We passed out in each other's arms.

When I woke the next morning, Shannon was already in the shower. "Damn, this bed felt good." I thought as I stretched and sat up. I couldn't resist, so, I got in the shower with her. She soaped my whole body up and she took her time doing it. It was unforgettable and one of the best showers I've ever had. She told me she had to go to work, but, she'd pack me up a bunch of food, like peanut butter sandwiches, crackers and cheese, some apples and oranges. While she was packing up the food, she told me she'd take me out to the interstate on the way to work. "Cool. Thank you for everything, Shannon."

She looked at me and moved in close for a warm hug. "We had a great night, Stormy. I'm glad we met. You really are a perfect gentleman with a good heart. I can tell. You can come back here anytime and stay with me as long as you want."

"Hmmmmmmmmmm... What a nice thought. I may surprise you and come back one of these days."

"I hope you do."

We hopped in her car and off we went. She drove to the interstate as far as she could and still make it to work on time. Then, she pulled over and got out of the car with me. Standing right there on the shoulder of the road, we hugged and kissed for a good ten minutes. Then, she jumped in her car and off she went.

I never saw Shannon again.

I stood there on that interstate for about ten minutes and a semi pulled over and picked me up. "Hey there. Where you headed?" I asked.

The old trucker with his big ol' cowboy hat on, looked over his shades and said, "I'm headed to Chattanooga, Tennessee. Hop in."

"Hell yeah. Sounds great. Thanks man."

It was about noon when Joe, this cowboy trucker, woke me. I remember now. He literally talked me to sleep. Telling me some story about his ex-wife and wife not getting along. They'd found out he was screwing them both, or, some shit like that. He went on and on about it. The dude must've been on the road a lot. I think he was high on speed. It was like he didn't get to talk to many people and he decided to unload all that drama on me. It got old.

"I don't care, man." I thought to myself. So, I crashed while he was talking.

"We're in Chattanooga. End of the road. We're at a truck stop here. Hey, I have to drop my load close by and I'm headed back north to Chicago."

"Well, thank you a lot. I appreciate the ride." I grabbed my bedroll with the food tied to it, in a bag, and got down out of his truck. I figured I'd better go use the john and freshen up a bit, since I was back out on the road.

So, I go in this bathroom and do the deed, wash my hands and face and start to leave. I opened the door to the john and walked right into two long-haired dudes, laughing and carrying on. We all froze for a second, analyzing the moment and all just shrugged it off and walked on, our separate ways. But, they were cool about it. I remember shit like that.

I had a little cash stashed back in my sock, so, I figured I'd go buy me a bungee cord to wrap the food and blanket up better. I'm browsing the trucker section looking for a bungee cord and I see three hot girls about my age. They're grouped up in the next aisle over, talking real quiet to each other. Me being silly and all and them all being sexy as hell, I made my way to their aisle and walked up to them real fast. "Excuse me, ladies, I'm Security, you're going to have to break this up. You're blocking the aisle and people are complaining."

They all stopped talking and just looked at me, not knowing what to say. They were all so serious and I could no longer hold a straight face. "Okay, okay, I'm joking! It's just a joke. I'm actually a yo-yo head!" They all burst out laughing. The little hot blonde in the group turned and faced me.... Oh, you thought we actually took you seriously?" "Uhhh, well, I hope not."

They were very cool people. We start talking, small talk, what's your name, where you from, what's going on, that type of stuff.   As it turns out, they were sisters. Two of them were dating the two long hairs I ran into at the bathroom. Gypsy, the oldest and the hottest one, I thought, who also happened to be the little blonde I'd first talked to, was single. They were all headed to see "Black Oak Arkansas" and Blue Oyster Cult" at some big arena in Chattanooga. Gypsy told me they were from Cleveland, Tennessee, about fifty miles north of Chattanooga. I told them I'd be glad to wait near their car at the arena if they'd give me a ride back to Cleveland after the concert. They all laughed and looked at me. Gypsy said, "I have a better idea. Why don't you go to the concert with us and then, we'll all go back to Cleveland afterward. I said, "That's cool, but, the thing is, I don't have a lot of cash. I'm really headed south to Florida and, and..."

Gypsy leaned into me, "I'll buy you a ticket, silly. We got some acid, too. Let's party and by the way, Cleveland's not on the way to Florida.

It's north, but, who cares. We're partying, right?"

I'm like, "hell yeah, Cleveland suddenly sounds good to me. I'll worry about Florida later. I say let's do it!"

So, we all load up in Billy's car and head to the concert. They were cool people. Gypsy's sisters were Sally and Sookie. Billy and Sally were together and Sookie was with the other dude, Mitch. Gypsy and I clicked immediately.

She was into me and I was into her. It was obvious. Billy reached in his shirt pocket and grabbed a big fat doobie and tossed it over the seat to me. "Light this up, brother."

"Oh yeah."

As we were passing the joint, Sookie pulled a bottle of Strawberry Hill Boones Farm out of her purse. She'd just bought it at the truck stop. Sally passed around hits of orange sunshine for everyone. We all took our sunshine and drank it down with a swig of Boones farm. The joint tasted good, too.

By the time we pulled in the busy parking lot at this huge arena, we were all pretty toasted. Everything was funny and we were having a blast and we hadn't even got in the arena yet. Gypsy bought me a ticket and in we went. There were thousands of hippies everywhere. We went to the last row in the top, right in front of the stage. No one was behind us and it's a good thing, because, we all started getting off on the acid. Thank God we found our seats and a cool place to be. The people started hallucinating into each other. Gypsy and I acted like we'd been together forever. We clicked. She kissed so well. Maybe I was just high as fuck. She still kissed well.

So, I can remember the bands playing. I know we were there. I know we had so much fun it's hard to even describe. Gypsy, that girl was crazy as hell, especially when she was wasted and God knows, we were all high. I know we had a hell of time. We got so wasted out of our ever-loving minds. I'm amazed I can remember any of it. Somewhere, in the course of that night, I can vaguely remember Gypsy handing me a little baggie with a half-dozen blue valiums in it. I don't even know why. Thank God I put those in my pocket and not in my mouth. I was messed up. We had fun. It's all really a blur.   I do remember pulling into an all-night gas station and restaurant. It had a big flashing sign out front that said ERNIES. It looked like every drunk in town was in there having biscuits and gravy.   Billy and all of them were saying how much they loved meeting me. We all talked about going in to eat, but, we were all tripping our brains out from the acid and everything else, so, we all passed on that idea. Gypsy gave me a big hug and kiss as they got back in the car. I remember her saying she and her sisters lived a few blocks down the road with her parents. Otherwise, I could come crash at her house. I assured her it was all good. I was used to crashing just about anywhere. Off they went. Suddenly, it's 3 something am in the morning and I'm in front of probably the only place open in Cleveland, Tennessee. I didn't know a soul in this town, except for Gypsy and her crew. I was wasted.

So, I staggered down the road toward where they drove. I don't know why. About a block down, I saw a big graveyard on the right. I stumbled my way quite a ways into the graveyard away from the road. I found me a grassy knoll between two graves near a big tree. I spread out my old blanket between those two tombstones, stared at the stars and passed out. It was about 4:30 or 5 am in the morning when the slivers in my eyes cracked open.

The first thing I saw was the stars again, all over the sky. I don't know why I even opened my eyes. Something woke me up. All I do know is, I was lying between two tombstones near a big tree, and my eyes were pointed toward the big sky above. All I could see was bright stars spread across the night. But, then, I saw 7 lights that looked like stars. The difference was, they were lined up and moving together across the sky. I locked in to watch them.

That woke me up. I'm lying there, now, and I'm not moving. I watched as the 7 lights flew in a long pattern, together, and stopped in the sky above me. They just hovered there. I couldn't believe this was happening. As they hovered there, the one in the front of the line, suddenly, flew toward me and stopped just above the tree lines. This circular object just hovered over me about 200 feet in the air for about 10 minutes. I froze. I couldn't move. Inside my head, I was freaking out. I didn't know what to do. So, I didn't do anything. I watched as a light came streaming down from this round object, I guess it was an actual UFO. It hovered as the light streaming from it shone all over the area. It was checking everything out. Curious, I guess.

All of a sudden, it shined the light right on me. I was scared out of my mind. This got serious, all of a sudden. I just laid there and didn't move. After about 1 minute of that light shining on me, it stopped. Then, a moment later, the spaceship shot upward to the front of the ship formation, where it had been.

It startled me. Just as mysteriously as it all happened, they all took off like a light streak across the sky, all moving together. It was the most amazing thing and I didn't imagine it. I laid there petrified and finally, fell back to sleep. It wasn't a dream. It really happened. Believe me, I've thought about that a million times. It happened.

I woke up again, about 9:30 am. What a hangover from that Boones Farm! Damn. So, I laid back for a while and just stared at the sky and the big tree I was laying under. "Seeing spaceships now!" I thought. Eventually, I got up and rolled up my blanket. I walked down to the store and got me a big drink of water from their hose on the side of the building. It was unbelievable when I walked around to the store to use the bathroom. There sat Gypsy and her sister, Sookie, eating breakfast. I walked in and I knew it was cool,

112

when Gypsy jumped up and gave me a hug. She had such a big smile on her face.

"I thought you were long gone. I'm so glad you're still here."

"So was I."

I joined them and we talked for the longest time. I told them about being on the road and meeting so many good people. They didn't seem surprised and agreed with me. They were both so cool. After we had a really good breakfast and we all took an Excedrin for our hangovers, Gypsy drove Sookie to her house and we went driving out on the back roads.

The back-roads in Tennessee are like driving right into a post card. There are so many bright and gorgeous colors in all the trees. She knew about a park with a gorgeous lake that was way out in the country. Gypsy called it Fire Lake.

As we pull up to the lake, it almost took my breath away. It was spacious and beautiful. Bright colorful lilac bushes were sprinkled everywhere. There were big red maple trees all around the lake. Planted around the grassy hills were wild flowers and there were nice picnic areas. I could see a campground down at the end of the lake, near a boat dock. It was a well-kept area, too.

Wouldn't you know it, she had a pillow and blanket in the trunk of her car. We spread the blanket on the carpet-like grass near the water. The mirror of the quiet and still lake showed a big blue sky. It was a sunny day. I felt at peace with her. The view sitting next to her was like a dream. Almost surreal. We walked all the way around that lake later in the day, as the orange sun set over the distant trees.

The smell of wild azaleas filled the air. Holding hands and enjoying the day together is what we did. We also made an elaborate plan for me to sneak into her bedroom, later, and spend the night with her. I thought that was a bit crazy, but, it was her idea.

We left the lake and headed back toward her house. It was dark when she dropped me at Ernie's and headed on home. I sat in Ernie's for a couple of hours, drinking coffee and passing the day with a few old farmers. After they left I sat there for another half-hour talking with Ginny, the store clerk, who was Ernie's daughter, I found out. It was about 8 o'clock. I decided to walk down to their house and check it out. Gypsy had told me which house it was, so, down the street I go.

About a block down, I see the graveyard I'd crashed in the night before. I kept walking past it. Another block or so, I see Gypsy's house. The front porch light was on and a garage light was shining through a window. I walked up to the side of the garage and peeped in. Nobody was in there. That was good. I quietly made my way to the back of the house and looked in the window Gypsy had told me about. There she was on the bed. Damn, she looked good. One of her sisters that I'd never met yet was sitting by her on the bed. I waited for a few minutes until her sister left the room. I lightly tapped on the window. She came to the window real quick and opened it. "Crawl in." she said. In I came through the window. We both laughed quietly.

She leaned into my ear and said, "My mom and dad are on the other side of that door at the dining room table. They'll go to bed soon. Just sit over here by the bed and be really quiet."

"You won't have to tell me that again." I said grinning. She sat on the bed and we joked around and suddenly, there was a knock on the door. Gypsy jumped right off the bed and ran for the door. Out she went. I sat there alone for about ten minutes. Then, here she came in the room saying good night to everyone as she shut the door.

"Yes, now what?" I thought.

Gypsy turned out the light and we both crawled into the bed. We played for the longest time, had sex and then passed out. The next thing I know, she's telling me I have to slip out the window and go. I'm like, "What time is it?"

"3 o'clock in the morning. My dad gets up in a couple hours and you should be gone before then." She was nervous, I could tell.

"Oh, okay."

We had a quickie, said our goodbyes and out the window I went. She ran over to the window as I was about to go. "Hey, you, you going to be down at Ernie's later?"

I didn't want to lie to her, but, I wasn't sure if I'd be there or not. I nodded my head up and down meaning I'd be at Ernie's later. But, I had a feeling I wouldn't be. So, I turned back to her and said, "Hey, I might not be, but, if I'm not, I may stop back by on the way back up North. Is that okay? I don't know how long from now though."

"Yes, stop by if you leave. You better. Okay?"

"Deal." I ran back to her and got a kiss through the window. "Hey, I'll be at Ernie's unless I get on the road, okay. I really like you, no matter what. Remember that." Then, I was gone.

It was time to roll further south.

After a quick stop at Ernie's to grab something to munch on and drink, I decided to leave Gypsy a love note saying I'll be back through someday and I'll stop to see her. I was writing the note and it occurred to me there wouldn't be any traffic out there so early in the morning. She woke me up way too early, so, her dad didn't catch us. I thought, "Hey, I could go down to the cemetery and crash for a couple hours and then, later, there'd be more traffic. Then, I could walk out to the interstate. Shit, I've already crashed for a while at her house, it'll be hard to go back to sleep. Then, it hit me. I could take those blue valiums. That girl back in Chattanooga told me to take them to go to sleep, when we were tripping on that acid. "Oh, hell yeah!" I'd never done valiums before, so, I wasn't sure how many to take to make me sleep good.

It had 5 in it, so, I went ahead and took all 5. They were little bitty pills. "They couldn't be that strong", I thought. Hell, I'd been a junkie. I thought I'd better head down to the cemetery, so, when I got sleepy I could have my blanket spread out in the grass and be on it.

I don't remember anything after that. Nothing.

Not until some old farmer was sitting me up outside.

"Hey, there, you okay? You weren't moving. Didn't look like you were breathing, either. I was just making sure you're okay."

The sun was up and I felt like I was in the Twilight Zone. I was on the sidewalk outside of Ernie's.

"Wow. I must've passed out when I ate the valium. They knocked me out. Wow. Little bitty pills, my ass! Just like that. OUT. "

I was laying on bare concrete. Damn, my head hurt. I felt like I'd been hit in the head with a jack-hammer. I sat up next to the front of Ernie's and looked back in to see if anyone was in there. The place was full of people eating. It felt like they all stopped eating to look at me at the same time. Weird.

"So, they must've all walked in right next to where I'd been laying. They all saw me laying here." I thought to myself.

I was just a little bit embarrassed about that. I ask the old farmer if he'd mind getting me a bottle of coke or something to drink. "Oh yeah, you look like you might need it." Shaking his head...

He brought me out a coke and I just about drank it all in one drink. I was dried out inside. After about a half-hour or so, I finally tried to stand up. I felt like shit. "Damn. I was foggy." I slowly, but surely started making my way toward the interstate. It took me quite a while to get my blood moving again. Those valiums kicked my ass. I was groggy as hell. Finally, I got to moving again. After a while, I still felt like shit, but, I was back on the interstate with my thumb in the air. Some guy in a white Cadillac picked me up minutes later and like dust in the wind, I was gone onto the next adventure. Down the road we went. "This feels a little strange," was my initial thought when I got in the car. But, hey, everybody has a dose of weird sometimes, so, I let it go. Wouldn't you know it, right after this guy crossed the Georgia state line, he offered me 30 dollars to give me a blow-job? Obviously, he was gay. That was a 'no thanks' from me and there I was, once again, standing on the interstate. But, just before he let me out, I felt weird as hell. The air got thick. It felt like he was thinking about some evil shit and weighing if he could get away with it or not. It was all around me. The darkness of it. My third eye cued in or something. I know when he stopped, I jumped out quickly and watched him drive off before I even took another breath. It was a freaky feeling, like I'd just escaped something pure evil. I kept my eye out for that car while I was standing there. After a few minutes it occurred to me, "I still have a dad-gum pounding headache and I think that gay dude was planning my demise. Damn!"

About an hour later...

The sun was just starting to climb in the sky over the line of trees in the distance. It was going to be a scorcher. I was standing at an on ramp with my thumb in the air, talking to myself like a crazy man. I'd just talked myself into eating the last of the cheese and crackers that fine looking nurse, Shannon, had packed for me a few days back in Hazard, Kentucky.

That's when it happened. That's when the ball started to unravel a little bit more. That's when the soup got cold... when the 'hitchhiking was a great idea' started to fog up in my cloudy head. Here's what

116

happened. These two guys pull over in an older model Mercury. My head hurt, I was dehydrated and the valium still made me feel drowsy. So, I was ready to sit down. They just look like two regular old hillbillies. No big deal, right! There shouldn't be a problem. Everything's cool! I'd just escaped the gay guy by the hair of my chinny chin chin. Um hmmmmmmm. Now, finally, I can sit down for a while.

Well, I got in the back seat, shut the door and we took off. Right away, the glue holding the baseball together started to pop loose and the ball started to unravel. (That's a metaphor.) The one on the passenger side turned to offer me a swig out of the half-empty quart of Jack Daniels they were drinking. Then, he proceeded to tell me his name was Clayborn and the man driving was his brother and his name was Buford. They immediately started talking over each other. Buford was telling me he'd just picked up his brother, Clayborn from prison. He'd just served 11 years for a murder he did years back. That's just what I needed to hear. Great! So, they start arguing back and forth about the exact amount of time Clayborn had actually served because Buford hadn't counted the year and a half Clayborn was in county jail.

Then, they started arguing about whose fault it was he was in prison in the first place. It was important to him that this time be counted and the proper blame was stacked in the right place. They start screaming at each other and both of them kept trying to get me to agree with their side of the argument. How in the hell did I get in the middle of this shit? Oh shiiiiiit! It gets even better.

Clayborn takes a huge swig off the whiskey and lunges at Buford while he's driving down the highway doing about 75 or 80. So, if you can picture this. Two crazy, drunk hillbilly's fist-fighting while driving 80 miles an hour down the interstate. I'm in the back seat about to jump out of this car. They're both screaming at the top of their lungs at each other.

"I should've stayed at Ernie's and waited for that chick, Gypsy! Why in the hell didn't I just chill there? First I almost got killed by a gay serial killer and now, this? What the hell."

Then, it popped in my head and all I could do was shake my head, "What could possibly be worse than a drunk hillbilly? Well, TWO drunk hillbillies, of course! Oh my God, I can't believe in the midst of all this bullshit I just thought that." I asked myself that while this old

Mercury was squealing across all the lanes at 80 or so miles per hour. Right about then, the damn car throws a rod. No shit! It threw a rod!!!! Don't you put oil in the car, dude? What the hell else can happen? It was loud as hell! It sounded like a bomb went off under the hood. Buford jerked the wheel to the right and over we went to the side of the road.

The Mercury rolled to a halt. All of us climbed out of the car and Buford opened the hood. They started screaming at each other and fist-fighting again, right in front of the car. I didn't say a word out loud, but, in my head, I thought, "Would you look at that! You two fuck-heads are crazy as a 3 legged monkey! I'm getting as far away from you ass-wipes as I possibly can, immediately!" I just started walking as fast as I could down the interstate away from both of them and their car. I got about 50 yards from the car and when I looked back, they'd finally stopped fighting. Clayborn started yelling at me. Where am I going and all that kind of shit?

I don't answer because I know they're both drunk as hell and this fruitcake just did 11 years for murder.

I'm thinking, "Get me away from these backward-ass drunken dweebs."

I started walking real fast away from them. I was almost running. Right then, a baby-blue and black leather 1972 Lincoln Continental zipped up and pulled over next to me. This jock-looking guy in the driver's seat looked at me and said, "Want a ride!"

Done. "Hell yeah!!!!" I jumped in and off we went down the highway leaving those two drunk nuts in the dust. I looked back and wouldn't you know it. Buford had ran up on his brother and there they were fist-fighting again.

"Adios amigos! Straight-up idiots, I swear! " I thought.

"Hey, man, did you see that shit? Those two guys?"

"Yeah, what was happening there?"

Two hillbillies. They're brothers. The one did a life sentence for killing some dude a long time ago. Both of them crazy as hell, I swear! He just got out. His brother picked him up. When they picked me up, they were already half-drunk. Then, they got all the way drunk. Oh shit!! Check this shit out, that car on the side of the road, the one back a ways parked there. Did you see it?" My adrenalin was sky high just talking about it. "Did you see that car by the road?"

"I think so."

118

"Anyway, it threw a rod when that drunk ass was going about 90, no shit, 90 fucking miles an hour man. I was in the back seat. For real. Car went all over the road. Scared the shit out of me! I don't even know those guys. They almost killed me and hell, they almost got killed, too. Damn!""

I think this guy just saved my life. Those two were insane. I swear!" He was smiling and listening to how this all went down.

"Where you headed?" he asked.

"OH, hell, Nashville, Chattanooga, maybe Atlanta, I don't know, really.

What about you?"

"Headed back to Atlanta. Been in Chicago for a couple of weeks, the ol' lady raking in some cash."

"Really? What's she do?"

"Stripper. Good one, too. Makes that money."

"She looks out of it."

"Yeah, she worked last night till daylight. Anyway, what's your name?

"Stormy."

"Cool name."

"What's your name?"

"I'm Bo. Old lady's Tess. He pointed toward the back. "She's crashed, I think."

I looked back real quick.

"Son of a bitch!" I said to myself. I was thinking, "She looks like a goddess."

I looked quick to be cool about it, but, she looked Latin or something. I wasn't sure what, but, even sleeping, she looked really good. I had to be cool, though. After all, this dude's giving me a ride south. Not to mention, he saved my ass from those two Hillbilly drunk nut-cases, hell, they were killing' each other on the damn interstate.

"Straight-up crazy!" I thought.

I was glad I got away from that shit.

Bo and I listened to some tunes while we rolled down the highway. Tess slept just about the whole way, till we stopped in Chattanooga for gas. Bo was in the truck stop paying for gas and whatever when she sat up. I saw her in the rear view and looked around.

I introduced myself. She said her name was Teresa Martinez, but, her friends called her Tess. That explained that. Wouldn't you know it? What are the odds? Another stripper. She started telling me everything Bo had told me when I first got in the car. I just let her talk. She had really sexy lips, so, while she talked, I couldn't help it, I watched her lips move. They were hypnotic. She said they were headed back to Atlanta. She'd been working in Chicago for a few weeks. She had coal-black hair and deep black eyes, dark skin and probably about 5'3 and a hundred pounds. Smoking hot!

"This Bo is a lucky man." I thought as she kept talking.

She got out of the car to use the john. I figured what the hell, so, I went in, too. Bo started washing the front window. I came back out with a bottle of lemon water and they're both already in the car.

Tess had gotten in the front, so, I got in the back.

Bo says, "Did you guys meet?"

We both nodded yes. I look at Bo and say, Hey Bo, what's worse than running into a drunk hillbilly on the highway?

He looks at me. "I don't know, man. What?" They're both looking at me to hear the answer.

"Running into TWO DRUNK HILLBILLIES! We both laughed. Bo says, "Tess, when you were sleeping, you wouldn't believe the shit happening when I picked this dude up. I think we saved him." "Oh, you did, my friend. You saved me for sure. Those two hillbillies were killing each other.

Thank God you stopped and grabbed me. I do appreciate it. I do."

"Oh, I know you do."

"Ooooh, that's what that joke's about! Two hillbilly's fighting? I didn't get it. Now, I do!" She said

"Yep. Sure was! You guys saved my ass from certain ruin!! We all laughed.

We all got along fine. I found out Tess was actually from Austin, Texas. She heard there was good money in Atlanta for a good stripper, so, that's how she ended up in Atlanta. I also found out her and Bo met in Atlanta. He was actually from New York and was trying to talk her into moving there with him. He was about to go back to New York to live and practice law. He'd just passed the Bar.

It's the same reason they'd both just went to Chicago. They knew he had to go back to New York. Come to find out, Bo doesn't drink, smoke dope or use drugs of any kind. He spent his time going to law

120

school to be an attorney. Now, it was almost time for him to go practice law. How about that?

We were all feeling good, rolling down the highway. We pulled into Atlanta about midnight. She didn't even say anything about me staying at her crib, till we got to her apartment. Come to find out, Bo had his own place. We were all tired from the road. They hugged and kissed and Bo left in his car. He acted like it was no big deal that I was still there when he left. He, obviously, didn't feel threatened by me at all. I was about 5 years younger than both of them. They seemed cool about it all, though. I was still young.

She's like, "Stormy, help me get my suitcase and bring it in. I don't know about you, but, I'm tired. I'm going to take a quick shower and go to bed. Make yourself comfortable. You can crash on my couch. I'll get you some blankets and a pillow when I get out of the shower. Okay?"

"Sure, thank you, Tess. You sure you don't mind me crashing here?"

"Yes, baby doll, I'm sure. It's all good. Glad I can help. Here's the remote for the TV."

"Thank you." I smiled at her as she handed me the remote.

Then, she disappeared into the bathroom. Her crib was set up nice. It was pure class. She was making good money dancing. It was easy to see that. I sat back and chilled on the big, comfortable leather couch.

She came out of the bathroom drying off and said, "Hey, Stormy, you're welcome to take a nice, hot shower. Mine felt great." "Would you look at that?" I thought to myself. "Smoking ass hot!" "Oh yea, that does sound good." I replied. I was being cool. I didn't want to disrespect her in any way. It was a nice place, she was a cool lady and I was tired.

I walked by her and went on in the bathroom. I took a nice, long, hot, much-needed shower. She had huge, clean towels, so, I grabbed one and dried off. Following her lead, I wrapped the towel around me and walked out. Tess had candles burning in her bedroom and Pink Floyd playing on her system. But, mostly, she had the covers over her in her King-sized bed and she was snuggled in. We were both tired. I laid back on the couch, closed my eyes and listened to Dark Side of the Moon, playing softly from her room. She'd left her door half open, so, I could hear it. Cool lady. Sleep came quickly.

Two days of partying later... Tess and I, coke, rum and weed...

I'm staying with Tess now. We haven't seen Bo since we got in town. Turns out she's a cool lady. No romance. It's nothing like that for us. She was just someone that felt alone and met someone who was alone.

We grew to be friends. I stayed in Atlanta with Tess for about 2 months and I swear I'll never forget a minute of it. We found out Bo had left for New York and he never even said goodbye to her. But, sometimes goodbyes are hard to do. She was mad and hurt about it, but, I understood where he was coming from. After I'd lived with her a few weeks, I started going to the club she worked at. I'd get wasted while she worked. She kept me flush with cash and drinks. We started doing lines of coke together everywhere. Behind her back, I started copping coke from one of our stripper friends whose old man was a dealer. Then, while Tess worked, I'd stay home and I started shooting it. We never had sex. Maybe she thought I was too young for her. I'm not sure. Once she told me I reminded her of her younger brother, Tony. He'd overdosed and died 2 years earlier. I think I reminded her of Tony a lot. I'd see her staring at me sometimes. And it was never sexual for us in any way. I would've gone for it, but, she never gave me any energy like that, so, I respected her feelings. I'll bet she was thinking about her little brother when I was around. Eventually, she found out I was copping coke from her friend and got really pissed at me.

One day, she said she wanted to go back to Austin, where she's from, to work. That was cool with me. She was making a thousand or more a night working on Peach Tree Street. But, she knew what time it was in stripper world, so, off to Austin we go. We'd grown into a family, like a brother and sister. You could almost say we loved each other and for me, that was scary. I don't think I loved myself, so, there was no way I could love somebody else.

One day, she'd been gone for hours and I started shooting coke. A few hours into it, she walked in and caught me. She went off. We both got pissed and it turned bad. We both said things we didn't mean. It hurt. I left and stayed gone for a couple of days. I was partying at a friend's. Well, I don't know if friend is the right term. We shot dope together.

After we'd both gotten wasted, we went to her work at a club in Austin. I met some dudes this guy knew and we started drinking and talking. They all had dancers working there, too. They were a crew. I

122

don't know if they grew up together or what, but, they seemed tight. This crew and I clicked. I thought these guys were cool as hell. So, we started getting together at this club where Tess worked and hanging out. We'd all get drunk as hell and I find out they can get pure coke, too. So, I start copping coke from them and we're all partying our asses off. After a few months, we'd gotten pretty tight. One night, they confided in me that they could use me in their crew if I was interested. I'm a young guy, looking to get into shit, so, here I go. They tell me they're robbing dope-dealers, houses and whatever else they could break into. There I was, in the middle of this shit now. But, I was always about the hustle. Like I've already stated, I'd do about anything except gay shit. Well, we robbed several houses all over South Texas. Then, we robbed a jewelry store and a couple gas stations. I ended up with a whole bag of diamonds, watches, rings and other assorted shit. One of the guys had a fence (somebody that would buy stolen jewelry, drugs and whatever else) and we sold a bunch of the jewelry and some weapons to him. We met him at a strip club in San Antonio.

During all that, unbeknownst to the other guys, I took about ten of the nicest diamond rings and tied them all together. I put that in my pocket and kept it. It was my secret payoff to myself for robbing this shit, in case they tried to fuck me over. After all, I was new blood in the crew. I still had that in my head. If I was anything, after the shit I went through in Hawaii, I was street smart.

Menard Max- Brothers doing time- South yard- early to mid-70's...

123

Chapter 5

STRIPPERS

A few months later...

The first thing I noticed was my disheveled face, almost plastered onto the cold, nasty concrete.

There was dirt in my mouth and I could feel I'd been slobbering on myself. Without moving, I opened my eyes to the immediate area. I could see through the haze, just enough, to know I was in a strange space. I could see bars on a door, and I knew right away, this wasn't good.

"Jail, man! Dirty-ass floor, shit smell and all!"

Slowly sitting up, I tried to get my bearing. All I could see around me was about a hundred Mexicans in a long, dreary looking jail-tier. This was messed up.

"Would you look at that?" I thought. "Damn!" As I scoped the area, I thought back to the night before.

It all came flooding back to me.

The crew and I had rolled up to a Strip Club, somewhere, in San Antonio, Texas. Something we did a lot.

Walking in, I knew this was going to be some kind of night. Six stages, and they all had smoking hot dancers making a lot more than their rent money. The place was filled with bikers, players, drug-dealers and hot, sexy nearly naked babes. I made my way to the bar and within minutes, I was at a VIP table with our crew and a half-dozen other partiers. We were all buying shots and the women smelled the free ride. They were everywhere. Of course, I didn't trust any of these other dudes or strippers. Hell, I didn't even trust Jo Jo and those guys that much. But, just meeting these other dudes, made me overly cautious. So, this one dude, Slick Rick, sitting to my left, he seemed alright.

We got along fine. We went outside to smoke a doobie and he showed me his Harley. Damn, that was a clean bike, not like my ol' Rat bike. I wanted a really nice Harley like this. One I could ride more than I worked on it. I was young.

Rick was cool. He was a Paul Bunyan looking dude with a flashy personality. You know the kind. Handsome, badass type, very cued-in on the ladies. They were cued in on him, too, it seemed. The man was a big, hard-ass player and the women loved it. That tripped me out.

I'm thinking, "They know he's a player and they're still all over him. Hmm, they love the bad-boys. WOW. " Being young, I had to file that info away for future use.

So, our table stayed filled with the dancers and soon enough, it was filled with empty shot glasses, too. Jo Jo and those guys got wasted and all left. I stayed at the Club for just one more. What the hell, I'm partying. It wasn't too soon after that, we're all out back, smoking herb, snorting coke and Slick Rick had slid up next to a stripper named Traci. I'd been hanging with two others, named Jane and Renee, barely old enough to dance. They were a little younger than me. They weren't identical twins, but, they were twins and they were beautiful, each in her own special way.

They both had long, beautiful blonde hair and big blue eyes. Neither one of them weighed more than a hundred pounds, soaking wet. We proceeded to drink, smoke and parrrrtttyyyyyy! About 4 am, when the Club closed, Jane and Renee said let's go get a nice room at a Motel they knew about, so we could finish our party. Slick Rick, Traci and I all said let's go. Out the door we go. All five of us. We get a nice room, like a suite. Rick looks at me and says, "Hey, bro, let's go to the room and just have one more." We all burst out laughing.

"Just have one more? Right."

(Lessons in life... This night would prove to be yet another one of those memorable events. Some memories we flash back on are just things we couldn't even make up. The reality of the events, far outweigh, whatever the imagination could conjure up. So many times in life, we'll look back and just shrug our heads in disbelief that we even lived through some of the unbelievable shit that happens.)

We're partying, wasted from all the booze and drugs. We were just one big happy, wasted bunch. Do you see a problem? I don't see a problem. After a while, Slick Rick and Traci were out in the living room, probably somewhere between the couch and the middle of the floor. Jane, Renee and I were all naked in the big bed in the bedroom.

We were fooling around with each other, having foreplay fun. That's when it happened. That's when it flowed through me. I didn't know what it was, but, I knew it didn't feel right. The vibe got funky all of a sudden.

I jumped up from the bed and ran over to the window. I peeped open a little piece of the drape and looked outside real quick. "Kiss my ass!" I said in a low tone. Outside the window, I could see cops in position, everywhere, circling like wild Indians on a wagon-train. Thing is, they're all trying to be slick, ducked down behind cars all over the parking lot.

But, I could see heads bopping around. I had to look really hard to make sure I wasn't hallucinating from the cocaine. I wasn't. Those cops were there. I looked again to be sure. Yep. They're there. I'm thinking to myself, "Would you look at that! Damn man, I just slid up here trying to get some poontang, slide in and slide out. "What the hell is this bullshit? Renee, Jane, hey Rick, COPS ALL OVER THIS BITCH!"

With my pants in one hand and my boots in the other, I head for the bathroom, screaming, "COPS," again, to Rick and everybody. The girls and I went into panic mode, trying to hide dope, booze and get dressed. In the meantime, Rick has a pistol out and is peeping out the window. I'm like, "what the hell, man? Hey man! Time to get the hell out of here!" I'm thinking, "I don't even really know this dude."

Here's the thing...I'd just got out of the Army not that long ago. I'd almost got killed in Albuquerque, twice. That son of a bitch shot at me 6 damn times. I'm lucky to be alive! Not to mention the hooker's crazy-ass dad, the Spanish dude, shooting at me with that 22. To hell with all that. Enough already. I'd been through that whole trip and I was just trying to get some party on. You know what I'm saying. This is NOT part of the party! Now, I'm thinking out loud, as I noticed this small window in the bathroom in the back of this motel. All three strippers ran into the bedroom throwing their clothes on.

Renee ran over to their bedroom door and looked at me and shut the door. They were freaking out. We all were. Ricks over there in the front room with a pistol in his hand, looking out the window. What the hell's that about?

"Hey, I just met this dude. I don't need to be loyal to him. I was here for the party. This dude's jumping off the deep end. Shoot out with the cops? Oh hell No! We're just partying, man. What the hell? I'm 19. Shit! Not me. Got to be more to this! Whatever! I'm out of here. Jail ain't on my schedule."

I tie up my boots real quick, pop open a bathroom window and slide through it. Slicker than owl shit, I drop to the ground. I don't move.

"Okay, so far so good. Right now, getting my ass away from this heat and all this bullshit is at the top of my list."

All the dope and booze had me head-tripping.

"It's going down. Hmmm." After a quick trip back through my thinking, while I stooped down behind that bush. I realized I had to get away from this.

The strippers would be fine. I'll talk to them later. For now, to hell with this shit! So, I froze where I was at. I look around all the buildings and I see cops through the bushes watching the back of the building. I just froze there and watched them for quite a while. Then, finally, they walked toward the front for something, but, I knew I had to hurry. I knew they'd be back, so, ever so carefully, I slipped quietly away from the back of the apartment.

At first, I felt nervous as hell, knowing Slick Rick was in there about to shoot it out with the cops. Far as I was concerned, I didn't sign up for all that shit. I was just here for the drugs and hot women. All this serious shit, screw that! Like I said, I'm only 19, maybe just turned 20. So, across a field I go and then, across some tracks and down a road and,

"I'll be damn...I'm getting away! I don't know how I pulled that shit off. I figured those cops would've grabbed me, going out that window."

Truth is, I thought those cops would have the back of the building covered better. But, somehow... I slipped away and down the road I went. That still amazes me, thinking about it.

By now, I'm almost running. "It sounds simple and thought out. Ya know, out a window, like a ghost... across a field, ninja-type shit, down some tracks, across a street, down the road a half-mile or so ...simple. So easy." I just snickered at my clever ways.

"Am I really this slick? Looks like I got away!" I'm walking fast and starting to smile real big at my smooth get-away.

Yeah, I was starting to feel pretty good about myself. So, I walked another half a mile, or so, turned down a few streets and came upon a McDonalds.

"This is a perfect place to chill, regroup and start over. I could use a good cup of coffee, egg mcmuffin, maybe," I thought.

I took my first deep breath and headed across the parking lot. I stopped to let this car-load of long-haired biker dudes go by. I'd done it. I'd gotten away. I stopped to slowly exhale my breath and enjoy my new-found freedom.

I thought to myself, "Now, would you look at that! There's a cool bunch of motherfuckers right here. I wonder why they're not on their Harleys."

There were four of them and they all had big beards and hair to the middle of their backs. They were all wearing shades. Biker rings on, leathers and all! They were a rough looking bunch, but, still, cool looking to me. As they drove by, I kind of nodded at them. The driver nodded back and stopped. A couple of them smiled.

"That was cool." I thought to myself.

It looked like he was going to ask me something, like how to get somewhere. Literally, in the blink of an eye, I had four, count 'em, four, "Texas Rangers" badges, flashing in front of my face. The driver quickly shook me down and put the handcuffs on me.

I was arrested for "Suspicious Activity" and leaving the scene of, and, in the company of a convicted Fugitive. "Aiding and abetting a fugitive". They charged me with that shit to lock me up. Later they added more drug-related charges. Here's how crazy I was. The ten diamond rings I had tied together and had stuffed in my pocket,

128

well, when I got busted by the Texas Rangers and they took me in and booked me. I turned the rings in with my property when I was getting booked. Some of that street hustling behavior.

I told the cops they were heirlooms that had been in our family for many, many years. I said my grandmother had passed away in Tennessee and had left them for me in the will. I've been carrying them because I didn't really have a place to keep them. The cop in the property room says to me, "Sorry about the loss of your grandmother." "Oh, thank you. I appreciate that." Then, he put the rings in my property in the booking room. No biggie. No biggie, my ass! Those rings were physical evidence in a jewelry store robbery. Oh well.

Turns out, my friend, from last night, Slick Rick, had just broken out of prison. This is what I was told later.

Then, he went in a garage, at some house about a mile from the prison and stole a Harley. That must've been the one he was riding, when I met him. This dude, man, damn! He was doing life without parole, and, I guess, after fifteen years, had made it to a work farm. I'm betting the thought of free life, good sex with a woman, good drinks and dope, just took him over.

One night, he simply walked off the work-farm. Slick Rick disappeared into the night. I think this is where he messed up. He forgot to stay disappeared. Once he stole that Harley, it was ON. He said "Let's do it" and began to party it up. That's about the time I ran into him at the strip club. We made some pretty good memories. Some pretty good memories for a man, to take back to life in prison, anyway.

So, that's how I ended up on this dirty-ass floor in this stinking-ass jail. I'd been locked up in Texas for several months. It seemed like forever. It was the first time I'd ever stood before a judge, too. That Texas judge sentenced me to 'five to life' in prison for drug-related crimes. It was hell. By the way, I never heard from any of those women I met hitch hiking ever again. They were just good times along the way. I guess that's what we all are, really, right? Are we just good times along the way? I hope not. I'd like to believe somewhere down the road, life becomes more than a series of good and bad times. Surely there must be more. We shall see...

Anyway, Bexar County jail in San Antonio was a hi-rise building in downtown San Antonio. It's worse than most prisons. Believe me, that's an eerie distinction. The jail tiers were 99 % Mexican gangbangers. The tiers were designed to house about 40 inmates. Our tier had well over a hundred Mexicans in it. All straight-up thugs. Talk about some primitive shit. We slept all over the floors. Some had to sleep by the toilets and these nasty asses would get up and shit right next to people laying all around the toilets. All night and day listening to everybody yelling, "aqua, aqua!!" It was filthy in the tier. There was constant screaming and fighting. There was nowhere to get away from all the bullshit. It was packed with cons, so, tempers were short.

Dudes would be having sex right in front of everybody. It was disgusting. Dudes jacking off and not caring if anybody seen them. They hated whites and they hated blacks even worse. I lied for the sake of survival. I said my Mother was Mexican, so, I was half-Mexican.

The shot-caller that ran our tier was half-Mexican, too, so, we got along okay. One of the dudes told me the leader was in for three murders, so, he wasn't going anywhere, except to prison for the rest of his life. Crazy man.

But, dude was cool with me and that made my life a little easier in this madhouse.

Anytime a black would come into our tier, he wouldn't last more than an hour or so. They would jump him and literally beat him nearly to death. After he was beaten unconscious, they'd pull his body over by the front tier door and leave him. Eventually, the Mexican guards would drag him out and we'd never see him again. That happened several times while I was there. Because it was my first offense, after several months, my court-appointed lawyer finally got me another hearing before the judge. He presented my case straight-forward. I was young, a veteran, this was my first offense. I was from out-of-state. So, he requested the court suspend the sentence, give me 5 years of paper and send me back to Illinois. Let me tell you, Texas doesn't play very well with dope-heads and criminals from out of State. Especially from a Yankee state like Illinois, where my folks had moved to. But, the judge listened to my case and gave us what we asked for. He suspended my sentence, gave me 5 years of paper with the understanding that if I violated the terms of parole, I would have to come back to Texas and complete the 5 to life sentence in Huntsville prison. The judge kicked

130

me out of Texas and sent me back home on a Greyhound bus, to Illinois. My God, I was relieved to get the hell out of Texas.

Like I said earlier, the jails down Texas way are filled with Mexicans. The Texas guard drove me to the bus station and told me not to get off that bus till I was in Illinois. No problemo. Ya think? All the shit I'd been doing, strippers, robbing houses, stores, drug-dealers, shooting all that dope. I was done here. I was lucky as hell I wasn't locked up forever. I'd had all the Texas I wanted. I didn't get off that bus except to piss until it pulled up in Peoria, Illinois.

"All you have to do is NOT violate your parole, Mr. Monday, you'll be fine! Keep your ears clean." resonated in my head over and over. Those were the final words the judge had said to me. All I had to do is NOT violate parole and I'll be fine!! Then I could go on with my life. Okay. That's the plan. Freedom's a lot more than a word, I'm finding. I'd just got off the greyhound bus from Texas, after being locked up there for eight or nine months. I had a 5 to life suspended sentence hanging over my head. I was trying to get my bearings, now that I was in the Midwest. They'd transferred my parole there, where my people were living now, with the understanding I couldn't go back to Texas, while I was on paper. If I did, that would be a violation.

So, here I am, in Peoria, Illinois. My family lived a few blocks from Taft homes. These were the projects, on the North side. North-enders! Our home was at 411 Evans Street, and 2 houses from Greeley Elementary. Greeley was about 98% black, from the projects, a few Mexican kids and a few white kids. While I was in prison, my five younger sisters were in Greeley and Woodruff High in our neighborhood.

The neighborhood had some whites and Mexicans, but, it was mostly black. Welcome to the ghetto.
My parents couch was a temporary bed for me while I figured out what I was doing. I didn't like the scenario, sleeping on the couch, but, just getting out, I had to sleep, somewhere.

That lousy paper from the parole office, let's talk about it for a second. It's like an eye that follows you, wherever you go. But, listen to me. It beats the hell out of celling with a mentally deranged murderer that thinks of killing as a general past-time. So, I was on paper with a five to life suspended sentence from Texas. Texas is rough, but, I was now under the watchful eye of the State of Illinois.

They had me on maximum security supervision. I had to report, in person, to the parole officer, every Friday before 5 pm. Prison-life, from Texas, still had me caught in some kind of psychosis from the bullshit found behind those dreaded walls.

Peoria. The heart of Illinois.

My first future ex-wife, Brenda and I met soon after I got there from the road. Let me tell you, the sparks went wild and our feelings for one another were mutual. I guess some of that bad-boy mojo rubbed off on me. She bought me a beautiful 1966 Ford Thunderbird. Badass ride! I picked it out. My partner, Skeeter, got out of the Army a month or so later and showed up at my parent's house. I just happened to be there, so, we were off and running. What timing! I'd been hitch-hiking all over the damn country, been in jail and finally made it home. Then, out of the blue, here's Skeeter. What a trip! So we dive it head first. We're partying heavy, shooting dope and raisin' hell, almost immediately. We honestly didn't realize we were so out of control. One Friday night, I went to jail on a battery charge, yet again, and while I'm in jail, Skeeter borrowed my ride and robbed a Kroger store. We're drug-addicts. He was broke and needed to get high. We're on a wild ride, shooting cocaine and drinking whiskey during all this.

Anyway, I don't know anything about him stealing my car and robbing the Kroger that's a few miles away. I bonded out on the battery charge. Two nights later, Skeeter had tipped me about the robbery by then. The cops show up at my door to bust me for robbery, because someone took down my license plate at Kroger's. The only reason I didn't go back to jail was, I told them I was in jail when somebody stole my car. It was parked down the street from my house when I got out of jail. I was glad to get my car back, so, I didn't report it. Because they could confirm I was already in jail that did save my ass. Of course, on the flip side of that, months earlier, Skeeter and I made our way down to Lexington, Kentucky, where his roots are. He had a Trans-Am put away in storage. We got that bad boy out of storage as soon as we got there.

We partied our asses off and Skeeter introduced me to several of his old friends. We were having one hell of a time. His grandmother let us crash at her house in the extra room in the attic. I believe with the whiskey and drugs, we were a bit too crazy for her. That all ended one night when I used Skeeter's Trans Am, to take this chick I'd met, out for a few drinks and a good time. Coming back, later that night, I was drunk and got in a high speed chase with a cop. He caught me speeding and I just said, screw this and took off like a bat out of hell. Well, that didn't turn out too well. I ended up crashing into Skeeter's grandmother's house. I tried to take the turn into the driveway at about fifty miles an hour. That's about forty miles an hour, too fast. I slid across the front yard, took out the front porch and ended up in the front room, car and all. Lucky as hell I didn't kill myself or anybody else when I hit that house. Well, I went to jail. I sat in that damn jail for several days. They finally gave me a personal recognizance bond, or, a PR bond and then cut me loose. Skeeter and I hit the road and headed back to Peoria, Illinois. I was an outlaw and I never looked back. As far as I can figure, the statute of limitations ran out on those crimes, after eight years, or so.

One night in Peoria, Illinois, we were smoking angel dust and drinking whiskey, wasted out of our minds. I saw him pick up and throw a 300 pound bouncer through the front window of Sgt. Peppers, in Peoria, Illinois. After that, my brother, Skeeter, took off with cops looking for him, and I never saw him again.

Chapter 6

Living in an addicts head is like living in a bad neighborhood.
You should never go there alone.

A TASTE OF FREEDOM

Adios Texas....

Some friends I'd met from before, heard I was free and I was back. The shit got crazy. So, they scooped us up and we were off into the night. Here we are, all of us, drunk as all get up and high as hell, in that 1973 purple Thunderbird of Wild Billy's. Raising hell and not giving one shit about it!!! We had zero fucks to give.

They turned me onto a hot spot on Farmington Road, called, Sgt. Peppers. On the way there on Nebraska, above Bradley Park, Billy came up on some barricades doing about 70, where they were working on the road, earlier in the day. It was right before Sterling Avenue. He floored it, his brakes went out and we tore through those barricades and ended up sideways in a ditch. Just like that, it happened. It scratched and beat the hell out of every one of us. What do we do? We're all bleeding like stuck pigs.

But, we're all messed up and crazy as hell, every one of us. So, we start laughing about this shit. We're just whiskey drunk, high as hell on weed, and dusted. We're bleeding all over the place. Well, we're close to the bar, just down the hill. We all get out, badly messed up, bleeding and shit, looking around, laughing, and all start running down the hill toward the bar. Billy says, "To hell with it, I'll get this bitch later". We're off down the hill, trying to get to the party.

This place was lit up! Sgt. Peppers! As we stumble up like we'd all just got our asses whipped, we're laughing like nothing mattered in the world. Well, the wreck did beat and scratch us all up, but, we were partying and trying to hook up with some babes. Priorities, man.

This is a perfect example of how messed up a man's priorities are when active addiction pounces into a life. Priorities go right out the window. Nothing matters anymore, except finding dope, using it and an occasional piece of ass. That's all that matters.

Sgt. Peppers...

The front of this place is lined with Harleys. Then, the next thing I see are gorgeous babes in these little mini-skirts standing around everywhere, smoking weed, partying and shit. Of course, dudes were hanging out, too, but, I'd just got out of the joint. I didn't even see those guys, other than, mentally checking out who had what weapon and who might be a threat if shit went down.

Analyzing who I'd take out first and how I'd do it. The kind of shit some crazy dude might think of that just got out of the joint and was skittish as hell. We're about to walk in and here comes two dudes rolling out the front door, beating the hell out of each other. I felt right at home. I'd been living in Gladiator School, anyway. Plus, my brother Skeeter was there, too, so, I'll have a pitcher of Crown and seven, and let's tear this bad boy up!

The band was "Eyes". They were badass. They were a great band. I remember the band saying they were from Cleveland, Ohio. Many years later, I found out they were a local band. It didn't much matter. Great marketing, right! Anyway, they were wicked! They also had a great stage show. I was having a good time listening to them and checking out the babes. Then, I find out, a band called *Eargasm* was playing the next night. Dig that! It seemed planning shit to do was going to be easy around these parts. The nights almost planned themselves. Let's go out and get wasted. That was the plan, every day and every night, that was the plan.

Anyway, we tear it up that night. The angel dust had kicked in and we were running all over the bar, drinking pitchers of Jack and coke, Crown and seven and smoking weed right at the table. Angel Dust is some heavy shit. It makes you lose track of where the floor is. I'm serious as hell! When you try to take a step, the floor seems like it's up near your waist. Crazy!!! It also makes you feel like King Kong. That's not good. I found out later that Angel Dust is an animal tranquilizer. We were injecting animal tranquilizer into our bodies. Anyway, I'm on parole. This is how an addict in active addiction acts, when he doesn't understand what he's caught up in. The deadly path in this lifestyle are disguised with parties, fun and good times, without structure, there's zero discipline and any sense of responsibility goes out the window. Working from a priority list doesn't even enter the picture when getting wasted all the time. We all needed to figure these things out in those days. We didn't have a grip on the dangers lurking at every corner in the streets! It was fun, though. Well, for a while, it was. We thought. But, good God almighty! Here's the truth of it. We were like maniacs running around with our heads cut off. We didn't have an ounce of structure, any plan whatsoever and one by one, we've all paid the price. Most are dead now and it's directly because of drugs.

One night we were all partying at a close friend, (Randy S) Rebel's house. There was about 7 or 8 of us getting high, smoking, drinking and shit. Our plan was to party for a while at Rebels and then all go to the Koliseum over in East Peoria. That's a 4 am club, live music, hot women, good times, etc. So, I got a good line on a couple grams of dust, a hundred hits of acid and a kilo of weed. The dudes with the dope lived on the other side of Pottstown, which was a drive out a country road for 12 miles or so, but, the good dope and good deal would make it worth the drive. Together, we decided to put our money on the table and count it, then, I'd go cop the dope from these dudes, since, I'd dealt with them before. Then, we'd split it up, all get high and sell the rest at the Koliseum for party cash. That sounds like a plan to me. Right. Together, we all pulled a shit-load of money out, counted it and I put it in my pocket. Rebel had a red Volkswagen full of gas and said I could use it to drive for the dope. So,

I head out with around 500 bucks in my pocket. Rebel lived off Western, so, I took it to Farmington Road then, veered right to head out toward Pottstown. It was about 12 miles out. I head out and about 5 miles out, I had to go through this railroad tunnel and around a sharp curve. Everything was cool. I was cruising along, just trying to get there and get back so we could all party. I go through the tunnel and around the sharp curve and BAM. There's a car up about fifty yards, sitting sideways in the country road. Two dudes are behind the car and they opened fire on me. I had bullets going all around me. Through the windshield, front end and all over. My adrenalin went straight out the top of my head. I slammed on my brakes and thank God I was in a small car. I did an instant U-turn, hit the gas and went back around the curve real quick. Both dudes were shooting at me the whole time. Those son of a bitches were trying to kill me. I believe it was a robbery attempt. Somebody thought they could kill me on that country road, take the dope money and disappear. That's my theory. It takes a real punk to kill a man over 500 measly bucks. Rebel's car had over a dozen gunshots all over it and for some reason, I didn't get shot once, not even once. So, we talked about it when I got back with no dope and the car shot all to hell. Hey, I still had the money. There was no way of deducing who did that. To this day, I've never found out who those low-life scum-sucking bastards were.

Speaking of the Koliseum, I remember another night, flashing back, we're drunk as hell and somehow, for some reason, Tommy, another crazy brother, throws a chair into a table full of drunk bikers. This was some more wild shit at the notorious Koliseum in East Peoria. I'm sitting there with Dave W., BJ, and Tommy sipping my drink and minding my own business. Skeeter was off with some woman, so, he wasn't there. In the blink of an eye, Tommy jumps up with a chair in his hand and throws it at about 8 bikers sitting at a few tables across from us. Well, it was on like donkey Kong. So, we all roll out the door and Tommy and this one big ugly biker that had gotten hit by the chair, well, they're eyeball to eyeball screaming at each other. The rest of us are circled around those two watching each other in case somebody else got Froggy. I'm cued in on all of it and I notice this biker that Tommy's screaming at is sliding a long-neck beer bottle down into his hand from inside his leather sleeve on his left side. I just watched it slide down his arm. At about the same moment he got a good grip on the neck of that bottle, I round-house kicked the dude in the face and I swear his head hit the ground before his feet did. The shit hit the fan! See, here's the thing, we'd all just got out of prison. We had a shit-load of built up frustration that these bikers weren't quite aware of. So, we unleashed the lion on these fella's. They were probably great dudes, too. In the midst of all the chaos, how could we know? As the bodies started hitting the pavement, here comes the cops rolling in the parking lot from up the Creve Coeur hill. At the same time, these 3 women we were messing with rolled up real quick with passenger doors open and in we dove. As the cops were pulling up, we drove off and went real quick over the bridge and into Peoria. Twenty minutes later, we're all at Patty W's house, (a girl I was seeing) naked and doing the wild thing all over the living room. Like nothing else even happened.

I'll discover in life that Tommy, Dave, BJ, Mingo and I do that kind of shit, often. We would do that, especially, when we're all drunk as hell. In those days that was all the time. So, my next memory is, a few nights later, again at Sgt. Peppers, some dude knocked me over two Harleys with a good sucker-punch, right-cross, and I sprawl out in the gravel in the parking lot for half a moment. The mistake he made was jumping over those Harleys on top of me. By then, my adrenalin had kicked in, all that time in prison kicked in, and as he came over those bikes and landed on top of me, I used his own momentum and adrenalin and flipped his ass off me. Like a well-oiled machine, I spun over on top of him. I was strong and filled out from pumping prison iron for a few years.

Pumping that iron in the yard every day is a necessity inside the walls for the sake of survival. So, as I start pounding this dude's face in, I see Tommy C roll by wrapped up with some other dude. They're trading punches and we were all just hog-wild. A few minutes later after we'd both beat these dudes senseless, a county cop rolls into the parking lot, lights flashing, and we jump up real quick. A crowd of party people had gathered around to watch the fights.   The cops run up and we're just standing there, while the other two dudes are just trying to stand up. I've discovered an ass-whipping will do that to you.

It's obvious who these dudes have been fighting with. All four of us have little gravels stuck all over our jean jackets, our blue jeans and I even had gravel stuck to my face.

The cop looks me right in the eyes and says, "Who was fighting?" "Not me, sir!" He looks me over and sees all the gravel stuck all over both of us. He just shakes his head, "Lying to me won't help you. Let me get your ID's and wait here."

We stand there picking gravel off our clothes and faces and the other dudes are wiping off their clothes, too. We forgot what we were even fighting about. I was thinking I was going back to prison. It was just a matter of fact, kind of thought that ran through my head. I told Tommy to go by my Mom's and let her know tomorrow, or something.

He says, "Oh yeah, man. I will if I'm not in jail."

Fifteen minutes go by and the cop finally walks back up to us. He hands us all back our ID's. Then, he looks at me. "You're on paper."

"Yes sir, I am".

He's like, "are you an idiot? I could violate you right now. I could call your Parole Officer right now. I know them all. Right now, you could be headed back to prison. You're not even supposed to be at a bar, or drinking, or around other felons and you're fighting too! Listen to me, son, you better re-evaluate your life. You're on a bad path, a rough road. He said, "Listen to me! This is your one and only chance with me. Go get in your car and take your ass home right now. All of you! If I see any of you here again tonight, I'll take you to jail. Is that understood?"

"Yes sir!!"

"I should take you to jail now. Don't make me regret letting you go free. Now go!"

We turned, started walking, quickly away from the cops and I see some dude we didn't know, headed to his car.

I caught up to him, nodded and said, real low, "Hey man, this cops watching us, can we catch a ride to the top of the hill, at Sterling? He's trying to burn our ass."

He says, "Sure." So, we hop in the dude's car like we knew him forever and off we go.

He drops us off at Billy's car. Billy had the hood up, messing with the car, trying to get it running. I don't know how, but, he got it started. We all hopped in, and we're laughing about the whole night. We started talking about how crazy shit got, and how we had this brotherhood thing going on, neighborhood and all. We decided to do the same shit, at the same bar, the next night. By then, it was about 2 am, when they dropped me off at my parent's home. Thinking back, this was how we lived. We were drug-addicts caught in the insanity together. We went out, got drunk, abused drugs, treated women like shit, lied to everybody, fought all the time, with whoever was crazy enough to fight us, and then, we staggered our asses back to whatever crib we were sharing, or, renting, or, living off of with whatever chick one of us was messing with at the time.

Going to jail, going to prison, overdosing and even dying. Normal procedure.

The Psychology of doing time...

When a man's in prison, he'll do some crazy shit to survive. It was a war-zone when I was there in the 70's. I ask God to forgive me for all I've done. Prison makes a man hard and the truth is, I'd rather die a man than live like a bitch.

Prison made us battle-ready. We'd go outside the bars, fight the rowdy, drunk dudes, like us, and then go back in, have some more drinks and do some more dope. In truth, I think prison actually saved me from myself. Throughout a good part of my life, I've been a serious danger to my own being. Looking back makes me realize how much kinder and nicer I am to people in the now. I reflect back to those times and realize just how much I've grown. Not just as an addict, but, as a human being.

PTSD and the nightmares of WAR...

It was just before dawn. We were wasted. I was out with the fellas again. Wild-Billy and the brothers dropped me off at my parent's house. I was crashing there quite a bit, but, I was also doing a lot of couch surfing and hanging with strippers for a crash spot. I staggered my drunk and high ass to the door of my parents crib. My mother unlocked the door, looked at me briefly, and disappeared into her bedroom. I made my way down the hall in the dark, to the couch and fell into it. In less than 5 seconds, I was dead asleep. Down for the count! Done! I was out.

I don't know how long. I know I was messed up from the dust and the booze. I'd, pretty much, blacked out, when I hit the couch. The next thing I remember was gunfire. It was all around me. There was a battle going on in the house. Damn! I freaked and rolled into the floor, looking around, in the dark. I was, instantly, wide awake and my adrenalin shot straight out the top of my head. I tried to get my eyes fixed to the dark, so, I could see. I was frozen, because, I didn't know who was doing the shooting.

As my eyes got used to the dark, I could feel my heart, beating out of my chest. Then, I heard a voice, in the dark. It was my dad. He was

140

talking real low, almost frantic, but, like whispering. It was like I didn't know him.

He says, "Don't move. I got this. I'll get 'em. Stay there."

So, he's crouched real low, moving forward in the prone position with a rifle. He's shooting in the other room and moving aggressively through the house. He made his way back to the recreation room. I could see him from where I was laying. He was screaming out shit in some other language. It was like Korean. Then, he let loose a bunch of firepower. It got quiet. I didn't move. I didn't have a weapon, other than a knife. My daddy taught me, when I was young to never take a knife to a gunfight. So, I slowly slid in the carpet, back to the rec room. It was real quiet. There wasn't a sound. I'm wondering who was stupid enough to roll up in our house. My old man was intense. Scary dude. I peeped around the corner of the room, very slowly, so, I wouldn't get shot. I saw my dad. He was sitting in the corner, in the dark with a rifle next to him. He was just sitting there, not saying a word. He was staring straight ahead.

I said, "Dad, are you okay?"

Let me just say this. I hadn't been out of prison too long. I'd seen shit people wouldn't even believe. This sobered me up, and quick. I wasn't ready for this shit. I looked around the room and I didn't see anyone else in the room. I turned the light on. My mother and sisters came out of their rooms and walked in the rec room with us. The piano was shot up, with twenty or so shots in it. The pool table and the windows were shot up and my dad was sitting there, just staring out.

Mom said, "Virgil, are you okay?" We'd been here before with my dad.

"I thought I was in Korea, Barb. What did I do? Is everybody okay? What happened? What happened?"

We didn't know what to do, or say. I hated seeing my dad like this. He was a mess. Combat in Korea had his head tangled up. He'd come back from Korea, but, he'd never really come back from Korea. Struggle was at this address.

"Virgil, we have to take you to the VA. You need to be back in the hospital for a while."

My mother was at wits end. Dad just nodded and stared straight ahead. I hugged my mother and my sisters. This freaked every one of us out. Dad had a hard time after coming back.

I was too selfish to think of anything, except, getting high and partying. When a person is caught in the grips of not giving a shit, we don't even see the hurt, the pain and the misery, we create, around us. I know I didn't. If I did, the drugs, women and booze were more important to me. These are the kinds of things that catch up to a person, later in life. Believe me, I know. You sit back and think about that for a while. I know I have. I know I do. My dad went back to the psyche ward at the V A.

I moved into a house on North Street with one of my best friends in life, my brother, Wild Billy Hansen.

Billy had a hot and sassy girlfriend named Vanessa. She was a beautiful, scorcher blonde, with a jalapeño personality. Perfect for wild Billy! I used to sit back and watch their crazy fights. They'd throw pots and pans at each other, claw and slap each other. They were two hot pistols and for me, in those days, it was free entertainment. Vanessa was a firecracker and took no shit from Billy boy. Believe me, she had to be, too.

Billy was a volatile man when it came to a woman. Anyway, they had one bedroom and I crashed in the other bedroom. It was the time for crazy fun. The other bedroom was me and whatever women wanted to crash over. Plus, the half a dozen or so that crashed there just about every night. We had mattresses spread all over the floor.

We'd all get wasted and just fall all over the mattresses. We'd be naked most of the time, of course. Every day, we'd sit around and shoot angel dust, smoke weed, listen to rock & roll and party, like there was no end. Billy never shot dope. But, he partied his ass off. All of Main Street would stop by North Street for the drugs and parties. All the chicks sold dope, cleaned and cooked and we had a lot of sex. We all had a lot of sex back then. Nobody gave a shit in those days. Not really. We had an electric spool in the living room. We'd all sit around the spool and smoke from the big pipe with six lines in the middle.

As far as ladies, Carol, Gina, Vanessa, Darla, Crystal, and so many more were always at the crib. Most of these people are dead now and Grateful Ed, he somehow survived those wild days like I did and thankfully, at this writing, he's still around. Matter of fact, we're still very close brothers. All those party women, unfortunately, most of them are dead, too. Vanessa's doing well these days. She's a nurse in

142

Texas. We had some times. I remember one time, a girl showed up on the scene from New York. Nobody knew her, but, damn, she looked good. She was an Italian, black, curly, long hair, big eyes, and a hard, sexy body.

Of course, being the southern gentleman that I am, I offered her a spot on our mattresses, in my bedroom, for a place to crash. At the time, I was sleeping with about a dozen other women, sometimes all together. We'd pile on our mattresses in the bedroom, wasted, and whatever was whatever. So, on this night, Claire and I did the wild thing a few times and didn't think anything else about it. She hung out with us for 3 or 4 more days of wild partying, and then, she disappeared.

That was our lifestyle, so, it was no big deal. About 7 or 8 days later, I go to piss during a party one night, and, oh shit, it burned like hell. The next day I went to the Health Department and found out that Claire had given me the clap.

The doctor tells me to bring in all the women I was having sex with in the past month. So, the next day I showed up at the Health department with over a dozen girls. The nurse came out to get us all and just shook her head. She looked at me and said, "REALLY?" All the girls and myself at the same time, said, "YEP, REALLY!!!" We all busted out laughing. Sex, drugs and rock & roll. That was us. Wild, young and for now, free! Well, everybody was tested and everybody had the clap. We all had heavy doses of penicillin poked in our asses and it got rid of it. It cleared it all up in all of us. Whew!

We never saw Claire again. She left us the clap and boogied on. Life, for us, was a big party. So, we thought. Our music was Wild Billy's turntable, some big bad-ass Aztec speakers, and every rock & roll album known to man. We rocked Zeppelin, Kiss, Aerosmith, Pink Floyd... well, you get the picture. North Street was always filled with hot babes, bikers, dope-heads and crazies. It was who we were and what we did.

This was back in the days of long hair, patched hip-huggers, bellbottoms and, everybody had a head-band or a fancy hat, sitting sideways on their head, and a pair of wild-ass shades. We were the coolest of the cool! So, we thought. This is the deception of the disease of addiction. It will lure you in and without warning, kill you.

Looking back, it was all so superficial. One by one, it took all these people and killed them all, except for Ed and me. Oh and my dear friend, Vanessa is still alive, too.

Main Street was the place to cruise and find the dope and chicks looking for a good time. Our crib was right off Main Street and down ten blocks or so. 2202 North Street. Our front yard was always filled with Harleys and our living room was always packed with babes, good rock & roll and plenty of good-ass weed. North Street was the HOT SPOT. Go figure!

I remember Buddy, this mid-level drug-dealer stopping in about once a week from Chicago, Rockford, and all over, dropping off our angel dust, white cross, coke, dilaudids and weed. Buddy would front me a bunch of dope one week, and collect a week or so, later. I'd front it out to my ladies, partners, and the like, and the next week, I made sure I had the cash, when Buddy stopped by. He only wanted to deal with me. That was good and that was bad. This dude was very serious. When he sat down, he laid his 38 on the table, next to him.

This guy was one gangster-down piece of work. He was several years older than all of us, so, he never stopped by to collect, and left empty-handed. We always collected our money, and I always paid Buddy, on time. One thing Buddy would always do when he showed up was use me for a Guinea pig. I didn't mind at all.

In my sick mind, I thought it made me feel important. That's some twisted shit, I know. We'd gather around the dining room table and he'd toss me a package of his new dust to try. I would start with about a dime and shoot it. If that didn't kill me and I didn't get too fucked up, which was often the case, I'd shoot the rest.

When we shot dope and stood on the edge, the high felt as good as it possibly could. There was no getting any higher. Dropping dead was the next place to go! This dust Buddy was bringing us was like no dope we'd ever done. No one took the time to tell us it was actually animal tranquilizer. We're young, remember. But, when I'd shoot a half a quarter of this dope, I'd have to step up about three feet to find the floor. I would lose my hearing for a bit. I would lose track of who I was. My eyes couldn't focus. It sounded like I was in a wind-tunnel. I was some kind of wasted. This dope would make me feel like King Kong. It made me feel like nobody on this earth could possibly whoop me. That was a good feeling to me. I truly believed it gave me super-human strength.

So, one day, I had packaged up all this dust, handed out all the dilaudids, weed and white cross to sell, and the last thing I remember was no one was there. Everybody had gotten their dope and everybody was gone, except for Vanessa, Billy's girlfriend.

Suddenly, I woke up in intensive care and I didn't even know how I got there. I didn't know how long I'd been there, either. Talk about a strange feeling of what just happened and how long have I been here? Weird shit.

I found out I'd overdosed, yet again, shooting too much of that angel dust.

I had no understanding that idle time for me would or could be very dangerous. It was. My sick thinking took over and I decided it would be a good idea to do a couple of quarters of that dust. Don't ask me why I'd think that might remotely ever be a good idea.   I was young. I wanted to see just how high I would get off this. Yes, dumbass move! Since the only way I did dope was shoot it, I took out the spoon and poured the first quarter in there, and broke it down with a few CC's of water. Right about now, I should tell you, this dust was very, very good. For that reason, I sat there a minute and processed whether I should really put another quarter in the spoon. See, usually, partiers would buy a quarter and split it. This dust was that good.

A dime of this would completely mess you up. I mean a dime would make you forget who you were. The floor would be knee-high when you'd try to take a step. Seriously! With this in mind, I started to draw the dope up with my rig, but, being an insane wild-man, my insanity kicked in and I went ahead and dumped another quarter in the spoon. I broke that down and pulled all of it up in my rig. It had this certain smell. I can smell it right now, inside my head. It was that unique. It wasn't a bad smell, but, it was different.

(You have to realize, as insane as this behavior sounds as you read it right now, to an addict, this insane behavior is normal. This was just another day for a using addict. Chaos and self-destruction were always on the menu. I didn't think two thoughts about the absolute madness of my actions, ever. Active addiction will lead you into hell and anyone chasing a high will dive in head-first without hesitation.)

In those days, I had big veins, so, popping it in my arm was quick and slick, usually. But, this time it went a little different. I remember pushing the needle into my vein and I remember starting to push the dope in. Here's where I black out and hit the floor. I had overdosed many times before in Hawaii. Big surprise, right? I have no memory of what happened next. Vanessa said I blacked out before I pulled the rig out of my arm. By the grace of God, right when I overdosed, some mysterious dude walked in to our crib to buy dope, saw me unconscious on the floor and loaded me in his car, then, rolled me out at the back door of the Emergency Room at OSF. I'm glad he walked in when he did. He really did save my life.

I don't, to this day, know who the dude was. Vanessa said she was in the kitchen cleaning the dishes and heard me hit the floor. She said she ran in the living room and I was lying there with the rig still stuck in my arm. I was white as a ghost. Then, this guy she didn't know, came running in the front door, out of nowhere, and grabbed me. Then, they both carried me to the car, took me to the E R and dropped me off at the back door. Vanessa said he never said his name, never spoke, never said why he stopped by, or, if he even knew me.

He just appeared, saved my life and disappeared. That's some heavy shit. I never really thought about it, but, sitting here flashing back on this, right now, and the way it happened, him appearing at the very moment he needed to and out of the goodness of his heart, saving my life, this guy, who had to be an angel, is a phenomenon to me.

Today, forty-seven years later, seriously, 47 years later, I can, for the first time in my crazy life, actually say how grateful I am that he and Vanessa saved me from certain death.

In those days OSF emergency room was in the back of the hospital. Vanessa said they pulled up to the door and the guy pulled me out of the car and dragged me over to the door. He laid me down on the ground and they left. They didn't want to get busted and this was our protocol, in case this ever happened. I have no memory of any of that. All I know is my first thought was me, opening my eyes, and I was in a hospital bed, with all these things attached to me.

A nurse was standing there and she immediately started questioning me and telling me how blue I was when they found me by the door. Now remember, I'm a drug addict in active addiction, so, I'm all about the street game. My addiction survival persona was in full gear. When I was a teenager, I'd come up with the name Tommy Miller, if I ever got pulled over by the cops. There was no social media back in these days and Tommy was a common name, so, in places and situations like this, I was Tommy Miller. Life was messed up for me right then. I told them I shot some angel dust and overdosed on it.

After the nurse put something in the IV, in my arm, I got the sermon about the dangers of drug-abuse. What they failed to recognize at this time, was that I was a dope-head, with a dealer's habit. That meant I could shoot all the dope I wanted. I had plenty of dope. Her words went through one ear and out the other. Even lying in that hospital bed, nearly dead from overdosing, I still refused to acknowledge that I had a drug problem. Addiction is very cunning.

Anyway, this was before technology and computers, so, my fake identity worked. That afternoon, I was released and by that night, I was shooting a couple Dilaudids to chill for a bit. The Dilaudid hit me hard all over again. It made me puke and then, I felt great. I laid back, smoked some weed, with all these partiers at the crib. We sat around our electric spool coffee table, and smoked some good redbud.

Then, I laid back with Darla, my girl, for a while. We slid into my bedroom, both wasted.

At the time, I didn't realize that down the road a few years later, Darla and her beautiful sister, Crystal, who both lived at our house most of the time, would both die of drug overdoses.

Anyway, so, later in the day, Ed came in and asked me if I wanted to ride down to Slick Rick's in the South end. He lived next to the Coca-Cola plant, near where South Jefferson and Western meet. He tells me Buddy's stopping by there with fifty Dilaudids and I could get some if I wanted. Of course, I wanted some.

That's synthetic heroin. I hadn't been back from overseas that long and I still had that junkie mind-set, crawling all over my back. The thought of cold-shaking some synthetic heroin for a while sounded real good to me. Off we headed to Ricks.

THE DEEP END...

We pull up at Ricks and I see Buddy's car parked in the alley. That's cool. The drugs are here. We go in and Buddy and Rick are sitting in the living room, doing a dope deal. After we sat down, I made a deal with Buddy and copped a kilo of weed, a thousand hits of white-cross, fifty Dilaudids and a quarter-ounce of angel dust. It was party time. So, we're sitting around, smoking dope, getting wasted and I go in the kitchen to sit at the table and shoot a Dilaudid. I dropped the hit in my rig, pulled up some water and cold-shook the pill in the rig. It broke down clear and I banged it.

I had to run to the john because it made me puke again. After that, I was in a full nod. I staggered back into the living room. Buddy says, "Hey bro, you ever shot any of those white cross?"

"Hmmmm, nope, I haven't. But, that Dilaudid got me knocked out. I need to wake up some. I'll shoot some.

Buddy just grinned. "You're crazy dude, you know that?"

"Sho do, my man. Yep, sho do! Insane in the membrane"

I pulled the white cross out of my bag. They were broke down and bagged in hundred lots. I looked at Ed, Rick and Buddy and I say, "I'll shoot this whole hundred lot."

"You'll die if you do!" Buddy shoots back real quickly. They thought I was joking.

"Not if I wash it real good, break it down in a cereal bowl and keep doing that till I got a clean rig full."

"Dude, seriously, do NOT do that! I swear that's certified crazy shit!" Buddy fires back. "Man, really, nobody's ever shot a hundred white cross. That's just crazy shit. Don't do that, man. Shoot three or four of them! Ten of them will kill ya. "

Ed chimes in, "Brother, you sure about that? That's a lot of dope. Shoot 3, maybe 4 of 'em. That'll kill ya, man!"

"I'm going to check it out! I'm going to see what a hundred feels like."

Buddy grabs his shit and says, "Brothers, I'm gone. You ain't gonna feel shit. You're gonna die. You got a death wish, dude. I thought I was crazy! I don't want to be here when you shoot that many white cross." "Oh, I'll pop it in slow." Don't matter! That'll still kill you man, I swear. For real, I wouldn't do that, brother. This can't turn out good, but, hey, you do what you going to do. It's your world. Look

148

here, though, you guys ain't seen me. I'm not here. I'm gone from this shit." He looks at Ed. "If he does this, I'm telling you he'll die, just make sure I get my dope, or, the money for the dope. Okay? Next week."

"Oh yeah, okay! Cool" So, Ed and I head into the kitchen. Ed pulls me out a couple of cereal bowls from the cabinet. I dumped a hundred hits of white cross into the first cereal bowl.

Then, I filled my rig with water and pushed it out all over the speed. It slowly started breaking down. After a long process of chalky, watery bullshit, it started breaking down, then, finally, it was broke down pretty good. I just kept pulling up dope and shooting it into the other bowl. It took me a long while, but, I finally got a good amount of the dope moved over. It was much cleaner.

Then, I pulled a big rig full of the speed into the rig. It filled it up. There was no more room in the rig for any more of the dope. Rick walked in and said he was going to get some gas in his car. I can dig it.

So, he left Ed and me sitting there.

Ed says, "Hey brother, you sure you want to shoot that many white cross? That's some crazy shit, man. Seriously bro, think about this. Dude, what am I supposed to do if you OD? You sure about this?"

INSANITY! WARNING! NEVER TRY THIS ANYWHERE!!!!

"Yeah, I'm sure. Time to shit or get off the pot! Time to rock & roll!" Ed just shook his head.

"Damn brother. Damn man!!! Come on, man. Come on, brother. This is heavy shit. You sure?"

"I came to party!"

I shook my arm down and stuck the needle in my vein. I started pushing the speed into my arm. I could feel the speed kicking in to my heart and head. I got about half of the dope in my arm. I felt like the top of my head was going to blow off my body. My heart was racing over a hundred miles an hour. I was over-amping. I quickly jerked the rig out of my arm and ran, as fast as I could, right through the storm door.

I knocked it right off the hinges, broke the glass and everything. It just flew in every direction. I started going blind. I ran into the street and fell to my knees. My blood was pulsating through my body completely out of control.

"OH NO! Oh shit! Oh man!" I'm in deep. It's too late now. There's no coming back from this shit. My body went into total over-amping, insanity and way too high to survive this shit.

I screamed out to Ed. "I'm dying, man! This is it! This is too much! Oh, God help me! Too much! Too MUCH! TOO MUCH!"

I'd never felt this bad in my life. The top of my head starting pounding out of control. It became even beyond a horrible migraine. I lost my sight. I literally couldn't see. My skin was crawling and my heart was beating out of my chest. I started sweating profusely. I was dizzy as hell. I could hardly stand up. Ed ran out to the street. He was screaming and freaking out. "You okay, brother? You alright? Hey man, hey man, hey man, Stormy, brother? Hey man...." "HELL NO, NO, NO, NO, NO, NO, I'm not alright! I'm not! I'm not! Ed, take me to my parent's house and do it quick. I'm dying, man! This is it! I'm done. Dying man... dying...I'm dying man... OH man!" I lost my ability to think and function. God had me here. I sure didn't. Ed ran and got my car and drove me to my parents in the north end. I felt like I had several heart attacks on the way. I might have. I don't know how I lived through this. Intervention, I'm sure!!! That's the only explanation. I ran into the house and quickly told my mother I had a horrible headache, worse than a migraine, and I was going to lie down. I could barely see where I was going.

Everything was a real bad blur and my hearing was completely shot, too. There was a loud ringing in my head that wouldn't stop and it sounded like real high wind blowing all around me.

Ed took my car and left. I lay in that bed at my mother's house for 3 full days and 2 full nights. I felt like I was going to die. I thought I really would. I didn't think I'd make it. My heart continued to pulsate! My body wouldn't stop moving around. I was soaking wet with sweat.

My head continued to throb. It hurt and the pain wouldn't stop. The ringing in my head wouldn't go away either. My vision kept going in and out. Everything was very blurry. I was scared out of my mind. After a couple of days of my mother feeding me and making me drink lots of water, I started thinking, maybe, I was going to survive. Slowly but surely, the ringing in my head stopped, the headache and throbbing in my head, finally, went away, the

150

pounding in my heart, finally, went away and finally, my vision got clearer.

Then, thank God, I stopped sweating. This was a close call! I almost died... again. This could very well be the worst three days and nights of my life. But, it didn't stop me.

Not long after this, I'd copped a thousand hits of 8-way windowpane for fifty cents a hit, in Chicago. I thought that was a good deal. I could sell them for 2 bucks a hit and stay high for free. My brother, Ed and I went to a brother's house on Western in the south end of Peoria. Another close brother, Rebel wanted 50 hits of the windowpane to sell over the weekend.

He was doing something out behind his house and I was sitting in his kitchen waiting for him to come in. I tell Ed, "Hey, brother, I think I'm going to shoot one of these hits of windowpane. See what it's about!" Ed's like, "Hell no! Are you insane? Man, don't even think about that crazy shit." Well, that's all I needed to hear. So, I grabbed a spoon and dropped a hit of windowpane in it. Then, I shot about 10 CC's of water over it. I let it sit there for a few minutes to see if it was going to break down.

After stirring it for a while, it finally did break down. I pulled it up in the rig and popped it in my arm. What happens next is nothing short of a journey through Disneyland on steroids. I have a first-hand account of what happened next, because, well, because, it happened to me. So, grab hold of your seat. This is a wild ride!

First, as I slid in about half of the hit, my auditory went away. It was gone, no more. Then, it exploded all around me. It went hay-wire. As I was trying to program my brain to accept what was happening to my hearing, then, my vision went ape-shit. As I looked around, my vision, at first, got blurry and, then, it turned into a million dots bouncing around all at once. Not for the weak, let me tell you! All around me, it sounded like I was in a huge wind-tunnel, or, what I imagined standing in a huge wind-tunnel would sound like. That's all I could hear.

It took me over for a few minutes. I tried to lean against the table, because, I couldn't tell if I was still sitting in the chair.

There was no longer an up and down. I stopped pushing the dope in, because, I started hallucinating so bad, I couldn't see my hand, or, the rig. Everything had turned from the dots to millions of tiny rectangles fluttering all together and completely surrounding me. I

151

couldn't tell where the rig ended and my hand started. It was all one thing. Everything was one thing. Millions of little rectangles fluttering like the wings of a hundred whippoorwills. My arm, hand and rig all seemed to become part of everything else and I didn't know what to do about the rig in my arm. I was hallucinating way too bad.

Ed appeared from somewhere and every move he made created a million trails. They were everywhere. He didn't even look like a human. He was a moving entity that was now a million rectangles, too, like everything else.

He was saying something to me, but, it sounded really muffled and I couldn't make out a single word. He grabbed the rig that was in my arm and pulled it out. Everything was still a million little fluttering rectangles and the sound was overpowering and muffled. I was the most high I've ever been. I couldn't stand up or stay seated. My movement had no sense of what is. I was part of the molecular structure of the entire space.

There was no up or down. I was floating out in some vortex of timeless insanity. I wanted to panic, but, a voice inside me kept telling me not to panic. It kept saying to hang in there. It was way too much for one brain to process and mine wasn't processing all this very well at all. After 4 or 5 minutes of this, I begin to start understanding what Ed was saying, "Heeey brooooo. Heeeeey.... Hey, bro, you okay? Are you okay? Brother, tell me something!" Talk about intense! Whatever far beyond intense is called, labeled or tagged, that's what I was. That what this was. That's where I was. Say it slow... Dweebling un-orthadoxed, maniacal meandering... comes to mind.

I felt like I said, "I'm okay. I think I'm okay." But, the truth is, I'm not sure if I was thinking that, or, actually saying it. I was so far beyond wasted. I was way, way, way over the top! It took me about a half-hour to come down enough to think I might survive this.   I finally started peaking on the acid, meaning, things were beginning to taper off enough for me to no longer be in panic mode.   It was very scary, but, at this time in my life my mind-set was bordering on insanity, anyway. I was willing to try anything that had to do with drugs. Anything. Obviously. Looking back, that's very unintelligent thinking. I'm not sure what bus I missed to get to these situations, but, I'm grateful I'm still around to catch it now.

152

(RAW TRUTH. What I did on those particular days are a few of what I believe to be, the most unintelligent acts of self-destruction, I've ever perpetrated toward my own life. I look back at this and all I can do is shake my head in disbelief and gratitude that the Lord above allowed me to survive those acts of insanity.)

Let's examine this suicidal behavior. Why did I behave so irresponsible? My mind-set wasn't to kill myself. I don't think it was. That's not what I remember. Quite honestly, I think it just comes down to a simple, elementary fact. I was very young and I didn't stop and think it through. I simply didn't play the tape all the way through. The possible consequence of my actions never even entered my mind. That behavior, so many years ago, really bothers me. Even today. Oh, I own it and I don't wallow in it, but, it does give me cause for a casual thought or two on a Saturday afternoon in a park on a beautiful day. I call that sort of behavior, long ago, being completely lost and devoid of self. My sense of reason must've went on vacation. It never occurred to me that doing some crazy shit like shooting a hundred hits of white cross might very well kill me. How could I not think about that? Sitting here, right now, I wouldn't shoot a hundred hits of white cross for a million dollars. Not for ten million dollars! I wouldn't even shoot one hit for a million dollars. I really wouldn't. The thought of that is too much, really. Disgusts me. My, how we've changed, right! That's truly crazy as hell, I know. That's not even typical addict behavior. Think about that. This behavior is several notches past typical addict behavior. It's more like insane behavior. Typical addict behavior is in another universe, compared to this. Wow! This is an example of that chaos and self-destruction we talk about. Just on a much deeper level. I'm shocked that I lived.

I've asked myself why on earth I would do such a thing, a hundred times. I still don't know. What's baffling to me is I perceive myself as an above average intelligent person. Addiction really is cunning and baffling. This is a prime example of that.

UNDERCOVER...

Did all this crazy shit, suddenly turn into an imploding shit storm of "What in the actual hell are we doing"? Hell yes, it did!

One of us, a brother named Dan C, was always, at the crib. He left one day and died in a wreck off Knoxville Ave.

Was he high? Who knows? He was a great dude. I still miss him and I think about him a lot. We were tight.

Soon enough, a brand new undercover drug enforcement group got wind of our parties, drugs and wild lifestyle. Tri-County Multi-Enforcement Group found out about us. They were the new Sheriffs in town and they hadn't nabbed a good bust yet to help them get more funding. We hadn't even heard of them, yet, and that was surprising. We had a notorious underground paper that came around, all the time. It was always in the hands of the drug dealers. It fronted off snitches and undercover cops. You could get it from head shops if they knew you were cool.

But, it missed this important info, at first. They had just set up shop in three counties. Guess who one of their first undercover busts was? Yep, it was me. The MEG crew, probably saved me from myself, yet again. Undercover set me up good. I was selling drugs everywhere. My life had no meaning. It just didn't matter. They busted me with six suppressed drug indictments.

Goodbye freedom...

Did it eventually get out of hand? Ya think? Hell YES! For several months, for a whole lot of party people, North Street was an unforgettable experience. If you were one of the wild folks from that time and place, you know exactly what I'm saying here. But, everything has to eventually end, doesn't it? Life's about change, right?
Fact: Most of the people from the North Street days are dead now from drug-related deaths. It was a wild ride!

I don't think it'd be fair to talk about North Street and not tell you why and how it all ended. So, here goes...

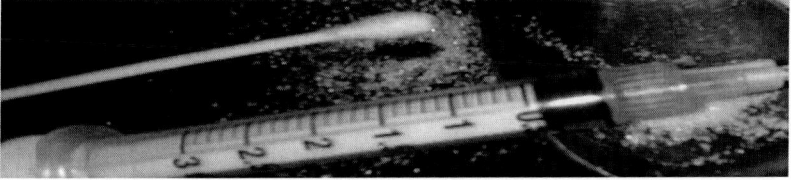

Chapter 7

THE DEMISE OF NORTH STREET

1974...

We all heard about a huge festival about to happen in Missouri. So, we all got together and made this elaborate plan. Sedalia Music festival, here we come with a van loaded with freaks and dope. We'd been putting this together for a while. Our plan was to load the van with dust, coke and weed and sell it at the festival. We had it all figured out. We were going to spend a week there, stay wasted, see some great bands, make a fortune, meet hot, sexy chicks, find the ultimate utopia with the hot chicks in some imagined erotic fantasyland and then, do dirty things with all the women. Sounds like a good plan, right? Right!

Then, we were going to come back to Peoria, our souls full of good dope, lots of money, great sex stories, music and memories and live happily ever after. Now, this all made perfect sense to us. This was the perfect plan. Inside our thinking, us thinking we were so clever, and all. We thought this was the best idea ever. Let's not forget, young addicts and wild decision-making skills were us. So, with that in mind, we're chewing at the bit to get on the road and head to Sedalia, Missouri, raise some hell and make some badass memories.

Our Plan and HIS Plan...

In life, we'll always have our plan, and we'll stroll through life-shit, with every intention of doing the plan a certain way, at a certain time. But, what we don't take into account, when we're young and trying to figure shit out, a using drug-addict, partying, living the fast life, living hard as hell, and focused on our self-centeredness, is this... shit changes in the blink of an eye!

Let me say that again. Life changes in the blink of an eye! It does. I mean, spin your toe on a dime-type changes. In the blink of an eye, life flips upside down. Well, these are the unfolding's of the events that soon transpired in the midst of our brilliant plans. Those plans we had all carefully and ever so cleverly put together while we were all dusted, high and quite literally, out of our ever-loving minds.   So, here goes. Let me tell you what happens. The shit got heavy and quick, straight out of nowhere. The very day before we were leaving, the very day before... I walked into the house on North Street and one of my partners, Ed, who I love to this day like a brother, well, he was getting loud and pushy with a chick at the crib that was special to me. It was Darla.

At the time, I was sleeping with Darla about every day and every night. The woman was a wildcat and we were into each other. One might say, she was my girlfriend. I know, in her head, I was her boyfriend. She and I were close. Yes, I was sleeping with lots of other women at the time, but, she knew it and hey, it was the seventies. We did that shit. It was all about the party.

This was before aids and all that foreign STD shit, being spread around. So, I'm going to tell you what happened next. The truth. We were drunk and high every damn day. That's what we did. We partied. We got wasted. We got drunk. We got high. We had a lot of sex with a lot of women and vice versa. So, what happens might sound a little crazy, or, over the top.

156

Whatever is whatever? You have to realize, drug-addicts do drug-addict shit. This is how this situation unfolded. So, I walk in the house on North Street and I, immediately, had a problem with Ed being loud and aggressive with my girlfriend, Darla. He was yelling at her and getting right in her face. What was happening wasn't cool with me and it wouldn't have been cool with anybody, so, I stepped in. He was about 6 feet away from me. I pulled out my blade and told him, "Leave Darla alone, man. Keep your hands off of her"... something to that effect. He's staring at me and says, "Fuck you man. What are you going to do with that blade? You ain't going to do shit!" Well, let me explain my mind-set right then. Because of my childhood, severe beatings and physical & mental abuse, I'm very hyper-sensitive about a guy, any guy, trying to intimidate me. It's not a smart move. I take that shit personal.

Think about it. I had a switchblade in my hand. His words and his tone hit me wrong. His tone hit me wrong the most. We'd been friends for four or five years by now. I mean I'd been all over the country for a while, but, Ed and I knew each other in High school and we ran together. We were tight friends, but, tight friends don't disrespect someone close.

Well, he did. I felt he disrespected me and it pissed me off, so, I didn't hesitate. Maybe it was temporary insanity. I'm not sure. I'd been locked up not that long ago, so, I was still in jail-house mentality. I threw the knife fast as lightning and stabbed him deep in the chest. It should be noted, I grew up throwing a knife. I practiced throwing a knife all the time. As a matter of fact, I still do. Truth be known... I can stab the hole in a gnat's ass from 5o feet away. Well, maybe part his wings for sure and get real close to his ass. Alright, I might get somewhat close. Okay, I'd probably miss the little son of a bitch by a foot or more. Anyway, back to the events that were duly unfolding...

Here's the thing, my dad did teach me, well, at a young age. So, I knew exactly where that knife was going to stab him. It wasn't reckless. That's a good thing. I missed his heart by a hair and the blade went through his left lung.

So, it's no wonder, he went down and started struggling for air with this switch-blade knife stuck in his chest 3 or 4 inches deep. I ran over and stood over him. He looked up at me and said, "You killed me, man." Well, remember, I was still in snapped mode. I said,

"You ain't dead yet, but, you will be." I reached down to pull the knife out of his chest. My girl, Darla, screamed right then, "Stormy, NO, please No. Don't kill him!"

That scream brought me back to reality. Thank God. I think I would've stabbed him, twenty, maybe thirty more times. I believe, at that moment, that was my thinking and my intent. I'm not sure. Like I said, I think I experienced temporary insanity for a few moments. My rage took over. Mix that with the dope and the booze and, for me, it was a one way ticket to life in prison.

Thank God I didn't lose it and keep stabbing him. I love my brother, Ed. I'm glad I snapped back to sanity. One of the reasons I'm glad I didn't kill him, besides having to spend the next twenty to fifty years, or, the rest of my life in prison, was this dude would turn out to be one of my best friends in the whole of my life. Life works in funny ways. Ed and I would grow to be tight brothers, like family. My family considers him to be family to this very day.

Well, another dude was in the kitchen, Dan W. and he witnessed the stabbing, too. So, one of those two called the cops and the ambulance took Ed to the hospital and the cops took all three of us downtown.

They separated us real quick and I'd already told those two to stick to this story that he staggered in the door, had been stabbed and he said some dude robbed him. That would have worked had it been just me. But, cops got that good cop, bad cop routine down to a fine art. As soon as they told both of them that I'd told the cops each of them had done it, they both ratted me out. Of course, the cops didn't tell me that.

They took me in a room and asked me what happened. I said he fell in the door and said he was robbed. They told me they were homicide cops and that he'd died. I told them I didn't know anything and I needed a lawyer. Then, I zipped my mouth shut. They took me to a holding cell and those bastards left me there till about noon the next day.

That was some cold shit. All night, I laid in that nasty cell, freezing my ass off, thinking I'd killed this dude. I find out later, Ed was hurt pretty bad. His left lung was punctured and being drunk and on dope all the time, he's lucky he lived. I guess we're both lucky he lived. He didn't press charges, but, the State picked up the attempted murder charge. We talked about this, but, I'll refresh your memory. While I was in the old county jail, at 310 Hamilton, in Peoria County, the Detective brought up six sealed, suppressed indictments against me, for serious drug-charges, in two Counties. They got me for Distribution of heroin, coke, LSD and PCP. These were all felonies. I'd been busy.

The busy madman. He also brought up a parole violation from Texas, informing me that after I got finished with the time in Illinois, I'd have to go back to Texas and do the complete 5 to life sentence that I was on parole for from Texas. The detective said since I'd stabbed a dude and it was a violent charge, they'd make me do the entire life sentence. Damn!

That was hard to hear. That was the suspended 5 to life for the robbery while chasing the strippers and dope. That's why I called the charges drug-related. Once again, the consequences of my actions had turned into pure hell. It seemed, in the blink of an eye, my life, once again, turned upside down. One day I'm shooting angel dust, smoking dope and dealing, partying my ass off, with a house full of hot babes, sleeping with sexy women every night, usually 2 or 3 at a time and the next thing I know, I'm locked down, for what will most likely be the rest of my life.

Welcome to hell! While I was doing the time in Illinois, Texas had a parole hold on me. Their plan was to extradite me to do the complete 5 to life prison sentence for the parole violation because of the violence. Consequences, it seemed, were my middle name. I found out in prison that when I stabbed Ed on North Street, it put eyes on the place. The cops were watching. So, that ruined it for the bikers, dopers, dealers and partiers.

No more North Street.

Everybody went in different directions. Some moved out of State. Some were homeless. Some disappeared. Some overdosed and died. But, me... I became property of the State of Illinois, inmate number 41937, in maximum security, Menard prison.

Confinement

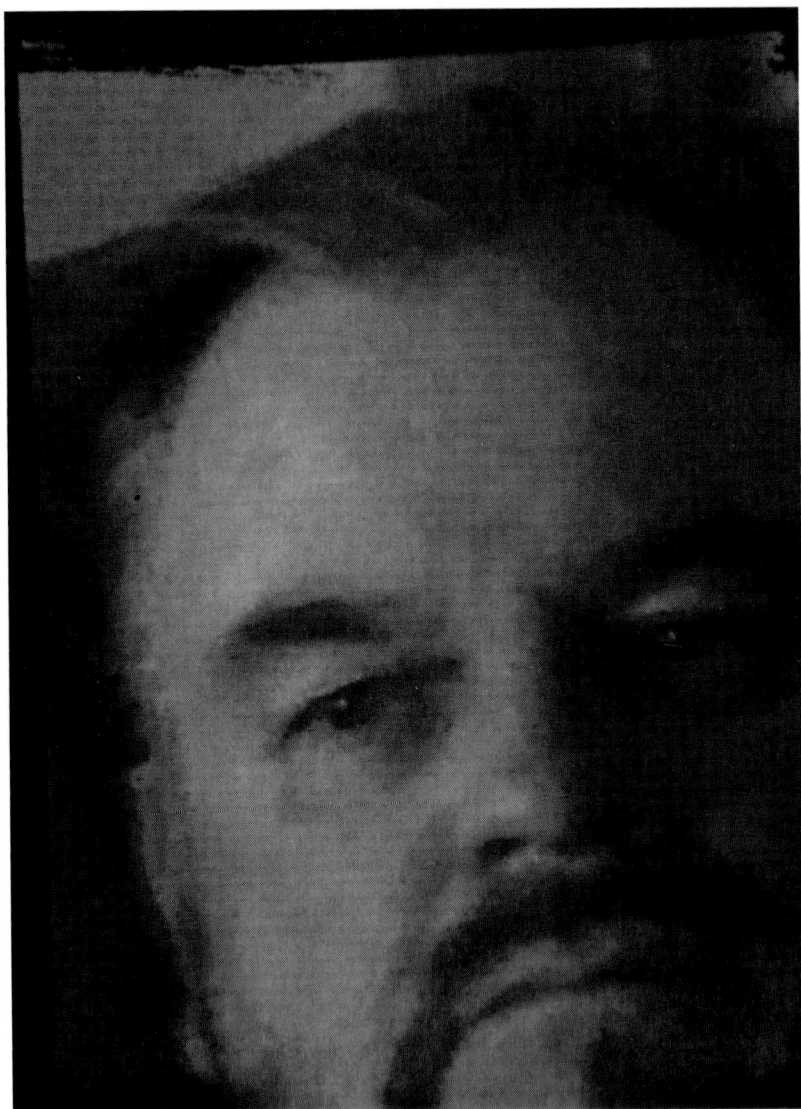

Chapter 8

STRUGGLE WAS THE ADDRESS

I was locked down with a bunch of nasty, stinking, smelly, psychotic, crazy-ass convicts, I wanted nothing to do with. I spent the rest of fall and winter in that cold, nasty county jail. I'll tell you again... I was sentenced to 3, three-year sentences in Peoria County, and then, 3, three year sentences, in Tazewell County. Also, stacked on that was the 5 years to life from Texas. They had the 'Parole Hold' on me from Texas because I'd violated parole. They were going to execute that when I was released from prison in Illinois.

I was supposed to be transferred to Huntsville prison down Texas way, at the completion of my sentence in Illinois. I had to do the entire 5 years to life sentence because I violated with a violent charge. The attempted murder was pleaded down to a battery and my other sentences ate that sentence up. The point is, this is some depressing shit and all of this, all of it, is a direct result of MY consequences from MY insanity in the drug-life. I mean, damn man. I have nobody to blame for all this mess but myself. I'm not proud of it, either. It's damn sure no badge of honor. This took valuable years of my youth away from me. I made the choices that did all this. I'll never get a minute of that back, either. I have no recourse in the matter. I own all this shit. I did every minute of the time, too, and if I said it was easy and I'm hard now... blah, blah, blah, I'd be lying. Oh, it was hard. It was hell on earth and I don't say that lightly. But, all it really did was scar me deep down in my soul. It scarred the man I really wanted to be before I went down the wrong path. It affected my psyche intensely. It made my life-journey longer and so much harder. It didn't have to be that way. That's the sad part. It doesn't have to be that way. I think about the lifestyle, the flash and the cash, the dope, all the times in the streets, fine women on my arm every night, the respect from the street people, dressing smooth, everybody loves me, but, not really, the life, man. The life. Oh, sometimes the life made for some good times, but, listen to me and take note... when I balance it all out, when I sit back and soul search my self-worth and my potential as a human-being, what I'm now discovering I'm fully capable of... giving up ONE minute of my youth to be controlled by an asshole with the only keys to my cell door, in a nasty-ass iron cage, on a long gallery filled with killers and crazies, day in and day out, for days, weeks, months and years, telling me where to shit, where to eat, where to sleep, when to do this, when to do that, believe me when I tell you, it is not worth it. It doesn't balance out at all. Most in the life don't even make it to prison. They die. Weigh that out.

When this crap went down, I stayed in county jail and the day to day bullshit is like living in a nightmare. This was the old County Jail at 310 Hamilton. Nobody was happy or smiled. It was a bunch of gang-banging assholes, all piled together. In the summer, it was a nasty, stinky sweatbox. In the winter it was nasty, cold, the food sucked and it was crowded.

We played cards and fought every day for something to do. Finally, in January, on a very cold and somber day, I was shipped, by bus, to Statesville prison up near Chicago. Richard Speck was there, when I was there, too. He was serving 8 consecutive 50 to 150 year sentences for raping, torturing and murdering the 8 nurses in Chicago. I would sit on the steps of the tomb, where he stayed and talk to him, some days, when we went to the yard.

I just wanted to get a peep inside his twisted head. I discovered he was truly one sick piece of shit. Later in life, he'd be bitched-out in this very same prison by a black gang-leader. He'd grow tits with hormone pills, have coke shoved up his nose daily, black dick shoved up his ass nightly and down his throat, whenever, and would eventually die of a heart attack. In Statesville prison, a white man walking down any gallery looks like a light bulb in a long dark hallway. I'm thinking 98% black, mostly thugs from Chicago, locked in a concrete jungle. You never want to be there.

Then, they shipped me to Vandalia. Vandalia was a medium security unit. We were in dorms that held about 50 inmates each. I was assigned to B dorm. There were other inmates there from my hometown, like Tracy D. He was from Pekin. In the short time I was in Vandalia, Tracy and I clicked. We were good friends. Both of us were artists and bikers and we were from the same neck of the woods. I lasted 21 days in Vandalia. A black dude purposely bumped into me in the lunch-room, so, I wrapped my tray around his head. Down we went fighting. The guards broke it up and sent us back to the dorms. Now, had I been a little more street savvy at the time, I'd have let that go and moved on with the day, just watching my back. But, I was a young, ignorant hothead back then. I wallowed in the fight for a few minutes in my head and got to thinking the dude might be conspiring in his dorm against me.

So, I admit I made a dumbass move. I decided to go into the dorm where he was housed and threaten him. When I did, I was loud about it, too. Hey, I was young. I was letting him know I'm not to be fucked with. I wanted to look strong to the other cons. Well, this just shows how green I was. A screw overheard me threaten him. Hell, I threatened the entire dorm like an idiot. Foolish move on my part. So foolish.

They threw me in the hole, immediately. A week later, in the middle of the night, guards came and shackled me and threw me in a van. The one guard said they decided since I liked to fight and they charged me with inciting a riot, they were shipping me to a maximum security prison at Menard. In the 70's, Menard is where they housed the violent, the criminally insane and the worst of the worst in Illinois. They threw me in a dark hole for six months. By the time they came to get me, I swear I was mentally ill, literally a nutcase.

I'd gone closer to mad than I ever wanted to be. It's like I stood on the edge of a thousand foot cliff and swan-dived straight off that son of a bitch. Have you ever had a good mind-twist? Better yet, have you ever had a deep-shit mind-twist? That's not good. I did that to myself. Sitting in a dark cell and the only contact I had was when they would slide a food tray in the crack at the bottom of the door. Three times a day, this happened...

We could hear the Iron door to the cell-house open and we could hear the loud food cart being pushed in. That was literally the only thing we had to look forward to. That and that moment of light a few times a day when they slid in the tray. On three occasions, they pushed in the food cart, gassed the entire cell house, locked the iron door and left. They ruined our food and damn near killed us.

This was their way of reminding us they controlled the environment. Yes, they DID do that! God help you if you had asthma.

Stick your head in the shitter and keep flushing. Tough shit and hope you don't die. Prison's a cold and cruel place.

Six months of near darkness...

I was damn-near in the dark. I could barely count the cracks in the floor or on the walls. A little more light could've, at least, kept my mind busy enough to not be idle in thought, since I was locked in damn-near total darkness. I could barely see my hand in front of my face. I felt like I was destitute on an island, filled with eerie near-blackness and there were no voices for me to hear, no matter how hard I listened. There was no kindness to feel, no matter how much I missed it and there were no smiles from anyone, because, I could barely see anything. I had no human contact in a miserable, really dark, small, scary space. Twice, sometimes three times a day, the little slot in the metal door opened for about three seconds and they'd slide some crap like an old bologna sandwich and a small cup of Kool aid through the slot. Then, just as quickly, it would close. It was a quick blink of light, then gone. Then, later and who knows when, they'd open the slot and grab the tray and cup back. We usually kept the door open with the tray for some extra light until they grabbed it. Even though I hated the food, that light through the tray door was priceless.

Claustrophobia ripped at my soul and chewed me into tiny, frantic pieces of myself. I needed space and lots more light, soon, and for more than three seconds at a time. I believe I went through many, many levels of insanity. My sense of reason prevailed for quite some time. False perceptions surrounded me. Voices from around me faded into nothing. I felt touched by things I don't think were there. My reason left.

I held onto it for as long as possible. But, reason in the near-blackness can only live so long, inside a mind with nowhere to go. My will to live wouldn't allow me to give up. I held on with every last fragment of my being. I had no idea when or if I would ever be let out of this maddening darkness. The days and nights all ran together, and, at no time, did I have any idea which one it was. I was floating in a universe of complete anxiety, confusion and turmoil. My reason fought with my ability to reason, and then, my ability to reason, questioned if I had any reason at all. This flowed through me

164

all the time. It was like a continuing, recurring lapse of flashes, of dwindling, desperate thought patterns, without any sane sense of time and space. I fought as hard as I could to hold onto the depth of that.

I felt fear, too. It was a vicious dark animal that constantly stalked me in this small nearly all-black space. I was scared for a whole lot of the time. So many times I'd see an animal standing near me. I would see its eyes staring at me and I'd hear it growling in the dark. I'd reach my hand out to see if it was real and it wouldn't be there. Just the image of it in my mind, standing near me. I'd wake up and feel its presence and wonder why I woke up. What touched me to make me wake up? Something touched me. Maybe not. I had no idea who was around me, or who had the key to let me out. There were constant shadows of people who weren't even there. I had no idea if they'd forgotten about me, or, if they were doing this to mess with my head, or, they were just inhumane and this was procedure.

That was possible, right? I mean, they'd brought me in the middle of the night and thrown me in this dark, nearly all-black space, locked the big iron door and left. How long ago, I had no idea. I was just there. Perpendicular to perceptible time and space in some lost vortex. There was an eerie vacuum of mysterious, stale air in a continuum of emptiness. I felt it clawing at the inner-workings of my calloused delusions.

Hopelessness and confusion floating all around me... a black and wretched abyss of fear. There was a foul stench consuming all of the air. My lungs would fill with the funk and then, cling to the last bit of it as it seeped from inside me. I think I was breathing the same stench over and over. Then, the questions in my brain wrapped around my head like barb-wired chain.

Maybe they lost the paperwork on me and I was an unknown entity? I wanted to scream, but, I forced myself not to. For now I won't. Maybe, this is a nightmare? Entity? Why did I say that word? Entity. Why entity? Hmm. I should try to wake up. Is this happening? Really? I'm trying not to panic. Don't panic. Don't panic. Don't panic. Don't panic. Why did I say entity? Is there an entity? One I don't see? Do not panic. I need to wake up. I might even laugh about all this. No, I won't laugh. No... won't laugh.

My thinking had stepped off some empty space in almost total blackness to some fucking crazy place I'd never been before. I mean, that could happen, right? There were moments when I'd burst into tears and they'd flow down my face, then, I'd have to convince myself, I had to be stronger. Somebody might suddenly unlock the metal door and rush in and I need to be ready to deal with whatever. My conscious thought slipped into some remote lost space in time and I fought with all my might to keep my sanity intact.

This was nearing an impossible place inside my head when, all of a sudden, out of the darkness, one day the cell door opened. The burst of light blinded me. I shut my eyes quickly and slowly opened my lids to let tiny slivers of light in. It took me a few moments to see the two guards standing there looking at me. "Come on out, Monday." I had difficulty walking out. When I did, I had to cover my eyes again. The light hurt and I couldn't get my bearing. Plus, my depth perception was off. I felt like I was hallucinating. I was hallucinating.

This time in that nearly all-black darkness, I'll never forget. I've had nightmares. I've had more than a few nightmares about being trapped in that shadow-filled darkness. It scarred me. I believe it affected me deeply. In fact, I know it did. This scar runs seriously deep. One of the guards told me to follow them. He said, "Looks like you're going to gladiator school." I'm like, "What do you mean?" He glances back at me and says, "Menard maximum security, East House, 10 gallery, cell 50. Keep walking. You'll figure it out."

Welcome to the Real World...

The East house was 98% black. I could see that when we first walked into the front door. All the galleries were filled with black dudes. In a few of the cells by the front door to the cell house, I saw guys with panties and high heels on. I'm thinking they locked them by the front door to keep an eye out for sex assaults from the other inmates. Crazy place. Then, the rest were thugs and the like. Most of those were the Black Nation. As we made our way up to the tenth gallery, I noticed it was loud. This sure wasn't Vandalia. This was the real World. I'd just entered the gates of Hell!

As we got to the top step and onto the landing of ten gallery, I was following the guards down the gallery. There were fifty, 2 man cells, on each gallery. There was not one white dude all the way down ten gallery. In every cell there was a wooden stick on the front of the cell that said the same thing, in front of every cell. "Black Nation."   If I said I wasn't scared right there, walking down that gallery, I'd be lying. See, I was scared shitless. But, my daddy taught me something about fear when I was still shitting yellow. He told me, "Son, you have to face your fear. That's the only way you can whoop it." When my dad was teaching me that, it seemed like sound advice. But, right here, right now, even with me being a strong, white dude, I was starting to question those wise words. Facing 98 gang-bangers who hate whitey, alone, is a task NOT for the weak.

As I walked by each 2-man cell with my eyes hidden behind my shades, and there was fifty of those cells to walk by, they each had something to say, to me. "Fuck you, white-boy. Hey Cracker. This the real world, motherfucker! Suck my dick. Go fuck yourself, white bitch-ass." These were some of the things getting slung at me as I made my way down that long nightmare of a gallery. Hey, we're in prison. We're in the real world, alright. This is the shit your momma and daddy warned you about.

Now, here I was knee deep in the shit and I have some bad news... there's no turning back. I kept my head pointing straight ahead in my own business and finally made my way to the last cell on the gallery. I'd just walked by 98 Black Nation. In cell number 50, they opened the door for me to walk in. My Celle was from the same streets as I, in my home-town of Peoria, Illinois. Butch Bo. There we were. Two white dudes from P-town and 98 Chicago Black Nation.   So, Butch and I were immediately brothers. We earned each other's respect and had each other's back, no matter what. To the day of his passing and beyond, our loyalty and brotherhood remains intact. We celled together for a while. I finally made it to the South house and Butch made it over, too, not too long after me. (Years later, we hooked up in the streets with memories of hard times long ago.)

The South House had all the races, but, the whites were a bunch of Chicago lifers, outlaws, murderers, Arapahos and crazy Chicago gangbangers, like the Chicago warlords. Most of the whites rolled with the White Nation. They were members of the Chicago West side, Wilson Avenue Warlords, led by Juvenile, doing 80 years for murder.   I remember one day, he'd gotten out of the hospital so he could walk the yard and get some fresh air. I walked with him around the track to wish him well. He had terminal cancer. It's a strange feeling to be flanked by a half-dozen convicted murderers, while we walked. They were there to protect him. We were on dangerous ground and he had a contract on his life. But, he was well protected. He wasn't in denial. He knew he was dying. A few months later, he did die. Then, the Nation was ran by M N, doing 14 years and a day for a murder in Chicago.

M N was one of the most dangerous men I ever knew. I could go on and on with names of dudes, but, why would I. We were tight brothers. Loyal. We know who we were and to the many that are now gone.... Rest in peace.

We ran together. We were family and inside those Menard prison walls, we were a tight crew. After that, the White Nation became the Shackled Outcast, then, the Brotherhood. No matter the name, the White Nation always ran the South House and the whites made sure it stayed that way.

The Black Nation ran the East house. The riots were frequent, but, that's how prison works. You better know who your people are. When I was locked up, I stayed with my people. That's called survival. Prison is racist. Period. There's no delusional bullshit going on. Blacks stay with blacks, whites stay with whites, Mexicans stay with Mexicans, and on and on and on.

You might have a black dude running with a white gang or vice versa, but, that shit's always short-lived in prison. Both races end up hating the dude for riding with the wrong race. So, for the most part, we stay with our own people. We sit with our own people, we eat with our own people and we ride with our own people. Even if we ride as friends and do business in the streets, when we get locked down, it's better to save the friendship for the streets and understand that's life behind the walls. It's just the way it is. Well, that's the way it was in max prison back in the 70's. Brothers from different races can always reconnect back in the streets. The rules are different in the real world.

(If I do time, I'll be fine. I'll just mind my own business and do my own time... said about every fish coming inside the walls for the first time. No. Unfortunately, it doesn't work that way. Different set of rules at work inside the walls. Say you're a white dude, or, a black dude, or, a Mexican, or, whatever, it doesn't matter... and you go inside the walls to do time. It's best to ride with somebody. Loners don't do well in population, in the yard, or, walking down a gallery riding alone. Everybody gets tested. Everybody. We all know there's strength in numbers. Convicts sell wolf-cookies on the gallery every night 24-7. Talking shit through the bars. Keys clanging, non-stop. At first, it's un-nerving, but, eventually, it is what it is. When the doors break, every morning, the real shit goes down. The wolf-cookies don't mean shit unless the mouth selling them backs them up. I don't care if you think you're the baddest mojo in the world. When you first go into somebody's turf inside the walls, let's say prison assigns you a cell and it happens to be in some gang's real-estate. If he has to, if you don't want to cooperate with their insanity, the chief shot-caller will put a goon squad like six bad motherfuckers on your ass. You'll be dealt with. Population has its own ways. Prisons have their own rules. The Real World. We stay with our own people. We watch each other's back. Plus, you got to earn your way. You have to do work. What's work? There's shot-callers, chiefs and soldiers. If you're on a gallery riding with a gang, (because, remember, you can't really ride alone, unless, you want to live in a little cell in segregation in protective custody) so, anyway, back to it, let's say somebody messes up, even in your own gang and your chief says you got work to do, which, that hit orders really already been authorized from the shot-caller... then, it's on you to beat the target's ass, or, shank him, or even worse if the infraction calls for it. If you don't do the work, then, the work gets done to you. Simple deduction. The problem is, I saw dudes go into prison with 1 to 3 years for trivial bullshit, then, have to shank some dude to keep from being shanked and, then, no shit, from this, catch a beef. Then, this guy that really just wanted to do his own time and mind his own business has to go to court now, and get 10 more years on top of the 1 to 3 years. Oh, and now you can forget about good time and parole because your violent behavior means they'll take that shit, too. Prison life is rough. That shit happens. (That's why anybody that's done time in maximum security will tell you it's the real world and it's no place to be, ever, no matter what color you are.)

INSIDE...

Since coming to Illinois from Texas, while on maximum supervision paper, I was running with the wrong people, doing the wrong things and going to the wrong places for all the wrong reasons. I didn't get it. By my own actions, I'd shoved my own ass so far into the system, it's a wonder I was ever set free.

How someone could be so involved with the cops, be watched like a hawk because of insane and crazy behavior, have a life sentence hanging over my head if I mess up and still, I'm acting completely insane, like it doesn't even matter. So, I screwed up big time. It took me several months, but, I succeeded in failing real well! Menard. Illinois Maximum security prison.

I'd been in Menard for over a year. It was the middle of 1975. I was in Vandalia before that and Statesville prison in Chicago, before that. Just 3 or 4 months at each place. Before that, I was locked up in Texas. But, let's talk some more about hard time in Illinois.

First off, let me tell you a little more about the prison numbers. My prison number was so old school, I didn't even have a letter in front of the number. 41937.

I remember when they first implemented letters in front of the numbers. A12345 and so on. I think they've already went through the alphabet a hundred times since then. But, my number was before all that. Old school as hell.

The nightmare was, I had a parole hold on me from Texas. After I got out of Menard, Texas was supposedly picking me up and taking me to Huntsville to finish my 5 to life sentence there. Talk about the never-ending feeling of impending doom. I just shared with you about North Street. I'd stabbed Ed and violated my paper in Texas for a robbery charge and they were pissed. They were pissed that I'd violated the 5 years of paper with violence. Oh, it gets worse.

Then, wouldn't you know it, they stacked six felony drug-charge convictions in Illinois on me...I guess the craziest part of this is what I'm about to tell you. The irony. In Menard, I celled with a close brother of mine for a couple of years. Every night we celled together, we got high. You can use your imagination on how we got it in. I'm no snitch. I'll never tell.

It was excellent weed. We stayed high. One would gap the gallery and the other would toke and blow the smoke down the shitter while he flushed. For a couple of years we never once were suspected or got caught until the very day I was leaving prison. No shit. The guard came to get me out of the cell to roll it in. He opened the cell door and I was picking up my bag to go. All I had was a shirt, pants and a toothbrush. I gave my brother, Mingo everything else.

170

So, I'm about to walk out of the cell, to go, and I turn to shake Mingo's hand, as I'm leaving.

The guards just standing there and looks down. He sees something strange, so, he bends down and picks up one pot seed. I went to process out and Mingo went to the hole for ten days. Ironic bullshit. I mean in a sick and twisted kind 'a way, it's almost funny. It wasn't too funny then. I remember coming out of the office from processing and my brother, Mingo's standing there in handcuffs. I stopped and the screw let us talk briefly. He said they shook the whole cell down and that's the only thing they found... one tiny little pot seed. Ten days in the hole for my brother. Damn. Out the front gate I went. I hated seeing him go to that damn hole.

But, there was always shit going on inside the walls. More serious shit. Riots and skirmish's happened all the time. It was almost every day. So much shit happened all the time that it was the norm. When we call it gladiator school, we're not bull-shitting. In max prison, usually, we'd take it to the shower room for a head to head fight. We'd always take enforcers to watch our peoples back while the shit was going down. So would they. That was all the time. We'd face off in the yard if we wanted more soldiers in the mix. Sometimes, we'd have full-blown riots in the cell house. We had at least two or three of those every year. It helped us get rid of some of the anxiety. Then, they'd carry the wounded and dead out in bloody sheets and the rest of us would get locked down for a while.

After 3 or 4 weeks of that miserable torture, it was back to general population and psychosis life. Everybody riding with us would pass around shanks to our people, and when the doors broke, it was a blood bath. Maximum security prison is a serious place. More cons die inside those walls than they want you to know. There's an ever-growing grave yard behind the walls of Menard. You die, they quickly bury you in the prison graveyard and its business as usual. I know this for a fact. I don't care how much they deny it.

Violence is a way of life in there and if you can't hang with that, I suggest you stay away from shit that'll get you locked up. Nobody wants to go to prison. Out here in the streets, nobody thinks they're ever going to get caught. All the prisons are full of cons that didn't think they'd ever get caught. Hell, I didn't think I'd get caught either. I was too slick. I thought those smooth, calculating thoughts, too. I was the master of silky smooth. Whatever.

I went straight to prison. So, don't start thinking you're too slick to get caught. Reality is, and I've said this before... it's a different world inside those walls, with a whole different set of rules. I saw dudes commit suicide, try to commit suicide, get raped, murdered and turned into women and I don't mean by choice. Fighting and stabbing somebody was something that happened all the time. You have to put in the work. Punks and snitches are real things, too. In a cell house riot, the doors would break and out would jump everybody with shanks swinging to stab the enemy. It's not a fun place. It's THE REAL WORLD. Riots are a fact of life inside the walls.. More than a few times. A gallery of cons would line up to go to the yard, when the doors break on their gallery. Now, that's every day. But, sometimes, the guards would pull a surprise shake down while we're standing there, or, walking out single file to go to the yard. As soon as they'd call, 'FREEZE...HANDS IN THE AIR,' you'd hear 30 or more shanks hitting the concrete. Then, the guards would gather all the shanks and walk us to the yard. Get caught with a shank on your person and you'll spend a year in the hole. They don't play. That's serious time in the hole. Make a man crazy.

So, we're in the south yard, one day, pumping iron. That's something we did every day to stay war ready. It was Stef, Mingo, Smokey, Flip, Ike, and me, working on one of the bench's, taking turns and watching each other's back. We ran together and one of our people, JB, from the East yard yelled across to us.

Two big wire fences separated the yards. They were about a 12 foot walkway between the yards for the screws. That's the guards. Stef, Mingo and I walked over to the fence. JB says a dude that had raped and tortured his sister in Cahokia, Illinois, had just got there and was in our yard right now. He pointed over to the ball field at the dude in right field.

The fish gallery had just came on the yard and was just getting a ball game started. So, we made a plan. Let's walk across the ball-field to the picnic tables, like we do anyway, and as we pass the dude, we'll surround him real quick and one of us slap him upside the head with a 5 pound weight. Then, if we don't get shot from a gun tower, whoever has the weight can drop it and we'll keep stepping. We look at each other and smile, "Yeah, let's do that." We all look over at JB and nod, "We got you, brother." So, we work out for a little bit longer to blend back in, then, with it being busy, everybody walking

172

the track, pumping iron, playing ball, shooting hoops, playing handball and the like, we look around, the yards busy, so, one of us grabbed a five-pound weight from our bench and stashed it.

We all walked across the field, together, like we were cutting across to go start a card game, which we did a lot. There were tables on the other side of the yard we would play cards on. As we came up on the dude, we circled him, like a bunch of dudes talking, just normal shit. Next, real quick, the weight came out and the dude was blasted hard across the side of the head with it. At the moment he turned to look, startled, and said, "What the fu..?"

As his head hit the ground, the weight was quickly dropped next to him and we immediately kept stepping. We didn't miss a beat and quickly went to a picnic table. A moment later, the gun-tower saw him lying there, shot off a shotgun blast and everybody on the yard hit the ground. The dude was unconscious. They carried him off the yard. We were questioned separately and nobody saw shit. We got away with it.

We never said much about it after that. Business as usual. Just another day. JB appreciated it, I'm sure. I don't even know what happened to him. We never saw him or that fish again. He might have been transferred. That kind of shit happened all the time, so, it was no biggie. Max prison, man. This was before they installed cameras, so, they could play that shit back and know what happened. Cons couldn't lie about what happened after cameras were installed. We did time in the barbarian days, when they depended on seeing shit happen first-hand, or, from the snitches.

We all worked back in the kitchen for a couple of years. All the Hunt brothers, Country, Shorty, Stef, Flip, Mingo, Lurch, Foots, Null brothers, Rabbit, Smokey, Cowboy and others. We were united and strong, always making hooch and hiding it from the Chief Steward, Ashton, the sniffing hound-dog. He could smell that shit, I swear. We'd make two gallons of peach hooch and get away with it, too, until he finally found our hiding spot above the ovens. It took him a couple of years to find it. Of course, all the names have all been changed to protect the guilty... and the innocent. Except for Mingo, all these brothers I mentioned are now dust in the wind.

Anyway, we'd be drunk as hell and he couldn't figure out how we'd all be so wasted. Time and time again. We kept shit tight in the kitchen and dining room where we worked.

One day a young white dude that didn't ride with us, named Randy, approached Ming, Flip and I. He was in line with a bunch of blacks from the East house. The East House was a bad place for a young white dude to be housed. It was 98% black. They were lined up to eat. He pointed at a black dude, name unimportant, and said he was taking his commissary. I asked him, 'So, what you doing about it?" He said, "Nothing. I came to you guys. What should I do?"

I went over and pulled a metal Vat paddle handle out of a big vat used to cook in. It looked like a boat oar. I showed it to him and said, "You go out there in the dining room with this and crack that dude across the head with this vat paddle. You do that and drop it. Then, lay down real quick on the floor. A warning shotgun will go off. Everybody else will be hitting the floor too. After that, we got your back." So, we distracted the kitchen steward that had the door key to the metal door between the kitchen and dining room. One of us carried a coffee bucket through the door and while it was opened, I handed this Randy dude the vat handle and he headed straight for this black dude.

He was standing there in line to get his food. Randy hit that dude so hard with that vat paddle his head hit the floor before his feet did. Warning shotgun blast went off, everybody hit the floor and the screws carried the dude out of the dining room, still unconscious. Randy went to the hole and while he was in the hole, we pulled some strings and had him transferred over to the South house with us. Another day in Menard.

Like another day, Mingo, Flip, some white dude we didn't know and I were sitting at a table in the dining room about to eat. You got to understand everything's segregated in prison. Blacks stay with blacks and whites stay with whites, etc. Blacks ran the East house and whites ran the South house. The whole dining room is packed with cons eating, lined up to eat and there's gun towers all around us. We'd just sat down with this dude to eat. Three seats open and we wanted to stick together, so, in unison, we all decided, yeah, this'll work. We sat down with the dude. Ten minutes to eat and gone, anyway. No biggie, right? Wrong! Everything in the joint is a potential biggie. You learn that quickly if you want to stay alive. About 3 minutes into the meal, Mingo, Flip and I are talking about after chow, going to the yard, pumping iron and shit. Suddenly, the entire dining room got so quiet you could've heard a pin drop.

There's like four distinct seconds of complete silence. Everybody freezes. That's when shit jumps.

We hadn't heard about a riot jumping and we were in the shot-caller circle, so, we should've known. Just as we all look around to see what's going down, this black dude dove right between Mingo and me and stabbed this dude we're sitting with, right in the chest with a huge shank.

At that moment, two seconds later, we knew it was coming down, we all jumped for the floor as the shotgun blast from the gun tower behind Mingo shot the black dude and sent him flying, blood everywhere. So, the one dude has a ten inch shank in his chest and the other dude just got blasted with a shotgun, all within a 3 second time frame.

Most of all, all of this crazy shit went down at our table. We almost got shot. We dove to the floor, knowing a shotgun blast was coming. I mean the whole damn dining room was on the floor. Both dudes were bleeding everywhere. We didn't move. Here come the goon squad to clean up the mess.

The dining room fills up with guards and they're hustling all of us back to our galleries. The goon squad carried the two dudes out toward Medical. We were all back in our cells in under three minutes. Then, we were all on lock-down for a whole damn week. Both cell houses. North and south house. One meal a day and locked in a cage. Period. This is where riots come from. Not letting us out to the yard, kitchen and all, for days on end. Not good for a man's mind. We're all crazy, anyway. Tired of being locked up. So, being on lock down for several days is a special kind of... go to hell.

So much shit happens inside the walls, it's literally too much to talk about. One day, middle of the afternoon, Mingo and I are standing on Main Street inside Menard walls. We're talking about snatching sandwiches from the Officer's kitchen to sell on the gallery later. We were planning that shit before we went to work in the general population kitchen. Out steps this huge black dude, a few buildings up from us. We're both watching him to stay on top of shit. As he walks up to us, to walk by, we both look at each other.

This dude is calmly walking down the street toward medical, we realized, with the big handle of a butcher knife from the kitchen, stuck in his chest. He nodded a hello as he walked by. None of us said a word. We nodded back at him and watched him walk calmly on by us. After he got past us, we both couldn't help but notice the three or four inches of blade sticking out between his shoulder blades, with a blood trail running down his back. Just another day in Menard.

Another time, Mingo and I had gotten off work in the kitchen. It was early afternoon, after the lunch meal. We both had shower pillowcases packed with sandwiches from the officer's kitchen. That was one of our hustles. Cell house help would sell them on the gallery later in the evening. Crazy Carl was on cell house help, so, we had a good gig going on. He'd sell them for us and take a cut. Worked out great, since he was a brother to us. So, Mingo and I take off from the kitchen and head to the South house, where we lived. Three gallery, cell 27 was where we both lived.

The screw opens the front iron door with his key and says a guard in the front office would let us in our cell. Cool with us. He didn't check our bags, so, we were good. We step in the cell house and he locks the big iron door behind us. We walk over to the front office and no one's there.

Then, we hear 5 and 7 galleries both open all the cell doors. That's fifty 2 man cells on each gallery. Like a real bad nightmare, it sounds like thunder. Five gallery was all blue flags. Seven gallery was all yellow flags. I'm purposely not naming the gangs. Why would I? The point is, they were at war and we just walked into a fucking riot. What I'm saying is this. There's a hundred blue and a hundred yellow trying to kill each other. The guard had been tipped off and split. He probably got paid to leave, so, they could go to war.

Anyway, here, we are, the only two white dudes out in the cell house with 200 pissed off gangbangers stabbing each other all to hell. Real shit.

Mingo and I both froze against the wall. We didn't know what to do. It wasn't our fight, but, we're both white, so, there's that. There's at least 200 black gangbangers loose in the cell house that most likely, hated whites and damn sure hated members of the White Nation. True shit. It lasted about five minutes. It was five minutes of hell. But, throughout the entire riot, we were invisible to them. Not one of them paid us any mind. I guess yellow flags were told by their shot callers to kill all the blues and all the blues were told to kill all the yellow flags. So, they didn't give a fuck about us. Technically, Mingo and I got a ghetto pass for this riot, or, maybe,

176

God put a shield around us. I don't know. I don't know how we weren't stabbed to death just for being white dudes in a cell house full of black gang bangers, in kill mode. I don't know. But, they were stabbing each other all around us and didn't even look at us. Damn, I was glad of that. Are you asking me if we were scared? Do you have to ask? No doubt we're both crazy as hell, but, we weren't stupid. It was a bad place to be.

Put yourself in that spot. Exactly. I don't understand it, either, but, I'm damn sure grateful we survived that. Five minutes later, the cell house filled up with guards locking us all down real quick to contain the situation. They shoved Mingo and me in a cell with 3 black dudes. We didn't even talk. We stood there and watched the guards take bloody sheets filled with bloody dudes, out of the cell house, for about an hour. Then, they took us to our cells. I'll never forget that day for as long as I live. That was a spooky situation from beginning to end. I'm grateful to be alive. I guess it wasn't our time to go.

It could've went another way so quickly.

We always had a bad riot in the summer when it was real hot in the cell house. The, we'd have a bad riot in the dead of winter when it was cold as hell. Then, we'd have a couple of skirmishes at different times. When the doors broke, you run out swinging your shank. Sometimes, we'd have dining room's jump and start fighting. Then, other times, in one of the yards, shit would go down. We'd fight in the shower room if it was one on one. Like I mentioned before, we'd always have a few others in the shower to watch both fighters' backs when the shit went down. Protocol, so we didn't kill each other. Another time, there was this white dude that lived 2 cells down from Mingo and me. His name was Dave. Dave was a quiet dude, long hair, tied-back, drug-dealer, like a hippie guy. He was from Peoria, Illinois and he'd lived in that cell for well over a year. He didn't wear our colors, but, he was on our turf and he was a homeboy, so, we let him be. It's just another day behind the walls. The doors break on 3 and 5 gallery for yard.

We all step out and go to the yard. Business as usual. Out in the yard, Mingo, Flip and I pump iron and enjoy the yard air. An hour later, we all line up to go back to the cell house. No big deal. We get back to the cell house and start walking down 3 gallery. I get to cell

25, 2 cells before my crib, in 27, and I, instinctively, take a 2 second scan in each cell, before I walk by, to make sure nobody's going to stab at me or throw hot coffee in my face, as I walk by. Yeah, it's like that.

Well, every cell has a shiny piece of steel about 8 x 10 on the back wall, we use as a mirror. Dave was standing in front of his mirror, naked, covered in blood. "Damn man!" He had a homemade shank he was using for a razor and he'd stood there the entire hour we'd been out in the yard and butchered his scalp with this dull shank. He was trying to shave his head, and, instead, he was slicing the hell out of his scalp. Most of his hair was on the floor now, mixed with skin and blood. It was something I'll never be able to un-see in my head. "Dave?" I said. "Dave, you okay, man? Hey dude, what are you doing?" He turned and looked at me.

His eyes were dead inside. I couldn't really see any of his face. It was covered in blood and it was still pouring out of his head all around his body. He just stared at me and started waving his bloody head back and forth. Then, he said, "Stormy, I can't take it in here no more. I'm done man." The guard came walking up to see why we were stopping at this cell. He didn't say a word. He got on his radio and called for his Captain.

We went to our cell and got locked down. Everybody on the gallery stuck their little piece of mirror out of the cell and gapped the gallery.

We were all watching this shit go down. They opened the door, threw a sheet around Dave's body.

By the time he walked out of the cell, the sheet had turned mostly red. They took Dave to the Prison hospital, then, on to North 2. North 2 is where the mentally ill are housed in Menard. I never saw Dave again. Then, just a quick segue on this. I guess it was several years later, I was out of prison. I'd somehow survived it. Well, computers weren't happening then, so, anyway, I got the Journal Star newspaper delivered to my door. One day I'm reading the paper and I'll be damned, there was a story about Dave in the paper.

He had driven his car about a hundred miles an hour off Creek Road right at Farmington Road and went airborne into the creek below, according to witnesses.

He died instantly. Do I think it was suicide? Yes, I do. I think prison killed Dave long before he drove off that embankment.   Hey, I

178

don't care what anybody tells you... maximum security prison is tough. Especially back in the 70's, when men were men. These days, hair in a bun, panties on, mascara and lip-stick, men dressing like women, it's downright sad, well, I'll leave it there. I know back in the seventies, in prison, dudes dressed like that were giving up that bootie and giving head, but, hey, I'm not judging. Now, back when I was locked up, I damn sure belonged there. My consequences put me there and I deserved my fate. I own that. Addiction had me by the ass. Every day I was free, my life was chaos and self-destruction. Hey, it was my own doing. When I was in the streets, I didn't think drugs were a problem. That reality, in itself, is messed up. Man, I was lost. I thank God he saw fit to slap me down and lock me up.

Listen to me... the following, are just suggestions from an old guy that's seen more than many live to see. I've survived more than many have survived. I've endured more than any man should be expected to endure. I've grown to believe, from it all, I've learned certain things in life. I just want to share with you, a little bit of what I've grabbed hold of, along the way. Of course, if you already know everything, what's the point, right? If your mind is closed to the possibility of positive abundance and you simply refuse to remain teachable, actually, these words are directed directly to you whether you like it or not. Did that get your attention? Good. You can choose to let my words bounce off your hardened bullet-proof soul, or, you can open yourself up to the possibility that I might share something with you that could help you. You get to choose. While you're deciding, the rest of us will dive in!

I just have a few suggestions... First of all, don't let your life be frivolous, meaningless or pointless. There's nothing any of us can do about time. It moves quickly, so, use it wisely. Dare to be bold. Take risks! Constant failure will actually lead to success. Just refuse to give up. Show true empathy with others. Show compassion. Honestly try to do the next right thing. Help somebody that needs help. They're easy to find. There's struggle everywhere. Hey, I want you to know something.., when I was young, I thought for sure I knew everything there was to know about anything. All you had to do was ask me. I'd tell you anything. But, looking back, those word were the words of a young and foolish boy. Time opens our eyes. Now I can say with certainty... I know far less than I used to think I knew.

I suggest, now, think about this... if you're NOT really aware that you don't appreciate life very much, go ahead and say it again so you know you grasps what I just said... maybe you're really not in touch with the fact that you're not paying attention to those little things that are happening in your life. It happens all the time, all around us. We move around too fast and key things of potentially monumental importance slip by, unnoticed. Maybe you should really soul-search that. I'm not the Captain of your ship. Believe me, I'm not trying to be, either, but, honestly, you better wake the fuck up while you have free will. The only thing you'll find inside prison walls is HELL on Earth, evil psychos and cold-blooded scenarios played out on a daily basis. It'll snatch your sanity without remorse. Get into your NOW. YOU'RE FREE RIGHT NOW! Embrace that. Enjoy that. Appreciate that. Dirty deeds are done dirt cheap inside those walls! For real. Pure miserable Hell! Even smiling makes you look weak and don't dare say, I'm sorry, for anything. No kindness allowed! I don't care how tough you think you are... taking your time, your free time, and those years off your youth, that precious THING that gives us precious memories. Well, it can also give us horrible nightmares, if we don't respect it with positive life. My suggestion... find your purpose and truly focus on that. Keep doing the next right thing. Give your life the right path and refuse to stray from that. Your rewards will be many.

TIME IS PRECIOUS...

Moment by lonely moment, second by dreary second, day by miserable day and time slows waaaaay down when you're locked up. I don't know the why of that, but, I do know it does. The saddest part of this is, as bad as prison is, it still didn't stop me from jumping right back into drugs when they opened the cell door and cut me loose.

180

Time is precious- a truly awesome dude. Wild Billy-RIP, Lived too hard and died way too young, RIP my brother.

Stormy Monday & Smokey G. & Stef C.-RIP my brothers

FRUITS FROM THE POISONOUS TREE

Several years later... back in the streets...
77, 78, 79... Consequences of active addiction...

So, here's what I had hanging over me. After I was released from prison in Illinois. I had a parole violation hold on me from Texas. Talk about deep levels of anxiety clutching and ripping at my insides. What that means is, Illinois was supposed to contact Texas when I was about to be released from prison, so that Texas could extradite me there to complete my 5 years to life sentence in Huntsville prison. By mistake, they didn't. But, God was at work here and I didn't even know it.

I was completely oblivious to the good going on in my life, while I was existing in the midst of the insanity. Here's what I'm talking about.... I was released on 3 years parole from Menard prison in Southern Illinois. They sent me to my home town of Peoria, Illinois. Remember, I also had 5 years paper from Texas that I'd already violated. That's hanging over my head.

In Illinois, they'd sent me home on maximum security parole from a max prison. Here's why I was on max supervision... I'd lost all my good time when I was locked up, because, I'd been charged with inciting a riot in the joint. That meant every Friday I had to go report in person to my parole officer in downtown Peoria. My parole officer was a dick.

with a capital D. When we first met, he had my criminal file with him on his desk.

Then I realized why he was being such a dick to me. I'd been convicted of a half-dozen drug charges in two counties, inciting the riot in prison, gang affiliation, robbery in Texas, plus, an attempted murder charge that was dropped down to an aggravated battery. On top of all that, my file was supposed to show that I had a parole violation and hold on me from Texas. Hey, my momma didn't raise a fool. I'm not saying a word about any of that. I did all my time in Illinois thinking I had to go back to Texas and spend 5 years to life in prison, in that shit-hole, for violating my parole.

I did time there before I went to prison in Illinois, so, my mind-set was fuck that place. I'm not saying a word. I just pushed that under some invisible rug and acted like it never existed.

For seven months, I reported to that PO's office, like a clock, every Friday. Just like I was ordered. In the meantime, I fell in love with my first wife, Brenda. Out of nowhere, there she appeared. She was sitting in a booth with her girlfriend, Julie. They were both sexy as hell and smoking hot. I'd just gotten out, so, they looked especially damn good to me. Anyway, they were listening to live music in a place called Sgt. Peppers. That's in P-town. Brenda and I clicked right away. We ended up going to her place and literally talking all night long about everything. We got close and watched the sun come up together.

By then, there was no question. We fell in lust and in love. Not long afterwards, we got married and in no time, she was carrying my first child, Misty, inside her. I was so proud. After Misty, we had a son, Jesse. I also got a job at the Southside Foundry on third shift. Hard-ass work, but, I was a hard-ass man. That was a rough job. Then, a few months later, I was hired at Caterpillar in East Peoria, Illinois. I worked in Building HH on second shift. They started me on a multiple drill and after six months or so, I finally landed a good job running a surface grinder. I was sincerely trying to change my life. But, here's the sad truth. I was still living a secret life. All around me, I still lived in denial and chaos. I continued shooting coke on weekends. That went on and on and on. Obviously, there was something wrong. I had problems everywhere. There was self-destruction and chaos at every turn. I was blaming everybody for everything. I started dealing drugs, then, that turned into large quantities. I'm thinking I'm literally on parole from two States. All this time, I'm secretly wondering why in the hell Texas never came and picked me up when I was released from Menard. I'm not saying one word about that. I was hoping maybe they just kept me on the paper and let me do it with the Illinois paper. Yeah, right! Even with all that shit going on, I'm dealing large amounts of weed and coke. Complete insanity. But, in my fervor to maintain control of all situations, I refused to accept my uncontrollable dilemma. I had a serious drug problem and Texas was hanging over me like a huge black cloud. Everything going on around my marriage and seemingly normal life was complete insanity. I lived like a chameleon. The stress level to manage this madness within my realm of being was catastrophic.   Brenda had a great job at Commercial bank in downtown Peoria. She took me out one day and bought me an entire wardrobe, since my clothes consisted of a pair of blue jeans and a prison t-shirt. Then, for my birthday, she bought me a beautiful 1966 T-bird. It was baby blue with black leather interior. She was a beauty and the ol' girl ran like a charm! Right after that, I got a call from Caterpillar for an interview. I got the job! We were so excited. It was like a series of incredible events unfolding. "I have some great karma going on here." I thought to myself. Life seemed to be falling into place. Then, they assigned me a different parole officer.

Thank God, he was cool as hell. The wife and I were renting a nice house on Gale Avenue. After a few months of marriage, I approached the landlord and told him we were just starting a family and really wanted to buy the house. To my surprise, he sold it to us for not a lot of money with no money down, to help us get a good start. What a guy! I immediately remodeled the home and landscaped it.

Three or four months later, during this process, I met a lady friend through my sister, Susie. She was a cat executive. I found out she was very independent and was looking for a home. I offered to sell her ours. She accepted after she saw all the improvements I'd done. We made $30,000 on the transaction after I paid the bank down to zero. We used that money and bought us a really nice home in Norwood. Now we had 2 and a half wooded acres and a beautiful home.

One really nice and sunny day, just before we moved to our new home in Norwood, I kissed my pregnant wife bye at the door and headed to my second shift job at Caterpillar, in my baby-blue 66 T-Bird. It was just another day in the city! Uhhhh NO! I drove onto the ramp off University to get onto 74 east. As I rounded the ramp,

184

suddenly, I had a dozen or so cop cars surround me in every direction. I was ambushed by the man. Cops were standing everywhere with weapons drawn. My adrenalin shot out the top of my head.

I stopped and quickly put my hands out the window, so, I didn't get shot. The cops, I'm told, are under the impression that I've escaped from Huntsville prison in Texas, and they have a fugitive warrant for my arrest. They handcuff me and take me to jail. Then, a few days later, I'm informed that The Texas Rangers are coming to take me to prison in Texas and I don't even get a hearing before a judge.

They'd found my parole hold and found out I'd been released from prison in Illinois. They were pissed that they weren't informed about my release. So, they were hell-bent on coming to get me immediately.

They were also pissed that I'd violated their parole with a violent charge, when I stabbed the guy in Illinois, while I was on parole from Texas. So, here I was, sitting in jail. My entire world collided with a cold and harsh reality. It all came tumbling down. My parole officer came and visited me. He told me the Texas Rangers were being assholes. He said he thinks they're on their way, that I wouldn't have a hearing. I was going to prison in Texas and spending life in prison, because I'd violated with violence. "Damn."

I sat in that cell that day and night mad at the world. I'd done so much to live a life in society like most people were doing. I was happily married, we had a child on the way, we both had nice cars, we both had great jobs and I'd busted my ass to get us a nice house. To my complete surprise, my parole officer went to battle for me. He came to my cell one day and said he had to act quickly. Those Rangers are in a hurry to get you to Texas. He pointed out all the good I'd done in the last 7 months. After numerous calls to Texas, Harold, my PO, finally called the States Attorney's office in San Antonio, where I'd originally gotten busted. For several days in a row, Harold was on the phone with these guys.

Finally, he made a deal with Texas. One chance. They ran my parole from Texas consecutively with the 3 years in Illinois. That meant I had to do 8 years of parole. Fine. I'll do 8 years of parole. Peoria County released me back to the streets. I went back to work and, incredibly, I still secretly shot cocaine.

EMPTY VESSEL

Continued from 1st Chapter...

(Remember where this story began at the beginning of the book. Think back. When I was chasing that high I could never find. I compared it to climbing a hill to get to the top, so, I could feel that sense of fulfillment after finally reaching the top, but, I could never reach the top of the hill.... So, there was never any fulfillment. In other words, I kept running. I kept shooting more and more dope. The past ten years have led to this night.) Death is a stones-throw away...
April, 7th, 1983.

Like a child left to play in a room filled with toys, I continued...

I have 2 ounces of coke, 2 ounces of Brown Mexican Heroin, a big bag of new rigs and, deep down, I have to admit, maybe I did have the inkling of a death wish. It's hard to admit that. There was too much mental anguish for far too long and, honestly, I think I wanted to be done with it all. Mentally, spiritually, physically and emotionally, I was tired. I was very, very tired. Just let me die.

I continued shooting dope in that bedroom for God only knows how long. I was blasting speed-balls, one right after the other. I'd cook a pile of heroin down and then I'd drop a quarter rock of coke, or more, in the mix, (that's $25 or $30 worth of coke) and let the rig cool for about 5 seconds. Then, I'd shoot it. The blues would crawl on me 5 or 6 minutes after I hit up and, I'd frantically start making another hit. Schizoid level. The hits just kept getting bigger and bigger. I was chasing that high and no matter how much dope I'd do, after so many, I'd do an even bigger hit. This kills people. Imagine being my body organs!

Over and over and over! After a lost haze of days, of me, staring out every window, in the house, for at least a thousand times, the hallucinations consumed me, and the paranoia had taken over.

Outside the windows, every tree, post and flowering bush, started turning into cops that were watching me. My brain melted. My soul was dead. My wife thought I'd lost my mind. Maybe I did. She was freaked out, but, she went downstairs to be out of my way. There was nothing left inside me, except psychosis. All hope for any semblance of survival was gone. That place inside my head, between what's going on, and what my thinking thought was going on, merged, into one another.

The coke and the heroin was all that mattered. There was nothing else. This monster was left. My spirit succumbed to the darkness. As soon as the rush from the dope blast passed, I was filling the spoon up again. Between nods, I'd put a bigger pile of coke in the blackened spoons of cooked heroin. Finally, several days into this insanity, my worried, pissed-off and scared wife, said I'd been in the bedroom for a long time and she'd hear me doing stuff, then, all of a sudden, she noticed it got quiet. She'd been outside and downstairs, cleaning and staying out of my way.

She said she started beating on the door, trying to get my attention, just to make sure I was okay. Thankfully, she had just enough love left in her, for me, to not give up. She said she pushed the door in and found me on the floor in the bedroom, unconscious and unresponsive. I was bluish-purple all over. I had overdosed. Unresponsive. In shock and scared to call the police or an ambulance, because she knew I'd freak out about it if I were actually alive, paranoid from prison and all, so, she called my parents and they called an ambulance.

When I woke up, 2 or 3 days later, I was in intensive care, at Proctor. I didn't even realize that, until a nurse told me they'd lost me in the ambulance. The ambulance EMT's had brought me back and I'd slipped into a coma. After that, I'd been unconscious for a couple of days. Then, I finally came to. I woke up. The next afternoon, I was moved to detox. It was next to Proctor treatment center. I was miserable. The monkey was on my back big-time. The next several days were hell. Then, I was given a set of stern rules by a nurse, I was supposed to agree to follow to be a patient in the treatment center. The whole idea of that pissed me off. I was sick as hell, since my body was still going through serious withdrawals, but, none the less, I was still pissed. "I didn't sign up for this shit. What happened here?" I knew one thing and that's all I could think about.

I knew that in my bedroom, I had a whole lot of dope just lying on that bed, in that house. I desperately needed to find out what my wife or parents, did with my coke, my heroin and my rigs. Plus, were the cops in my house? If so, am I busted? What now? But, Proctor wouldn't let me call anyone.

So, to hell with Proctor, I walked out! I walked out against every body's better wishes and judgments. Cell phones didn't exist then, so, I made it to a pay phone, and called Brenda, my wife. This was my first wife. I was so caught up in my addiction at this time in my life, I didn't even realize the absolute hell I was putting this good woman through. She put up with this madness for almost six years. That shit doesn't even enter the mind of an addict in active addiction. It sure didn't enter my sick mind, at this time, in my life. The entire marriage with two beautiful children had come down to this. Brenda was dumb-founded, that I'd walked out of Proctor. She was done.

Then, she said, "Stormy, your father poured all that dope down the toilet. He threw that bag of syringes in the trash."
I'm screaming, "OH my God! That was almost four thousand dollars. No, Brenda, no!"

She said, "We thought you were dead, Stormy. You weren't breathing. Your skin was blue, for Christ's sake. So, he flushed it. He flushed it all!"
"Wow … Oh my God, oh man, oh no! Oh no, oh no, oh no." was all I could say. "Well, fuck it all then."

"One other thing" my wife said. "Listen to me… I'm taking the kids and I'm gone. I'm sick of your shit. You scared the hell out of me this time. You're going to die, Stormy. Those drugs are going to kill you. I can't watch it anymore. You're crazy!"

"To hell with you, Brenda! You're going to take my kids and go! You're just going to leave me. I need you now more than ever. What the hell! Threw my damn dope away! Now what? I hate this shit! This is some bullshit! " I screamed.

Life on life's terms…

I had an amazing and gorgeous wife, Brenda, who loved me with the heart and soul of her being. I had two of the most beautiful and
188

amazing children, Misty and Jesse, that cherished the ground I walked on. We had this circle of really cool people always stopping by, for cook-outs, parties, and the like. We had a beautiful home in the country with three acres of landscaped land that had big, red maples and Colorado blue spruce all over. Blue spruce that I'd strategically planted for appearance and privacy. It was a beautiful property. The back acre was covered in trees. We had a beautiful hundred year old, weeping willow tree in the back yard. The home had a walk-out patio, from a gorgeous recreation room, with a gym in the next room.

I'd worked very hard to create this gorgeous setting. I built the rec-room, the gym, the walk-out patio, planted the blue spruce trees, put a beautiful fence around the property and on and on and on. I put in a circle drive and remodeled the inside of the home. I had so many material things, so many toys, nice Harley, camper, great dogs, Zak and Abby, both AKC registered Dobermans, and everything else a man could want... and with all of these amazing things, in the midst of all that incredible stuff going on in my life, my soul had died. I wasn't there. I don't know where I was, but, I wasn't there. I had all the toys, a great job, beautiful home, awesome family, a great life really, and I threw it all away for a needle and a bag of dope. Why? That's the million dollar question. Why? Addiction is truly cunning and baffling.

(Back to the story...)

YOU THREW MY DOPE AWAY?

I'd walked out of Proctor Treatment Center and called my wife from a pay phone. "So, my dope's really gone? Are you serious? What the hell, Brenda!" Think about it. I'd almost died. I'd overdosed, yet again. This time, I'd been in a coma from heroin and cocaine toxicity. I'd worried the hell out of my wife, my children, my 5 sisters, my friends, my mother and my father. I'd been in detox. I'd almost got in a fist-fight with a drug counselor and walked out of treatment. I had warrants out for battery charges from a month back.   Two dudes had been put in the hospital downtown at about 4 am one morning. The cops had several written statements from people who didn't want to be identified that stated a few of my partners and me had fought and beat the hell out of 4 guys in the middle of Main & Monroe street at 4 am. So, the cops wanted to put me in a police line-up. Screw that. Plus, I owed a drug-dealer money. I didn't give a shit, I figured I'd deal with him later. My entire life was spiraling out of control. I was at the end of my rope. I kept thinking, if everybody would just leave me alone, I'd be fine.

This is the definition of a neurotic paradox. I had all these problems going on in my life and I was pointing my finger in every direction, placing the blame on everyone but myself. The truth of it is this... there was only one problem. My drug problem. If I'd take care of my drug problem, all the other problems in my life would work themselves out. On top of all that was the self-centeredness.

Think about it... Was I concerned about my wife, my home, my children, my health or my mental state? Was I the least bit worried about whose feeding my dogs? Where's my car? Were my bills paid? ARE MY CHILDREN OKAY? Are they safe? Have they eaten? Am I losing my family? Does my wife still love me? Is she leaving me? Was I concerned about ANY OF THAT? Did any of that matter? ANY OF IT? ONE THING MATTERED.

I was freaked out over one thing. MY DOPE. Where was my dope?????????????? That's a clear-cut symptom of the disease of addiction. Self-centeredness.)

I hung up the phone and puked right there in the gas station parking lot. My stomach was knotted up like a hardball, so I went back to detox, suffered through it for about a week and then, back into treatment.

I just wanted to die. But, as it turns out, I guess I hadn't suffered enough. Even now after all that hell. I didn't know anything about hitting my bottom. I didn't know we all have different bottoms. All those things were like fog in the glass to me. This was in April, 1983.

Even after all this hell, after all this bullshit, all this pain, all my deep, mental very real suicidal THOUGHTS and near-death experiences, once again, I still wasn't ready for recovery. Unbelievable, I know! Sound familiar? Hey, did you know, addicts have far more similarities than differences... neither did I. Well, it's true. Finally, I sat back alone.

I searched my soul.

I did. I even told myself, this is it. No more! I wanted to live in recovery. I even believed it. But, the truth is, beneath all that, I refused to be willing. Willing enough to do what was necessary to live a clean life. I refused to be open-minded about my situation. Oh, I said I was being open-minded. I was lying to myself. I wasn't honest with me. I still had reservations and I didn't want to admit that. I didn't want to miss the party. I thought living clean meant no more fun.

When I did complete thirty-two days of treatment at Proctor, I left wanting more than anything to try to live life without drugs, including booze. In treatment, I met a counselor named Randy McG (RIP). He was a Vietnam Vet and he'd seen action in the bush, boots on the ground. Randy was a recovering heroin-addict. The dude was a hard-ass. That's exactly what I needed to get my attention. We were eyeball to eyeball, the moment we met. Randy wouldn't take my shit and I needed that. We almost came to blows and like I said, I even walked out. He pulled me back with his words.

What he said actually made some semblance of sense to me. I was a mess. He ended up being my sponsor for a couple of years. Randy warned me when I didn't go to many meetings that it'd catch up to me.

At the time, I didn't want to hear it. I should've listened to him. He worked extensively with me on my rage and addiction issues. I went in mad as hell at my dad. He'd beaten me bad, way too much and way too often, throughout my early childhood. It scarred me. I carried that rage inside me for a long time. I really tried to open myself up to the whole concept of life without drugs. I discovered the treatment offered at Proctor was a course in self-awareness, as outlined by Maslow's humanistic theory. This would be my journey toward the pursuit of self-actualization. This would be my attempt at fulfilling my basic needs to reach a beautiful level of enlightenment. My journey of self-discovery!

That's just what I needed to help me figure out who the hell I really was. I'd been so wasted since I was thirteen, I had no idea who this person was that I saw in the mirror. I spent my childhood running from myself. Running from this weak kid those beatings had destroyed. The bottom line is this. That weak kid had to die, so, I could emerge from the wreckage. Well, I went through thirty-two days of treatment at Proctor and they released me back into the world. Talk about culture shock. My world was different. I was going to Alcoholics Anonymous meetings a few times a week, because that's where the treatment center had taken us. I didn't know of any other place to go. Right away, I didn't feel like I fit in at Alcoholics Anonymous. It wasn't me. After all, I'm a drug addict.

I did a whole lot more than drink booze. I shot dope and lots of it. One of the old-timers at one of the AA meetings told me in front of the group one night that I couldn't introduce myself as an addict. He pointed at me like he knew me and said, "In here, you have to introduce yourself as an alcoholic." "Really? Excuse me, uhh NO. The only thing I HAVE TO DO is die. I'm an addict." So, that turned me off to going to AA. The old man embarrassed the shit out of me. This was all new to me. Let's talk about this...

Here's what I'm saying. I hadn't grown to an enlightened place inside my recovery.

I was new. I didn't understand to not let anyone keep me out of meetings.

I didn't even know our recovery must come first. We grow to that place by coming to meetings and listening. We learn to talk to our sponsor when we have an issue before acting on it, impulsively.

I wasn't there yet. We have to surrender to a Higher Power of our choosing, and to the program before we get to that. I was still trying to figure out how to use and still be okay.

Here's the bottom line... Nothing will make a man leave a meeting that truly wants recovery. I wasn't there yet. Also, one other thing, don't get this twisted. I know a lot of alcoholics that love AA. That's great for them. It just wasn't for me. I did all the dope I could get my hands on. So, because, deep down, I was looking for any excuse I could find to use again, I turned that old man's words into a resentment.

RELAPSE

1986...

It's about 3 years after I'd went to Proctor Treatment Center and if you were around me, or, saw me out, you'd think I had it all together. I wasn't using. I wasn't drinking and I was busy working, going to Tae kwon do, doing family activities, fishing with friends, picnics and the like. Thing was, on the outside I showed quite a different person than the screaming and clawing animal inside me. It was horrible.

I was white-knuckling my so-called recovery, every moment of every day. What that means is this... I was staying clean, but, I sure wasn't working any program. All I was doing was making myself not use or drink. It was hard, too. I still had the cravings, but, after three years, they weren't as bad as they had been. The sad part is, I felt no harmony in my soul. I was still empty inside.

I had no spirituality at work in my life, whatsoever. I was just trudging along trying to figure out how to keep staying clean. I didn't know what I was doing wrong to keep living clean and still feel so unhappy. There had to be a better way. I just didn't know what it was. Why can't I be happy, too? I wasn't happy. I was just going through the motions. Then, the worst thing happened. One of my favorite people on the planet, my grandfather, (Dewey Monday) Papa passed away. He was one of the two kindest men I ever knew. The other one being my other grandfather, (E. C. McClung) pop Gene. They came from another time. They were real men, kind, brave and patriotic. Anyway, one of my dope-shooting partners stopped by to show me love, because he knew how much I loved Papa. My partner, Bingo and I were close friends. So, when he told me he was sorry about my grandfather, we hugged with brotherly love. I appreciated him remembering how much I loved my grandfather. He knew I was clean, but, he didn't know that I'd been white-knuckling my recovery since I'd left treatment. I was forcing myself to stay clean because the last dope frenzy almost killed me and it scared me. So, I was holding on to that fear to continue to stay clean. But, like I said, I had no inner-peace at all. None. I was still a mess inside.

My brother Bingo said, "Hey brother, since I'm here, you mind if I do a hit of this brown? I just copped from Chicago. It's brown Mexican, almost pure heroin."

I said, "Go ahead, man, not a problem." I sat there like a fool and watched his ritual. I watched him get his dope ready.

Watching him was a mistake and when he shot that hit, it took me about 10 seconds to decide I was doing a hit, too. I didn't think anything through for a second. I dove in head-first.

Even after going to treatment, all the sessions with Randy, all the counseling, all the pain and suffering, all the fights with my wife, all the hell of her leaving me, the pain of her taking my children, all the suffering and crying alone, I still shot that hit. I didn't think it through or anything. Let's STOP right here.... Are you paying attention? Okay, here's what I said....

I didn't think it through.

Chapter 9

A PERFECT STORM

So, I was back out in the streets...
Mid 80's... (After relapsing in Peoria, Illinois...

City lights pierced the black of the night sky and broke the narrow shadows of taller buildings into partial silhouettes. A million stars filled the blackness and lit my way almost every night. I had a closet filled with black suits, black shirts and flashy silk ties. My Italian loafers sat next to my Harley boots. Black biker leathers filled the other end of the closet. Some nights, my mind-set was a smooth and sharp, clean look. Inside my brain, the committee bartered over my apparel from night to night.

Some nights, I'd catch the back roads on my Harley seeking that ever so rare and priceless spiritual enlightenment. It was always tucked out there somewhere in the wind. All for the taking, for the chosen few. It's still the best therapy I know.

Anyway, black leather hugged my skin for protection against the endless miles of asphalt. I'd carry that look on through the night. Downtown at 2, 3 and 4 am. Hell, all the way to sunrise. On the prowl almost every night like a lion stalking feline prey. Other times, on the hunt, I'd dress just for the ladies, mysterious and bold, out and about in my clean, fully-loaded RX 7. It appeared the ladies loved both looks, the wild, yet, flashier look with the clean black threads and loafers and the Alpha male black leather biker. Early mornings found me in the smoky downtown clubs, catching sexy curves and pitching clever fast balls. This was my domain. Where my dark-side would push me into the crowded dance clubs filled with cocaine and whiskey. Anything goes in the wee wee hours and the club scene downtown was like the Wild West!

If the drugs didn't kill us, the lifestyle did.

The shadow people were all around me, whispering their game and pitching there clever angles to all who would listen, selling their wares, drugs and promises of good times. Sex was a popular tool for trading. Players shaking down the money tree wherever it grew. Rolling in the snow and shopping for the next good time. Live bands played their beat and the street hustlers prowled for a new and sweeter flavor. I didn't care if I lived or died. I'm living high on cocaine and whiskey, wild in the streets nightly, doing whatever I could to get that dope in my arm. I always had a sexy, fine woman on my arm. Everything around me was insane and complete chaos. I was comfortable in that. The allure of the lifestyle had pulled me in. After my wife moved out and took our children to her mother's in Iowa, I met a fine little woman downtown, named Mellie. We got close. She was gorgeous, sexy, fine, hard-body, all those adjectives a man looks for in a woman. Mellie was also the kind of wild I loved in a woman. We had a thang for quite a while. But, overall, I still partied with lots of women, mostly strippers, like Steph. Fine and pure class. She was a top-shelf woman. Steph and I had a beautiful thing, too.

Strippers like her seemed to understand me.

This was about the time I was introduced to crack cocaine. Bad idea. Talk about addictive. Talk about chaos. Everything in my life at this time was focused on getting high and wild sex. I always thought shooting coke made more sense, but, that sure didn't stop me from smoking the shit. I'd smoke crack, shoot heroin and coke all at the same time. I didn't discriminate. Believe me, you'll never meet a social crackhead. That's an oxymoron. I lived the life of a maniac. Thing was, I ran with guys who were all convicted murderers.

This time of my life turned out to be another bout of insanity. Downtown Peoria, Illinois was a much different place back in those days. This perfect storm would, unknowingly, deeply affect my life. I'd bought a Harley in 1978. It was a 1976 kick-start Sportster. I named her "Foxy". It was early to early eighties by now. Like I said a minute ago, I was bar-hopping the biker-bars, the 4 am downtown bars, the after-hours joints, drinking Crown Royal whiskey like it was water and shooting cocaine like a madman. The suppressed rage from my childhood started pouring out. I wasn't happy inside. I was filled with rage and going to jail, constantly, for assault and battery. I was literally just stacking up battery charge after battery charge. If my parole officer hadn't been an okay dude, and I wasn't friends with shot-shot lawyer, I'd have gotten violated several battery charges back. I was back into heroin and a crew of us ex-cons started hanging out. We knew each other from doing time and the downtown street life, plus, all the biker bars. We shared a mutual respect for one another.

So, we hooked up and became, like a blood in/ blood out, family. Brenda, my wife, stuck around for a while, but, eventually, in 83, when I ended up in treatment, she took the children and left. It was crazy all the time. My partners had strippers working, hookers in the game and we were deep in the street-life. I was also at the animal level in the dope game. This was about the time I met the little sex kitten, Mellie. Together, we would prove to be a very wild and dangerous bunch. It was complete madness. In this time and in this place, these guys became like my brothers from different mothers. Who were we? We were Dave W, later convicted serial-killer, now dead. Billy K, convicted violent madman and was later murdered by Dave W. based on Dave's confession on Dateline News.

He'd made a deal to give up a murder for 30 years off his 60 year prison sentence. What a story! Then, there was B J, convicted murderer, boxer, player and another tight brother. Let's not forget Chris A. (Mingo), convicted of drugs and explosives. He was a danger to himself and others, nothing short of a violent madman. Mingo was a biker in the streets, ruthless and a very smooth player. We met in Menard prison where we celled together for over 2 years. True brother. Then, there was Tommy C. Tommy was also a wild man and a very close brother. Also, there was Carl. Carl was and is a very serious man and close friend to this day. Enough said there. Then, there was me.

We were a tight-knit group of guys. This was the early 80's. If you were downtown P-town in the late 70's and early 80's you knew who we were. The third shift cops like Skallion and his trained German shepherd damn sure knew who we were. My addiction during this time was intense. I was existing on coke and heroin. Deep in the game, getting fronted quarter-pounds of cocaine from a friend who was bringing it back from Bogota. Then, I'd spend days on end with shooting partners in bathrooms, shooting it way past hallucination level. I was shooting way too much dope. I overdosed twice more. I almost died both times.

I'd shoot coke till I couldn't hold the rig in my hand anymore. Literally be near-dead, completely drained, then, I'd drink a fifth of Crown Royal, so, I could come down off the coke enough to go downtown.   Maniac shit. While I'm writing this and thinking back about it, I can't help but think it sounds like I had some crazy death wish. But, sitting here right now, analyzing that, I don't believe I did. I was consumed in the dope life. Buried up to my neck in addiction. Deadly stuff. "Amazing to be here writing this" surfaces from my subliminal, often.   David W, who was later found to be a serial-killer is dead now. He died of lung cancer in prison doing time for multiple murders. Nowadays, there's lots of books and movies about his path of terror. Dave W is the man who kidnapped, robbed and murdered the Madelyn Murray O'Hare family.

Madelyn Murray O'Hare was the woman responsible for taking prayer out of school. She was also the founder and President of the Atheist Foundation. News outlets all over the country tagged her the most hated woman in America.

So, anyway, before all that happened, after we left Peoria, when the shit got deep, Dave and I traveled all over the southern and southwestern parts of the country. We went to Atlanta, Georgia, Clearwater Beach and Tampa, Florida, to Mobile, Alabama, New Orleans to Corpus Christi, Texas. For a while we moved around quite a bit. I was shooting dope all the way. I was trying to get Brenda, my first wife, out of my head and Dave, was searching for his ex-wife, Lola, with devious plans. I didn't realize that at the time. I will say this. We did find her in a swank restaurant in Clearwater Beach. She was a waitress, working, just trying to make a living. Well, when we first got to Clearwater, Dave had one lead.

Let me explain something. Dave was a brilliant man, criminal as hell, but, he was a very cued-in man. He found some guys house that knew her somehow. I don't even know how he found any of this shit out. I do know this. We went to the dude's house. He was happy to let us know where she was working.

So, we go where he told us she worked. It was a very classy spot. We were seated by the kitchen doors and who you think came walking out of those doors right after we were seated. There she was. He immediately pounced on her. It even caught me off a little off-guard. The cops were called and he went to jail. I didn't do shit, but watch it go down, so, they let me go. Shit, we were in Clearwater Beach. It was gorgeous everywhere. When they took Dave to jail, I went out and partied. After a week or so, he got out on a PR bond. It was business as usual. We hung out in Clearwater for a few more days and hit the road. We were traveling around the country, places like Tampa, Jacksonville, Mobile, Austin, San Antonia and Corpus. We stayed in weeklies in all these places.

In answer to the questions running through all your minds, I know with 99% of certainty, he was not on a killing spree. Nor was I. I'm not a killer. There's a hundred percent certainty of that. Unless you harm one of my children. But, on our journey, there were no dead bodies along the way. Not to my knowledge and we hung out in bars, strip clubs and the like, daily and nightly. Dave and I were just about always together. There was no killing going on.

We were friends and brothers, getting our ex's out of our systems. Also, he just happened to be an actual maniac. Who knew? I didn't. Sure, I knew he was a convicted murderer, but, none of us were squeaky clean. We were a tough crowd. That's all I knew.

Relative to that, this happened in the early 80's, I think it was. Billy K had gotten murdered while we were all out one night in Peoria, Illinois. Our crew partied all day at the Gaslight on Main Street. Thank God I'd ridden my Harley. We got drunk doing shots of Redeye and drinking Crown Royal, literally all afternoon and night and when we all left to go downtown, I went home instead. I was too drunk to go downtown and I knew I had cocaine stashed, so, I wanted to go home and shoot some dope. Thank God! I'm surprised I survived riding my Harley home that night. I was way too drunk to be riding on a bike.

Well, after that night, Billy disappeared and there were witnesses that saw us spend the day and night together getting wasted. Plus, they had us on surveillance cameras partying together and leaving together. Just like that, Billy vanished. I had no idea where he or anybody went. Like I said, I went home. We were all questioned and I honestly had no idea what actually happened. Whatever happened, happened, after I went home.

Thing is, we were downtown almost every night, all night. All the club owners, all the downtown partiers, everybody knew who we were. We were VIP everywhere. No matter what club it was, when we walked up to the door, the bouncers stepped aside and shook our hands and nodded as we walked in. The drinks flowed freely. We did whatever we wanted, wherever we were. I was going to jail for assault & battery every other week and I was on parole. Thank God I was close friends with my P O. I really didn't give a shit, though. I didn't even think about consequences. That never entered my mind for a second. All I know is we controlled every space we entered from minute one and we got respect no matter where we were. Maybe it wasn't respect. Maybe it was fear.

We had our hands in about everything illegal. I mean, unbeknownst to us, one of us is a serial killer, for Christ's sake, and the rest of the crew had all done serious time for heavy shit, drugs, murders and the like. But, here's what I saw a lot of in the streets. Everybody's savage until it's time to do savage shit. Believe this... When we walked through any door, here's what you knew... you were good with us, most likely, bad without us... let me say that again, you were good with us and, unfortunately, for you, bad without us

I've never talked about this time in our lives. The only reason I'm sharing it now is for the sake of helping others. I believe in order for addicts to give a shit about anything I say to help them, they have to know a little bit about where I've been and what I've been through. The only way my words will have any weight to anybody, that would make them want to stop and pay attention, and think about what I'm telling them is for them to see that even after all this, I've changed into a better person than I was. I very carefully kept particulars of many instances out of this story. I did that on purpose. Details aren't important. What's important is the still-suffering addicts read this and know there's hope for change.

Many years later, after Dave was busted for torturing, robbing, and killing the Madeline Murray O'Hare family, Madeline, her son, her niece and, another dude, Gary F, Dave W. also confessed to killing someone we knew real well. Billy K. It was part of a plea deal Dave had worked out with cops. Billy K. use to run with us in Peoria. We partied together all the time. Dave, BJ, Carl and him went all the way back to Juvenile as kids.

So, they all had history. Dave was a scary dude to a lot of people. True sociopath. He was a dangerous man. The dude always had a

200

cigarette in his mouth. He could pierce a hole through concrete with his gaze. I saw more than a few jump in his face and regret it. Hell, he spent twenty plus years in maximum security prisons for murdering a guy when he was seventeen. Rough.

Anyway, in the deal he made in the O'Hare case was this... they knocked thirty-years off his 60 year sentence for possessing a firearm while being a convicted murderer. (They found a 38 in a search looking for evidence of the O'Hare family's disappearance.) I was as shocked as anyone when I saw him confess to killing Billy on Dateline News. There he was with a Peoria detective sitting next to him. He was locked up in Texas at the time. I was honestly shocked to see him confess to that murder. I knew we'd partied all day and night together, the night Billy K was killed, but, I damn sure had no idea Dave did the dirty deed. No knowledge.

After Billy's funeral, everybody moved away in different directions. We were all burned out from the street life. So, it seemed normal that everyone wanted to do something different. I was at Cat, so, I stuck around for a while longer. I eventually moved away, too, after I was laid off from Caterpillar.

Mingo, he moved back to East St. Louis, continued to be his crazy self, infamous tattoo artist, druggie and maniac, for many years. In the years to come, he turned his life over to the man upstairs. Mingo, who goes by his first name, Chris, now, is a preacher and helps at-risk youth. His addiction survival persona that he'd created for the streets and called Mingo with the huge beard and long crazy hair was no more. This particular Hedonic Calculus ended and a great and honorable man emerged.

The crew ended. Everyone went to different States. Tommy C. died. Drugs and alcohol took him out. He was one of the best friends I ever had. B J went somewhere South, Dave went to Texas. Carl went off in the woods away from people. That's a good place for my brother, Carl. I visit Carl from time to time to this very day. He's found a certain peace in his soul after surviving hell for so many years.

Me, I stuck around Peoria for a while, then, I hit the road. I had to deal with a divorce first. We weren't happy. I'd been married to a pissed-off wife. She had every right to be pissed off, too. She was married to a drug-addict that had checked out of our marriage and our family long ago. I was working at Cat, so, I stayed in town, until after I was laid off. Billy's murder remained a mystery for many years. I didn't think we'd ever find out who killed him. Not until I saw Dave W. confess to it on Dateline News. It about knocked me out of my chair. I actually thought, at first, that he'd just drove to Chicago or somewhere to hook-up with some woman and was on a big party binge. We did that kind of shit. Then, when they found his body, I thought some random dude coming through the alley in the back, saw him after I rolled out on my Harley, robbed him, he resisted and got shot several times. But, as it turns out, I was wrong. I lived for many years with death on every corner, a mere stone's throw away.

~ IF THE DRUGS DON'T KILL YOU...THE LIFESTYLE WILL. ~

Stormy Lee Monday
1980's

THE IMPERFECT CHAMELEON

I didn't treat cocaine like a weekend party, do a few lines, go out, dance, have fun and be ready for work on Monday. That wasn't my life. I couldn't stop. I had a circle of dudes that would stop by to sit and shoot dope with me. They were strung out the way I was. I'll respect their privacy. No reason for names. They'd buy an eight-ball or quarter-ounce of cola from me and we'd sit there and they'd do all of it while I was doing my own. A strange reality is addicts using at this level gravitate to one another. All these dudes I'm talking about are dead now, from drug use.

After I was laid off from Caterpillar, I started doing what all the Monday men grow up doing. Painting. I started my own paint company from nothing and slowly but surely watched it grow. I owned that company for years, no matter where I lived in the country. The business went with me. Drug-addict and all. I'd lose it all, then, clean up and do it all again. Insanity.

At the same time this was happening, while I lived in Peoria, I was studying Tae Kwon Do four days a week. At the same time I was doing all that, I was raising a family and doing family activities. All of this was happening, of course, before my wife left me and took my children. I mean, what choice did she really have? None. Oh, I was trying as hard as I could to be the perfect chameleon. I was trying to keep every different part of my life in balance, looking normal. That's an impossibility in this case.

It's not easy to juggle everything in your life when one of the things you're juggling is hiding out in bathrooms and shooting dope, especially on a Friday night, when Tae Kwon Do is at 8 am the next morning. Week after week. Then, trying to pretend I'm not high when I'm actually wasted.

A lot of times, I thought dying would've been easier. I put my first wife, Brenda, through absolute hell. Because of active addiction, I neglected my children, disappeared from my family and friends and there's no other way to say it... I checked out of life. Period. My children and I lost so many precious years because of addiction. My life experienced incredible times as well. Artist, writer, poet... showings all around America. There've been periods of time when circumstances would be fine, life would flow silky-smooth, work would be great, art would be selling, art showings packed with fans, media writing about my talent, television spots, family life would be awesome, we'd go camping, fishing, doing family functions, vacations and the people, places and things around the family would be amazing.

Life would, for all intents and purposes, look very normal to everyone around us. Even super special to some! But, here's the deal, throughout the years, it seems just when beautiful life-stuff would be happening and things would be great with the wife, the children, work flow would be ON, good money coming in, great benefits, everybody loving my art and my first book, "The Journey", I mean, smooth sailing ahead and just when my life-path is spiraling straight upward and we'd have every reason in the world to be happy... BAM!

Chapter 10

STREET LIFE

WARNING: The following lifestyle and behavior comes with very serious and harsh consequences. I am against all of this dangerous and deadly behavior. Do not think for one second I'm condoning anything you read in this book pertaining to violence or the drug-life. I'm NOT. Nobody wins with violence and drugs kill. The street lifestyle kills. STOP USING AND SELLING DRUGS NOW OR DIE. You get to choose. But, I promise you, stay on the path in active addiction and death will choose you very soon.

Drugs and violence played a part in everything I did in my early life. I honestly didn't realize I had other options that didn't have anything to do with intimidation or getting high. Somehow, that got by me. I was dealing coke and weed, so, I could use for free. For quite some time back in the 70's and early 80's, I was copping a hundred pounds of weed at a time from a brother of mine. He was making trips to El Paso and bringing back 4 or 5 hundred pounds at a time of good Colombian weed. As soon as he'd hit town, he'd call our tight circle and we'd pick up a hundred pounds each to sell. I'd break mine down in quarter pounds and ounces. (FACT: All four of these guys are dead now. They all overdosed and died.)

There were a few choice friends I'd sell pounds to. We'd do that about once a month. For a few years, we flooded Peoria with good weed and pure coke. Everybody in those streets knew what's up with everybody in those streets. Anyway, in the late 70's, I copped and sold a lot of dope around Peoria. I'd usually get a quarter or half-pound of coke straight out of Bogota fronted to me as soon as it hit town. I'd work and party with that until the next load came in. Then, we'd do it all over again. Insane.

So, with this lifestyle, it's no wonder my first divorce from Brenda was final and now behind me.

She left me for good. I don't blame her at all. She did the right thing.

I'd gotten laid off from Cat, too. So, my only source of income was dealing dope and lots of it. Then, one night, in downtown Peoria, I met, my soon to be, second wife. I'll respect her privacy. She was working as a waitress in Carnegies at the Pierre Marquette. We fell hard for one another. One sexy dance with our bodies wrapped round each other on the dance-floor, in Spirits nightclub, next to Carnegies, and we were both hooked. She was a very classy lady, very beautiful, dark-skinned Native American, with beautiful dark hair way past her sexy butt and a killer body. She had it all. I guess we balanced each other out in some twisted way. We had a lot of good times on our trips to California, Nevada and other places. That love affair lasted about three years. This was a crossroads time in my life.

I was still fighting my demons when we were together, trying to get my artist career moving in the right direction and be a husband to her, a dad to my two children and to her two sons. It was a bit much. Only because, I don't even think she realized the war I had going on inside my head. The voice of my addiction was always there urging me to get high.

I was still using coke, occasionally, and drinking like a fish. We had some good times. But, she had turmoil from her ex and that created turmoil with both of her sons. The pressure, eventually, was just too much. After three years, we divorced and went our own ways. By this time it was late eighties, somewhere around 1988. In the next year I'd spiral, yet again, into a deep dark hole. I overdosed on coke and heroin one night and it was serious. There were people in the house that said I looked dead purple and blue. I was probably dead. Some dude and I don't know who to this day, drug me in to the shower and turned on the ice cold water and left me. It had to be an angel from God that brought me back. Everybody there freaked out and left. Sometime later, I came to, wet and freezing. The cold shower was still splashing against my skin. Nobody was there.

They thought I'd died and was done. Somehow, I survived again. I did feel like I'd came back from the other side. Strange feeling and I never found out who drug my lifeless body into that shower that night.

206

OVER THE EDGE...

Around 1988, in P-town, Illinois, I'd moved to the end of a straight-up thug street, Freemont Street, back in the ghetto. I was the only white dude on the street. I had no problem with that. In fact, I welcomed the danger. Bring it! Thing was, I was dating Steph, a gorgeous stripper from Big Al's. I fell hard for her. I was a junkie and a bad one at that. Steph would leave Big Al's early so she could stop by my crib, at 2 or 3 am. We'd hang out in my bedroom. What she didn't know or realize was 99% of the time, I'd be shooting dope about every time she'd stop by. She was one of the most beautiful women I've ever known. She actually looked like Angelina Jolie, but, better. We were madly in lust. I messed that up with my addiction. I don't think she ever realized how much I actually felt I loved her. Probably to her, I acted busy, disinterested, whatever you want to call it. The woman had every man that laid eyes on her fall in love. She was gorgeous.

But, talk about messed-up priorities. My focus was the dope. This is a sad truth. We could've conquered the world had I been clean. She was special.

Before long, I had the shot-caller of these black gang-bangers, bringing his dope in from Chicago and breaking it down at my crib. The shit around my house started getting heavy. Black soldiers rolling up in the crib at all hours of the day and night.

Throw me out a pile of pure Mexican brown heroin, some golf-ball size crack-rocks and a big pile of pure uncut coke, as soon as he hit my door from Chicago with a new load. All this for opening my crib, to be the dope hook-up spot. That lasted a while, till my habit took over my soul, once again. I was living with a house full of thugs, a rig sticking out of my arm, a crack pipe in my mouth and strippers stopping by to see me all the time. The dope-man...

"How much can a man take?" I asked myself that, all the time, while I existed at this sick and twisted animal level.

For the longest time, I wasn't even human. My existence was miserable. It seemed, no matter where I went in the Country, that damn jones would follow me. Like I said, it was like my evil and dark shadow. I'd go somewhere different in the country to escape the crazy shit I was doing, then, I'd look around and there that motherfucker was again. I felt hopeless. I actually think I got used to the despair. Misery can feel normal after you swim in it for a while. About now, I can hear my little sister, June, a deeply religious woman, say, "but, Stormy, where was God through all this? Why didn't you ask God for help?"

Little sis, well, all my sisters, my answer to that is this. Maybe you can understand this and maybe you can't. To truly understand someone, one has to walk in that someone's shoes….but, maybe, this'll shine a little bit of light and help some people, maybe, even you, to understand.

First, 'think about' what I'm about to tell you. Addicts aren't like so-called normal people. Our brains aren't wired like someone who doesn't have the disease of addiction. Call it a chemical imbalance, call it a thinking disease, call it whatever you want, but, no matter, addicts have very poor coping skills. If you think about it, our best decisions led us into prisons, jails, hospitals and treatment centers, unless we overdosed and died, which many have and many more, unfortunately, will. Regardless, our self-esteem or, how we view ourselves, when we're in active addiction, is dismal at best. I'll explain this, but, don't, for a second, think I'm shooting for some pity pot. I'm not. I'm trying to describe for you, the reader, the thoughts and emotions that go on inside a person's mind that's caught up in addiction.

"Sometimes, while existing in active addiction, we can get so low in the perception of ourselves, our personal thoughts of who we are inside, that we don't feel any worth whatsoever. Drugs actually change our psyche and our emotions. Feelings become suppressed. For a great many years of my life, that's how I felt inside. I was ashamed of my life. I felt helpless and hopeless. I felt confused with no sense of direction. With that, I felt no sense of purpose. When I felt that insignificant, I ran from God and all his goodness. I didn't feel inside that I deserved his loving grace. What I did feel inside was empty, alone and consumed in inner-turmoil, chaos and misery. I felt like I existed in a big, dark, black hole and everyone around me was focused on their own lives, their children, their situations and it's so much easier to isolate during those times. I felt everyone was judging me and most people do. I didn't even want to be around anyone that didn't use drugs, unless they were giving me money.

208

The worst thing is watching someone you love, drown, and NOT being able to convince them, that they can save themselves... by just standing up.

LOSING FOXY

Late 80's, early 90's...

If you're an addict and you feel lost, I understand what that feels like. It's one of the worst feelings I've ever experienced. The feeling of being alone in the world runs really deep in the soul. When you're in that place, it'll make you question if God's even real. I remember that. Out in those streets, it's easy to feel forsaken. Sitting on a sidewalk, flat broke, with no shower for a month, begging for a few dollars to get high on and to hell with eating.

People passing by won't look you in the eye. Most of them look away to make you invisible to their world. It just makes you feel lower than low, like a piece of shit. Feeling worthless and hopeless is the worst.

When I was homeless, it was really hard to trust or befriend other homeless people, too. I tried, but, the rampant desperation makes people do crazy shit, like this... I was in a park once in Phoenix, in the south side of the city. I was by myself. The park was filled with homeless people. This rogue group of ghetto-rats were bullying everybody in the park, so, I kept my eye on them. Wouldn't you know it... they confronted me one night under a palm tree where I was sitting, just minding my own business. The one leader of their group pulled a knife on me and threatened me with all of them standing around me. There was four of them. I literally laughed like I was crazy, when I saw the blade pointing at me. I'm thinking, "You are some genuine pieces of shit! All of you! I'm sitting here on a worn-out piece of cardboard by a palm tree in a park full of vagrants, scattered everywhere. I'm a broke-ass junkie, starving to death and homeless as hell. I don't know a soul in this big-ass city. Here I am with nary a penny in my pocket and you son of a bitches want to rob me. To hell with that shit!" I said, "Hey, look here, man. I'm broker than you guys are. I ain't got shit."

The dude said, "Empty your pockets." I replied, "Look here, the only thing I got left is a little bit of my self-respect and man, I'm holding on to that. So, hell no. Fuck you!" The guy slashed quickly at me with the knife. My adrenalin shot sky high! He missed my face by a half inch as I bent backward quick as lightning, away from that blade. Just as quickly, I turned and ran. I'm tough, but, I'm not stupid. Starvation had clamped into me and I didn't have the strength to fight four dudes. Especially a crazy desperado with a knife. Besides, I didn't want to die hungry. This was serious shit. I kept running long after the bastards stopped chasing me. So much for crashing in that park. I never went back there. For that same reason, I stayed away from homeless shelters. They lock the doors at 10 pm or whatever. They're filled with conniving and untrustworthy folks that are struggling to survive, too. It's a tough environment and, for me, if I weren't with my cousin, Sonny D (Michael J) then, I stayed to myself. He and I were in Phoenix and homeless together for quite a while. We had each other's back, too. We were walking down Indian School one night, late, homeless, hungry, just struggling to survive. We were looking for a place to lay down for the night. The night before we'd crawled in the seats of an unlocked car in a parking lot and slept there till sun-up. Then, got out and walked away before the owner showed up. We did that several times and it worked, too. We never did get caught in somebody's car. That could've been bad. Looking back now, that sounds messed up, like, I'm thinking right now, how the hell could somebody do that? Crawl in a stranger's car and sleep in it and get up before dawn to not get caught. Over and over, night after night in downtown Phoenix. As crazy as that sounds now, back then we thought it was normal. We had to get warm. We needed to lay down somewhere. Why not find an unlocked car?
Crazy.

Anyway, one night, we were on that same major street named Indian School and two dudes got off a bus a block down. We watched as they came walking toward us, scheming the whole way. As they approached, they pulled knives on us and tried to rob us. A

210

broke-ass robbing a broke-ass! Now, double that! Crazy shit! We were hungry, tired and pissed-off about our situation, anyway. We didn't give a shit about their knives. The fight was on. Sonny jumped one and I jumped the other one. We took their knives and beat the hell out of both of them. I slashed one of them across the stomach with his own knife, before I dropped it to beat on him. I beat him in the head with my fists till my fists hurt. Sonny D sliced the other dude across his forehead and arm. Then, he beat the hell out of that guy. We left them lying on the sidewalk next to each other, bleeding like two stuck pigs. We figured another bus would come by and see them. Maybe call some help for the thieving bastards. I ended up having to go to the ER. I'd crushed my knuckles on his hard head. I ended up having surgery to put my boxer's fractured knuckles back together. They ran wire up my fingers and through the knuckles of my little finger and ring finger. The wire sticks out of your knuckle for 6 to 8 weeks. It's no fun. I did that a few times through the years. Being homeless is rough. This is just a small glimpse of the hell that's out there when a man has a hole in his soul and nowhere to go. So, man, I've been there. There was a time when living in the streets was my normal way of life. It was every day and every night. I slept everywhere. I've laid down in graveyards, behind dumpsters, in bathrooms, behind bushes, you name it. Another time, in Phoenix, Arizona, I'd lost this little place I was renting. It's no wonder. Hell, I never paid rent. I'd buy dope instead. I'd literally use any money I had for dope. Even my rent money. I would always justify in my head why I had to do this deal or why I had to use that money for that dope. Of course, it was all bullshit. I'd lie to myself and even believe it so I could feel a little bit better about getting high on all my bill money. I did this all the time.

When I was strung out, really bad, I never worked either. I made a job of going to the strip clubs and while the strippers worked the Johns for money, I'd make friends with the strippers. Money, drinks, places to crash, etc. were there for the right conversation. It's not like I hustled them. Shit, they were the hard-working hustlers. We became close, we were tight. We all got high together. We partied away from the club together. They knew me. The real me. I knew them, too. The real them. They knew I could usually cop dope and quick. Most of them could, too. They found out real quick I was like one of them. I wasn't a money man they could play. Who's playing

211

who, anyway? Everybody wants money, right? It's a street lifestyle. We were in the same circle together. Dancers make fat money quick. So, we helped each other. A lot of times, I'd move in with one for a while, till I'd meet another one with a better deal, or, a better ass, or, a better hustle. It was street life. But, many times, I'd get consumed by the dope and wouldn't see the dancers for a while. I'd be too strung out to go to the clubs. These were bad times. Once, for months, I slept on a piece of cardboard behind dumpsters that were behind a supermarket off Indian School, again, in Phoenix. It was close to the Bourbon Street Circus strip club.

I'd go in the store and eat food while I walked around, stuffing packages of ham down my pants for later. I'd grab a chocolate milk, or, a soda and drink those, then, walk out. I think after a while they caught on, but, nobody ever said a word. I looked homeless. I was. There was a restaurant nearby, too. I'd walk in, get seated, order a big meal, eat it, go to the bathroom after I ate, sit there for a while, then, I'd walk out without paying. The third time I did that, I went in, got seated and this really cool waitress came to the table. She was inked up everywhere, and had long dread locks tied back. I don't know why, but, this waitress had a great vibe about her. She told me, "Hey, last time you were in here, you walked out and didn't pay me." I started to get up to run. She stopped me. "NO, no, it's okay. It's cool. Really. It's okay. Hey, I know you're homeless? Been there."

I felt so ashamed. I nodded my head, yes. She said, "Well, listen, like I said, I've been homeless, too, baby. It'll get better. Hang in there. Okay, now, eat what you want. I'm going to pay for it." I didn't know what to say. It touched my heart. I wasn't use to anybody being good to me, or, caring about me. Not out here in the streets. It's a cold world. Very cruel and very cold. She caught me off guard. But, then, she really tripped me out. She said, "Hey, I'm Sandy. They have me working different shifts through the week, but, I'm always here Saturday mornings. You come in here every Saturday morning, ask for my section." "Really?" "Yes, really. I'll buy you a good meal every Saturday." I was speechless.

I'd been ripping her off and now, here she is, reaching out and helping me. I've never forgotten Sandy. She was probably about ten years older than me. She was so good to me. She had such a good heart. I went there several Saturdays and just like she said, she was always there working. She paid for my meal every time. We became

212

good friends. She inspired me to do better. Sandy was a rare gem. When I think about someone giving me a flicker of hope in a desolate situation, I always flash back to Sandy. She did that for me when I needed it most. Some guy somewhere was blessed to be her man. One day at the Bourbon Street Circus, I met an Asian named Melee.

She was drop-dead gorgeous. We had an immediate connection! It was powerful. Melee and I became very close. She'd feed me drinks and cash when she was working her shift at the Bourbon Street Circus, a huge strip club. She worked every day on the day shift. When we first hooked up, she'd feed me and then, after work, drop me off behind the huge grocery story down the road. I was sleeping behind the store on a piece of cardboard behind the dumpsters. After 3 or 4 days, she took me home with her. Melee had a cozy apartment in a weekly and she made great money dancing. We fell in lust and I moved in with her. A few weeks later, we moved in with one of her girlfriends, who had a nice home with a beautiful pool. Her pool was full of dancers most of the time. My kind of place. I never saw Sandy again after that. Before I met Melee or Sandy, I remember one night in Phoenix feeling so low, I was suicidal. I felt horrible. I don't think I've felt so miserable before in my life. A Sioux Indian named Dawn had left me. We had a good thing, but, I messed it up. So, I spiraled straight downward into hell. Then, here's what happened... I had a badass black and chrome kick-start Harley named Foxy. A few years back, I'd been on the run with warrants out for several batteries in Peoria, Illinois. So, a friend of mine named Doug S. from Peoria was moving to Phoenix. I was hiding from the cops, so, I asked Doug if he'd put Foxy in the U-Haul and take it to Phoenix with him. I trusted Doug.

Several months later, I hitch hiked out to Phoenix and got Foxy from Brother Doug. I'm loving having my bike back. I rode it for a while and was loving it. At the same time, I'm falling deeper and deeper into my cocaine addiction. One night I snagged a girls credit card and robbed her through an ATM. I used that money and bought an eight-ball of coke from a coke dealer I knew. He let me sit at his house and shoot the coke. I sat there for several hours and shot the whole eight ball. Then, I sat back and checked out.

I was trying to get over the cocaine blues, so, I could leave. I was too wasted to ride my bike. While I'm sitting there, another dude walks in to buy a quarter-ounce from the guy. I'm sitting there watching this deal go down. The blues were crawling all over me. I didn't have any money. Now, I didn't have any cocaine. I had the blues from shooting all the coke, so, now, I'm broke and miserable as hell. I needed to get high really bad. The one guy cops his dope and he leaves, so, he wouldn't have to share his dope.

I'm looking at the briefcase this dude has. There must've been 4 ounces in it, broke down in quarter ounces and eight-balls. He sees I'm going nuts needing a high really bad. He looks at me and says, "Hey, I can help you out if you're interested." "I'm interested. What are you talking about?" "Well, I'll give you seven grams for your bike. Straight deal. Coke for title. Then, you can party." "No way, man. My bike's worth 4 times that." "Yeah, you're right. Okay. It was just a thought." My mind went into overdrive. Hmmm. What will I take for my bike? I can get another bike." Then, he says, "Okay, what would it take for us to trade?" My cravings were going ape-shit. I had the blues bad. "I tell you what. I'll take 3 quarter ounces for the bike." "That's 21 grams of coke, man." "I know what it is. Well?" "Okay, this is pure coke. Here's what I'll do. I'll give you one half of an ounce for the bike. That's the deal. That's as high as I'll go." "Okay, let's do it. But, I'm going to do the dope right here, cool?" "Yeah, no problem." We traded. I signed my title over and gave him my key. He laid a half-ounce of coke on the table. We shook hands.

The dude went about his business and I sat there and shot cocaine for the next three days and nights. I literally shot coke till I couldn't hold the rig in my hand. My arms were literally worn out. So was my brain, my body and my soul. I died inside, one hit after another. Then, I passed out in that chair. I slept for God knows how long. When I woke up, the dude was just coming out of the shower. The sun was just coming up. I don't even know what day it was. I sat there and spaced out. I was worn out, hungry, thirsty and I felt dirty. As he got dressed, he looks at me and says, "Hey, bro, you're welcome to take a shower. It might help you feel better. I'm going to take a ride on my bike." "Oh, okay, yeah, sounds good. Thanks man." I got in the shower and he walked out the door, went out to the bike and fired it up. He sat there on it for a few minutes and then, took off. He never looked back. That's the last time I ever saw my Sportster, Foxy. I felt like a vegetable. The shower felt good and drinking water felt good. Eating a bowl of his cereal gave me a little

214

bit of energy. I sat there and regrouped till the afternoon. He never came back with the bike.

I left his house, walking. I felt like I'd crawled into some big black hole and there was no way out. I was empty inside, alone and pissed at myself for trading my bike for coke. I walked around aimlessly the rest of the afternoon. I didn't even have a destination. I was depressed as hell. I couldn't believe I'd given my Harley away and for what, more hell and misery.

It was the last thing I owned from my first divorce. Now, it was gone. Later that day, the sun started going down. It's the desert. When the sun goes down, it gets cold. Before I even knew it, it's cold as hell outside. I realized I didn't have anywhere to sleep, I didn't even know if I could sleep. I had nowhere to go. I was walking down the sidewalk trying to find somewhere to be. I felt lower than low. This man came out with his garbage as I was walking by. It must've been about 9 o'clock at night. I stopped him and ask if I could sleep in his garage, or, in a closet, maybe.

Anywhere. It was cold out and I just needed to get warm, I explained. He looked at me like I was crazy. He said, "I don't know you man. I have two children inside. I wouldn't be comfortable with that. Sorry, but, NO." He turned and walked back in his house and shut the door. I felt humiliated. I felt lower than a cockroach. I ended up sleeping behind a big bush that was behind a shopping center. I almost froze that night. I didn't even have cardboard to lay on. I felt so alone, so hungry, so empty and so dead inside. Just a few days ago, I owned a beautiful Harley. Now, all I have is a really bad drug problem.

Now, all I have is nothing. It was just before sun-up and I'd moved from behind the bush. Now I was sitting behind a nasty dumpster, trying to stay out of the cold night air. I just started crying. I felt so alone. I'd broke down. I felt empty and hopeless. I got on my knees on the cold concrete and I looked up to the heavens. I didn't know what else to do. All my options were gone. I asked God, "How much pain do I have to go through before its okay to give up? How much?" It's in those times, when it's easy to question God and get mad at him, it's easy to let Satan in and just say 'to hell with it'. Just remember one thing, in those very times, when you don't think God's there, is exactly when he's making you stronger for something up ahead. You just got to put all your faith in the man upstairs.

Just because your life's a bucket of shit, doesn't mean you have to stand in it.

Chapter 12

OBSESSION & COMPULSION

Throughout the years, I've often wondered how anyone who's never experienced cravings the way an addict does during active addiction, could possibly understand, or, ever begin to understand what that feels like. How in this world could I express it in a way that would help someone truly understand, or, even attempt to grasp the absolute insanity that transpires inside the mind of an addict in the midst of active addiction?

I thought about that for a long, long time. It gets so old, not to mention, annoying, when someone looks down at us, like it's our fault we crave our drug of choice. Like we could snap our fingers and it would all go away? Like we actually choose to destroy everything in our wake to get high. If only there was a way I could help this person that wants to judge so much, that wants to put us in a box and label us a certain way, or, even, just someone that really doesn't get it... how can I use this time right now, these pages right now, to help them understand the insanity of our cravings?

Then, one night, I was really hungry, about to sit down and eat and it hit me. So, I'll share it with you. Maybe, just maybe, it'll help you begin to understand, or, at least, try to...

No matter what, when an addict is caught in the grips of active addiction, those cravings must be fed. So, go on this journey with me. It's like this... ask yourself this question, when you're hungry, what do you want to do? You want to eat, right? But, what if you don't eat most of the day? There's no food. The hunger really kicks in. It becomes a little more important, right? Of course it does.

216

Now, think about this, what if you don't eat all day and into the night and you start feeling really, really hungry. Starving! The food, any food becomes even more important, right? Like next level important. Priority one. Okay, let's go ONE MORE step deeper. Even with no food to eat now becoming your first and only priority, what if you can't find a speck of food to eat at all and can't find one drop of drink to drink for two full days and two full nights? This is the PANIC ZONE! Your brain is screaming out loud, "I'M STARVING... I'M DYING OF THIRST!" This is that place where finding food is all that matters. Finding water is all that matters.

Nothing else even enters your mind and it won't until you feed that starvation and that thirst. You have to feed that hunger and thirst, or, you'll have a complete and utter mental, emotional and most of all, physiological meltdown. The minutes are passing and you have to eat something, anything, and you have to taste the delicious wetness of a simple drink of water. You feel your brain signaling the rest of your body to go into shock. Time is passing. The moments feel monumental. Your entire psyche is completely freaking out. One by one, your organs are shutting down. Without food and without water, the once-clear reality you knew so well begins dissipating among the rubble of the nearing and terminal disaster.

Suddenly, panic does set in. Every moment counts. Every second without food is another second gone forever, and you're still empty. Panic is exploding inside you! The screaming you hear loudly within is your body, your mind and your soul teaming up to unite for the sake of survival in the final fight, in this war for more life. Just one drink of water! Just one bite of food would change everything! Your taste buds are screaming for something, for anything. Denial has turned to anger, anger has turned to manipulation and manipulation has turned to pleading and begging. Pleading and begging has turned to whatever is necessary.

Parched lips, dry throat and even dryer inside your whole body. Starvation and thirst, ripping at your soul, tearing your brain apart and shredding your soul into little slivers of who you used to be. Your insanity is driving you in to the ultimate panic zone to find food and water immediately, no matter the cost.

You get my drift?

(Just one cracker and one small sip of water would give you a small semblance of relief. It would give you the drive to hopefully, find more food and more water. Somewhere, surely, somewhere, there must be some food and water. Just anything would help console your mental breakdown, demanding these necessities! Just a little food and water would give you the strength to go find more. You starting to get the picture?)

DRUG CRAVINGS...

Let me put it another way... You're minding your own business and it's a beautiful day. You go hiking in the woods to join all your friends. Plus, it's nice to be closer to nature. You know where there's a beautiful waterfall. Lots of awesome friends and family will be grilling food, listening to music and playing in the water. So, you head through the woods to join every one, excited to be a part of this fun-filled day. Suddenly, a fierce tiger appears out of nowhere and this huge beast has zeroed in on you for dinner.

You are about to be eaten by this gigantic animal. You immediately panic and run as fast as you can to get away from this hungry beast. Right now, even with all the friends and family cooking out, even with the good music playing and the gorgeous waterfall and all the fun that you know is going on.... Instantly, none of that matters. Now, just like that, only one thing matters! You have to get away from that tiger. That's all that matters. Nothing else even enters your mind. You're too busy running as fast as you can to get away from that fierce tiger. Until you get away from that huge, hungry beast, this is the only thing that matters in the world. This is all that matters.

This is an addict in active addiction.

No matter what's going on all around this person, that craving to use must be satisfied. Period. Until that happens, nothing else matters.

This is what the cravings of an addict feels like, every moment of every day when they're in active addiction.

Addiction is NOT a spectator sport. Eventually, the whole family gets to play.

MY EARLY YEARS

Life, for me, started in Tullahoma, Tennessee.

On the first few pages, I mentioned one of our child-hood homes. It was the one we lived in under a viaduct, next to railroad tracks and down the alley from Ike Brown's junk yard. That junk-yard was my play-ground. That boneyard for old classic, beat-up cars was my Disneyland. Every other kid on the poor side of town that wanted to shoot junk-yard ball or play horseshoes, football and all the other things kids do, would be there, too. Life, back then, was much simpler. There were no computers, no cell phones, hell, the TV's were black and white with three channels. The phones were rotary dial with a three foot cord. Fancy! Back then, every other kid in that junk yard, just happened to be black. That didn't mean a damn thing to me, or, to them. To me, this was like an escape from my dad and all the Brown kids were like family. We played together as often as I could slip off to go there.

When I was about six years old, we moved to Athens, Alabama. My father had moved us way back in the country, outside of Athens. Our tiny home sat at the end of a long dirt road that ran through corn fields for the longest of time. I remember a big, old barn sat behind our home and our yard was filled with thirty or forty chickens. There were also two big, mean roosters that did one hell of a job of controlling the entire yard. We lived so far back in the sticks, there was a grocery truck that drove down the old dirt road to our house every Saturday.

My mother would buy things like bread, milk, sugar, flour and meal off the truck. Every Sunday, my dad would grab a chicken out of the yard, and chop his head off. We'd watch that chicken run around the yard for twenty or thirty minutes, with no head. Then, my dad would pick up the dead body, pluck the feathers, and hand it off to mom, for Sunday, fried chicken. Well, actually, mom would pluck the feathers.

It was just another regular day, like any other. I heard birds singing, and the chickens were all over, running around the yard. It was beautiful out. There wasn't a cloud in the sky. I remember because I was always out running around and getting into stuff. I loved to play outside and seek out adventures.

I'd play in that big barn, run through the cornfields, go play in the woods, or find a big dirt pile, and build little roads all over it, for my play cars and trucks, to roll around on. Most of the time, I'd just explore all over the property. This is how we lived in those days. My dad had gone to work, leaving my mother to tend the four children. I was the oldest, then, my sister, Barb, she was three, my sister, Jackie, was two and my newest sister, June, was just a little baby.

Mother was ironing clothes, and I was playing in the front yard, out by the dirt road. I first noticed it getting real dark, off in the distance. It seemed like it happened just like that. One moment it was bright, and sunny, and the next, the wind started kicking up, and the ominous black clouds started rolling in. It was kind of spooky, so, I ran in to tell my Mother. But, it was too late.

Everything happened so fast, it's almost surreal to relive it for you. There was a weird silence and stillness, for a few moments, then, all of a sudden, it sounded like a hundred jet planes, were flying right over our heads. My Mother was praying out loud, as she scooped up June with the baby, Susie, in her other arm, then, she grabbed Barb, and yelled for me. I was scared to death, so I was already glued next to her. She laid us together on the floor in the bedroom and pulled the mattress off the bed over us. I didn't even have time to panic. The whole house started shaking, like it was going to blow up. Everything went crazy, for what seemed like forever, but, really, it probably wasn't more than a few minutes. My mother lay on top of us screaming, "Dear God, have mercy on us, please help us! Your will

220

be done, dear Lord, Your will be done!" We were all crying. It sounded like World War three all around us. In my mind, it lasted forever, when, in reality, everything was so surreal, it was like time stopped, and complete chaos erupted. The sound of a hundred jet planes actually only lasted about 30 seconds.

Then, just as quickly, it got quiet again. For a few moments, you could hear a pin drop. We laid there for more than a minute, frozen in fear. Then, my mother pushed the mattress off of us. If you knew my mother, you'd realize that was quite a feat for her. She was and is a very tiny little lady. Standing only five feet tall, barefoot, you'd never think she'd be so strong. On the other hand, as soft spoken as she is, I've seen dynamite come out. Anyway, she and I stood up in disbelief.

Our home was gone. The barn was gone. The chickens, the corn and this farmer's tractor that sat in the barn... they were all gone. The only thing left in the house was a coffee table, some of the floor, part of a few walls, the mattress, and us. My mother dropped to her knees and began thanking God for sparing us. My sisters were crying, and I was in a state of shock. It wasn't very long till my dad came barreling down that dirt road, in his old work truck, to see if we'd lived. All our clothes, furniture, and everything, we had in that house, were lost in that tornado.

I stood there for the longest time, staring across an emptiness that used to be a cornfield. There was nothing. Not even a chicken left, or a stalk of corn.

Just like that, the sky was clear blue, and the sun was shining, like nothing had ever happened. I could hear birds starting to chirp again. That was a day my mother, dad and I'd never forget. I thank God my three sisters were too young to remember it. The next day, we moved back to Tullahoma, Tennessee.

We moved right back to our old neighborhood. Right next to the junk yard, by the viaduct. The house we moved into under the viaduct didn't even have a bathroom. The outhouse was at least a hundred feet behind the house in the woods and we tried to make sure there'd be newspaper in there for those night-time trips.

Something interesting I learned about being dirt poor. When being poor's all you know, there's nothing to miss. So, we didn't have anything to compare being poor to. Because of that, having almost nothing was everyday life and we made it work. We had a garden, worked it faithfully for food. We found wood for the fireplace and coal for the potbelly stove. We always had a big pot of pinto beans on the stove and cornbread was a treat. Polk salad grew out back and Church was every Sunday.

I realize today my dad was actually a great teacher. He just had unorthodox methods. Back then, I had no idea. I didn't appreciate his capacity to teach me valuable life lessons. After all, he only went to the 4th grade and that was a little one-room shack in Valley Creek, Tennessee. That's way up in the East Tennessee Mountains. My dad gave me the education I didn't know I needed. Without even knowing it, he planted me like a seed. A seed he pulled out of his pocket and dropped on the ground to grow. That's when my mom and dad connected. Mom was my angel. Always. The balance between them made me who I am.

Every day was a life-lesson to my dad

When I was young I was so wet behind the ears, it's a wonder I didn't drown. I was shy, scared, withdrawn and confused in the ways of life. I didn't get IT at all.

Whatever IT was, and is, I didn't understand. Maybe that's the irony. Learning as we go, and messing up along the way. Then, hopefully, we can learn from that.

Meeting Brother Ed...

I always wondered why I started using drugs so early in life. Thing was, I was never able to be myself with my dad. I know as I got older, being under his complete control really seemed to affect me. I just couldn't shake it. Does that make any sense? Up to that point, I had pretty much grown up around that viaduct and in that junk yard. We had railroad tracks right next to the house and I was burnt out on the train traffic, too.

It was about then that my dad decided to move us to Illinois to find work. So, in my sophomore year of High School, we moved to East Peoria, Illinois. Soon, thereafter, my dad found us a house in Marquette Heights, Illinois, just across the river. This is where I started using drugs. I think I just wanted to fit in... I was trying to fit in with a bunch of hippies that hung around this corner next to our home. There was Mark H, Roger K, Bud S, Dudley and Rich B. They hung out by the road, next to my house, so, what the hell, I started hanging with them and getting drunk and stoned. A week or so later and fifty or so doobies of good Colombian weed, Roger started calling me Spok of all things. He said the weed opened a lot of doors in my head and my conversations were getting deep. Hell, I was a country boy. I don't know. We were stoned all the time and I loved to psychoanalyze everything when I got wasted. That's all it was really. The shit made me laugh. Anyway, I didn't really like the name, but, I was trying to fit in, so, for the time being, I let it slide. One thing led to another and pretty soon, I'm eating acid, mescaline and mushrooms, damn-near daily. I heard about this cool spot outside of Peoria called "The Barn". This place was having concerts like Alice Cooper, Uriah Heap, Styx, Brownsville Station, and on and on and on. So, I eat a couple hits of purple dot acid and hop in a car with a couple of hippies to see Alice Cooper. At the time, I thought that was some chick band. I didn't want to sound like some hillbilly, so, good for me, I didn't say anything. Obviously, Alice Cooper turned out to be an ass-kicking rock & roll show. But, that night I didn't get to see it. I couldn't find the front door of the Barn. I really couldn't. I can remember, I was standing in front of the place and I heard a thousand or so people screaming and the band blowing the place up with their music. I was going along the front of the building, feeling for the door, but I couldn't find it.

The wood kept sliding down into the ground and it all kept melting together. Nothing would open. I was hallucinating my ass off. Also, it felt like the building was breathing. I had to walk back away from it to get a better look, but, the building kept moving with me.
Everything sounded muffled, too. I was wasted.
Out of nowhere, this dude walked up to me and said,
"What's happening, brother?"
I replied, "I wish I knew. Do you know where the door is to this place? Dude, I'm tripping my brains out. Man, look at you...Wow... you're melting into yourself, dude, you're sliding down a wall of vibrating time. Seriously, you're energy mass is reverberating with some kind of flowing waves and I see revolving doors. It's far out, man. I see trails dancing down around the building with big shadows but where does the shadows come from man? Tell me, man! There's no reason for shadows to be there, man! Do you see them? Really? Do you? Whoa! Your face, man, it's doing some weird shit right now. Purple dot, two hits. Want one?"

"Ohhh, yeah maybe. Sure, why not. Man, I'm tripping, too, right now. I'm Ed. Did you say shadows? Wow! What's your name, man?" "I'm Spok." "Wow, trippy name, man. Ed continues talking, "So, I'm in there and I started getting off on this orange sunshine. Alice Cooper says real loud, "I got to get out of here!" I'm wasted, man, tripping my ass off. I screamed back at him, "No man, I got to get out of here!" We both fell out laughing. We were way beyond high. Well, I know I was way beyond high. The acid had me by the balls. I felt like I was flying in some parallel universe caught sideways inside a time continuum stuck on reverb, with multi-colored flashing lights streaming around me, in me, on me and through me. Wicked shit. I'm pretty sure Ed was wasted, too. I discovered through the years, Ed would give a man the shirt off his back. We became the best of friends, immediately.

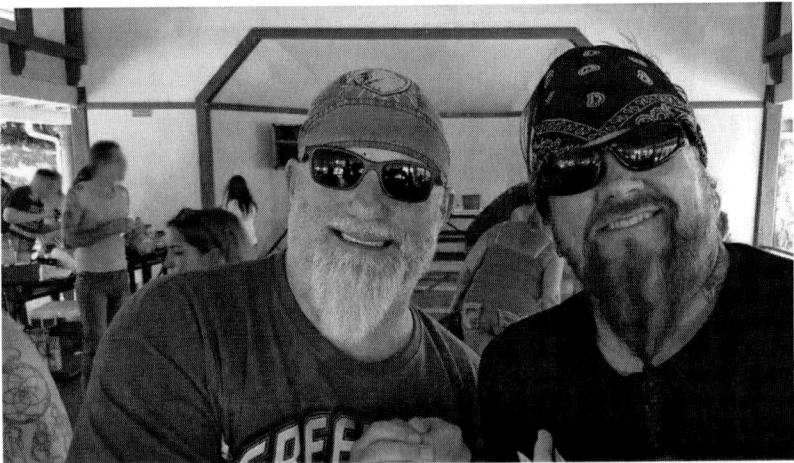

Ed Moore & Stormy Monday
Brothers from... different mothers

We felt a brotherhood bond. The party was on! We were immediately and literally out of control. I bought a 1963 primer-

224

black, Ford, Falcon, 2-door and that became our second home, almost our first. Ed showed me around at the school and introduced me to some of his friends. Some of the female friends liked me and some of his male friends saw me as a threat when it came to the girls. See, I didn't forget my lesson about the birds and the bees and my hormones had kicked in. Quite honestly, I guess I was a threat on some trivial high school level.

After all, I was the new kid in town and I heard some of the girls said they liked my southern charm. What? I was so young I didn't even know what that meant. I could work with it, though. I'm willing to learn quickly. That was my thinking. Hey, I was seventeen and slowly, but surely, getting more and more confident. So, it seemed some of those same girls were a little curious about me and I seemed to be getting over my shyness. The timing was perfect. On any given day, Ed and I would load up the ol' Falcon, with a pocket full of acid, a case of beer, a bag of weed and some of the hot chicks, like Linda B and Barb R. Both beauties our age and then, we'd pick up whatever other good-looking chicks we could find. Usually, they found us because we had a cool car and good drugs.

We'd pop some Black Sabbath in the eight track and trip our brains out. Looking back, it's hard for me to believe people would act and carry on the way we did, way back then. Hindsight is 2020, after all! We were at the beginning stage of active addiction and we didn't even realize it. Because, after all, it's just good, clean fun, right? We weren't out to hurt anybody. We were just looking for the best time a couple of out-of-control hippies could have. Nothing more! Just a couple dudes eating acid, picking up sexy foxes and tripping our brains out!

For an addict, many times, this is how it all starts. This is how it slips up and grabs your soul and be aware, it won't let go, either.
This is one of the major paths to active addicts. We get caught up in all the innocent fun. For many people we call normies, it stays innocent fun. They're capable of partying all weekend and back to focusing on the work week on Monday morning. For addicts, this behavior plants the seeds for a horrible life-path that, for far too many, leads to pain, struggle and death. Be cognizant of that.

My mother, for the whole of my life's been there for me and for anybody that she could help. I mean, in my childhood, when dad was reliving combat in our home. She was there. When my dad severely beat me, she was there. She saved my life so many times, I lost count. My sisters were there, too. Many times, getting the same beatings. I know my mother jumped between my dad and I multiple times to get him to stop beating me. He wouldn't hit her. I saw him throw hamburger meat against the wall, ketchup bottles, he'd break chairs and tables and whatever he could get his hands on when he'd lose it.   He shot the house up, too. My dad was a mess from what he'd been through in his life.

I don't know what else to say about it. I know combat messed him up and he'd just come home. I know he suffered from PTSD. I know I was scared most of my childhood. I was scared he'd beat me to death. So, I'll leave it at that. I also know, years later, I was diagnosed with PTSD. How I lived through a lot of that, I don't really know.   He must have been pretty messed up in his head. I'm sorry my dad had to go through that. I always believed he was a good man. He just had combat wounds that were with him all the days of his life. I know that for sure. My earliest memories of my dad are him beating me up and down my body with a bunch of switches and then a belt. He whipped most of my sisters, too. Well, the 4 older ones, for sure, except maybe, June. June always had a way of sneaking off and hiding in a closet when we were getting whipped. Seems she got away with that about every time, too. She was a tiny little girl, though. I believe she'd have broken like a twig if he'd gotten hold of her. I'm glad she escaped most of the wrath.

By the time Markie, my youngest sister came along, I wasn't around a lot, military, jail, prison, etc., but, I'm told he'd mellowed some. The times I was there, between the army, jail and prison, I saw Markie run to our grandfather, Papa, a lot. I don't blame her at all. He'd let her sit next to him and protect her from dad. Dad wouldn't mess with Papa. When I was young, my dad made me stick a butcher knife in this big tree in our yard. This was so I could cut switches out of that tree for the beatings. I had to cut at least ten or twelve switches and they had better be pretty big ones. That way he wouldn't go cut them himself. He always cut big ones and he'd beat me till, either my mother would get between us, or, the switches would wear out. Like I said earlier, my mother ran between my beatings, many, many times. Then, she would take me to the hospital ER for treatment on my legs, butt and back. I remember how much the bleeding welts hurt after the blood dried in them.

226

STORM SHELTERS...

When I was a kid, about ten years old, my dad started taking me to this old fashioned pool hall, located right in the middle, of this little old country town we lived in. The name of that spot was Red's Pool hall, in Tullahoma, Tennessee. He taught me to play about every pool game ever created. We'd go there on Saturdays, a lot. Pretty soon, I got really good at pool. Really good!

That was one thing my dad taught me that allowed us to share time together in a good way. We'd go and spend hours shooting straight pool, or, bank pool. He even let me work there sometimes as a rack boy. You'd be surprised at how many old timers in that place could shoot a really good game of pool. There weren't money slots in those old Brunswick eight footers. Shooters would beat the floor with the big end of their stick and yell, "rack". I'd run to their table and rack whatever game they were playing.

After a while, I started playing the old-timers for two or three dollars a game. By the time I was twelve, I was playing for five or ten dollars a game. A lot of times I'd skip school just to hustle pool. Here I was twelve or thirteen years old, walking around with forty or fifty dollars in my pocket at any given time. We're talking in the mid-sixties and we were poor. Fifty dollars in the mid-sixties to a poor kid was a lot of money. I can't tell you how many times my dad would bust me hustling pool, when I was supposed to be at school. Usually, he was pretty cool about that. We'd end up shooting pool together. Those days I'd get away with NOT working in the garden, or, digging in the storm shelter.

I think my dad always had the best of intentions for me. The war messed him up, his broken childhood messed him up and I was in the wrong place at the wrong time, caught up in his mental illness. Psyche Doctors diagnosed my dad with PTSD and labeled him with schizophrenia. This was after they noted he talked to God and said only God could heal him. I agree with my dad completely and, actually, I talk to God, too. He was messed up when he first came back from Korea. I was born a few months before he came back. There I was for all the ass-whippings. Then, two years after I was born, here comes my five little sisters, one after the other to share in the grief. It's all surreal to me now. I think back to getting beat so many times and so often till, finally, my brain just snapped. This is a book marker in time for me.

My emotions turned into some metamorphosis of "Go to hell, I'm done here". I was fourteen when that happened. I had slipped off after school to play football with the neighborhood kids.
I didn't want to dig any more dirt out of this big hole my dad had instructed my sisters and I to do every single day. It's like I was trying to dig a hole to China. With every shovel of dirt, I'd suck in a little more resentment. With every shovel of dirt, I'd get just a little bit older and a little bit madder. Just to frame it in with concrete, tie rods, bedsprings and metal bullshit.

So that, somehow, once again, this concrete room was going to save the Mondays from an absolute nuclear holocaust that, someday, inside my dad's mind, and a great many other peoples, was definitely going to happen. So, the plan was, according to my dad, I would dig this big hole, and my sisters would carry this dirt out of this hole. Then, we'd create a concrete room and when Russia, China or whoever, dropped five hundred nuclear bombs on the world, we, the Monday's, would run out to this amazing concrete castle. The concrete storm shelter that the Monday kids, blood, sweat, tears and way too many ass whooping's made in a big hole in the ground. Then, somehow, we would be saved. SAVED!!!!! Saved to continue mankind and start the world over. I added that last part in to be coy. Anyway, damn! I'm so done with digging a hole. This was my thinking inside my fourteen year old, pissed off head! So, I slip off to the neighbors and we're playing football, like neighborhood kids should be doing. Right? Boom!

My dad shows up madder than hell! "Git home boy!" he screams! "You got work to do?" (What's wrong with this picture?)

"I've got work to do? Man, I'm a kid!!! What the hell, MAN!" "So," I'm thinking to myself, "Oh my God, are you kidding me, He's going to beat me to death right here in front of my friends! This is going to be bloody... again! HELP!!! Somebody!!! Please!!!! HELP ME!!!"

No-one there. Just my dad, and me and my friends watching! Traumatized, I'm in panic mode.

So, completely embarrassed, I run home as fast as I can, scared to death. Because I'm playing with the neighborhood kids and that's what they did every day. But, not me! For me, that was next to a sin. How dare I be having fun with the kids in the neighborhood? Playing a stupid game called football and laughing, having fun and interacting with the other kids. How dare I! I ran up in the yard and he was furious. He goes into a manic frenzy and pulls his belt off. Before I had time to think, he grabs my left arm.

The man has, once again, lost all control! That's what happened a lot. He'd grab me by the arm and when he beat me, I'd run in circles around him. I was terrified. That's being a few notches more than scared. I was freaked out. I thought my life was in danger every time this happened. I'd always end up in the ER with my mother explaining the welts up and down my legs and back to the doctor. It was a small town, the doctor had delivered me, when I was born, and they knew my dad. They never called the police, but, they told my mother every time, "one of these days, Virgil is going to kill this boy, Barbara." I agreed. I was always trying to run away from him. I stayed away from him, out of fear, when I was younger. I'd piss on myself, with blood, running down my back and legs. It happened a lot and it's not easy to relive it, to write it, right now. At the same time, I love all my sisters and they went through a lot of this shit, too. Oldest to youngest, they were Barbara Lynn, Jackie Claudette, June Elizabeth, Susie Q and Markie. I don't want any of them to be mad at me for pouring this out of my heart, but, I can't hold it in anymore. I've carried it too long and it's weighed me down for most of my life.

I just can't carry it inside me anymore. To be honest with you, I'm sitting here writing this and yes, the tears are flowing. This is painful to relive. It's not easy to flash back to these times. They were hard on all of us. You have to realize, we loved dad. I miss him so much to this day. I didn't want this to be happening in our childhood. What kid does? But, I didn't know how to get through to him. I tried.

His childhood was hard, too. Really hard. His mother, my grandmother, died when he was 7 and he raised himself, after that, way up in the Smokey Mountains. His dad, Dewey Monday, was a boot-legger and coal miner in Egan, Tennessee, an old coal-mining town. It consisted of 20 or so homes. They've all since been destroyed by a tornado.

That's way east over the mountain from Middlesboro, Kentucky. So, my dad ran wild and sold ginseng root for money. He'd dig it up in the mountains and take it down and sell it. After that, as soon as he was old enough, he joined the Air Force and went to Korea. He served 14 years. So, he had it rough and unfortunately, I caught, and then my sisters, caught the worst of his PTSD.

Here's the thing... I have to write this for the sake of the children out there, that don't have an answer. The child that feels scared and alone in the world. The child that's going through what I went through. This is for that little boy or girl who's scared to say anything in your home, for fear of being beaten. The child that has no free will. This is for the child whose movement is controlled by the mom or the dad. The child being beaten severely and most of the time, not even sure why. This is for the child who, sometimes, thinks it'd be easier to end it, it'd be easier to die. You listen to me, don't short change yourself. Don't leave this world because you're unhappy right now? It'll get better. It will. None of us can stop time. It keeps moving forward. You get a little older every day. Keep pushing through it. I promise you, one of these days, you'll think back to all the struggles you survived and be you'll be damn proud of who you've become, against all odds.

Anyway, I think you understand my soul and I understand yours, too. So, you live your life the best way you can right now and do your best to look forward to the time that's coming... in front of you.

Let's get back to this ear-marked day, in my life. Back to my dad, and this beating. I would run around him screaming, and crying, because he beat me hard, and for a long time, every time. He'd always use the belt for a while, and then, like a well-tuned guitar, he'd throw down his belt, and grab three or four switches, and they were like torture. The switches had all these little arms that went in

230

every direction and as they would penetrate my skin, as they would cut into my back, or my butt, or my legs, my mind would blow a fuse, because there would be so many places for the pain to come from, all at the same time. He'd wear those switches out and he'd grab three or four more. He'd do this till I was covered in bleeding welts, or my mother would run in between us, to stop him. She did that many, many times. To this day, my Mother is my hero. Anyway, since he's holding my arm, the only place to run is in a circle. The routine was real familiar to me.

But, something happened this time. I don't know how to explain it.

He grabbed my arm and laid into my back, butt and legs, with his big belt. I didn't plan it, and I didn't even know it was going to happen. But, I didn't start running in circles. I didn't start screaming and crying. Something inside me snapped. I mean I snapped, in my head.

There was no pain. No emotion. I just stood there. I stood there for, at least, two or three minutes, while his rage and his belt, once again, brought the welts, and the blood to my back, butt and legs. I felt nothing. I was numb to it all. Numb!

About that time, my mother ran out on the porch to revisit the nightmare we knew so well. I was different! I stared right through him! No fear! A calmness swept through me I can't explain.

I still can't explain it. It was a monumental day for Terry Lee. He went away...forever. He closed up shop, left, never to return, he was truly gone. See, he died inside, so another soul could be born. In his place was a soul, that wasn't going to take these beatings from any man. At last it was peaceful inside. My dad was frantic. He was a madman. He kept beating me harder and harder. But, I was a statue. I stood there, stoic. I was concrete, steel, iron and calm, all rolled into one. I was a superhero! Finally!!! I was in charge. That defenseless boy, that Terry Lee. He died. The serenity and rage swept through me, in unison, like a song, singing to my soul, with a voice many will never hear or understand. My dad jarred the moment, as he screamed at me with an overwhelming intensity,

"AINT YOU GONNA CRY BOY...AINT YOU GONNA CRY?"

He stared into my eyes like a challenge to my spirit, as he yelled those words. I looked right through him. I stared back. Imagine that! I stared back. I LOOKED THROUGH HIM! I was fearless! Done! No more! THIS WAS IT!!!! Believe me, that took all the courage in me, but, I was beyond courage. I was somewhere else. Gone. Nobody's going to kick this dog again and if they do, I'm kicking back a hundred times, as hard as I can!

"NO! You might as well keep on beating me. I ain't crying and I ain't running! You hear me daddy! You hear me! Just keep on beating! Go ahead, BEAT ME... Do it, BEAT ME! Beat me to death, I don't care! Beat me...Beeeeeat MEEEEEEEEE!!!!"

I screamed it at him. I was screaming as loud as I could. Quite simply, I'd snapped. I LOOKED RIGHT THROUGH HIM! I saw him tense up. I saw him think about that for five or six seconds, really soak it in. He looked away from my eyes and let go of my arm. As he folded his belt up in his hands, he paused, took a breath, and looked at me again, as the words rolled off his lips, "Well...if you ain't going to cry, then, I ain't going to beat you anymore. That's it. That's enough. We're done here. Now, go in the house!"

I just stood there, staring right at him. Finally, he looked away, mumbled something under his breath, like he was talking to God, and walked past my mother. Suddenly, void of emotion, he went inside. His eyes stared straight ahead as he disappeared inside our house. This memory scarred my soul. It's given me nightmares, throughout the years. It's a thought that haunts me, even now. I cannot shake it, and I've tried and I've tried. It won't let me go.
My mother looked right at me. She was both startled and shocked," Are you okay, Terry? Terry Lee, are you okay?"
"Don't call me that, mother! I'm not that person. That boy's gone. He's dead. He's gone. Don't call me that name anymore. It's not me. He's dead."

We hugged for the longest time. I was different, numb and in shock.
We didn't speak. My mother just kept hugging me.
"We're going to be okay, Mama. It's okay. I'm tired of this. I ain't getting beat on no more. I'm tired of it. Ain't going to happen no more, mama. Not to me!"
"Okay son." My mother didn't know what else to say.

"Call me bubba. Call me anything you want, Mother. But, please, please, don't ever call me, ya know, that other name...that name... No more, Mother. He's gone."

She didn't know how to respond. She stood there quietly, looking at me. I went to the back porch where I slept and sat down on the couch that was my make-shift bed. I was different. I'd changed. I wanted to cry, but, I didn't. Not for a minute or two. Then, I did cry. It was like a pressure valve and I couldn't hold it in, anymore. I couldn't help it. I cried for a long time. I shook all over and the tears poured down my face. I was fourteen years old when that happened.

On that day, I think my dad had an awakening. During that beating, I know I did. The way my dad stopped hitting me. The way he looked at me when I stood up to him for the first time in my life. He realized, he'd taken me 'to that place'. Some of you know that place. It's a few steps past the edge, where a man loses sight of his actions. That's a place no child ever deserves to be.

Here's my thinking on that...

Let's say you kick a dog all through the week. Like clock-work, you kick that dog, all the time, or, you slap it, or, you're just mean to it. Mad, glad or sad, eventually, one of two things are going to happen. Some dogs, after a while, they've had enough, they lose their spirit. A little at a time, it goes away. Then, as time passes and the beatings continue, they lose everything. The broken spirit succumbs to the endless emotional pain. The physical pain after so many beatings become non-existent. The body goes numb. It becomes emotional and mental.

They'll lie over in a corner and fall prey to their own submission. You'll see them walking with their head down and they won't look you in the eye. They'll get scared of everything and everybody. They're forced to turn into a weak, miserable nervous wreck. The spirit within them has been murdered, taken from them. Their soul is wrecked and fallen in demise. Now they isolate.

Then, they lose their heart and their sense of self-worth! This poor dog will end up alone, scared of the world and everything in it. What a horrible thing to put on a dog. All because you felt it was so important to beat the shit out of an innocent creature all the time. Now, you're left with a dilapidated critter, with nary an ounce of self-esteem, or, positive energy to bestow upon the World. A broken-down, mentally, crippled, totally dysfunctional dog, with zero-flicker of what could've been a happy little fella'. You decided to abuse him and constantly treat him like shit and this is what you're left with.

Imagine how this affects his life and everyone around him, because of your senseless acts of constant abuse. The sad part is this. These effects will be life-long. So, in essence, the happiness in this dog's life has been stolen and ripped away from the very core of the dog's soul.

Then, there's the other kind of dog.

Let's talk about him for a minute. You kick him every day, push him around, slap him and manhandle him. It's what you want, or, feel you need to do. On and on, this continues and time passes. He becomes your release, every time you get pissed off, or, you think he's done something wrong, you kick the shit out of him. Maybe your days messed up, or, people around you didn't act right. Maybe you didn't get a certain job you wanted, or, the sun didn't shine that day, just right, in the big ol' sky. Maybe the lady didn't give you any. You just keep on kicking, kicking and kicking that dog. Soon enough, as time passes, you don't even think about it. Way too often, that dog gets kicked up side his head, or, in the ribs, or, in the ass for general principles. Just kicked and kicked and beat-on, till the kicks get lost in the haze of day to day living.

One day, out of the blue... you kick him and in the blink of an eye, he reaches out with his open mouth and viciously grabs on to your thigh, chewing into muscle and tendon and he's not letting go, now, my friend. He's chewing to the bone in a mad frenzy. He even gets excited because he realizes who he's chewing on and it's a sick kind of happy for him. This dog's lost it! Snapped! I mean lost it! Or, maybe, he finally found it! His breaking point and with it, his savage courage! That's a dangerous mix. That's when all bets are off. That's when the crazy shit gets done! That rage-filled dog chews your leg off. I promise you, he'll work his way on up past your leg and then, given the chance, he'll chew your face off, too. Happily, with vigor and finesse!

234

See, here's the thing... The nicest dog in the world can only take so many ass-whippings, before Captain Snap to the Lou breaks off in that ass.

Don't take this the wrong way, but, I do believe when I was 14, I became THAT dog. I believe on that day when I was fourteen, my dad saw that inside my piercing eyes.

I believe that. He saw that mad-dog in me. It was there inside my eyes. There was no mistaking it. Over time, with all the bloody slashes up and down my back and legs, all the hospital visits, all the shaming at school, the embarrassment, the endless pain, the confusion, just all of it, evolved, merged and exploded into that one moment, into that one final beating and I snapped. It'd turned me into that crazy, raging, spitting, clawing Bull Mastiff and on that day, in that moment, my dad knew it. We never talked about it, but, after that day, my dad treated me like a different person, with a whole lot more respect. He treated me with that respect, right up to the day he died, some sixty years later.

Maybe in some sick, twisted way, my dad put me through his own carefully, well-planned, and intricately designed Basic Training. After all, he was, for several years, a Drill Instructor in the Military. He did survive combat in Korea. Maybe, after all his survival training as a child, first hand, that is, having to grow up like a wild animal in the Great Smokey Mountains, maybe, he decided he would prepare me for the madness running rampant in the world.

Well, I have to say, based on my personal perception of that particular theory, I'd have to applaud my father. I think he was a true visionary with the unique and uncanny ability to truly see into the future, which, actually, may have been the case. I do have to applaud his focus on shaping my thinking to such an extremely keen point. In the coming years, little did I know these same survival instincts and masterful training techniques would prove to save me, time and time again?

Both in the inner-city streets, across the ocean, in the military and inside prison walls.

The Bible says, "Honor thy Father and Mother". I do. I never hit my father or my mother and I'm proud to be able to say that. I don't hit women either. Never have and never will, unless I'm physically attacked and have no other recourse.

Soon after my fifteenth birthday, he started taking me to jobsites. I fought it tooth and nail. I hated the thought of painting. Time and time again, I would scream out, "I'm not growing up and being a stupid painter. I missed the nail on that one! My dad taught me to paint, and he taught me how to deal with people on a business level. At the time, it was like pure misery to me. It seemed like such work. The caulking, scraping and taping seemed endless. But, that's what he did for money. He created a small paint company, painting residential homes and new construction. His crew consisted of his brother, my Uncle Earl and his father, Dewey Monday. (They both moved in with us when I was about five or six.)

Then, as a teen, they added me, as their flunky or apprentice, as a beginner is called, to learn the business. They were all excellent painters and my dad, somehow, had a knack for getting the work and making sure everyone was always happy with the finished paint job. As much as I complained about having to work with them, they taught me so much about the business.

Like I said earlier, in 1969, my family moved to Marquette Heights, then, Peoria, Illinois. A few years and hundreds of hits of acid later, I went into the military. They lived on North Jefferson Street across the street from Matthews Market. My mother was the produce manager. My father was a paint contractor. My five younger sisters were all in the schools around the north-end. They were in Greeley and Woodruff High School.

There was some very cool families that lived on both sides of my parents. Billy M and his family lived on the right and Marie M lived on the left. She had a bunch of beautiful daughters, and some cool sons. This family and our family became very close and still are to this day. I made friends with a lot of cool people through Dave M. We call him Mully now. Mully turned me on to a bunch of the north end. The Travis Brothers, Mike, Joe and Butch. Larry and Terry W, The Cooks, Jerry, Tommy, Carol Lee, Joe, Debbie, Cookie and Becky C. Arnie, Roosevelt, across the street from us. There were just so many cool people in the north end. There was Stef, Mike, Sharon, Sandy, and Gail, Crazy Richard and all that crew. We're all brothers to this day. Many have passed on.

One day, I met a dude named Joey B in Matthews's market. He seemed cool enough. Joe tells me he's into music, big time. I say, yeah, me too. So, Joey takes me to a dudes house in the

236

neighborhood, named Tim H. Tim was this slender kid, about our age, with real long blonde hair. He had hundreds of rock & roll albums. When I met Tim, he had a guitar, strapped on him. We were all drinking wine and smoking weed. It all seemed so normal at the time. He says to me, "Pick out any album there and I'll play any song on the album."

I'm thinking, "Sure you will! I know this is some bullshit." But, hey, I'll play along. Besides, Tim had this one slender, beautiful, long-blonde-haired sister that was hot and she kept smiling at me. Believe me, I was smiling back, too. Anyway, I'll never forget it. I went digging through these albums. I went deep into the stack to find an obscure album. I just knew I was going to trip this dude up. I found this album called, "Wishbone Ash." I'd never even heard of them, but, I liked their album cover. So, I pull it out and handed it to Tim as he handed me a doobie.

As I took a big hit, he put the album on and it started playing. Tim started playing along. I mean, he didn't miss a note. He was damn good! Hell, he was excellent! Yes, I was stoned, but, I was impressed beyond words. After a few songs, I pulled out, The James Gang, then, Montrose, then, REO, then, another, then another. This dude was badass!

While we're tripping on the music, I met a Mexican dude that was there. His name was Roy P. We clicked right away, like instant blood. Little did I know, at the time that my sister, Jackie, would end up marrying Roy and they'd have the most beautiful little girl, my niece, Christina?

I also didn't realize that Roy's huge Mexican family would become very close family to my family. All his brothers, Eduardo, Speedy, Mike, Richie and Steve, would all become very close family to me. So would all their children. So, would their mother, Father, their sisters, cousins and everyone. We became very close and still are today.   I did so much shit with Roy, Ed, Speedy, Richie, Steve and Mike, I don't even want to go into it. But, I will say, the years only brought us closer together. Hazel, Steve's wife, would end up being my sister, Jackie's, best friend. Hazel, God bless her, was a very generous and amazing woman. We also became very close. I loved her like a sister. She left us for a Heavenly journey, but, she will always be with us. So will Steve, who is also gone. The oldest Ponce of the brothers, Mike, passed away in 2017, also. Steve, Mike and Speedy all served in

Vietnam. The P's and C's, all the same family and always will be very close in my heart. I remember after I went to Roy's house on Voris Street, the first time and met his mom and dad. They were awesome people. His dad, May God bless his soul, would have these get-togethers at the Legion or VFW. About every Mexican in Peoria would show up at these parties. I went to a few of them, also. They were a good time and I met a lot of life-long friends at these parties. Joey B became a life-long friend. He's a big record producer out in Oklahoma now. They also have an office in Nashville. Landline Records. Anyway, we started out getting high together and hanging out at Tim's, or, another friend's house, guitar wizard, Mirty Mi. Then, we started stealing cars together, just to joy ride. We were both very adventurous when we were young. We ended up hitch-hiking for a while, like I'd done after the Army. Joey and I ended up in San Antonio, Texas for a while. He had a sister that lived there named Barb. Barb was a nurse and let us stay with her. She literally worked all the time. We rarely even seen her. She also lived a nice neighborhood. We ended up meeting all these hot women. Life was one big party after another.

Once we found a nice home that someone had told us the people were on vacation. That's all we needed to know. We were on vacation, too. Well, in a homeless, hitch-hiking around, selling drugs, raising-hell, picking up girls, kind of way. So, I was seeing this girl, Marsha, and Joey was seeing this hot neighborhood girl, also. She was a sexy brunette, named Tracy.

We break in this house and the girls start cooking us all dinner. I got the music on and we're drinking, smoking dope, jamming and having a blast. All of a sudden, a cop walks in the front door and yells "FREEZE", and one walks in the back door. We all about shit! I jumped up and the cop grabbed me, just like that. Joey dove through an open window in the living room. I got to admit, that was slick. The one cop from the back darted back out the door, after him. The other cop walks me quickly to the cop car, throws me in the back and

says, "I'll be right back. Sit tight, don't move!"

"Who me? Move! Right! Never."

As he disappeared around the house, I immediately kicked out the rear passenger doors, window. Thank God, he was in such a hurry, he didn't handcuff me. Out the window I go! I see the girls at the side of the house, just standing there, freaking out. The cops were zipping and gone after Joey. I ran up to the girls and we all rush off, down the street. We cut across a field, cross some roads, through a neighborhood, and take a short cut to Marsha's house. We go in her garage and hang out for a while, while we catch our breath, then, we all go in their bedroom and hang out.

We actually succeeded in getting away from the cops. So did Joey. He circled around and followed us to their garage. I couldn't believe it. But, we did that and got away with it. We were wild. Joey liked to call us Deuces Wild. He was right.

Black out...

One weekend, Joey and I go to a three-day festival in Sunken Gardens. That's in San Antonio, Texas. All kinds of great bands were playing. Everybody was there, from Steppenwolf to Santana. We bullshitted our way back-stage. We were drinking beer, smoking weed and having a blast. After a while, we started partying with some of the bands, like Carlos Santana and Steppenwolf. We got wasted. We got very wasted!

Flashing back. I honestly can't remember much past us going backstage. I vaguely remember somebody pulled a bottle of Tequila out of a big travel bag. I think it was one of the dudes in Steppenwolf. This was late into the first night of the 3 day Festival. He also had a tray with a cut up lemon on it and a salt shaker. I remember some shot glasses, too.

I lost a few days and nights after that. When my eyes opened, it took me a few minutes to focus in. I was lying on a bed and my face was between a pair of brown, naked legs. My face was pressed against a really pretty flowering lotus. It was well-kept. I was glad to see that. The smell of sweet strawberries filled the air. I pulled my head back real quick and shook it for a moment, to get a bearing of my surroundings.

"Would you look at that?" I said to myself.

There's this really good looking Spanish girl lying here with me. Okay. I don't even know her. She's out. I mean, she's probably asleep." It's crazy, I know.

I was trying to figure it all out. What the hell happened here? I was groggy, everything was blurry. I just laid there for a few minutes to clear my head. So, let me see. I must've been pleasuring her and passed out. "My, my, my, she looks good." I thought. "Whew. Glad of that! This could've been bad." I chuckled.

Then, I noticed her dark skin and how flat her tummy was and how perfect her breasts were. They were full, perfect in size and beautiful, too. Then, I wondered, "Who the hell is she?" She had long black hair laying tussled around her body. I slowly lifted one of her naked and sexy legs up, so, I could crawl up next to her.

She felt me. Her body pulled in close to me and she slowly opened her eyes. They poured right into mine. She had beautiful, big, brown eyes. They were dark, in fact, they were almost black.   As she looked into my eyes, her little voice purred to me,
"Stormy, you're awake. You woke up."

I melted right there into the bed and I pulled in tight to her body. I pulled back for a moment and looked around the room.
"We're at Barbs. How'd we get here? When did we get here? Hey, I don't mean to be mean, but, how long have we been here? You're beautiful. Who are you?"
She giggled. "You were so high. Si, Te entiendo. You were wasted out of your mind. I'm Anna. Anna Trinidad. There was a bunch of us. We all came here last night and partied for a while. I think almost everybody left, except us and your one friend." "You mean Joe?? Did you meet Joe? Where's he at?"
"Si. I think he's in that other room over there. I think he's with some girl, but, I don't know who it is."
"I don't remember shit. How long we been partying? You know, you and me. Where'd we meet? I don't remember anything." She looked at me, smiling just a little bit. "God, she had a nice smile.
Her teeth, so white and perfect. Wow!" I'm thinking to myself. "Si, it's okay. You were really drunk. We met at the Sunken Gardens Festival a few days ago. Do you remember being there?
"It's foggy. No, I don't. Well, maybe a little. It's almost a blank."
"We drank some tequila and smoked some weed. I think you and your friends were doing acid. You don't remember?"
"Hmmm, I don't think so. I'm blank."
She smiled and said, "I was watching a band play. They were moi bueno. You walked up out of nowhere and took my hand. We started talking. That was a few days ago. We've been together ever since. You really don't remember?"
240

"Wow! I don't remember. I don't know how I could forget you. Look at you!"

I took her in my arms and rolled back over on top of her. It felt like we were floating on an ocean. I stared into her brown eyes and I swear, we traveled through time together. One thing I discovered that Anna and I could do well and I mean really well was slip- slide away. We made it an art form.

Those brown eyes had me. She spent the next two weeks with me. Joe's sister, Barb, was cool about it. Hell, she was hardly there, anyway. Being a nurse, she worked all the time.

Anyway, after a few weeks, one day, Anna says to me while we were sitting in a park, "Stormy, I don't want to, but, I should go home. My mother's sick and I should help her."

That killed me. If I'd been a bit more together, I would've probably hooked up with Anna Trinidad for a long, long time. But, I was a drug-addict, deep in active addiction and still searching for myself. She was a poor Spanish girl from the South side of San Antonio. Her mother needed her. Joe and I took her home two days later. I walked up to her house with her and her mother's eyes lit up when she opened the door. I met her mother. Rosa, I think, was her mom's name. I talked to Anna on the front porch for a while, then, we hugged, said our goodbyes and I went my own way.

I never saw Anna Trinidad again.

Chapter 13

~I just want to spend the rest of my life laughing!

EIGHT-WAY WINDOWPANE

An old friend of mine and I were flashing back a few years ago about old times. We were laughing about stuff from the old days. It was Tommy. The dude and I did so much together back in the day. He was truly like family to me. Drugs and alcohol took Tommy from us all way too soon. Before he died, we'd gotten together and were flashing back to this story I'm about to share with all of you. It involved a couple cousins of mine. I have two cousins that are brothers, named Danny and Timmy. We grew up together. They're around my age, just a year or so younger. We'd always be outside playing Army, wrestling, exploring, or whatever. We were family and this was our early childhood. That's what we did in those days, for fun. We didn't have computers, cell phones, and any of these other fancy doohickeys. So, we went outside and found stuff to do. If Danny and Timmy weren't around, no problem, I'd run down to the junkyard, but, when they were hanging out, trouble always seemed to find us.

Move ahead a couple of decades, and we're all married and having kids. We still hung out when the family's got together, but, other than that, we did our own things. I'd went in the Army, came back, once again got neck-deep in the drug life, went to jail in Texas, then, went to prison again in Illinois. Finally, I got a good job, got married and had kids. Of course, I didn't know how to live a normal life, because of my addiction, so, time and time again, I messed everything up and then, I'd have to start all over.

Anyway, all of us, Danny, Timmy and myself, got into partying. We all got into it heavy. The following drug-infested story is one of those times.

242

I hadn't seen Danny or Timmy for several years, so, my partner, Tommy C and myself decided to swing by their crib in East Peoria and pick them up. It was snowing like hell outside, but, we didn't even care. This was back about 1979 or so. I owned a beautiful 1976 Sportster. She was Foxy, my smooth, sexy, black bitch. Foxy was stored for this cold, dreary and snowy winter.

So, we all loaded in my 66 Ford Thunderbird and talked about what we were going to do. This was probably our first mistake. That, thinking shit will get you every time, especially a dope-head. Remember, our thinking's messed up. I had about a hundred hits of 8-way windowpane tucked down in my pocket. I hadn't said a word about that. Let's just say it was a party surprise. It was called eight-way windowpane, because, it'd fry eight people with one hit, but, really, I wasn't into cutting little bitty squares into tiny winy squares, so, we just ate a hit each. Then, we grabbed a case of PBR, in the cans and headed to the back roads.

We headed toward Farmdale, behind East Peoria and I just kept driving. Before long, we were all tripping our brains out. The beer started tasting like cold water and we went through that case like a windstorm. So, we bought another one in some small town. I have no idea where we even were. It was a complete white-out. Blizzard-like conditions... Back out on the back-roads we went. By then, we were tripping our brains out.

Right about here, I should mention something about eating acid. See, for me, anyway, when I ate acid I'd get high as hell, twisted out of my bell-bottom, patched-up blue jeans and like some hungry stork looking for little fishies to munch on, I'd think it was a great idea to eat more acid. I know that's some messed up shit. I don't deny that. I know this books about addiction and I shouldn't be glorifying a good time, but, let's be for real, if you think about it, that's part of the allure. Sometimes it is fun as hell, but, trust me, the good times that we're talking about are short-lived. It does all come crashing down. In the big picture, it's not worth it. But, we have to get to that and on the way there, sometimes, some crazy shit happens... anyway, I found that out more than a few times all on my own. See, when I was in high School, around that age and a little older, I enjoyed melting my brain with lots of acid. As I've grown older I realize how truly lucky I am to have survived that insanity. That's dangerous turf, so, do not try this.

These days, I couldn't imagine doing a hit of acid. Even the thought leaves my head spinning. But, when I was young and not as cued in, I swear I was about ten cards shy of a full deck, too. Maybe more! This meaning I'd do about anything, except, like I said before, gay stuff. I have zero interest in having sex with a man. That's just not my cup of tea. So, anyway, let's get back to this story.

About now, starting to get off on the 8-way hit's we'd taken, I pulled out the acid again and in our inability to process reliable thought, we all decided to eat another hit. There's that hungry stork again looking for those little fishies to munch on. Bad idea. Anyway, try to imagine the genius of that fleeting decision. Little did I know, this particular hit would take us far beyond the edges of our twisted mind-juggling to an out-of-body astral plane on a parallel universe, where we could flicker and flutter the audio vibrations into the ever-fluctuating time continuum and from another view of ourselves, off to the side, we could watch our more wasted selves party and melt into a million tiny squares of a hundred different bright and brilliant colors, as they flowed into one stream of magic dust under a rainbow bridge. Did you get that?

At least, that's what I figured out as I drove us deeper and deeper into the lost and blinding back roads. The snow was a torrid blanket of white flying sideways. It was hitting the windshield like big white baseballs splashing all over the glass. It was way past hypnotic. We traveled down this long stretch of road that was a literal white out. That's all we could see in every direction. There was white snow falling into white fields of whiteness. Still, the T-Bird kept chugging along and the tasty beers kept flowing.

Steppenwolf was playing in the CD player and we were far beyond higher than men should be. Everything was funny! I mean hysterically funny and for no damn good reason. Beer cans were flying over the back seat, or, out the windows. One right after the other one in every direction. The more we drank, the more wasted we got. Hallucinating our asses off! We had less than zero shits to give about anything. Laughing about everything and laughing about nothing. Losing it, too. Logic and human conceptual thought went right out the window.

Well, we're cruising along having a blast with nary a care in the world. Just moving through time like an episode of the Twilight Zone. The whole vibe was transcendently strange like we were the only

244

people on some planet far away and our iridescent conscious thought had just realized it. Then, BAM, son of a bitch! In the rear view window, I noticed dazzling red flashing lights coming up behind us in a barrage of whiteness from the storm. For some reason, we all thought that was funny. We were definitely in the twilight zone! So, right when none of us could possibly contain ourselves for one second, infiltrating paranoid set in...

I immediately turned the music down and tightened up as a flash of reality crossed my thinking. Ten and two on the steering wheel! Sitting straight up, overly perfect posture, eyes straight ahead! "Whoa! It's the man! What the hell! Oh hell no! Don't panic! Don't panic, Oh shit, I'm the one panicking. Stop it! Stop it!" My mind was in over-drive.

My cousin Danny, well, you'd have to know him to understand what I'm saying. His hands always shook anyway. He's since been diagnosed with Parkinson's. We didn't know it then, but, we did notice he shook a lot. Now, with this cop rolling up on us and we're all wasted and NOW, paranoid as hell, Danny boy was flat-out tripping the hell out. He was flipping out, which made us all laugh even harder. Now, realize, we're not laughing at Danny. He's one of us. He's family. It's just that we're wasted out of our ever-loving minds and, suddenly, the monumental time continuum was splashing down all around us like an icy-cold waterfall in the pristine mountains of New Zealand. We were a mess in capital letters! We're all three sheets in the wind. I told Tommy to put his coat over what was left of the case of beer. Just as he was covering it, the cop walked up to the window. The thing is, I didn't even remember coming to a stop. I was that wasted. There were beer cans scattered all over the car, like his coats going to cover all the beer cans. Literally ridiculous to even think it.

"Damn!" I rolled the window down.

Here's this cop standing in what looked like a blizzard, high wind and snow blowing sideways and he's telling me to follow him into town. He didn't ask me for a driver's license or anything.

"Hmmm, okay. Wow! Alright, I'll do that!"

"You guys hang in there, I'll drive you out of here." I'm thinking, "What in the hell are you talking about?"

Then, it hit me. In this cops mind, this was a rescue mission. He was rescuing us. This cop was getting us out of this blizzard snow-storm safely. This same snowstorm that we didn't give a shit about, cause, we're all wasted out of our cotton-picking minds. The cop walks back to his car and drives around us. I look around the car real quick to gather my senses.

Like I said, there were beer cans lying all over the car. They were on the dashboard, in the floor, on the seats, everywhere!

I'm screaming, "Did that cop see these cans? Did he see the cans?" Tommy, being funny with his famous shit-eating grin, says, "What cop?" We all laughed our asses off. Then he added. "I don't know. There's a hundred fucking beer cans laying all over the damn car. Do you think he saw them? We lost it.

Now, I'm tripping! "Better yet, how could he NOT see the cans? You're right, Tommy! There must be a hundred of them." We all got real quiet. It was all sinking in.

I started to follow him. The super- paranoia set in again. I'm like, "We're going to jail! You know that, right? GOING TO JAIL. Parties over! Damn, OH SHIT! I don't believe this shit! Look at us! We're following a cop to the cop shop to go to jail! We're busted. Damn! How the hell did this happen?"

We didn't know whether to laugh, cry, freak out, or, run through a white field of nothingness and high wind in the freezing cold! But, run where? We're in the middle of nowhere, in a blinding snow storm and it was so bad out I could barely drive. "Damn! We can't even make a run for it. We're in a fucking blizzard." We all shook our heads and laughed, nervously.

Let me tell you a little more about my cousin, Danny. He's a genuine character. Even when we weren't high, he's a genuine character. His hands shake real badly when he got nervous and he'd start to stutter, just a bit. Otherwise, he was fine. It was just when he got nervous. He was diagnosed with Parkinson's disease. I'm sure that's the reason he'd shake so much. He also had this nerdy look about him. Don't get me wrong, I love Danny and Timmy. I just have to help you get a clear picture of what's about to happen.

It was like he was Timothy Leary or somebody really out there. His eyes were beady and he had this grin he could never wipe off his face. Like I said, I love the dude. He's family. Even when we were really young and I'd watch his mom beat his ass for anything, he'd have this smirk on his face.

246

To compound this dilemma, right now, remember, we're all tripping our brains out. I mean we're hallucinating really heavy. Now, somehow, I'm following this cop to a cop-shop and we don't even know where that is. We're in a white-out. My belly was aching from laughing as we finally pulled up to the station.

I honestly, to this day, have no idea what little town we were in. But, we park and it was a bitch to walk through this blizzard, into the station. But, after falling down about 4 or 5 times each, we somehow made it inside. That, in itself, was a comedy. So, we finally make it.
We follow this cop into this old jailhouse and he shuts the door behind us. We're all looking around and shaking all the snow and ice off. He was the only cop there. After we shook all the snow and the storm off of us as best we could, here comes the questions. Immediately, we all start laughing and freaking out at the same time. Ever done that? We can't stop laughing, but, we're trying.

"Contain myself. Contain myself. Contain myself." I'm saying this over and over like I'm a lunatic. The cops standing right in front of us and staring at us and that in itself was too much intensity all at once. It wasn't working. The vibe had exploded around us. We're really trying to contain ourselves, but, the windowpane had taken us over. We're all consumed by the wicked witch of the west, that damn LSD. Have you ever tried to contain yourself while you're tripping your fucking brains out, in front of a big, redneck cop, in a cop-shop, in the middle of nowhere, in a blizzard... while his big buggy eyes are staring right in your face? No shit. Neither had we. From our personal experience, it can't be done. Not on this night, for sure, anyway.

This big cop notices that Danny's white as a ghost, shaking all over and really nervous, I mean, 'over the top' nervous. Hell, he was wasted out of his ever-loving' mind. Well, this big cop figures it's time to make a point. So, he walks over to Danny real quick, bends down eyeball to eyeball with him and in his deepest, most serious, stern voice, he says, "What's your name, son?"

Danny just about shit all over himself. He tensed up like a starched shirt and his eyes about popped out on to the floor. "Uhhh, well, uhhh, Sir, uhhh, well, my name is uhhh well, my name is Danny C. "
We all fell out laughing. Cry level! We couldn't help it. Now, this pisses the cop off, so, he got more serious. "What in the hell's wrong

with you boys? You smell like a brewery. You better be over twenty-one. Is everybody 21 or more? Let me see some ID's."

I said, "Officer, we just needed help getting off those back roads. If you don't mind, we'll head on home now."

He screams at me, "You ain't headed no got-damn where right now, boy, ya hear me?"

We bout fell in the floor, again! Oh, this cop was pissed and confused. The acid had us by the balls. I swear, this should've been a sitcom. This cop's face was melting down the wall and the walls around him were breathing, turning colors, moving and doing all kinds of weird shit. Think about that shit. The pictures on the walls were sliding down the walls and the floor, the walls, the ceiling, hell, the whole room was breathing real loud. I could hear it. I know I could. The cop was turning different colors and his face kept "oinking" at me, like a big hog.

All of a sudden, the cop puts his face a couple of inches from Danny's face. BAM. He's going to make a serious point. He looked him square in the eyes and started to say something real serious. It scared the living shit out of Danny! That was it. Danny puked right in the cops face! Right in his face! It was a violent blast of vomit right in the cops face. We lost it! Fell on the floor. Done! That was it! Laughing till we cried. Just lock us the hell up! This happened. Oh my God!

The cop blurted out, "Son-of-a-bitch! You puked all over me! Oh hell no! You did not just do that! What the hell is wrong with y'all?"

He ran to the bathroom and started washing himself off, screaming, "What the hell? What the hell? You bastard! You puked in my face! You son-of-a-bitch!"

He screamed for us all to sit down. We're really trying to be serious now. It wasn't working at all. I looked over at Tommy with his crazy-ass laugh. He was turning colors. I swear he was. His face was red, then, it was green, and then, I swear it turned blue, then, all of a sudden, it was kind 'a purple. I'm like, "Tommy, for real, man, stop turning colors! Just stop. I can't take this shit. My sides are hurting from laughing." We were crying it was so damn funny.

We walked to the dude's desk and sat down, laughing hard and trying like hell to stop. My ribs hurt. The cop knew we were wasted. He wiped himself off the best he could.

"Git in that cell! All of you. You ain't got one lick of got-dam sense among you." He took us all straight to a cell and locked us all in. Then, without saying another word, he just up and left. He left us all locked in that cell. Remember, we're all tripping our brains out. Fried, like a deep-fried turkey. So, we didn't realize it, we didn't even think about it, but, the dude went home to change his clothes and take a shower. Of course, none of that entered our thinking for a second, cause, we're all hallucinating our nuts off in that cell. To us, him leaving was strange. Our minds went a million directions on why he left and who he's bringing back, when he's comes back and what will our charges be. We got into a deep conversation about how many cracks were in the concrete in the cell and the color of the paint on the walls, why the toilet was on a piece of floor that was built about a foot higher than the rest of the floor. I felt the axis of the earth shift a little and of course, I had to point that out in explicit detail and then, I spent an hour explaining why I thought we didn't just fall off the earth while we were standing in that cell. Tommy thought the cell floor might've dropped about 6 inches right under our feet. I leaned more toward 4 inches. Danny was in a trance. Timmy was muttering something about the stock market. I didn't know he knew anything about the stock market.

Timmy, Tommy C and I were a mess. Danny had freaked out. He was sitting there on the stool, lost, didn't know whether to laugh, cry, or what. He was red as a beet. He was having little laughter outbursts and then, he'd just sit there, staring straight ahead. Killing me! Danny boy had me over the top. I'd fell to the floor and my stomach hurt from laughing so damn hard. I still had a pocket full of acid and here I'm in jail now. That's felony charges. I was too wasted to give a shit. This should have been serious as hell and we should've been freaking out, like Danny was, but, we were too high to think straight, or, even care.

"Danny, you puked in that cop's face! Dude. Damn, man! I can't believe you did that. You really did that! Tommy, you can't top that shit. Danny Boy puked in that cops face! Never, for the rest of my life, will I forget that shit! Who does that?"

"I ain't even going to try!" Tommy slings out. "Hahahaha, damn! Puked in that cops face. Damn, Danny, oh hell yeah!" Tommy C. and I just laughed, high-fiving the whole thing.

"I'll never forget that shit. Oh man! I can't believe you did that shit, cuz."

Oh, we were wasted. My sides hurt from laughing so hard and I couldn't stop.

Tommy C has this laugh you can never forget. He's on the floor rolling around, laughing and wasted. Oh my God, I'll never forget this night for the rest of my life.

After a couple hours, we finally started coming down off the acid some. All of us had pissed a lot of the beer out of our systems and now, we're just a bunch of partiers with hangovers. I could see the sun starting to come up through the bars in the windows. The sunlight was streaking through the bars. I was laying back on the floor spacing out and that same cop came walking through the front door, just out of the blue.

He looked in the holding cell at us and said, "how you boys feeling' this morning?"

Tommy C was passed out on the floor. Timmy was laying on a metal slab and he was out, too. Danny boy, he was sitting against the wall by the stool, white as a ghost. He'd puked a few more times and I could tell he felt like shit. Me, for some reason, I felt pretty good, considering.

So, I answered him. "It's been a long night, sir. Hey, I'm truly sorry my cousin puked on you. Man, he gets nervous at the least little thing. Anyway, I'm really sorry that happened."

The Officer just looks at me and grabs the keys out of the desk drawer, opens the cell door and says, "git your friends up and meet me over here at my desk."

"Here's your ID's. You fellows look like you might be able to make it home now. The snows settled down, the suns up. You should be alright now." "Oh, yes sir, I can drive."

So, I loaded up my cousins, who were like zombies, and brother, Tommy, into a car still full of empty beer cans. The cop stood in the doorway of the jail house and watched us pull out of the parking lot. We were all stoic, sitting in that car, not knowing if cop cars were going to roll up on us or not. We thought this could maybe be some bad joke this cop was playing on us, payback for puking in his face. It was a strange few moments, like the twilight zone, or some shit. We all just looked at each other, shaking our heads in disbelief at what had just happened. We headed home on white-covered back roads

250

and no one said a word. I still had acid in my pocket. There were no charges filed for anything! It was a miracle. I'll never understand how we got through that without a single charge. He just opened the cell door and as nice as a man could be, said, "You fella's be on your way. Drive safe." It still baffles me.

Danny boy…

A month or so later, we had a big get-together at my house out in Norwood. I had a nice spot, a few acres out in the woods, so, we'd have some kick-ass parties there. Several of us started gambling on the pool table. We were all getting drunk, playing for shots and the like. We shot pool all day and listened to some great music on my reel to reel. It must've been about 4 o'clock in the afternoon and I get a phone call. It's my cousin, Danny. "Hey Stormy. I'd love to come over to your house and shoot some pool and hang out with my cousin."
"Hell yeah," I say. "Come on over."
"I would, but, I don't have any way to get there."
"Dude, not a problem. I have my old work truck sitting outside. I'll come and grab you. You can just crash here tonight, so, we can get party it up." We both laughed.
"Alright. I'm on my way, cuz."
"Cool."
I had a few more drinks, blasted a hit of coke and then, headed over to pick up Danny in my old 69 Chevy Pick-up truck. He jumps in the truck and off we go. Something I noticed when he got in the truck. He was completely straight and I was wasted. "Dude, you need to get high. You got to catch up! Oh yeah, we'll fix that when we get to the house."
Danny lived in East Peoria off of 150. We're speeding toward my house in Norwood. The blues from shooting' the dope was crawling all over me. I was craving another hit really bad, but, since I was driving, I was trying to be cool. Driving the speed limit and following all the rules of the road, I was trying to get us back to my house. We're cruising along, headed down Farmington Road at about 45. As we pull up toward the tracks by the speedway, I notice cars waiting for a train. "Damn!" So, I roll up and man, there's at least 50 or 60 cars waiting for the train. It hadn't come yet, so, there

251

everybody sat. There were businesses along the road there, so, it's hard to tell when the train will actually be there.

I thought to myself, "I don't have time for this shit, I can beat this damn train. It hadn't even got there yet, but, they had the guard rail down. "Such bullshit," I thought. "Damn, I need a hit of coke and a Crown Royal."

So, off I go toward the track, around the cars, in the wrong lane. I'm passing one car after another. There was a lot of cars waiting for this damn train. I started speeding up to get up to the track so I could beat that train before it got there. I kept speeding up and passing cars. I was up to about 70 and still had a half a block of cars waiting. Danny started telling me, nervously, "No, no, no, don't do it. Stormy, No... no, no..." I was drunk, so, I'm laughing about it and I kept speeding up. I was committed now. There was no slowing down. I was in fruit loop mode, fixated on crossing that track before that train got there. The speedometer said 85 when I made it to the track.

Total commitment! There's no turning back!

Too late to turn back now!

As I passed the last couple of cars, I saw an open track and the arm down blocking the road for the train. So, I go in at an angle to go around the arm. Just as I got to the tracks to cross them, there's the train barreling down on us at about the same speed, about 80 or 85. Too late now! OH SHIT!!!!!!!!!! I crossed the track with the train right on top of us. I could almost touch it. But, bam, we made it. Almost! Almost made it! Not quite. The front of the train clipped the back bumper of my old truck and sent us air-born and spinning. It shocked both of us so bad, but, we were in too deep now, we froze as we were flying and spinning.

We went across to the gas station parking lot, in the air, came down on the concrete hard and started sliding in the loose gravel in their parking lot. We slid up from a full spin, within an inch of the gas pumps and the tires caught traction right at the pumps and shot the truck off toward the line of cars on the other side. We slid over to the cars and within inches of a car, the truck caught traction again and we darted out and headed down Farmington Road, like it was no big deal. Like we planned ever bit of that. Like it never happened. Of course, it freaked me out, but, I'm drunk and high and I'm trying to be cool, but, it ain't working, so, like a crazy man, I'm laughing my ass off. I couldn't contain myself. We almost died! We're headed down Farmington Road about 60 now and I look over to Danny. He was white as a ghost and had his face buried in his lap shaking his head back and forth. "OH, Stormy, Stormy, Stormy, oh shit, oh shit, oh shit, oh hell no!!!"

I don't know why, but, I lost it. I couldn't contain myself. I literally laughed till I cried. My stomach muscles ached from me laughing. Oh my God, Danny's face was so funny to me. He was in shock and I'm not kidding, all the color had left him.

He just kept saying over and over. "Oh dear God, Oh dear God, Oh dear God, Stormy, Stormy, Stormy, no, no, no....

I had to pull over and park just to regain my composure. I sat there and laughed till I cried, for a long time. Finally, I looked over at Danny and said, just matter of fact, "Danny boy, we just about died right there!" He had this look on his face, just shaking his head back and forth. He was white as a ghost. I'll never forget it. I know I'm probably just a bit twisted, but, I found that shit funny as hell. For the rest of my life, I'll never forget the day I almost killed Danny and myself at the train track on Farmington Road. I'll never forget the look on his face after we survived. He really was white as a ghost and genuinely probably shit all over himself. Oh my God! I love my cousin, but, that was some funny shit.

At the same time, let's not forget the reason I was in such a hurry. Cocaine. We almost died because I put that cocaine above our safety.

There's no logic to it. It kills people all day every day with zero remorse.

I'm grateful we survived. Yes, it was crazy as hell. The train actually clipped my back bumper and sent us spinning in the air. We were flying and literally airborne! Hard to believe that actually happened and believe me, I'm grateful we didn't get crushed by that train. It must've been traveling about 80 miles per hour. I completely realize we're lucky to be alive! No drug is worth more than living.   Truth is, I believe the man upstairs had a whole lot to do with saving us on that day.

~ The best part of everyday... is right now. ~

Chapter 14

How can someone be so lost and not know it?

RUNNING FROM MYSELF

Late 80's...

Tired...I mean, I was beat like an old wool blanket strung across a clothes line in a wind storm. All the drugs and booze had finally caught up with me. I was dead inside. Everything and everybody around me was disappearing. My world was falling apart. I was mentally and emotionally exhausted. The only thing left for me to do, in my head, was either kill myself, somehow clean up, or, I knew I was going to end up in prison, yet again. Not very good choices in my messed-up mental state. If I didn't clean up I knew I was going to die. I'd been to treatment in April of 1983 and about 3 years later, I'd relapsed. So, I was essentially, once again, running from myself. It's the most hopeless feeling. I couldn't get away from the lifestyle, no matter where I went and I couldn't get away from the cocaine, either. I was staying on the move. This was so I could keep away from the coke-dealers that were making a fortune off me. People like Kelly D... He's another brother, dead now, to the drug-life. I loved the dude like a brother and he always had great deals on the pure coke. We had a guy making runs to Bogota, Colombia. Balls of steel. As soon as he hit town, Kelly would call me and I'd go straight to his crib. I knew I'd be the first person trying the new shit.

Then, after I'd shoot a blast to check out the new load and pick my ass up off the floor, he'd front me an ounce. I wasn't doing cocaine anymore. Cocaine was doing me. I knew I had to leave. I had to go or I was going to die. I knew it. My soul was dead. I was a walking shell of a man. So, one day, I flashed back to when I was hitch-hiking around the country after I got out of the Army. I thought back to that one day when I spread that blanket out under that big shade tree. I think it was in Kentucky. I laid there and smoked a joint and drank a bunch of rum. I remember I was trying to clean up off the coke then, too. Plus, I still had crystal meth in my system from New

Mexico. I hated that shit. But, laying on that blanket under that shade tree. Even before I smoked the weed or drank the rum. Just feeling the wide open sky wash through me and the freedom of it all, completely drug-free. That's a feeling I would always flash back to when life sucked. That's a feeling I needed to feel again and soon. So, I decided it was time to hit the road. It was time to get in the wind. Sometimes you just know. So, I rolled up a blanket and a few other things... and I hit the road on my Harley.

I'd been on the road for about a month, all over the south.

I was living in the wind and trying to jump-start my soul. The spark had went out and I was only a remnant of my real and true self. Many a night, I'd set up a little camp in an out of the way spot, spread out my sleeping bag by the bike, build a fire and go to sleep looking at the stars. No drugs. No booze. Just the feel of the wide open sky. Freedom, man.

I'd managed to get the coke withdrawals out of my system, somewhat. What a bitch that was. The cravings were still there, but, they were getting a little easier to deal with. I was feeling a little better. After a while on the road, I was starting to wind down a little. I'd been on the road all day on this particular day. Someone somewhere said something about a town in Arizona, called Jerome that was full of bikers, art galleries, artist and the place was mostly really cool people. I had to check that out for myself. I know I had over 400 miles on my ass from that ride. Four hundred miles in 110 degree weather with that sun barreling down can heat up a body and a bike. Hell, you can fry an egg on the road. That's hot. Foxy, my Harley, was on her last leg, I mean, she was on fire from that sizzling hot desert pavement. I could feel the heat billowing off the dirty chrome and the damn-near empty tank. The last few miles on that long road, I did see the most tranquil sunset, though, slipping down over the far-off mountain horizon.

Then, I rolled up on a long line of parked Harleys. It was a few miles out from the town of Jerome. How about that. This was, suddenly, my destination. I was riding solo and loving it. I brought her down to second gear as I pulled off the road and into a secluded spot behind some over-sized, red desert rocks. I noticed a bunch of bikers parked all over and some partying going on, but, I was too damn tired to even care. Talk about road-weary. I could feel the worn leathers vibrating all over my beat-up body.

Maybe it was just me still feeling the bike running through me. I kind 'a shook off the road a bit and grabbed my bedroll. After that, I forgot all about the party. Sleep came quick.

I still had my cravings here and there. They would eat at me when I'd least expect it. They wouldn't let me completely go. My solution, as crazy as it was, was to keep moving. I know, I know... any shrink in the world would tell me I'm running from myself. That I should stop and deal with my issues and embrace the much healthier NOW. Resolution brings peace. Well, I know this. I'd have to agree with every word, but, I'm not mentally, or, emotionally ready for all that yet. Not yet.

Anyway, I woke up about daylight to go pee behind a big rock and I didn't feel social at all. Somebody around another camp-fire had some Zeppelin playing. It sounded good. I just wanted to piss and get in the wind. Everybody was passed out all over the place. Biker's laying everywhere. It looked like some hard partying had happened. For the most part, it was all done now, though. Except for, maybe, a few speed freaks scattered about building campfires and getting into shit. Fine with me. I think the coke made me paranoid. Think? I know it did. Anyway, there was this one Native woman sitting alone by a campfire. She was sitting back against a big rock and had some bacon and eggs on the fire cooking. Our eyes met as I was walking by her. "Wow. Those big brown eyes and that smile." I thought. Somehow, even in my stupor, she took my breath away. She smiled so pretty with those perfectly beautiful white teeth, so, I sat down next to her by the fire and we started talking. Her name was Dawn and she was Sioux Indian. She was there with a girlfriend and they were about to leave and go back to Phoenix, she said. That is if her girlfriend, Jazzy, ever woke up. We both chuckled. She got up and made both of us a plate of bacon and eggs while we enjoyed the morning together. We ate and must've talked for an hour. Damn, that breakfast was good, too. The connection was obvious. Jazzy, her girlfriend, finally got up moving around, so, we said our goodbyes. We hugged a few minutes longer than normal. I gave her my mother's phone number and told her I'd always get any messages from her. Then, I fired up my bike and hit the road without saying two words to anybody else. "I have to stay on the move. Damn, that woman was a breath of fresh air. Just came out of nowhere." I thought. My bike roared like thunder down the long, winding

256

blacktop. She sure felt good between my legs. This was what I needed. The wind in my face and the sun just coming up. I needed this even more than I knew. I was the only one on that long road in front of me. So, just like that, POOF... I was gone. The black pavement rushed to meet my wheels as I shifted through the gears, to get on down the road.

A few hours later, I was in the zone, cued in to the sound of my motor, listening to it roar down that road.

The sign said, "GAS 2 MILES". I was running low, almost down to fumes.

"Oh yea! I can make that".

I'd been thinking about two things the whole way that day. How in the hell could I actually clean up off the dope? I was so sick of fighting the demons in my head and knowing I couldn't say no to the spoon.

I just needed to get that dope out of my soul. I needed to clean up. I was a mess and I knew it. Plus, I couldn't get that beautiful Sioux Indian out of my mind either.

~◇~

Stormy Monday on his 95th anniversary Fat boy - Image by Gary Taylor

IN THE WIND

One year later... give or take a month...

I'd spent the last several months riding my Harley all over the southern-most part of the country. I wanted to stay in the warm weather. That warm wind, just as the sun is going down is a spiritual plane. To feel that against my face and feel it blowing through my hair. Pure blissful heaven! I rode down to Clearwater Beach, hung out for about a month, then, rode over to Daytona and hung out there for a couple of weeks. The weather was beautiful. All I found wherever I went were brothers happy to take a wind tramp in for a few days. If I had to, I'd sleep on my road blanket by the bike. I'd just pull off under a tree, somewhere a little private and make home for the night. I'd been living like that for a while and I was as content as a man could be. I rode to Mobile, Alabama, partied a weekend and met some good brothers over that way. While I was in Mobile, I hung with a good friend from the old days there. Big Gary. He owned a strip club in Mobile and turned me on to some good times. He introduced me to a few of his strippers. Needless to say, I had a good time in Mobile. Other than one night, I was with a stripper named CC.   After she got off work, we were just chilling at her crib, smoking some weed and drinking some Bacardi and coke. Then, here we go, she pulled out a damn 8-ball. I didn't expect that, so, me being half-drunk and high, I busted out my rig and there I was, again, shooting cocaine. I hated myself for that a little later, when we ran out of the dope. Those blues made me psychotic. So, depressed, I crashed in her bed for several hours, then, got up and showered to get some of the funk off me. Afterwards, I rolled up my shit for the road and rolled out of Mobile, I was headed up to Tennessee. On the road I was weighed down with a hard truth. I couldn't get away from the needle and the spoon. All the constant chaos and self-destruction was hard on me. It was turning me into somebody I wasn't, somebody I didn't even know. People that aren't addicts will never understand the level of shit we go through. I mean, the road

258

for an addict is dark as hell wading neck deep through the never-ending thinking, all the misery and hell. I felt so damn hopeless. My mind wouldn't shut up. Always thinking of ways to get high. I hated that.

The hard times we deal with strung out on dope are like high walls for a reason. In the midst of all that, at this time in my life, here I am still running from myself and I don't see that deep shit. I don't realize this is God's way of preparing me for a real and deeper purpose. It's like a training session that, at the time, I wanted no part of. At the time we don't even realize it, but, these situations prepare us for the process of spiritual clarity, that plateau of deeper understanding and that hard-earned wisdom that lingers out there, beyond our own knowing. So, being where I was in life, like I said, I ran from all that. I didn't stop and think about the fact that DEATH was one shot of dope away at every turn. Hard-earned wisdom only comes to those who survive to embrace and share it.

But, there again, we have to accept a truth about our own selves. The road out there can get real dark on the way to a pathway lit with light. All we can do is pray there's some sense of purpose that'll eventually start making some kind of sense. Something that'll feed the soul. It's those hard times that steer us to the mountaintop of enlightenment. There are some beautiful possibilities when one has the ability to feel humble and grateful, to feel deeply thankful and to appreciate the little simple things when life isn't so hard. Eventually, after enough pain, sorrow, hurt, misery and life on life's unforgiving terms, the soul finds a level of personal understanding that many never know. I know, right now, as wise as all this may sound, sometimes on our journey, there's no choice. We have to wade through a lot of frustration, anxiety and bullshit to finally get to the good stuff. We have to peel back a lot of layers. This is that place where most people give up. But, a few of us, maybe you, refuse to throw in the towel and will continue to endure all of it with a determination and drive we didn't even know we had in us.

Because of this, the voice of karma will hopefully usher in love. It'll finally invite the weary soul inside the heart of another. Makes me wonder... maybe this is what's happening here with Dawn and me. Maybe this is what's missing in my life? I don't know. But, I guess maybe, I'll find out one of these days. I know I'm open for it. Maybe then, I'll feel more like I have some sense of purpose in my life.

Imagine a life with no wisdom to feel the need for purpose. Think about that. Here's what I come up with. Without the gift of purpose, life would be like a crippled bird found out in the cold, starving, no food, with broken wings. There'd be nowhere to fly and even less reason to go there. A crippled bird trapped on cold, barren land, sitting in a black-hole, starving. That's what hopeless feels like.

Back to the story...

I felt it was time to head to my mothers and clean up for a while. It was time to regroup. I felt lower than a cockroach, like walking death. I rode on over to my Mom's and sisters. They lived in Tennessee. I spent some much-needed time with my mom, letting her remind me of all the country cooking I'd been missing. Tullahoma was still Tullahoma. A much older Mount Olive Baptist church still stood on a hill off Rock Creek Road. Rutledge Falls was still a piece of heaven and I was still a coke addict. I was still fighting the insanity of it all. Rutledge falls is no more than 2 minutes from my mother's country home. The whole area is surrounded by beautiful lakes.

When I first got into town and rode to my mother's home, I no sooner got off my bike and my mom and sister, Markie, met me at the front door. We all hugged and went on in the house. We were sitting back talking about friends and family from around Tullahoma. My sister, Markie, all of a sudden, ran over to an end table and got out a notebook pad.

"Stormy, I got a message for you. Well, a bunch of them, actually. All from the same woman. Somebody named Dawn. Do you know somebody named Dawn?"

I just smiled. "I do. I do know somebody named Dawn. She's been on my mind."

I told them about how Dawn and I met. Then, I called the number she'd given my sister. The phone went to voice-mail, so, I left her a message. I was bummed. I really wanted to talk to her. I was road-weary and settling in sounded pretty good. I needed to make a home somewhere. About five minutes after I'd left her a message, the phone rang.

I answered it and it was Dawn. Immediately, we both felt IT. I guess we probably talked about two hours or so.

260

By the time I got off the phone, I had her address, where she worked and I realized this woman was as crazy about me as I was for her. She lived in Phoenix, Arizona and was a dancer at the Bourbon Street Circus on Thomas Road, near Indian School and 32nd Street. I stayed in Tullahoma for three days, getting rested up and spending time with my mother and kin-folk. The fourth morning I rolled out early, headed for Phoenix, Arizona.

Four days later, I rolled up to Dawn's apartment. She lived in a furnished weekly. They were cheap and easy to maintain. A lot of the strippers lived in those. They tend to move around a lot to the different clubs and it's easy in and easy out. It was about noon when I pulled in. She wasn't home, so, I headed over to the Bourbon Street Circus. That wasn't too far from her apartment.

When I walked in, I was tired from the road and I must've looked like warmed-over death. The place was busy, considering it was the middle of the day. I didn't see Dawn when I walked in, so, I grabbed a table next to a back-wall and ordered a drink. I guess I sat there about a half an hour and sipped my drink. Three or four strippers strolled by hitting on me for table dances, but, I wasn't interested. I had one thing on my mind. I started thinking, maybe, she wasn't there. I figured I'd drink this drink, go to the john and leave. I'd rent a room, shower and rest and then find her. So, I finished my drink, went to the john and when I walked out to leave, I was met coming out of the john by Dawn. She looked so good to me. After drinking her in, the next thing I noticed was the turquoise and silver ring she was wearing on a chain around her neck.

"Damn, that looked sexy around her neck". I thought.

We wrapped ourselves around each other and sat down at a table. Her eyes felt like moonlight washing through me on a warm summer day.

"I've missed you. It's been over a year. I thought you forgot about me."

"Forgot you? No! How could I ever? I've missed you just as much. I just had to do some stuff. Hey, I've been here a while. I didn't see you."

"Oh, I was in the dressing room changing outfits, make-up, that stuff." We smiled at one another as our eyes made love. I moved over to the seat next to her. I couldn't help it. I wanted to touch her, be near her and kiss her, everything. She leaned in closer and said,

"I'm going to take the rest of the night off. Let's go."

Later that night...

We spent the next few hours in a Mexican restaurant in Scottsdale having dinner and drinks. We lost track of time. If this woman was a magnet, I was definitely steel. After a few hours, we went for a ride in the long winding roads in the desert. One of the best feelings in the world, to me, was her body close to mine on my Harley. I could feel her pressing against me as the wind blew across my face. Her arms and legs wrapped around me had me spellbound.   Later that night, we ended up at her place, laid in bed and talked for the longest time. Wrapped together, we passed out. Dawn and I lived together for seven months. For that entire time, life was like a dream. When I looked in her eyes, it made everything okay. We were a great team. I don't know what the formula is for perfect love, but, I think we got real close to it. We had friends from the club and the Salt River would find us all tubing together, often, or, swimming in our friend's pools, or, our pool at the apartment. It was almost a daily thing.

If I had to gage how my life was with this woman, I'd have to say amazing. We'd go on the longest rides together, rolling out to the desert at sunset, making love on the sand, or, a big rock scattered among the flowering cactus. It was heavenly. Everywhere we went, everything we did, I'd take pictures, or, she would. This was before camera phones, so, I bought her a nice camera and she loved photography. We both got into it.

We were taking the best pictures ever. Once, we went up to the top of South Mountain and walked out under the stars. We got completely naked and made beautiful love on top of the mountain. It seemed like we could reach up and touch the stars. When we made love, it felt spiritual. She was a sweetheart. The entire time we lived together, I never once did coke. I never shot anything. Dawn was better than any dope I'd ever done. In my heart of hearts, I thought maybe we'd marry, have children and grow old together.

Then, after about six months, we met a guy named Bob through a stripper friend named Shelly, from the club. Bob rented a weekly down from us and we'd party with him and Shelly, quite often. We went tubing together a few times.

I even hung out at the club with him a few times when the women were working. But, I never considered him a friend. He was an acquaintance. I'm very perceptive and I saw how he looked at my woman sometimes. I didn't like it, but, I was trying to be cool. Not be psycho about it. I mean she was a stripper. Everybody would stare at her. It's part of the business. Thing was, this Bob dude was from Jersey and people from Jersey got this attitude that doesn't usually work with me. It's a rare thing if it does. We actually knew Shelly better from Dawn working with her. One day we were sitting at the pool at our apartment, just sunbathing.

This dude, Bob, comes out to us and says to us both, "Hey, you guys, Shelly and I broke up, so, I lost my transportation. Dawn, would you give me a ride to the gas station to get some cigarettes?" Because I didn't really trust this dude and he was from Jersey, I say, "I need to pick up a few things, anyway, so, let's all go. Dawn nods in agreement and we go to the gas station. On the way there, I notice him make a few coy remarks to my girl, which struck me the wrong way, and it red-flagged him to me even more.

When we got back to the apartments, I pulled this dude off to the side and I tell him, nicely, "Look, my man, Dawns my woman, so, you need to get your rides from somewhere else. Other than that, everything's cool, far as I'm concerned."
He just looks at me and says, off-handedly, "Sure, man, whatever you say."

Quite honestly, I didn't like his tone, so, I decided to talk with Dawn about this dude and cut into his little clever ploy. I mean, he wasn't with Shelly anymore, so, we need to back away from him. He was a player. Bottom line, he needed to find him another stripper and leave my woman alone. This was my feeling on this. That night I did talk with Dawn and she agreed. Our plan was to just back away from him and do our own thing, like we liked to do. For a few days, that was working great.

So, it was about three days later, and I'd rode my Harley over to a friends to cop some weed for Dawn and I. As I pull up to our apartment, after I copped, here comes my woman pulling in the parking lot with this dude in her car.

She gets out and tells me, "Don't be mad, honey, he needed cigarettes, so, I ran him to the gas station. No big deal. " She then walks toward our apartment.

I'm like, "Sure, baby, it's all good." Trust me, inside my head, it wasn't all good. I was pissed.

But, I was pissed at the dude, because he knew Dawn was kind and helpful by nature. It was clear to me he was taking advantage of her good nature. He also knew my feeling on the subject and made his play, anyway. That's disrespectful to me. Not cool with me at all. Down-right personal, really. But, I'm trying to be cool and just looking at him, as he slowly leaves the car and shuts the door.

Dawn was just opening our front door to walk in. So, I thought my timing was perfect. He was standing by the car, lighting a cigarette, giving me this smug look out the side of his face. I'm thinking, "This dude doesn't know me, but, he's about to."

At the same time, I see Dawn open our door to step in the crib. So, at that moment, with one hand, I snatch him by the neck and with the other hand, I pull my blade out of its sheath. It all happened in the blink of an eye. I bend him back across the car hood and put the knife to his throat. "Dude, you're crossing lines.

That's my woman. Don't even think about it. I'll pour honey on your dead carcass and bury you in the desert in a shallow grave. Let the coyotes eat you. You got that? I'll cut your throat, man!" I had the blade cutting into his throat. I was pushing it pretty hard against his skin. Blood was trickling down his neck.

"Okay! Okay man! I got it, I got it. It was just cigarettes, that's all, I swear."

"I don't give a shit. You better check yourself or I will. I ain't playing. Stay away from my woman. You got that?"

I'm piercing his inner-being with my eyes. I wanted to fry his brain. Felt like it did.

Then, just as quickly, I let him go and he shook it off for a minute, looked at me a second, decided against making a stupid move and then, he darted to his crib. We never saw him the rest of the day. I went in the apartment and everything was good. Dawn didn't work that night, so, we went out to eat and had a great night. We rode the bike for a couple of hours, watched the sunset in the desert,

264

then, went home, watched a movie together and, right before bed, we made love and crashed.

The next morning, the bright desert sunlight coming through the window, woke me. Dawn was already up, so, I figured she was in the shower. I laid there a minute and then, walked out into the kitchen. No Dawn. "Where you at, baby?" No reply.

Then, I walked into the bathroom. No Dawn. I walked out to the front yard and her car was gone. This was before cell phones, so, I couldn't call her. All we had was the land-line. So, I walk over to the land-line to call around to her girlfriends and see where the hell she was. That's when I saw it. The note. It was laying on the end-table by the phone.

"Stormy, Hey, It kills me to do this. Yesterday you scared me. I saw you put the knife to his throat. I thought about it all night. I'm gone. I didn't know what else to do. I took the camera. I know it has all our pictures in it. I'll always cherish them. I'm sorry. I'll never forget you. Dawn."

This hurt. She had my heart. I laid the note on the table and went to the closet where we kept the camera. Yep, it was gone, like she said. This was hard. Of course, I called all her friends and they all told me the same thing. She loves me, but, I scared her. That tore me up. The dude I threatened let another stripper move in with him, about a week later and we never spoke again. The owner of the strip club, Rob, told me, she called and said she was going back to South Dakota, or, maybe Miami. She knew I'd get that message. I was literally devastated. Our apartment was paid for, for the month, so, I stayed there while I searched for her, praying she would just show back up some night and surprise me. She never did. I still have her car tag memorized all these years later. FAE 5--. I still think about her. Her little brown car still runs through my mind.

But, she is no more, except in my memories. She visits me from time to time while I'm dreaming. I've googled her name, searched for her online in every way I can. She disappeared. I even wrote her a book once. It was a fifty-something page poem, titled, "Dawn". She'd read parts of that poem about every night before bed. Dawn was so sweet to me. I still wonder where she went. I wonder, to this day, if she's still alive. I pray her life has been amazing.

I left Phoenix after a few years of digging myself into a big black hole. I ended up trading my Harley for a bag of cocaine. Who does that? Me. It was my last meaningful possession. I sat at this dope dealer's house, shot all the coke and then, with the cocaine blues ripping my mind apart, I watched this dude ride off on my Harley. The same bike I'd spent so much money on, chroming it out and other extras. The same bike I'd poured my heart and soul into and put a lot of good miles on many times. Gone. Foxy was now his motorcycle.

This is a classic example of an addict in active addiction. I would never do such insane behavior, living clean. NEVER! This bit of insanity scarred me deeply. Then, as I wallowed in the reality of all this, trying desperately to accept the pain of actually giving my bike away for one sorry-ass night of shooting cocaine, I spiraled straight downward. I was homeless and felt like I deserved it. I was empty inside and hopeless, yet again. Night after night, I was walking around lost, sleeping wherever I could and eating whatever I could find in dumpsters behind restaurants. I'd steal food from supermarkets to survive and sleep on card-board behind dumpsters that were behind those same supermarkets. Life was a real struggle. It was no life at all, really. I don't know how I kept going. My self-esteem was in the toilet. I was still on the hustle to cop dope to shoot, too. I'd boost small tools from places like Walmart and then return them for cash. That money went straight to the dope man. I was in a big supermarket one day, on Indian School in Phoenix, actually boosting a pack of ham and drinking a chocolate milk, while I walked around. I met a beautiful Korean dancer named Melee. We talked briefly. She was a cool lady to be talking to a homeless and obviously dirty dude in a store pillaging for food. I guess she must've saw a spark of something in me. We clicked and I ended up moving in with her. She worked at the Bourbon Street Circus like Dawn had. We grew really close. It gave me a chance to gain some of my self-esteem back. It felt good to be able to shower every day once again. Melee helped me buy a few threads. I actually started looking rather classy for an imperfect chameleon. Life was just getting into a routine and you have to know what happened next. We lived together for a little over three months. She caught me shooting coke when she came home early from work one night. So, on the way out, I convinced Melee to buy me a bus ticket to Peoria, Illinois, so, I could supposedly clean up where my people were. I felt empty inside.

266

~We can never be what we want to be... if we continue to be what we are~

PURPOSE

How do you describe the feeling of empty inside to someone that's been blessed and never experienced it? I would say it's how you feel right after you lose someone you love with all your heart. A feeling so horrible it makes you tremble. But, in this case, the person you lose is you.

It's sad how many beautiful people we do lose along the way. Think about it. When we're younger, it doesn't occur to us that if it's God's plan to allow us to survive for a long time, most of the people we associate with for several years, many of them will go away and not by choice. They'll move, they'll die, get murdered, overdose on drugs and die in car and bike wrecks. There are so many countless other ways as well.

Along the way, slowly and surely, the faces and names will change. I've experienced that phenomenon in my life several times, through the years and all over the country. Everyone I knew in my teen years are all but gone. Twenty's, thirty's, forties and fifties are the same. Entire groups of people I would associate with, befriend and get close to have all disappeared. Imagine the depth of loss I feel now that I finally have clarity and can feel things. I didn't feel anything for many years, except emptiness and periods of chaos.

With time, I've learned to keep my circle smaller, so, it doesn't hurt so bad to constantly lose someone close. What many of us never think about is how everything is supposed to happen the way it happens. Things we don't expect to happen. Many times, it's a tragedy, or, horrific, and we don't think we'll be able to survive the loss. Losing a son, daughter, husband, wife, mother, father, sister or brother is an entirely different level of sorrow.

We manage to survive some things because that's the only choice. There's no other option. Have you ever really stopped and thought about that? At some time in all our lives, we have to deal with a traumatic or horrible event or situation. "It's too much. I can't do this. There's too much pain." Immediately, after all those thoughts flow through our heads and we're way past traumatized, we, somehow, reach deeper inside our psyche than we've ever been before. It's unexplored territory. But, none the less, here we are. We arrive at this deep, unknown stored and reserved supply of inner-strength that's been, conveniently, tucked away. We didn't even know this inner-strength even existed inside us. It's a paradoxical mystery. It's a mysterious and baffling part of our hedonic calculus that's never appeared before. It's right there inside our thinking, inside our hearts and souls pushed way down beneath the surface. Here's why it appears. The event or the situation is just too much. It's too much for your normal self to grab on to. It's too much when you reach and search within the parameters of your normal ability to deal with things. But, here it is, this heavy shit, whatever it may be in your world that flipped everything upside down! It could be a loved one overdosing on drugs and dying, maybe a fatal car crash, a death by heart attack, someone close dying of cancer, there are so many things it could be. This shit will break you down and make you tremble from the sorrow like you've never experienced. It is too much to handle. So, you reach deep. See, here's the thing, we have to survive to be able to move on in life. You can't go numb and tread water for the rest of your life and stay in the same place. You can only shut down, sit and stare out a window for so long before it controls your entire existence.

Things will knock us down at times, hard and it'll hurt beyond our ability to understand. I trembled in profound sorrow when Raina, my third wife, and I, lost our son, Elijah Blu. My body shook with more hurt than I've ever known. It was catastrophic. This was our son and he died right after he looked deeply into my eyes. I can still see his eyes looking into mine, inside my head. It fills me with such shame because when Raina rushed to the hospital because she'd started bleeding, she was alone in Denver, Colorado. She couldn't find me. You know why? Because I was sitting in a crack house smoking crack. I was spending all the money that I'd worked my ass off, all week, for, to pay our bills. I was an addict in active addiction in the midst of what should've been one of the happiest times of my life. It became one of the worst. Once again, my poor choices and drugs took my happiness. Addiction took my happiness.

It was January 20th, 1994. This was a profoundly traumatic circumstance like I'm talking about. After my son was born, I held him and was so filled with paramount joy, counting his toes, fingers and looking inside his big blue eyes that were looking right back at me. I was feeling so proud! He had a full head of black hair and this little guy looked just like me. The nurse had cleaned him off and handed him to me. A few minutes of holding him and I was feeling so happy, then, suddenly, he started struggling for air, so, I handed him back to the nurse. She rushed over, laid him down and yelled for the Doctor. Then, we started panicking when code blue was called out. Our son's lungs hadn't developed enough. Raina had lost amniotic fluid during the latter part of the pregnancy. We lost him. My body shook from more grief than I'd ever known.

I had no control over what happened. I was mad at God for taking our son. That didn't help. I couldn't help it and I couldn't handle it. This was too much. So, I had no other choice. I had to endure a lot of pain and hurt before I could even think about accepting this loss. This was my son. This was our son. In time, we were left with the guilt and pain of losing him. I blamed myself. I should've taken better care of Raina. We should've visited the doctor more. Should 'a, could 'a, would 'a! I lost it. So did Raina. I had to finally accept that God's will must be done. We create our own karma. It hasn't been easy. I've carried this pain and hurt for way too long. So has Raina.

The nurse had let me hold him to say goodbye after he passed. They had to pry him out of my hands. He had turned blue, purple and then black while I was holding him, because he was gone. My world changed in the blink of an eye. I'd never felt that depth of hurt before or since. Eventually, I had no choice in the matter. I had to accept it. It was the hardest thing I ever did. We're forced to eventually accept great loss. We reach for and find inner-strength that we didn't have before. Why? Because we have to in order to move forward. We do what we have to do when we have no other choice but to do it. It's the only possible way we can ever hope to move forward and begin to attempt to heal.

Horrible things like losing someone may very well happen to teach us lessons. Some people we meet are only with us for a short time for a specific reason that we're not even cognizant of. When they complete their mission, without even realizing they had a mission, they are taken from us. Maybe they have a higher calling we don't know about in this life.

If I'd only known these things when I was younger, I'd have held so many of my friends closer. I would've taken more pictures with people I loved. Thousands more. I would've shared my feelings more often with people that really mattered to me. Most of whom are dead and gone now. So many things and situations, I would've handled differently. Hindsight really is twenty-twenty. But, for many of you, this doesn't have to be hind-sight. Never forget as you proceed in life, to hold those you love like it's the last time.

One day it will be.

Chapter 15

ROAD RASH

Mid-nineties...

Throughout the years we've all lost friends and family to the drug life. Anymore it's an epidemic and one of the main reasons I felt the need to write this book. I've lost friends and family from all walks of life. Many of those losses were biker brothers and sisters. I've lost track of the number of funerals I've gone to, biker or not. I've owned and ridden a Harley since 1977, so, it's a huge loss to me when I hear about another biker brother or sister dying. There's one thing I've found that's always been able to clear my head, even if it's for just a little while. You already know, it's hitting the road on my Harley and heading into the wind.

Taking off with my bike-bags filled with things to make the ride better, along the way, and then getting in the wind. I'm talking about with no destination in mind, no route planned, not a care in the world. Just riding out into the wild blue yonder like some maverick dreamer piercing through time on a ray of streaming light! What could be better than just leaving all the bullshit, all the headaches, all the addicts, the pain, the misery and all the grief behind and putting the rubber to the road?

I'll tell you, though, stuff happens out there, I can't even make it up. The kind of shit those big action movies are made of. But, see, those big Hollywood writers make most of that shit up. Then, we see it on the big screen. Seems us bikers have a way of waking up every now and then on the edge of some wacko dream, or, the darker side of a Harvest Moon with nary a notion of what's about to unfold.

Sometimes I wake up and all I can do is shake my head. This is one of those times.

I'd been on the road for about two weeks...

Several hours of black pavement at 80 miles an hour was like a trip through heaven, but, I was beat. The lights of Denver were spread along the dark and distant horizon. My Fat boy was running well, but, it needed a well-deserved break. The ol' bones were vibrating and my ass was numb from the long ride. I'd lost all the feeling in my face from the icy chill in the Colorado wind. It was time for a break and a good meal.

Just on the outskirts, somewhere in Lakewood, Colorado, I decided to pull it in for the night. After all, I was a basket case. Well, this flashing bar sign just off the highway, coaxed me in with its "Bikers Welcome" and "Hot Food". So, I pulled in, got off my bike, locked her down and stretched for a minute. Then, I headed in. As my eyes soaked up the place, I could see a little sexy mama sitting at the end of the bar doing a quick glance at me. She was dressed like a gypsy with all this wild jewelry, cool necklaces and she had on a bunch of really unique rings on all her fingers. I dug that. Plus, she was inked up nice. I love the wild look on a hot woman. I love that look, especially, when she's a little, sexy, mama giving me a look. I'm a pretty good reader and it appeared to me, as I surveyed her eyes and energy…it appeared to me, that this little piece of sweetness might just be on the menu. At least she was on the menu I was holding. So, I sat on a stool next to her like we were old friends. She didn't seem to mind. Her big brown eyes smiled at me and made me tingle just a bit. I could feel the blood rushing back into different parts of my body. She could've lit up Cripple Creek.

There were a few other bikers drinking at the bar and other than that, the place was empty. She said her name was Lizzy. Lizzy was cool, it seemed like. We got to chatting about life, love and all that deep shit. A deeper soul wouldn't dare wander through. Well, maybe they would. I told her I'd just came out of a divorce and was looking to spread my wings and fly for a bit. That seemed to light her candle, so, we used that flickering possibility to talk into the night. We celebrated my divorce with some shots of Tequila and then we celebrated her leaving her old man and starting' her life over.

"Cool," I thought.

We're both single and after four or five of those Tequilas, I swear, she started looking like an Egyptian beauty. I love Egyptian beauties. Over a burger and some fries and after some long conversation, she whispered, "You going to give me a ride on that Harley?"

272

"What do you think?"

That worked for me. I was tired and with my renewed energy from the Tequila I was ready for anything. Plus, with her Egyptian look going on, I'm into that anyway. As we're talking, I'm checking out all her ink and jewelry. I couldn't help it. I was really high. She had some multi-colored, long, wild hair sticking out of this black and gold trimmed scarf and her eyes were big, dark and mysterious. They had a wicked vibe about them. By then, we'd both moved closer to one another for whatever. I was drunk and worn out from the road, so, I didn't give a shit about anything right then.

Here's where I have to ask you an unorthodox, particularly unique question. Have you ever just been floating through life, headed down the road and things appear to be just clicking along. Smooth, casual, care-free... Then, you do one simple little thing and that one simple little thing leads to another simple little thing and then, sure enough, you've started a series of simple little things, events, we'll call them, unknowingly, and these events are really going to affect your life in a major way. Now, this could be a great, fantastic, amazing, major way and then again, this could be an, 'Oh shit, what in the hell have I done, major way.' Well, the reason I asked is because I have often times through life, thought I probably shouldn't have ever walked in that bar, that night and sat down next to Lizzy. Looking back, I don't think I should've started up a conversation with that particular woman and I definitely shouldn't have went home with that particular woman. NOT THAT PARTICULAR WOMAN. As we get further into this, I'd love to be a fly on the wall and listen to your thoughts about it. Anyway...

So, we close the bar.

Turns out, but, of course, she works there. She's the damn bar manager. When we met, she'd just got off work and was having her after-work, "I'm unwinding", drink. Of course, that turned into our after-work mini-party for, at least a good couple of hours. After she locked it all up and put the bar's money in a safe, we hopped on my Harley and headed to her place. When we got there, we walked into quite an exotic little creative spot. Her home was tripped out with very creative ambience and I loved it. She was clever, this one! She let me shower and when I came out with just a big towel around me, she had a bowl of hot homemade soup on the table and some crackers. I ate while she showered. Delicious!

After about fifteen or twenty minutes, she came out of that shower with this little white robe wrapped around her. She looked beautiful. But, that didn't mess me up anything like the joint we smoked. The doobie was fire. She said it was from Humboldt County. (That's in Cali). Then, she lined out some coke rails. Long ones! All that dope and tequila made me want to do dirty, nasty things to her little body, especially with her big eyes zeroed in.

Her hands caressed me up and down my legs. I was tired from the road and after smoking that weed, I laid back on the couch. Next thing I know, Lizzy sat down next to me and she's pushing my towel to the side.

I just kind of looked at her.

Lizzy took her time. I liked it so much I started speaking in tongues. You know what I mean.

We fell asleep together on the couch.

A few hours later, about the crack of dawn, there's a loud knock at her door.

That woke both of us up. As she's putting her clothes on, she tells me to go lay down in the bedroom. She'll get rid of whoever it is and join me in there.

"Okay. That sounds good to me. I could use a quickie before I pass out again." I said to her just under my breath. She looked at me real quick, "You might get one, too."

Then, she adds, "It's probably my ex at the door. No worries. I'll get rid of him."

"Great! What did you just say? Your ex? Really? Did I just hear that right? Your ex?"

I'm still woozy from the Tequila and I'm betting she was, too.

But, what the hell! "Her ex? What the hell?"

Now, I'm in the middle of some bullshit. All I wanted was a sweet piece of pie and a quick goodbye. Sometimes shit just doesn't work out like you planned! Okay, okay. So, I'm trying to be cool about it. I go in the bedroom, like she asked, and I hear them out there in the front room arguing, but, I'm hanging by her bed like a good man. I'm in a strange place here. I don't know anybody in these parts, so, this was, let's just say...awkward. Then, I hear a couple of dude's voices.

Yes, I said, now I hear a couple of dudes voices talking!

"Oh shit! This ain't cool" Now, I feel my adrenalin shoot skyward. So, I grab my clothes and get dressed in the blink of an eye. I'm an

274

ex-convict, remember. I've seen some wild and crazy-ass shit in my day, so, this shit put me on RED ALERT! Running through my mind is number one... How do I get out of this shit and NOT go back to prison? Things ex-cons ask themselves during some bullshit! Now, I'm debating with myself.

"What the fuck do I do here? I mean, I don't even know her and I sure don't know these dudes out in the front room arguing with her." My mind's in over-drive. But, I sit tight. My better sense of reason tells me to just sit tight for a bit. I'm praying this'll work itself out. IT DOES NOT WORK ITSELF OUT! Shit got crazy as hell! "I'm like, what the fuck? How the hell did I end up in the middle of this?"

Gunshots start going off in the front room. Bam... Bam... Bam... 1, 2, 3, shots fired! My adrenalin is straight out the top of my head! Automatically and instantly SOBER! That was me in the blink of an eye!

"OH, wait, I'm cool. I have a pistol. I have a 9mm. It's all good! Hey, wait a minute! Are you kidding me? I don't have my pistol on me. Oh shit!!"

"But, of course NOT."

This makes me want to shoot myself in the head right now. I'm pissed off at myself just thinking back about it! I mean, I have a fully-loaded 9 MM out in my bag on the bike, but, NO, not with me. It's not on my person, so, it doesn't do me any good. Makes perfect sense, right! Lol... Not really. It's a dumbass move on my part. Carry a piece, but, NOT, carry a piece! What's the point, right! I hate to even admit it. Embarrassing.

So, I start talking to myself, "here I sit in a stranger's bedroom at the crack of dawn, high as hell, pistol blazing in the next room with at least 2 dudes out there I don't know and some crazy bitch, I don't really know and I'm back here in this bedroom and I must admit, tripping on this shit! I don't even know whose shot, or, for that matter, I don't even know whose shooting who! Plus, I have a loaded pistol in my hard-bags on the bike. Great!

Am I at a murder scene? Oh shit! If he shot her, he sure won't leave a witness. This a messed up."

"How in the hell did I end up in this bedroom right now?" I asked myself quietly inside my frustrated head. I was shaking my weary head, frustrated. The things we do.

About that time, I hear screaming. I can't make any sense of it, other than everybody is pissed at everybody. Here comes sirens blaring and then two Harleys fired up and then, two Harleys were tearing away from the place in a flash. Lizzy's at the front door screaming, "Fuck you's" at her ex old man and then I heard it. He laid his bike down in some loose gravel, trying to tear out of there real fast. Next thing I hear is Lizzy screaming "Good, you bastard, I hope you got road rash all over your ass." The other dude was gone.

"Damn girl!" is all I could think of. I look through the window and there he is, getting back on his bike as fast as he could. Then, he was gone, too. She's out there waving her pistol all around in the air. She's done lost her ever-loving mind.

I'm steady talking to myself, "How in the hell did I end up in this shit?"

Lizzy comes back to the bedroom, full speed ahead.

She's out of her head, screaming, "That bastard wanted to stop by for one last fuck like that's all I was. Man that pissed me off. I tried to kill both those bastards. Did you hear him? He laid his bike down out there. Hope to God his ass is raw."

She's standing there with this pistol in her hand, waving it around, and cops are getting closer, their sirens getting louder.

"So, you missed? You didn't shoot them? That's good, right? You don't want a murder charge. Believe that. Road rash? Damn, these dudes almost got killed, he laid his bike down, and got road rash, all in the same morning. Damn! Plus, didn't get any pussy. That's what I call a bad night. I got to go! Lizzy, you're a sweetheart, yes, you are, but, baby, I got to get the fuck out of here!" That's all I could get out.

She was actually trying to get me to stay. "Bitch, you crazy. I'm tafukouttahere!!!" I'm thinking to myself.

"Oh yeah, let's sit down here, and play a game of scrabble. What? Are you out of your ever-loving mind? Hell no, I'm not staying. Hell no, I got to go! It's in the wind time! I have no time for this crazy shit. Crazy! Not right now! I have to go. Suns coming up anyway. " I put my stretched-out hand to my ear, wiggled my outstretched fingers like I had a phone in my hand, as I made my way to the door.

"I'll call you." I was in a dead run.

It was time for me to get out of there. I don't need to be explaining any shit to a shit-load of cops. My mind was working... "I'm a

276

convicted felon, I don't know you people. I'm drunk and high on cocaine! I'm not even from here. I got better shit to do. I don't want to go to jail... yada, yada, yada...blah, blah and blah, to hell with all this!"

Have you ever said your goodbyes to someone in a blinding flash, heading out the door, ya know, like, if you blink, you're going to miss me? I told her in about 30 seconds that I was an ex-con and couldn't be around firearms, especially weapons that had just been used to shoot at somebody. Especially when I, a convicted felon, have a pistol on my bike.

In under 60 seconds, I'm on the freeway and headed to Colorado Springs. Time to fly. I kept right on riding. It's too cold around these parts. I kept riding. I'm headed toward the desert out Phoenix way.

One week later... somewhere outside of Phoenix...

I was camped out next to a nice warm fire, lying on my sleeping bag, smoking a big fat doobie under a night sky full of bright stars, staring up at the big, beautiful openness. Since I had no plans for the evening beyond exactly what I was doing, I continued watching this UFO off in the distance. It would zig across the sky like a flash of light, then stop mid-air. After a few moments, it would zip again in another direction like another trail of light, then, once again, stop in mid-air. It was way off in space above me and was fascinating to watch. To know that whatever that was, it didn't come from our planet. It was doing aeronautical movements with the zipping and zapping that was other-worldly. Stopping in mid-air? I wonder what that was about. Anyway, hey, it was cool with me. Through the years, I saw a lot of UFO's. I was used to them. They were actually fun to watch on a night just like this one.

My mind got to thinking about that night. I started flashing back... "Damn! That Lizzy. Damn." I smiled. "Now, that was good. What a crazy night! She was a fine-looking woman, though. We had some fun, but, damn, I sure wouldn't want to be her ex. That bitch is a bona fide psycho." I went to sleep shaking my head, still thinking about it.

The next morning, real early, I got up, built another fire, sat back for a few minutes and had me a cup of cream and sugar with a touch of coffee in it. I paused and took in the feel of the sunrise as it slid across my body. Then, I tightened up my gear on the bike and fired it up. I let the early morning wind push all the crap away and I settled into a good ride, feeling the warmth of the breeze, as it blew across my face. I let my thoughts all race away and I got lost in the atmosphere. It was going to be a great day.

After many, many perfect miles, while the wind stroked my gypsy soul and slapped me across the face, while my Harley growled across the blacktop and it felt like heaven had poured itself all over me, I was thinking, "It's time for a lot more wide-open desert nights. I need a big dose of that spirituality, I need some more of this wind. Last night felt really good. Even spiritual. Damn, I'm glad I'm not in jail. That bitch was crazy." I thought to myself. "Good time, though, for a minute." I had a big smile plastered across my face. "I tell you, some of the shit I manage to get myself into. Just another day in the life of a rambling man with a drug problem. That could've turned out real bad real quick."

I can't tell you how many times I've thought back to that night and just shook my head. It was a crazy night. I mean, I'd been riding all day, doing my own thing and this bar and this woman just popped out of nowhere. I mean, I rolled up to the bar to get off the road for a bit, and I walked in. I never thought a thing about it. Then, all this insane shit unfolded. The way it all happened was a twilight zone, type vibe. That's what trips me out. How shit can just happen out there on the road.

Riding is my escape from the complexities of addiction. My life would get tangled up and I'd wind up like a bass-drum, chaotic and down-right miserable, but, sometimes, sometimes, even strung out, life and the ability to breathe and figure shit out would feel pretty damn good. Oh, the whole world around me would just be falling apart and shit would be crazy as hell. To me, that insanity would feel normal. Total chaos would actually feel normal. Pause and think about that. That's active addition at work.

Needless to say, I never saw or heard from Lizzy again. I guess I forgot to call. No, I didn't forget to call. I didn't call.

Anyway, here's the thing. I actually think of her from time to time. I've done a lot of soul searching about her entire trip. She was unique, that's for sure. The woman was classy in her own way. All the real nice ink and bad-ass jewelry with a hot body to boot was a turn-on to me. I love that look. It must be the freak in me. Hey, a

278

sweet treasure like her is a rare find as far as I'm concerned. How are we supposed to know a sexy, inked-up beauty can be crazy as a rabid dog? Here's what I think about all that. I don't think Lizzy wasn't crazy at all. She's, most likely, actually a good woman, I think. She was just tired of getting screwed over by asshole dudes and she decided she wasn't having it anymore.

Let's face it, a lot of dudes are pigs! Regardless, I didn't see myself wanting to settle in with a wild woman that might shoot me at the drop off a hat. She was hot fun for a minute and there's no doubt she was sexy as hell. What I'd call an erotic and exotic woman, really. But, sometimes, some things are better left alone. Besides, I'm a free spirit.

The fun pulls you in...

Telling people that life is always misery, grief, rage and pain, when you're out there in the mix is simply bullshit. Along the way, partying, meeting people, having fun and doing cool shit can leave a bunch of unforgettable memories. That's the clever and deadly allure. There's danger in it. Death happens all the time, all around you in this world. So, be aware. The drug-death epidemic is real. It's not bull-shit or some scare tactic. It's real. It should scare you anyway. It's 2020 and people are dying in record numbers all across America directly from drug overdoses.

Let me be clear about something. I want you to understand. I share these ventures with you to show how you can be having a life on a good path, just rolling along and it can be deceived and diverted in the blink of an eye, to the wrong path. What seems like innocent fun can turn into pure hell right before your eyes.

I want you to read in detail about many of my escapades. This book only skims the surface of all the places I've been and all the insanity along the way. But, I want you to see how it appears that, along the way, I would be having a lot of good times with great people and in the midst of that, without warning, active addiction slips into my world, destroys everything around me and it won't let me go. The drugs killed about everybody I ran with. They're gone forever. I, by the grace of God, have survived and I truly believe I'm doing God's work. I believe he wants me to share with you the real-life dangers of this deceitful life and I pray, give you the idea that hope is possible. I pray some of this sinks in and grabs hold of you. The absolute point of this is to show clearly how addiction can slip up on someone that's just living life. I'm telling you about these parties and good times to show you the steady decline. To show you how the allure of it all, the lifestyle, the circle of people that seems to continue to grow with awesomeness can slowly, but surely, lure you in. How the lifestyle can romance you and make you think this is exactly what you want to do. These are the best of times. Everything is beautiful! It seems like everybody loves you. Just be aware. Chaos is coming. Self-destruction is coming, too. Eventually, if you continue on a path of active addiction, I promise you all the hell will catch up with you. Your soul will slowly die right before your eyes and inside, you'll believe there won't be a damn thing you can do about it. It won't be apparent. You won't feel your inner-self dwindling, but, that's the clever web of deceit flowing through you. I mean, think about it. How can you fix something when you don't even think anything's wrong? You might have a hundred good times and parties and get completely lost in the haze of it all. Just flowing along. Feeling popular! Friends coming out of the wood work. Then, one day, out of the blue, you realize your once great health is deteriorating, your friends that you thought loved you so much are disappearing, you're starting to feel empty inside where you once felt so alive, plus, the snakes and back-stabbers are surfacing around the parties and now you have to watch out for them, too. Close friends are overdosing and dying every day, everywhere. Some of them you didn't even know were getting high. Now dead forever. The fun becomes less and less meaningful and, before you know it, even stale. More than all that, here's the real bummer these days. Every time you get high anymore, it's a crap shoot. Is this fentanyl or not? Will I survive this? Every time. One wrong time and it's another death. Another statistic. Another friend gone forever. Another great person robbed of a potentially incredible life. They're adding up fast all over the country. Right now they are!

It's 2020 and they've discovered a drug in California a hundred times more powerful than fentanyl. Really? Why? It sounds like a terrorist plot to me. Anyway, eventually, it all catches up. It does. Just be aware of that because I promise you, if you stay on a destructive path, in time, and when you least expect it, your world will fall apart. Your life will change on a dime for the worst until it finally kills you and that, my friend, lasts forever. Forever.

~<>~

Chapter 16

Looking back...

TRUTH COVERS ITS OWN PATH

1980 something...
Protect me from myself...

During my second marriage... (I'll respect her privacy) I really tried my best to stay clean. When I say that, I mean I was determined to stay away from hard drugs. We still drank and went out for dinner. But, I never saw her use any hard drugs at all. I wanted this marriage to work and I knew if I started shooting dope again, it'd be over. That would, of course, ruin, yet, another marriage. So, I stayed away from the syringe.

Life went on for us. I owned a paint business. My company painted all the Jumer Hotel properties for Mr. Jumer. There were seven hotels scattered around Illinois and Iowa. Plus, Jumer's also had a winter home in South Florida and I'd paint that, too, just so I could regroup every now and then. I had a hand-picked crew of excellent painters and Mr. Jumer kept us busy.

Being so busy all the time helped me stay away from drugs, most of the time. Like I mentioned earlier, I still got into partying from time to time.

After about 3 years, she got a job as a dealer for the Casino in Peoria. It was all new and everybody wanted to work there. I had felony convictions, so, I couldn't. After she started working there and meeting new people, our relationship changed. We grew apart. After a little over 3 years, we split up. I immediately went nuts. I found an old drug-dealing friend of mine and had him front me 10 pounds of good weed. I broke that weed down into ounces. Because I knew the dude really well from the joint, he fronted me the weed really cheap and I sold my ounces for a good street price. This meant profit to me. It also meant money to buy heroin and coke which was definitely on my mind. Like I just talked about, I moved into a house on the end of a dead-end street deep in the ghetto. I immediately started selling the weed. The only white person that lived on the street was me.

Gang-bangers lived all around me. It didn't take me more than a day and I was shooting heroin, cocaine and smoking golf-ball size crack-rocks. I dove head first into complete madness. I knew when my ex found out where I lived, she wouldn't even come down there. Of course, falling back into full-blown addiction, that was my plan. It worked, too. She came down once and it scared the hell out of her. All black thugs everywhere and me. She stayed briefly, and left, never to return. I continued to dig a black hole in my soul, deeper and deeper.

My habit took me over. In no time, I had Chicago bangers bringing their dope back from Chicago, into my house and breaking it down. There was a steady flow of drugs and money in and out of my crib. On a regular basis, I'd have a house full of gangster soldiers stopping by to pick up dope and drop off money. The shot-caller figured out real quick to keep throwing me bags of dope and big crack rocks and all would be fine. So, I let them turn my house into a dope house. I took off on my Harley for a little over a month, but, then I came back.

Mistake.

For several months, I sunk deeper and deeper into despair. Now that I look back, I cannot believe how low I sunk. I saw so many things at that house. White, black and Mexican women would stop by and trade sex for a hit of dope. They'd be treated like dogs, but, they didn't care. They were strung out. I was strung out, too, so, I'd just shake my head when I'd see them coming. Some of these women were absolutely beautiful. They'd fell victim to the grip of crack or heroin and they had to have it. These gang-bangers knew this, too. These women would do some vile shit for a hit of dope.

Thinking back, it makes me sick. For close to a year, I lived in that dope house. Like I said, I saw some rank shit happen over dope. A dude was stabbed in the living room for being short on his money. They carried him out bleeding and freaking out, to keep heat off the dope house. I never saw him again. I don't know if they killed him or what. I never asked either. He just got raked under the coals of despair... and forgotten in the midst of run-amuck addicts, chasing their daily fix.

Sometimes, it's better to NOT know shit. This is another one of those things that stuck with me.

One afternoon, this fine and I do mean super-fine, classy lady pulled up in front of my house. She stepped out of her red corvette and she was smoking hot. This woman was dressed to kill. It was obvious she was loaded with cash. I didn't know her, but, I damn sure wanted to. She came to my door, said her name was Sandy, and dropped another name I knew and trusted very well. I let her in with hopes of becoming much better acquainted. We talked for a little while and I turned her on to a 20 dollar bag of heroin. That's what she was really there for. I slid her out a line of my own on to a mirror. I wanted to see her snort the dope, first-hand. Not a problem! She did that without hesitation. Okay, she's probably not a cop. That was cool. After we nodded for a while, she stood up and said she had to go and ask me if I minded if she stopped by again. "Please do". I'm thinking. Sandy told me she was a legal-aid for an attorney. I swear this woman was so together, I was thinking I might marry her ass and grow old with her. Change my ways and all that good shit. Time passed. She became a regular, dropping by almost daily for her bag of dope. A lot of times, she just grabbed her bag and left, but, she always made sure and got her 20 dollar bag. Through the next few months, I watched this woman deteriorate in front of my own eyes.   She spiraled straight down into being a full-fledged junkie. Her little bag grew into a fifty dollar bag, then, 10 bags for the price of 8, then, a hundred dollar bag. She eventually got very strung out. It got bad for her. She lost her corvette and then, she'd stop by in an old Chevy. It was nice, but, it damn sure wasn't that corvette. Of course, I was strung out, too, so, it was just a part of everyday life. We all spiraled down and the chaos and self-destruction seemed normal. I was okay with that and then, one day, my dope connect was there from   Chicago, dropping me a load of dope to sell. Sandy dropped by to get her bag. I was trying to be cool because I didn't want her to know my connection. My intent was to give her a hundred dollar bag, get her money and send her on her way. Dude saw she was strung out real bad and saw she was fine underneath her addiction. What happened next I still think about sometimes?

284

There was three other junkies and myself in the room at the time. We were all shooting up. My connection asked me if I minded if he worked a deal with her so she could get high. I thought "Sure, why not?" He looks over at her and says, "If you'll strip right now, I'll give you this 100 dollar bag of heroin." He held up the bag of dope and waved it back and forth in her face. She was a junkie with a big habit and came from pure class. But, when she was chasing that heroin high, none of that shit mattered. So, she undressed in front of all of us.

After she took all her clothes off, she was desperate for that bag of dope. I felt bad for her, but, I was caught up in the shit, too. Then, the dude said, "Now, for real, you have to give me a blow job. Then, I swear, I'll really give you the dope." She didn't even argue. She unzipped him and gave him a blowjob. He was a nasty dude, too. Filthy looking. But, none of that mattered to her right then. All that mattered to her was that she got that bag of dope in her arm. Yes, she shot over half the bag in one hit. I saw that woman shoot dope about every day and, it really didn't matter to her what she had to do to get the dope.

I watched her go from a gorgeous and very classy lady with a great job and a boss-ass car, to a nasty, street-tramp junkie with nothing, not even her self-respect. It's sickening for me to think back to that, now. She's exactly the people I put my heart and soul into helping now. But, that's now and this was then. I'm enraged at myself for allowing her to destroy herself like that. She was so together. I only helped her in her madness to keep spiraling downward. I pray for forgiveness for letting something like this hell, happen in my home. Anyway, after he got off, he threw her the bag of dope and within a minute, she had cooked it down in a spoon and she was shooting that Mexican Brown in her arm. I was so strung out at the time, this all seemed normal to me. Think about that. This is all existing at the animal level type shit, but, at the time, it seemed perfectly normal. I heard about a year after this happened, she overdosed and died in a cheap motel turning a trick.

The saddest part of this is... this is just one account of insane shit that happened in that dope house. This type of shit happened all the time. People dropping by willing to trade their soul for just one more hit. Of course, as an addict, I know, there's no such thing as just one more hit. That's a fallacy. It's not possible. Narcotics Anonymous says it best... One is too many and a thousand's never enough. For an addict, this statement couldn't be truer.

So, after about a year of this, I was deep in the shit. It started affecting my psyche. I started getting very paranoid. I was spending most of my days staring out the windows and I was running from window to window. The dope was affecting my psyche. One day I just snapped. I knew I needed treatment and I felt like if I didn't go quickly, I would die. There's where my head went to. I just reached a place where there was no turning back. I was as deep in a hole as I could dig. I went to the Methodist Hospital ER. I told them I was strung out really bad and I needed treatment. They turned me away. They said there was nothing they could do for me.

So, I went to St. Francis. They turned me away, also. Then, I went to the Proctor Hospital ER. They also said without insurance they could do nothing for me. The treatment centers all had waiting lists and I was told I had to have good insurance to be admitted. I went back to my house. I was determined to clean up. I was truly sick and tired of being sick and tired. At my house, I was going through withdrawals really bad. I was miserable.

Looking back, I can understand why the hospital wouldn't accept me to clean me up. For quite some time, I'd played most of the doctors in town at one time or another. I always had something wrong, my back hurt, my foot sprained or my shoulder hurt.
Anything that I could dream up to get pain pills.

So, they turned me away. Withdrawals were killing me. One of the gangbangers came to my door. I could barely walk to get to the door. I cracked it opened and he said he had quarter bags of heroin for twenty bucks. He said he heard I was sick. I bought one real quick to take the sick away. It did help. But, I knew in a few hours, I'd start getting sick again. I had ran out of options. I didn't know what the hell I was going to do. I just knew I wanted desperately to get clean. I was tired of this shit. Just all of it. The gangbangers doing a lot of business in my house, the junkies laying everywhere. People stopping by for dope at all hours of the night. I never knew who might show up at my house. It was all making me crazy.

I was sitting on my couch, high just a little from the dope, but, not much. My habit was way bigger than a 20 dollar bag. I needed a hundred dollar bag to nod. I was desperate. Then, it hit me. There was one last thing I could do to clean up. So, I got in my truck and I

drove to my sister, Jackie's. She lived in the Heights. When I walked in her house she knew something was really wrong. I told her. I was honest, finally. I told her I was strung out really bad and if I didn't clean up, it was going to kill me. She said, "What can I do, Stormy?" I said, "Jackie, I'm going to go in your extra bedroom and I'm going to stay in there for at least a week. You have to keep the door locked. A couple times a day set me a bowl of soup and some water in the door, then, lock it back real quick. Also, no matter what I say, don't let me out of that room." She said, "you sure?" I told her, "Yes, I'm sure. Do NOT let me out of that room. I'll get very sick. I'll be throwing up in the bathroom that's connected to that bedroom.
Don't let me out. I can't get in treatment and I have to clean up, Jackie." She said, "Okay brother."

For the next 7 days, I lived in that room. Jackie would set me some chicken noodle soup in the door and then, lock it. Later, she'd get the bowl and set another bowl in there with some crackers. That's how I lived. It was pure hell, but, I did it. Every second, minute, hour and day of every day was a miserable existence. I must have drove Jackie crazy with all my screaming, gagging and puking. I went into convulsions, body-aches, my eyes were constantly wet and they wouldn't dry up. I had restless leg and nausea, plus diarrhea, God, I got sick. I was so sick! This habit had my soul in its clutches and it didn't want to let go. It took all I had in me to kick it. Thanks to my sister, Jackie's help, I kicked the heroin jones, once again. I did it. Cold turkey again. If you remember, I'd done it before in a Marine stockade overseas. I promise, it was no easier this time, either. Believe me when I tell you, heroin is a monster. It's an evil, coldblooded, sick and vile monster. It takes no names and it kills. It kills a lot, all the time. Its euphoria is very deceptive. It feels so good at first.   It lures you in like a lion stalking prey. Almost immediately you get hooked and then, your life is turned upside down.

Everything becomes about you getting high. It becomes about you not getting sick from the cravings. You'll do anything and I mean anything.

Fresh start... 1992 or so...

The Harley ride cross country really helped clear my head, until I came back. But, the help I got from my sister, Jackie, saved my life.

287

Feeling like someone with a little more hope, I loaded up my truck with my stuff and my cousin, Michael, (whom we called Sonny D) and I, headed west. We'd planned on going to California. I was just about clean and I wanted to really try a fresh start. But those demons were still there. Even as I was loading up, one of the black dudes pushing the heroin showed up at my door with bags of dope for free, he said. Nothings free! He knew I was leaving and he was trying to lure me to stay and get me back into the dope. I thought about it for a minute. Hey, I'm an addict. I did. Then, I snapped because I didn't know what else to do. I pulled out my 12 gauge sawed-off shotgun from the truck and ran him off the yard and down the street. My truck was about loaded. I left everything else. I even left my 40 ft. ladder leaning against the house. I'd carried that ladder all over the damn place for my paint business. Left it. I threw my shotgun back in the truck and rolled out. I headed west. It was a great feeling driving away from the dope, knowing I could have shot some and I didn't. That felt damn good. The sick part is this. Even though it did feel damn good to not shoot that hit before I left, inside my sick thinking was a part of me that still regretted it. I felt like I could've hit the hit and then left. Oh well, I didn't. That's how an addict thinks. Part of me wanted to quit using so desperately. Part of me couldn't. Two days later we were sitting in a Denny's in Denver, Colorado, eating breakfast. I remembered I had a past partner's phone number in my wallet from back home. One of my old shooting partners. Here's another one of those places in life that we all earmark as a pivotal moment. I'm not stupid, but, I damn sure shouldn't have called Jake up. This dude's gone, but, for the sake of helping addicts find a new way to live, I'm going to tell you about the time I stopped to eat in Denver on the way to L A. Back in 92, when I called Jake, he answered right away. "Oh Stormy, did you bring your paint business with you. Do you have your tools? A truck? Your sprayer?"

"As a matter of fact I do."

"Well, I have 3 builders giving me homes to paint around Lake Stanley. Come on out here and I'll give you a builder. I can't keep up with them. There's big, nice houses out here just sitting that need painted. Too much work. Big money! Come on out. " "Damn. I should've brought that ladder." My first thought. "Okay. Sounds great!" So, we finished up our breakfast and headed to Lake Stanley.

We meet one of the builder's moments after I pulled up. Jake was right. There was a shit-load of new homes being built around this gorgeous lake. We immediately go to work. Jake and Big Chris, another buddy of mine now living in Denver, told me half the duplex he lived in was empty. Later that day, we moved into the duplex. As it turns out, Jake is consumed in active addiction. So is Chris. The duplex we moved into next to Jake had a front porch. It was full of empty beer cans. I don't mean 10 or 20 cases of empty beer cans. I mean 2 or 3 hundred cases of empty beer cans. Jake had drank every beer. This was at the corner of Colfax and Colorado Boulevard. This is a horrible area in Denver and full of dope-heads trying to steal and sell everything they could get their hands on. I just continued my own addiction as well. I was smoking crack, shooting coke and heroin. Once again, things got a little crazy as time passed. I was seeing this hot mama named Jenny, I'd met right after I'd moved in. She turns out to be the sister of another woman, Mary, I'd met at one of these parties I went to. She was married to a friend of Jakes. They were both hot. Mind you, I've only been in Denver about 4 months when this shit happened. Well, Jake got wind that I was sleeping with his buddy's wife, Mary. I wasn't. I was sleeping with his buddy's wife's sister, Jenny. My cousin, Sonny D, was sleeping with Mary. But, we're both grown men. It really wasn't anybody's business who we were spending time with. Jake got drunk as hell one night and decided to make it his business. He came around to my side of the duplex and started banging and kicking on my front door.

It would never be wise to get in my face and add to that, the hell and bullshit from the last year. I'd just uprooted myself to get away from my addiction in Illinois and now, I'm in Denver with no real friends around. Mentally I wasn't in a good place. Well, like I said, my cousin, Michael J. was with me. His life was a mess, too, so, we hooked up to go out west together. We're family. We lived in the duplex together. Truth be known, the woman that was married to Jake's buddy, she was sick and tired of Jake and her husband out all the time, screwing around, drinking and drugging, so, that's why she hooked up with my cousin. They were getting it on, but, there again, that was their business. Not mine or anyone else's.

Anyway, it's about 2 am and Jake's beating on my door as loud as he can, screaming threatening shit through my front door. This dude knows me well enough to know better than to do some shit like that, and yet, here he is at my door at 2 am, screaming he's going to beat my ass through the door. I looked at my cousin, Sonny D. Then, I grinned and said, "This fat-ass thinks he's going to beat my ass." I opened the door and in one fluent motion, grabbed him by the back of the head with one hand and pulled my loaded 25 pistol from my back pocket and shoved it down his throat, with the other. It's not a particularly powerful weapon, but, when it's shoved down a man's throat and he's got a mouthful of metal that might more than tickle if I happen to pull the trigger. These few moments in time are somewhat surreal to me.

It's like everything went into some translucent slow motion type-shit. Jay, well, he weighed in at about 340 pounds. He was well over six feet tall and just a towering, ugly, scary-looking dude in many ways and yet, here he stood, frozen in time, suddenly, not moving an inch, in my ghetto-ass living room with my pistol shoved down his throat.

Jake and I had a long history of drug-deals and wild times. We started out as friends when I first got out of the joint, many moons back. We shot dope together and he knew I was partnered up with some of my old prison crew, all killers. We'd been whooping dudes asses on the regular in downtown Peoria and flying out to other cities, collecting drug debts and the like, years before Denver. He also knew I was collecting money for some real unsavory characters. Years before this, I flew to Chicago to cop a quarter-pound of Mexican brown heroin from Jake. I did cop, but, I found out later, he'd fixed me a kill shot when I showed up to cop, hoping I'd overdose so he could rob me. I was told this by a reliable source. So, when he rolled up in my crib blowing shit out of his mouth, I was already holding some serious resentments against him, anyway. Now here we are at 2 am on a Friday night, my pistol crushing against his larynx, as he suddenly reversed his power surge and began to run backwards back out my front door.

Now, I was doing the threatening and he was walking backwards fast as he possibly could toward his own front door. In my mind, I really wanted to pull that trigger and plant a slug in his brain. But, that voice of reason kept pulling at my coat-tail, whispering in my ear, "Better not. Don't do it. Life in prison. Remember prison. You don't want to go back, right?" Reason man. Jake ran back into his own crib and locked his front door to keep the big, bad wolf out. Me.

That was a smart move on his part. In my chameleon phase for many years, while still shooting dope every chance I got, I still studied Tae Kwon Do and I stayed stretched out. I wasn't done with Jake. He'd pissed me off. I mean I was borderline homeless, so, I was unhappy, anyway. I'm a nice guy. I think I am. I've been around some not nice guys and I'm a lot nicer than them. I'm just speaking from personal experience here.

Literally, for the rest of that night, here's what I did. There was this big tree in Jakes front yard, just outside his front picture window, I stood next to that tree till daylight kicking side-kicks and jump reverse side kicks into the trunk of that big tree. I beat that trees ass! It was right outside his window and the entire time, I was yelling for Jake to bring his big ass outside for a genuine Southern style ass-whooping. As crazy as he was, he knew better. He saw me beat the hell out of a slew of assholes at Sgt. Pepper's biker bar, when I first came home from prison.

Anyway, Big Chris M rolled up in his van about 6 am to pick the dude up for work. I loved Chris like a brother. He was one of my old shooting buddies, too. He was also another brother that died shooting dope. At about 6'7", he was like a big teddy-bear, a gentle giant. He rolled his window down and very respectfully pleaded with me to just let it go. He said, brother, we have to go to work. Just forget all this shit and let Jake go to work.

I was spitting venom. I was pissed, even after kicking the shit out of a big tree for about 3 hours. Being a nice guy and being good friends with Chris, I backed up and gave Jake space, so, he could go to work. He came out and walked quickly to the van. We just stared at each other. "To hell with him." I thought. I went to bed and crashed. Later that day, I woke up and my cousin, Sonny D, was sitting in the kitchen. We talked about it. I told him I didn't trust Jake. He's a sneaky, conniving bastard and he's the kind of guy that would roll up with a half-a-dozen friends, if he didn't think he could handle it himself. This was that situation, in my thinking. He lives over there with a couple of his brothers and he's got that partner whose wife you're spending time with. I looked over at my cousin and he nodded in agreement. "We're going to slide out of here and get a weekly across town. We didn't know anybody else in town and I ain't stupid. It was time to regroup and get away from Jake." So, we loaded my truck with the little bit of shit we had and moved over to the other side of town, into a weekly.

A few days later, we had the sisters come by so we could party. Using deduction, I bet you can figure out what happened from there. We stayed out all night with them, partying. When they left the next morning, they swore they'd keep it a secret where we lived, so, we could move past that bullshit.

Well, the hot-mama that Michael was doing, went home to her pissed-off husband. He and Jake kept pushing her till she finally gave up where we were. I saw this shit coming a mile away. I told my cousin this shit was going to happen. Jake couldn't mind his own business. So, later the next night, I told my cousin, Jake would pull all his dick-wads together and probably try to jump us.

To hell with it! We could've left and got another weekly somewhere else. We knew that and we talked about it. We agreed if they jumped us, we'd be forced to deal with whatever. I ain't running' from shit. Never! That night, we both stayed on high alert waiting for some shit to happen. It didn't.

My cousin, whose 13 years younger than me, said, "Well, looks like everything's kool."

"No. Hell no, my blood, nothing's kool right now. These dudes are trying to be sneaky. Screw them!" All day long and nothing happened. I told my cousin, "Don't get comfortable. It's going to go down, you'll see".

Later that night, about 11 o'clock or so, there's a knock at the door. A voice through the door said, "Housekeeping." That might've worked except we don't have any housekeeping. This is a cheap-ass weekly. We're lucky we have beds.

We both jumped up and I told my cousin. "Here we go!" I opened the door, but, this time I had my 38 in my hand. I immediately had a 357 and a sawed-off shotgun pointed in my face. Dudes were on both sides of Jake. I quickly sized-up the situation. It wasn't good. So, I put the 38 in Jake's face with my finger on the trigger, so if I got shot, I was shooting him, too.

"What do you guys want?"

Jake said, "You're doing his wife?"

I said, "Is she the younger or the older one?"

Jake said, "She's the older one."

I said, "Well, no Jake. I'm not touching her. I'm into her younger sister, besides, it ain't none of your damn business who I'm doing or who I'm doing it with."

They just looked back and forth real quick, thinking about that shit. Then, my cousin spoke up. He looked right at the dude married to Mary and he said, "Hey man, Mary said she's sick of you running around with other women and out with Jake all the time. She said she's leaving you. I'm just telling you. She knows you're cheating." Jake said, "You better not be messing with her, dude." He's looking right at my cousin, Sonny D.

Sonny D. shot back, "Fuck you, Jake, this really ain't none of your business."

We all stood there for a minute, like a Mexican stand-off.

I finally spoke up, "Alright, here's what we're going to do. It comes down to this. Jake, since you're all up in this like it's your business, you go one on one with Sonny D., or, with me, either one. We'll even let you choose. Then, this shit's done."

(See, they don't know a few things about my cousin and they're about to get a monumental surprise. He's not a big guy, but, he's tough as nails. That runs in our blood. Like me, he's a Tennessee boy and, like me, he's been fighting all his life. I'm like his big brother and yes, we've fought a few times after we grew up, but, we're brothers and sometimes brothers fight. I can tell you, first-hand, he's a man. There's no punk in him. This is different. He damn sure ain't scared of any ass-whooping. One way or the other, I knew Jake was about to get his ass whooped.)

Jake jumped right on that. "Oh yeah! Sounds good to me." He looked at my cousin, Sonny D. "Well, you're fucking my brother's wife, so, I'm going to whoop your ass." He looks at his partners real quick. You guys keep those guns on Stormy. He knows karate, for real, and he's good at it, so, watch him." They pointed both weapons to my head. I jumped up on the bed that was next to me before they could even acknowledge that I'd moved. It surprised them, but, I got away with it. I wanted a fighting chance just in case it all fell apart. I said, "Alright, so you two go heads up and then, it's done." Everybody nods in agreement. "Alright, that sounds good." Jake jumps at Sonny D. They lock up, hit the floor and fists are flying.

293

Then, they jump up and box for a few minutes and Jake grabs on him again, because, he's twice as big as my cousin, so, he figured he'd slam him down and put all that weight on him. It didn't work. Sonny D's smarter than that. He saw that coming a mile away, plus, he's fast and greasy to grab a hold of. After several punches back and forth, Jake runs out of air, then, the fun began. Sonny D. pounced on him and started blasting him in the face with both fists. After a good minute or so, he jumped up off Jake and left his ass laying there. While he was standing there, he got his breath, Jake slowly stood up. Then, they tore it up for a good 5 or six more minutes inside the room. Punching and rolling around and the whole time, I had a loaded shotgun and a loaded 357 pointed at my head a few feet away. After they'd both about ran out of breath, Jake backed out of the room with Sonny D. punching him the whole time. Jake was out of breath and if you've fought much you know, once you lose your ability to breathe, there's not much fight left. They shook hands out of respect after the fight.

I know Jake felt like he'd just fought with a rattlesnake on steroids. Like I said, my cousin's meaner than hell when he has to be. That's the country boy in us. Anyway, the crew of misfits got back in their car and rolled off. Not another word was said about it.

Jake got deeper and deeper into dope and beer, lost his legs, and eventually was put in hospice and died there.

My gentle-giant friend Chris M. that I mentioned, overdosed and died shooting cocaine, several years later. I went to his funeral.

Chapter 17

Sometimes, you have to get knocked down lower than you've ever been...to stand back up, taller than you ever were.

OVER THE EDGE

2002... I was back in Peoria...

We are our own worst enemy. We have a thinking disease and it literally rips our brains apart. I would sit down alone and tell myself a hundred times all the reasons I needed to clean up and never use again. Then, that other voice in my head would tell me how silly that reasoning was and give me a hundred seemingly better reasons why I should just go get some dope, get high and forget about it. Just sitting here now reading this, it sounds so ridiculous. But, it's not. That same voice is killing addicts all over the world right now. Anyway, a dope-shooting buddy of mine that I've mentioned earlier, had went to Colombia and brought back a half-pound of pure coke. He immediately called me to check it out. When I did, we banged enough to blast the tops of our heads off, kicked shit up to fifth gear and we were off and running. He fronted me 2 ounces. I hopped on my Harley and like a streak of blinding light, I was gone. The next couple of weeks were a bit hazy. I literally sat in a chair in the dining room of this apartment I was sharing with my old partner and badass bass player, Chuck C. One after the other, I shot dope. Caught up in this insane psychosis like a madman, I focused on my hit, every five minutes or so, for several days in a row.

I got to a place where I was so weak from shooting the dope that I could barely raise my hand to do the dirty deed. I was on a mission I guess. Dying never occurred to me. Would I dare hop on my Harley for a midnight spin? Am I that nuts? Occasionally, dopers would stop by and grab a gram, or whatever. But, that didn't faze or stop me. I just weighed out their dope, took their money and kept on shooting. I lost track of time. I just kept shooting dope. The hit would knock me to the floor. I'd freeze there until I could stand up again. Then, I'd do it all over again. Never-ending.

About 3 days in, my brother, Deuce, stopped by to check on me and make sure I was still alive. He mentioned it was Friday night and maybe I should hit downtown about midnight to get out of the house. "Why not?" I thought. After Deuce left, I realized I needed to come down just a notch, so, people wouldn't see I was wasted out of my mind. I step in the john to check my look out. Damn! My eyes are big as saucers, my skin's white as a ghost and my lips are bluish purple. I was coked out of my mind. I thought about it for a minute and I figured it out. It was getting near midnight right then, anyway. So, I opened the cabinet and pulled out one of my fifths of Crown Royal in the blue bag. Anxiously, I took off the blue bag and opened the bottle. Grabbing a glass I started pouring. I filled up the glass and just about emptied the Crown bottle. Then, I threw a couple of ice cubes on the whiskey. It melted just like that. To hell with it. I went ahead and drank the whole glass down. Hmmm, what a rush! Afterward, as I was on the way out the door to go downtown, I felt sick for a minute, so, I stepped to the sink, bent and threw up. WHOA!!! It was solid blood. The whole room was really blurry and started spinning.

Then, before I realized it, I, somehow, stumbled along the wall and made it to my bedroom. I was gone. Passed out. A couple days later, streams of bright sunlight through a window woke me. It surprised me. Once again, I'd survived.

This happened many, many times.

There are moments in time that will linger in the soul forever.

SEEDS IN THE GARDEN OF LIFE

For years, I felt detached from myself. For most of my life, really! I had zero self-esteem. My self-efficacy was out the window. I think the real truth was, I didn't like myself very much. I'd never given myself the chance to be honest enough with myself to try and be me and like me for being that person. For me, that was scary. I'm sure all those factors played a bit part in my using hard drugs. It's not an excuse. I'm just pointing it out. I've always been a lot of different people in my head. In the past, the strong ones would walk right over the thoughts of the weaker ones. The nice guy. He'd be pushed aside. After so much heartache, pain, misery and suffering, I finally started to grow from that. Getting clean helped for sure. It was a big part of my growing stronger. I grew to a place that, when I walked in somewhere, I finally stopped wondering who might like me and I started looking around the room to see who I might like. That, for me, was major growth. It was a part of growing wiser, of growing more secure with who I was and who I am today as a person. Living clean promotes clarity.

For the longest time, I even tried liking everyone I met, but, my sense of perception taught me quickly that some people are just assholes; some people are just not likable. Jealous people are people I avoid. They live in misery and want everyone around them to be miserable, too. They're very toxic. From those people, I step away and I keep stepping toward the positive. I never take my eye off the prize. As my successes grew and my existence as a using addict continually had to be dealt with, I encountered street people who were straight-up manipulators. As I grew, I began to realize all addicts are manipulators. What's important is to be cognizant in every situation and continue to spiral upward.

Active addiction will sneak up and kick you square in the ass. It'll mess your head up, destroy your body and your soul and then it'll forget all about you. But, for some of us life gets very deep. Like we all say, shit happens. In the program of N A, shit happens translates to, living life on life's terms. What really matters on the deepest level is invisible to the naked eye, anyway. So, I kept trudging forward on my journey.

Most of us know all of that, already. But, some don't. I'm writing this for them. One thing's for sure, life's a learning tool, so, make the mistakes and, remember, don't repeat those mistakes. Always learn from them and, hopefully, it'll make your world a little better as you go. Right? Remember, we get one shot at this. You make the choices and decisions that create the path you're on. Regardless of what you hear, life's really not about chance, it's about choice. Don't live in the problems. Live in the solutions. I learned that from N A.

We've all heard what the definition of insanity is. Doing something that works to destroy your life, it's the wrong thing to do for a healthy life. Then, knowing that and realizing that and yet, doing the same thing again, anyway. That is insanity. Well, I'll bet a bunch of you don't know what sanity is. Actual sanity, to me, is living in harmony with your reality. It takes a while to get to that place and for many, that's a long, difficult, winding journey. I learned when I survived to find recovery, by the grace of God. But, I've discovered, the trip's well-worth the pain and heartache, along the way, if you survive. You won't think so, till, you reach a serenity you've never known, but, I promise you, true, inner-peace is waiting for you, if you're willing to work for it in recovery. I'm not talking so much physically as I am, spiritually.

Isn't it crazy how life works? An addict's life can spiral completely out of control and for me anyway, I couldn't figure out why my life was such a mess. That's where the cunning and baffling comes into play. That's a horrible feeling. There were moments of time where I was simply amazed I'd survived. So many times. Maybe some you knew really close didn't make it. God, I've lost so many really awesome friends from using drugs and abusing drugs. There's so many lessons we learn along the way. All of us, at one time or another's been backed into a corner. What do we do when that happens?

Life lessons are like arms reaching into a night filled with endless dread. See, in our youth, we always know the way. Even when we have no clue, we step up and step out. We find the road or the situation that fits. We seek the path of fun and we stumble and fall anyway. But, that's okay unless we happen to be an addict. That reality can change everything. We have to learn to make good choices. Along the way we cry at our misgivings, we laugh at our mistakes and then, of course, we make some more. As we grow older, something happens we don't even think about. But, it happens.

We implement hesitation in our thought process. What this is, is a prelude. We stop and think about things a moment longer. We think about a mistake we made or that feeling of standing at a crossroad. Maybe, we want deep down to do the right thing, but, then, no matter the outcome, we move forward, anyway. It's our deeper self, reaching for the pinnacle of wisdom, but, not quite achieving its humble grace. Wisdom is attainable, my friends, but, not found in youthful passing. Wisdom only finds us with an overwhelming, unbelievable and at times, amazing journey through the tunnel of time. Professor Will B. Experienced leads the way. There's an Ocean in the soul. Someone once said, "I'm insignificant. I'm only a drop of water in a vast Ocean." But, I say, and I mean this and I want you to soul-search this. "How could you not be significant? The Ocean MUST HAVE the FIRST drop of water and the LAST drop of water, TO BE THE OCEAN. Right? Without either, there could be no vast, amount of water, we've grown, to call, the Ocean. Plus, think about this... you're not one drop of water in the ocean. You're the ocean in one drop of water. WOW, right!

What a profound, yet simple, truth. We all want inner-peace. We want it so much! We reach for comfort in the arms of another and pray to the Great Spirit above that they yearn for who we are. We pray that we're really that one and only that they want as well. We smile, but inside, many of us are barely holding on. Helping others along the way, we discover a semblance of true, inner-most fulfillment. We forget in our haste, how fragile we really are. We lay to the side the value of time. Some of us become careless. We let memories pass in the wake of life as we trudge forward. We live and if we're blessed and lucky in the ways of life, love and most of all, a happy life filled with inner-peace and love, finds us. We begin to actually feel a level of enlightenment we've never known. Gratitude seeps in and a better life evolves. Hopefully, the addict finds recovery and then, you know what, as long as the addict stays clean, everything becomes possible. EVERYTHING.

Here's the thing. There can be great consequences like success with a great family, beautiful love, a nice home, a big, beautiful boat, a few classy cars, a custom Harley, matching jet-ski's and on and on and on, or, there can be horrible consequences like jails, prisons, homelessness, loneliness, poor health and an untimely death. Which path makes more sense to you?

Chapter 18

I didn't come this far, to only come this far.

LAST FLICKER OF HOPE

In 1978, I decided it was time for me to grow up and be a family man. Work, come home and raise a family. It was time. I was trying to do the right things for the right reasons. Wouldn't you know it, just when I get in the rhythm of things and I'm loving it, the cops in Texas realized my parole paperwork had been misplaced by the Illinois authorities. Thank God, when this happened, I was working, I had a great job at Caterpillar, and I was married to my first lovely wife, Brenda. We had a baby coming, we'd bought a couple of cars and we were buying a nice home. These were all reasons to give me a chance at life, right? Incredibly, even now, being completely honest, I was, secretly, still shooting dope every chance I got. So, after a fierce battle with Texas authorities, with the help of an attorney friend of the family and my parole officer, I was given one chance to live, work and be a part of society. I still had to do all the Texas and Illinois parole and for 8 years, I showed up at the PO's office and filled out a sheet, weekly, then, monthly. I did it all. Every damn day of it and I was finally released. Let's add the insanity to all this. I was still partying all the time. I was still fighting downtown, acting a fool. I was still inside the prison walls in my head. At this same time, Brenda and I had a gorgeous daughter named Misty Michelle and a handsome son named Jesse Miles. Directly because of addiction, Brenda and I didn't speak for 30 plus years after our divorce. Through recovery, we've grown. We even had Thanksgiving dinner together last Thanksgiving at my daughter, Misty's beautiful home. I have so much more clarity now. Misty and Jesse have grown into amazing people and I'm very proud of them. They're both very responsible and doing well in life. Between them, I'm blessed with 5 grandchildren.

I was married and divorced 3 different times. My second marriage was to a woman whose name will remain private. We had no children. Since we have no communication anymore, out of respect, I've kept her name out of this story.

My last marriage to Raina, lasted almost 19 years. I have to be honest. I believe there was good and bad in all three marriages. We all, in some way, made beautiful memories.

Unfortunately, I was distracted or afflicted, by addiction. I'm not making excuses for any of my behavior. I own it all. I'm just saying these three ladies, as beautiful and amazing as they all were and are, didn't realize, as our love grew for one another, that I was at war with demons in my head. They controlled my inner-self. These women I married never had a chance at a good marriage with me. I have to own that now and remember, I can't bring back that time, I can't fix all the damage my active addiction created, but, I can try to do better now and, hopefully, continue to learn from the countless mistakes I've made along the way.

Raina and I, literally, lived all over the country. I could write a book about our marriage. I guess I kind 'a am right now. Anyway, we were truly an adventurous couple. She helped me with countless art showings and poetry readings all over the west and southwest. For years I believed we were magical. Of course, you'd be hard-pressed to get her to admit that. She's remarried now and he's a good guy, so, I wish them both the best. For me, they were some of the best years of my life. All the trips to Vegas, San Diego, hangin' on the beach, Denver, Colorado Springs, Tennessee, up north, hell, Florida to California and all parts in between. We had a lot of fun and raised beautiful children, too. Our little girls, my beautiful Sunshine and amazing Breezi, were with us for all the trips and travels we had. But, this happened, too. In the course of our journey, we lost a baby in Denver, a very handsome boy named Elijah Blu. Because of my addiction, this was a very difficult time in our lives. I still blame myself for his loss. When this happened, when he was first born,

Misty, Sunshine and dad, Stormy Monday, on Ocean beach, in San Diego, California, Jesse, Breezi and Raina not in the pic, 1997

I held him in my arms for a few minutes and he looked just like me. He had a full head of black hair and deep blue eyes that looked right into mine, just before he passed away. Doctors tried to revive him, but, his lungs weren't developed and Raina had lost too much amniotic fluid. Like I mentioned, Raina and I also had two beautiful daughters, Breezi, and Sunshine, plus, a handsome son named Storm, who, at this writing in May, 2020, is seventeen years old. Storm's birthday is January 7th and he's growing into an incredible young man.

He's handsome, intelligent and smooth like his big brother, Jesse. We also raised one of Raina's awesome sons, Calen, who was a year younger than my oldest son, Jesse.

I have to say, we had some good years, too. Sadly, throughout all these years, I was in active addiction. No matter what was going on in my life, I had a secret life using drugs. I thought no one really knew about the secret life. That's so ridiculous, looking back. How wrong I was. Clarity now has helped me realize when people are caught up in active addiction, like I was, everybody knows you have a drug problem, except, maybe you.

Suicidal/ homicidal tendencies…

One of the things that happens to people caught in the street life and active addiction, is deteriorating health. Everything about life becomes un-important to someone chasing a high. I was very sick, too. I lived with Hepatitis C, heart disease and so many other serious illnesses I've already talked about. Then, around the latter part of 2013, I had spine surgery. I cracked some vertebra in a fall at Caterpillar. It was horrible and it was also a perfect reason to stay wasted on pain pills. I got intensely strung out on Vicodin, OxyContin and was in and out of the hospital for my chronic liver disease. I also had recurring pancreatitis. It was killing me. I got very, very sick. While admitted, a liver specialist came down from Chicago Northwestern. She talked to me and told me to get my affairs in order. I was told I had about 6 months to live. I was in 4th stage cirrhosis and with the hepatitis C attacking my liver for so many years, the prognosis was very bleak.

This made me very depressed. During this time, I began to lose all hope. I couldn't walk without a walker. All I could do is lay in one place and stay so high I couldn't move. My spine was pushed into my sciatic nerve and it hurt so bad I couldn't even think. It was horrible. I was mentally panic-stricken. The next year of my life was filled with hospital stays, depression, pain pills and intense misery. I was crippled, both mentally, physically and spiritually.

Talk about depressed… I found a lot of depth between empty moments, when the next moment doesn't matter. I, somehow, found an unknown inner-strength and made that moment, start to matter. That wasn't easy and I had no other choice, except suicide. I don't know where this sliver of desperation or this moments shedding of depression came from, but, I do know, it unfolded into something I could somehow reach into. I wanted it to make sense. I cried out to God. I had nowhere else to turn.

Making sense of anything had already set sail for me. Within those dark places, I crumbled, yet, never once, admitted my destitution of soul, to anyone. Being alone is for soul-searching. But, I must say… in this inner-searching are fragments of self, one might never have known. One might never come to terms with. There really is a

304

Highway of Hope. It's far more than a street sign. Many of us know that road well.

Some of us have traveled its length simply because all other roads had closed, long ago. So, it was the only road left to go. Believe in your ability to believe in yourself. Stand over your inability to find hope.

These are all things I really do work on every day. I'm far from a perfect human. I still have defects that ravage my thinking. At least now, I'm aware of the defects and I really try to be a better person in everything I do.

I mean, I've been to a dangerous place inside my head. I sunk into a very deep, black hole. I thought about suicide, constantly. I mean, I was dying, anyway, right. I panicked and called clinical trials all over America, trying to be part of anything that might save my life. It became very disappointing and very bleak.

So, I made a conscious decision to kill myself. I'd made up my mind. Suicide. I wanted to die. Well, I didn't want to die. I just didn't want to live in pain, waiting to die. So, I soul-searched it and made peace with my decision.

I called a crack-head friend of mine one day. He had worked for me for years in the painting business. Greg was an excellent painter, but, like so many, he was devoured by crack and beer addiction. He came by and I told him I wanted a hundred-dollar bag of heroin. It was my old friend, Greg. So, off we went to the dope house. I was so sick and crippled. I was completely depressed. Life felt completely hopeless. I felt helpless and empty. I couldn't wait to do the bag of dope and disappear. That's called losing all hope. I pulled into the drive of the dope house and he ran in with my hundred dollars to get me a bag of heroin. I thought, well, if I shoot it all in one hit, I'll just go to sleep with no pain, quick and painless. That sounded like a good plan to me. I could leave all this suffering and misery behind me. Greg comes running out and jumps in the car. I take off down the road and tell Greg to hand me the dope.

He says, "Alright, alright." He hands me the bag.

It's a hundred dollar crack-rock.

I screech to a halt. "Greg, you bastard!" I wanted to slap the piss out of him.

He says that's all they had. "Sonofabitch! The last thing I want to do is smoke some damn crack. I want to go to sleep, forever, not wake up from this shit. Dammit!" I was pissed.

Greg says, "Well, I'll buy it from you."

(NOTE TO SELF- Never send a crack-head into a dope house with money to buy anything except crack. Dumbass move on my part. In my defense, I was suicidal, desperate and mentally, physically and emotionally empty. Obviously, I wasn't thinking straight.)

"Sonofabitch, you ain't got no money."

"Well, I'll get it for you, just let me get that crack."

I wanted to reach across the seat and snap his head right off his neck. He reached in his pocket and pulled out fifty-five dollars. I snatched the money out of his hand and threw him the rock. "You owe me and you ain't smoking that shit in this car either." He's desperate. Well, let me out then. BAM! I slammed on my brakes and he jumped out. "Well, that didn't work." Pushing the gas pedal down, I took off toward my house, more depressed than I was. "I can't even kill myself and I'm out here driving with a broken back. I can't even walk. What the hell!" I thought. For the rest of the drive, the silence smothered me as the misery and depression chipped at my soul. I wanted to die. Just be done with it all. Impending Doom... That's what it felt like to me. I was in a black hole. I didn't see any way out of this, except death.

One of the things we suppress and stop caring about when we're in active addiction is our health. But, it all catches up eventually. Usually it's when we clean up and we start caring about things in our life. We start working down a list of situations to resolve. Inevitably, health issues are always on the list.

In 2005, I found out I had Hepatitis C, Chronic liver disease, stage 3 to 4 Cirrhosis. I continued to live in denial. The silent killer continued to attack the liver inside my body. I grew sicker and sicker. A year later, I seriously injured my spine in a fall at Caterpillar. This began a journey of self-discovery. After all, did I really think I could abuse the hell out of my body for so many years and NOT have any medical consequences? It had to happen. Tests confirmed my chronic liver disease had moved into 4th stage. My insides were covered in polyps and lymphoid and most of my liver, 80%, had no blood circulation. In other words, my liver was only functioning 20%. That's scary shit man. With recurring pancreatitis and heart disease, I was no longer a candidate for interferon and ribavirin treatment.

A few years later, a liver specialist came down from Chicago Northwestern Hospital and said it was her belief that I had been in 3rd to 4th stage cirrhosis for at least 10 to 15 years. I was living on borrowed time. Without treatment, there are only two lists I can go on. Those are the liver transplant list and then, death.

I came home and cried, alone, for a week. Talk about a pity pot. The death sentence freaked me out. I mean, were all going to die, right? But, this was directed at me and it forced me to face a very harsh reality. I couldn't talk to anyone. I'd lost all joy and hope. I fell back into that big, black hole, beyond hitting bottom. I'd never been this deep in this hole before. Death was eminent. But, we hear it time and time again...

MIRACLES HAPPEN...

It's in a time like this right here where the answer to that question is very, very important. Do I really believe miracles happen? Deep down in my heart of hearts, do I believe miracles happen? I mean, I was dealing with some heavy shit. Heavy shit. The year was now 2013.

My life was overwhelming pain and suffering. I was strung out on Vicodin and Percocet, along with OxyContin. I existed in a black hole waiting for death. My body had given up. So had my spirit and my hope had dwindled to nothing. My liver had stopped processing a lot. I was down to about 20% function. My body had swollen to 293 pounds. Then, I quit weighing myself. What's the point? Right. I was accepting that my death was coming soon. It was 4 am, sometime later. A hand from the darkness grabbed me by the arm and pulled me up in the bed from a deep sleep. I tried to focus in the dark to see who was there. No one was there. It had to be an angel of God or maybe even God himself.

I just know a voice inside my head that I couldn't see, said...."You have two paths.

There's the path of life, and then, there's the path of death. You have to decide."

I was fighting the urge to panic. At 4 am, filled with desperation, I went to my computer, got online and started searching. I thought,

307

"If I can't take interferon or ribavirin, this is the 21st Century. There has to be new medicine somewhere that I could take that would kill this Hepatitis C in my body. Then, with work, I could rejuvenate my liver and my life." After hours of research, I found two pills in Canada on the cutting edge of success. Those pills were Daclatasvir and gs-7977. Through third-phase clinical trials, these two pills had 90% success, coupled with protease inhibitors, for Geno-type 1a. This is my Genotype. For all other Geno-types, they had an 82% success rate. This was with no adverse side effects, except maybe a headache and some nausea. Those symptoms can be easily treated. Then, I sought out at clinical trials.gov, every Research Hospital in America doing clinical trials.

Never give up...

I found 3 that knew about these pills and I faxed them my medical records to pass the criteria to be placed on the list for upcoming clinical trials. I was told all these treatments were in testing and had rather harsh side effects. I figured I'd have to take the good with the bad. I explained I only wanted to be in clinical trials with at least one of these two pills. So, I wait for the clinical trials. I keep waiting and it's driving me crazy. It was like I was sitting there wasting away waiting to die. It was killing me, mentally as much as physically. Then, out of nowhere, I get a call. The voice on the other end of the phone said, "I'm Tammy. I want to help. I've been sent to you. I do all my work for God. Do you believe in God, Stormy?" I replied, "Yes, I do."
She replied, "Well, he believes in you, too."
She came to my home and was a very nice lady. I let her in. She explained everything she was going to do if I didn't object to anything. I was willing to do about anything to be able to keep living. So, why not. She sat over my body, meditated, then, she prayed and put her hands all over my abdomen, my feet and my head. She did this for hours. Seriously, for the better part of the entire afternoon. Tammy had a young man with her. While he was at my feet, she was at my abdomen. She kept pulling something from my body and throwing it away. Then, she looked me in the eyes and said, "I just want you to know, I'm not doing this. God's doing this. I'm here in the name of God. He talked to me in prayer and told me to find you.

308

He said you've got things to do in this life and it's not time for you to go. You'll be fine now. Medical tests will confirm this." I was speechless. I've heard of this throughout my life, but, I've never, first-hand experienced anything like this. So, the next day, it was already scheduled. I had to go to the Hospital. They did a sonogram of my stomach, liver, spleen and gallbladder.

My brother Ed took me to the hospital three days later and we got my results. Here's where it gets deep. Once again, I was speechless. I didn't know what to say. My liver was smooth and not swollen. Blood flow was perfect, going in and coming out. It was supple, like that of a thirty year old, non- smoker and non-drinker. The same was the case for my other organs. My spleen was still a little swollen.

All I can say is, I laid the reports down, ones from a few months back and these new ones, I laid them side by side and I mean it, the reports look like two different people. One of those people is definitely dying and one of those people is definitely living. I have only one clear explanation. This is a miracle of God! This happened. From my heart of hearts, I'd been truly humbled. I really don't know what else I can do right now, but, say, THANK YOU, GOD! Now, in my life, after actually living this, I truly believe, when the Great Spirit wants it to happen... miracles do happen. There is no way I can deny or change the reality that lies before me in black and white, in these Medical reports and especially, how I feel inside, now as a person. I've been healed. This, I know, is true. This crazy truth soaks through me like the rays of the hottest sun, scorching my soul with the most beautiful, real and amazing truth.

I'll thank God every single day of my life out loud and I'll sing his praises. I'll share my story with all who will choose to listen, or, read this book. You must first truly believe. Look at my medical reports. Study the results and read what they say in black and white. Then and only then, will you understand and see as clearly as I now do. You will believe. You will believe in miracles. I know I do.

Even with this miracle, months later, during testing, my liver specialist found that I still had Hepatitis C. My condition had improved. All my organs were better, according to testing, but, I still had the virus ravaging my organs. But, God's not finished here. The doctor said there were choices with varying percentages of success, but, still no cure. Through the years, I've had hundreds of friends and brothers die of Hepatitis C. This is a terminal disease. It kills with no mercy. The liver Doctor said in 6 months a pill would be approved that would cure Hepatitis C and the percentage was 100% for Geno type 1A and that was me. He also said this would be the one pill that had better side effects and a much simpler treatment.

Get your affairs in order...

Note the irony here. A week ago, I was told to get my affairs in order, I had about 6 months to live. A week later the liver specialist tells me in 6 months there will be a cure for hepatitis C. Sometimes, the irony just kicks you square in the ass. I'd been waiting on a cure for thirty years.

Miracles Do Happen...

You know what I got from that? Hope. I didn't want to die. I started thinking about my next step to get better. Here's another harsh reality. This is honesty.

Even with this miracle happening to me and me knowing, first hand, this miracle was a gift from God, I still abused pain pills. Remember the definition of insanity? Exactly. My back was a mess and I ate OxyContin and Percocet like candy.

My wife of 19 years had left me. I never for the life of me expected that. It knocked me down. I didn't know 'how to be' anymore. I'd lost the best part of myself. My life felt pointless. It was very painful to admit I felt like I had no purpose.

That's where I was in my life. I felt I was standing on a dead end street. The doctor's death sentence was catastrophic to my brain. The doc also said those days were flying by.

All I could think was, "I KNOW." I had nowhere left to go... even my wife had jumped ship. I was done. I didn't want to kill myself now, but, I didn't want to live like this. One night, I was alone, crying in a dark room. It took a lot of courage for me to do this. I didn't feel worthy. Filled with shame, I got down on my knees and prayed to God for help. I ask him to forgive me for all my years of insanity.

As I knelt there, I felt like a stranger talking to someone that had always been there for me... I'd just forgotten it. He was just waiting for me to come back home. I felt a very real sense of peace.

The Face of Active Addiction- Stormy Monday, Menard prison, 1974

There must be something better. I'm sick and tired of this shit. Just sick of it! I don't know how to stop. It's out of control. I'm done with it all! I don't care anymore. I give up. I can't do it anymore.

Does any of this sound eerily familiar? All addicts caught in active addiction go through it. Eventually, it hits us right between the eyes. Not all of us survive to find another life. Most of us die, overdose, liver disease, Hepatitis C, kidneys shut down, the pancreas gives up, or God knows how many other ways the man upstairs comes for us. But, one thing is certain. If you use and you don't stop using, you keep on drinking, shooting dope, snorting dope, eating pills and abusing weed, I promise you this, you will die way before your time. Self-centeredness is right there at the core of our disease. I, I, I, I, I, me, me ,me, me, me.

Just to feel, once and for all, "I'm done with this shit". It's a strange phenomenon and there's not a psychology professor, drug-counselor or mental health professional alive that can tell anyone why, one day an addict makes the conscious decision that they've literally had enough. No more! Done. "I need help and I'll go to any means necessary to get help, get clean and learn how to stay clean." Of course, by this time, the spirit's gone. There's nothing left to hold on to. Everybody left long ago and you've lost everything.

Treatment centers have about an average of 18 to 23% success with addicts and that seems low until you weigh in all the variables, then, you begin to realize it's much better than zero success. Someone's being saved. That's something, right?

Chapter 19

SEARCHING YOUR SOUL

The first symptom of addiction is denying you have a problem.

It's time to be honest with yourself and face your own denial and lies. Are you in DENIAL?
This is life on life's terms.
Search your soul ... Tell yourself the truth, or, what's the point?
Look inside a mirror into your own eyes...

Ask yourself these questions...

1.   Am I putting my family first? (Well, am I?)
2.   Do I break promises to my special someone (Be honest.)

3. Do I miss fun activities with the family, all the time?

4. Ask yourself this...Am I going to work on time?

5. Are my priorities in order? Do I work from a daily check list?
6. Am I lying to people for financial gain. (Do I hustle others?)

7. Am I stealing for extra cash to spend for drugs?

8. Are drugs beginning to be my focus? Or alcohol?

9. Am I isolating away from people? Family?

10. Am I spending more time out partying with druggies than I am with my family? (I want you to really think about that.) At first, it seems innocent. It might start with a cook-out, let's just have a few drinks, after all, it's a Saturday get-together. Someone suggests... let's just do a bump. Then, the coke comes out. But, we all know one bump is never enough. So, that turns into another and another and another. It's not fun anymore. Ask yourself... (Am I doing this?)

11. Do I hide cash from my wife/ husband? (How would I like it?)

12. Am I in the bar all the time? (Shouldn't I be home, family?

13. Do I use drugs or alcohol behind my spouse's back?

14. Are drugs or alcohol high on my priority list?

15. Do I party through the week, or, early in the morning?

16. Do I think about getting wasted a lot? (Is there a problem?)

17. Do I hide my pain and misery with drugs or alcohol?

18. When I drink or use, does that seem to hide my pain?

19. Do I hide drugs or alcohol around my home?

20. Do I pawn household items to buy drugs? Tools, jewelry,

21. Am I constantly living in the problems, not living in solutions? Have I lost everything yet? Is that coming?

If you answered honestly and the answer was yes to any of these questions, you may want to go somewhere alone, sit down, pause and search your soul. The solution could very well be detox, treatment and then, Narcotics Anonymous meetings. Make a plan or keep spiraling downward, till you die.

Process this fact... It's not our fault we're addicts, but, we are responsible for our recovery.

By the way, how's your health? Be honest. Do you have issues that need medical attention?

Four years after the twelfth grade, you can be an ex-convict on parole, homeless, broke as hell and flipping crack to satisfy your habit, that can never be satisfied, by the way, or, you can be framing your Bachelor's degree in the office of your awesome and well-earned career. You choose your own path by your own decisions, choices and actions. Why not, at least, always try to do the next right thing? Why not create a priority list and work from it? Check off each thing as you complete it... every day. WHY NOT? I mean this when I tell you...

Your tomorrows will show you the paths you choose today.

By the way, do you have any legal problems? Maybe it's not the legal problems that's the actual problem. Maybe it's a drug problem that you've been denying even exist. Have you considered that?

Do you blame others for just about everything that goes wrong?

Why not use that same energy to find solutions? All suggestions.

~<>~

~ SURRENDER ~

~RECOVERY BEGINS WITH SURRENDER~

What's that even mean... surrender?

Throughout my life, I honestly think I've tried every possible way to get clean and stay clean. I never could figure out a way to actually live without drugs sporadically and actually lose my desire to want to get high. I tried over and over to live a different life and I couldn't figure it out. After willpower failed me, over and over, after the methadone program failed me, over and over, after Alcoholics Anonymous failed me, after making promises and deals with myself failed, constantly, after switching out drugs to rationalize and make myself quit, failed, then, running away from myself, failed a hundred times, and on and on and on, all failed me... How can I get clean and stay clean?

(I've come to realize we really are all different. What works for one person may not work for another. That's a fact that I had to grow to understand.)

One day, like so many times before, I was at the end of my rope. So, I tried Narcotics Anonymous. Here's a little of what happened in my experience, when I first started going to N A meetings.

The questions are endless for a new-comer at N A and the classic answer from an addict in recovery is always wisdom from the Basic Text... "Keep coming back. More will be revealed." I remember when I first stumbled into Narcotics Anonymous. Like most of us, I was dead inside, lost, I mean, a mess. To begin with, I had no idea what to expect when I walked through that door and because it was such a mystery, it took even more courage. None of us like to walk into the unknown. Add to that horrible self-esteem which most of us deal with and then, pure shame from the way we've been barely surviving and it's a wonder anybody ever finally does walk into that first meeting, or, even second or third meetings. I was willing to do anything to get clean and I was past ready to do whatever I had to do to stay clean. Every day at first was a huge mystery, shrouded by the fact that I didn't have a clue how any of this stuff at N A worked.

The Narcotics Anonymous overview... from a regular guy. What I felt when I first walked in to a meeting...

As a new-comer, I felt alien because I didn't know anything about the N A program. I often thought it'd be really helpful to have some sort of book that explains some of the situations that unfold, when someone's new in the program and first walks into a meeting.

Just a step by step guide to help nudge new-comers along in the program. Almost like a map to highlight and share what to expect when someone that's already lost first comes into a meeting. This is the reason I'm sharing a small degree of insight into the Narcotics Anonymous program. Let it be known, I do NOT KNOW EVERYTHING. I'm also learning on my journey, even now. Please realize all of us should definitely remain teachable. There is so much more to learn. As I've grown older, I've begun to realize how little I actually do know. So, I'm here to learn all I can, also. REMAIN TEACHABLE. That's in a very important book in the N A program I mentioned a moment ago, called, "The Basic Text". It's obviously common sense as well. But, some come a few months and suddenly want to save the world. They truly believe they've got it all figured out. Watch for that. I do not, I repeat, I do not have it all figured out. I'm merely a student of life willing to share whatever I can. Above all, please, for your own personal growth, remain teachable and remember, the bottom line is we're all here for our own recovery, but, we can help each other stay clean. What we can't do is anyone else's recovery. I can't do yours. You can't do mine. Remember that. By the way, these are all suggestions. I pray to the Great Spirit above, Jesus Christ, who's my Higher Power, that this book is helpful to you. Writing this, for me, is like a very thorough fourth step. You'll understand that better as you continue to read.

Narcotics Anonymous works for me.

I don't know if it'll work for you, but, I do know it works for hundreds of thousands of people around the world. So, I'm going to share how I perceive the Narcotics Anonymous program. This program was created by addicts for addicts. As you know, I'm also an addict, so, in this book, I'm going to try to give you an insight into how I've been taught the N A program works. We have 12 steps and 12 Traditions among lots of other N A information. Let me be clear about a few things. I believe in the N A program. When you work it, it works. We do not change around the N A program to fit any of us. The N A program is the N A program. It's not the Stormy Monday program, or, your program, or, anybody's program. It's the Narcotics Anonymous program. I'll never try to change the N A program. It works fine just the way it is. I'll share some of what I've been taught by addicts with more clean time than me. I know this is an anonymous program. I'll not divulge anyone's name except my own. This is my recovery out loud. We have an epidemic of deaths by overdose, people.

The time for being hush hush about a program that actually works is over for me.

People are dying from overdoses, in massive quantities, everywhere, daily. Then, I think about how literally everybody has friends that have overdosed and died these days. Daily.

For me, the epidemic of dying friends from overdoses, plus, saving whoever I can, far outweighs a handful of naysayers.
Each of us, as addicts, should work on our own recovery. This is what I've learned from addicts in recovery with more clean time than me.

A JOURNEY THROUGH NARCOTICS ANONYMOUS

FREQUENTLY ASKED QUESTIONS

1.   What on earth is a pink cloud?
2.   What's a normie?
3.   Will I have to talk if I go to an N A meeting?
4.   What do those colorful tags mean?
5.   What are the coins for?
6.   Is it okay to talk back and forth during the meetings? 7.   Is it okay to question someone while their sharing
8.   What the heck is the 13th step?

9.	Is the 13th step actually mentioned in the N A literature?
10.	Is it okay to smoke inside the meeting?
11.	I can be in recovery and still take a few pain pills, right?
12.	What is the No Matter What Club?
13.	How long do the meetings last?
14.	What is step work?
15.	Is there a chain of command at N A?
16.	Will I still be clean if I just smoke pot?
17.	How about methadone?
18.	I'll still be clean when I'm in the maintenance program?
19.	How do I become a chair-person?
20.	What does service work mean?
21.	Closed, open, speaker, group conscience- differences?
22.	Are phone number available at the first meeting?
23.	What does, do your own inventory, mean?
24.	Have you ever met a social crack head?
25.	Is this a religious program?

Keep reading... I'll try to answer all these questions and more... with answers I was taught by addicts, in recovery, who've been there longer than I have. Just know, there's no advice offered in this book. There are only suggestions.

THE BIRTH OF NARCOTICS ANONYMOUS

What is the Narcotics Anonymous program?

After some research at NA.org and in the NA Basic Text, 6th Edition and talking to other addicts in recovery, I discovered a few things that I'll now share with you. Narcotics Anonymous was formed in July, 1953. Unfortunately, drug-addicts didn't feel included in the Alcoholics Anonymous meetings. This is because Alcoholics Anonymous was written by alcoholics for alcoholics. Spear-heading that was an alcoholic named Bill W. A group of addicts led by Jimmy K. formed and requested permission to create a group geared toward addiction. A place was needed that helped drug addicts find recovery and made them feel like they had a place to go, also. Permission was granted by A A to create and use the concept of the literature they'd written. The wording in this literature would be directed toward "addiction" and living clean rather than living sober. The very first meeting was held in Southern California. The fellowship spread around the country. But, N A struggled through the 60's with very little structure. Membership started to decline because a more specific direction was needed. This maturity came about in 1972, when a World Service Office opened in Los Angeles, California. The WSO brought the much needed stability and sense of purpose to the fellowship. Then, in 1983, the first publication of the Basic Text was created. Today, there are approximately 67,000 meetings weekly in 139 countries. The World Service Office now serves an ever-growing world-wide fellowship.

~<>~

CHOOSING LIFE

I finally decided that the thought of going to an N A meeting sounded better than staying in my current miserable existence, or, dying.

I gave up. I was finally ready to go to any means necessary to actually break down and do whatever I had to do to experience what the rest of my life would feel like, living clean and in recovery.

I finally did it. On June 3rd, 2014, I decided Narcotics Anonymous appeared legitimate enough for me to keep coming back to meetings and check it out for a while.

Very soon, thereafter, I began the process of trying to learn to live life, one day at a time. Don't be fooled or misled by my words that might sound courageous. It was really hard. But, it was worth it. I also discovered that in order for me to be accepted for Hepatitis C treatment, I had to be completely clean for 6 months, meaning, in order for me to be cured of Hepatitis C, I had to live without any drugs whatsoever in my system for at least 6 months. This was literally life or death for me.

This shit's not easy. In fact, it's hard as hell. A lot of people try the N A program and relapse. Somewhere it's said, relapse is a part of our recovery. I disagree. I don't think relapse has to be a part of our recovery. I think that philosophy gives an addict a way out. We are, by nature, master manipulators. It's like a cop-out. That's how I feel about it. Addicts trying to get clean come into an N A meeting and I hear it all too often, they go back out and hopefully, survive to come back. Their first words in the first meeting back, are, "Well, it IS part of our recovery." These are words they're taught. But, no. No. No. No. Listen to me. Get clean and NO MATTER WHAT, stay clean. Take the option of USING, off the table. If relapsing ceases to be an option... then, what's left? Stay clean. That's my perception.

Those first thirty days clean, for me, were brutal. They're hard. I'm not going to bullshit you. The cravings ate at my brain constantly. The desire to use still haunted me. It would've been so much easier to just go get high. But, something inside me kept pushing me to stay clean.
Something kept me going to those meetings. Then, those first sixty days went by and hey, I was still clean. It started getting a little better. It started getting a little easier. I thought, just maybe, I could do this. I could stay clean. I just had to keep coming to the meetings. They were my lifesaver. Listening at the meetings to others share their experience, strength and hope helped me so much. I thought, if they can do this, so, can I. Things started to matter a little more. The cravings started backing off a little more with every passing day. I could feel my spirit coming back to life inside my body. The darkness started slipping away. I could feel a new light coming on inside me. What a great feeling that is!

I could literally feel the spiritual awakening inside me! Those people's testimonies saved my life. God saved my life. Narcotics Anonymous saved my life. Everyone in recovery in those meetings saved my life. They kept me coming to those meetings by sharing their pain. I started feeling the feeling of hope again. That helped me so much when it got rough and there were days when it did get rough.

I had days where inside my thinking, I just wanted to say, "Fuck this shit". There were hard moments. Sometimes, I had to hold on, one moment at a time. There were times when I wanted to quit and just go find some dope, say to hell with it and get wasted. Just numb myself from everything. But, I held on. I didn't do that. I always did that before and nothing good ever came from it. So, no matter what, I stayed clean. The difference was and is, now, when those moments come, I let them pass through me and I move on in life. They usually come and go quickly.

I can't help it that some days just don't go as planned, but, what I can do is not use, no matter what. What I can do is stay clean. What I can do is not pick up. I refuse. I won't get high. I will not use. NO MATTER WHAT.

Believe me when I tell you, stay clean and growth will happen. Stay in the solution. You'll get an education you didn't even realize you needed. I know I did and I try my best to remain teachable. We suggest that everyone remains teachable. I wake up every single morning filled with gratitude. When I first started coming every day to Sanity for N A meetings, I was a mess. I was spiritually dead inside. There was nothing left inside me. Can you imagine how empty that feels? Maybe you can.

If so, I hope and pray my words help you to find your way.   Drugs had consumed who I was, as a person. I didn't even know who I was. I just knew that I was dying and I thought maybe that would feel better than what living was feeling like, at that time. Those first days clean were hard. But, something wonderful started happening... I reached a place where I was scared to not go to a Narcotics Anonymous meeting. So, I went every day at least twice, for the first 32 months of my recovery. Some days I'd go three times. The meetings became my refuge, my place of safety. Most of the addicts in recovery made me feel welcome, like they understood what I was going through. I knew no one else did.

So, I kept going and I kept going. I met a black dude that had been through a lot of the same shit I'd been through. I noticed he was very humble. His name's Larry. The more I listened to Larry share his story, the more I knew I wanted to ask him to be my sponsor. So, after I'd been to the meetings for about a month, I asked Larry to be my sponsor. He's been my sponsor ever since. One of the first things Larry said to me was this, "Stormy, you should join the No Matter What Club. I did. I'm still a member in good standing." "What's that?" I ask.

"That, my brother, is you deciding right now that no matter what happens in your life you will NOT use, you will not drink, you will not smoke, you will not pick up and you will stay clean."

"Hmmm... I love that." I replied. "Count me in." I've been a member in good standing since my clean date, June 3rd, 2014. Most importantly, today, I'm a member in good standing."

I was all in then and I'm all in right now, too. No matter what.

At the meetings, you'll hear, don't leave before the miracle happens. I used to think, what the hell's the miracle?

The miracle happens for everyone at different times.

What's the miracle? Hmmm... This is the miracle... You actually lose the desire to use.
NOW... Imagine that feeling!

WORK THOSE STEPS! This is the key to a robust recovery in Narcotics Anonymous. WORK THOSE 12 STEPS, in order, under the guidance of your sponsor.

As long as you keep coming to meetings and keep working the N A program, the desire to use will, someday, mysteriously leave you. I know it sounds crazy. I'd been going to meetings for about three weeks and I heard someone in a meeting share that they'd lost their desire to use. I, honestly, thought they were full of shit. They had to be making that up. I didn't believe them. They had to be lying. I've had this desire to use, I've had these cravings inside my mind and body for as long as I can remember. No way will I ever lose that. Not me. I've always had that. It's not going away.

But, I kept coming back. After about six or seven months, one day at a meeting, it hit me! I literally couldn't believe it. I had to process it slowly and accept it. I realized I hadn't thought about using for several days in a row. You could have hit me in the face with a hammer. That's what realizing that felt like. That was some eye-opening miracle type shit in my head. Hell no! This can't be! But, it was. It was true. It was really true. In my whole life, I never thought it would be possible for me to go through a full day and not once have the thought of shooting coke or heroin. That always happened in my head since I was 18 years old, strung out on heroin.

My mind stayed focused on getting high. No matter what I had going on in my life, that was always going on behind the scenes, in my head. If you didn't get high or have money I might be able to get from you, you probably had no idea I was in the hustle to get high. This was literally 100% of the time. So, what a revelation for me! Of course, there'll be moments in time that the thought of using will pass through my thinking, but, now, in recovery, we learn some important and valuable tools to help us. We call them tools for our toolbox.

FINDING A GOOD SPONSOR...

I cannot put into words the importance of a good sponsor. As we continue to go to meetings, here's some of what we'll learn. A very important part of the healing process is to work the 12 steps with our sponsor. We'll also continue to fill our tool-box with ways to fight this never-ending disease. The person you choose should be someone with a substantial amount of clean time. This means, hopefully, more than a few years. This sponsor has worked the steps thoroughly with their sponsor, hopefully, more than once. Keep in mind, a good sponsor is someone you've gotten to know and you both click as potential friends. You develop a friendship relationship based on trust. After all, when you work the steps, specifically, the

4th step, you'll be sharing a lot of very private information with this person. You'll be telling your sponsor things you may not want anyone to know. Sharing that information with your sponsor and letting that suppressed pain and anger go is the best way to peel back the layers inside and open yourself to a healthier level of spirituality. So, choose your sponsor wisely. Remember, working the 12 steps is not a race. I suggest you set aside a half-hour at the end of each day and work on your steps. Start at one and work them in order.

THE RECOVERY TOOLBOX...

One of the most important pieces of knowledge you can place in your recovery toolbox is this... just because the thought of using might pass through your thinking, doesn't mean you have to act on it and use. I suggest you get busy and let the thought pass on through. Play the tape all the way through. Think about the consequences of active addiction. Think about all the crap you've went through directly because of you saying fuck it and using. Those thoughts of using usually pass through rather quickly. Life goes on. That was huge for me to learn that simple thing. As an addict in active addiction, when I'd have the thought of shooting dope, drinking or whatever, I was off and running, no matter what. There was never a second thought, or, any thought of the dire consequences. I didn't play the tape all the way through at all. It was just spontaneous insanity. How refreshing to leave that behavior behind me and move forward. I feel so grateful. How refreshing to think it through and realize I never have to use again. I have the power to choose to decide not to use... and let life move past those insane urges and carry on, on my path spiraling upward and onward in the forward position with robust recovery.

I will say this. Life does suck sometimes. Sometimes, some things don't go as planned. Sometimes, people will disappoint us. Sometimes, we just want to kick the shit out of somebody or everybody. We all know this. But, at least, for me, anyway, even when life seems to be really hard and I want to just jump up and down and scream, I have to always remember, as long as I don't use, things will work out the way they're supposed to, even if we don't agree with the outcome. God's will must be done. In recovery, I continue to learn.

I honestly don't want that to change. I live every day and every night clean of all substances, including booze. After all, I have a lot of reasons to continue to live clean. My amazing family and my incredible new life are at the top of that list. Plus, I have a much better relationship with God, who is my higher power.

DID THEY REALLY FIND A CURE FOR HEPATITIS C?

I'd somehow survived to at least be on a waiting list for an actual cure for Hepatitis C. It's called Harvoni. I was told it was just one pill a day at the same time for twelve to 24 weeks. I've actually been waiting for a cure for Hepatitis C for at least 30, if not forty years. I think I got it when I was shooting heroin in Hawaii in 1972 and 73. So, it's currently 2014. Irony. I chose to wait for the Harvoni. I've waited all my life. So, now, I've been in a race against the clock to get the Harvoni treatment and be cured of Hepatitis C before it kills me. This is a serious race. The doctor recommended I not wait. He said the best, wisest thing to do would be to do what is available now. OH HELL NO!!!! I didn't agree with my liver specialist and I waited. It was a hard decision. Do I most likely die waiting for the cure or do I go ahead and do the one treatment available that's so harsh it's killing everybody? I was nearly dead already. Hmmmm. I waited.   Battling the insurance company for this treatment was another war I didn't anticipate. It was a very, very expensive treatment. I'm talking a few hundred thousand dollars, plus. It was new on the market and everybody dying of Hepatitis C was begging, demanding, strong-arming, whatever they had to do to get it in their bodies, they were doing it. So was I. I was cued in. I had friends like Jeri Lyn and my liver specialist working on this for me, too. She needed the treatment, too. I had to get this Harvoni treatment in me or I would be dead and soon. That was my reality. I looked like walking death. I was walking death. After I waited for what seemed like forever, they finally did come out with the Harvoni.

It took my doctor working with my insurance Company seven months for me to finally be approved for the Harvoni treatment. Drugs are expensive and life is precious. We're all shocked that I'm still alive. God, I was sick. Life has no price. So, finally, I was counseled by the nursing staff at the pharmacy dispensing this pricey pill and was sent my treatment kit from the doctor.

For twelve weeks, I took one pill a day at exactly 10 am. I, also, stayed in contact with a nurse I was set up with, to monitor me for the twelve weeks.

Finally, I WAS CURED! The harvoni worked! There's actually a cure for Hepatitis C.

For the first time in a lifetime, they found my enzymes in normal range and there was NO Hepatitis C found in my body. Six months later, I took my six month checkup and still NO hepatitis C in my body. One might ask, what I think about this result. I put myself through absolute hell to finally be free of hepatitis C. Let me tell you something. I'm more grateful than words on paper can describe. Consequences to my actions cost me dearly. For a lifetime, well, for forty years, I never gave the care of my health or body, a second thought. I was an active hard-drug user. I would do anything that I thought would make me feel euphoria. I lived in the problem for forty years.

I felt like I always had hepatitis C, I flashed back to the countless friends through the years that had died of this very thing. I lost so many friends. So many great people that I was close to, died from drug use.

I went through my entire life with a feeling of impending doom, knowing I had a virus in my body that was aggressively attacking my organs, destroying my life and killing all my friends, too.

The only out we had from that for many, many years, literally almost all of my life, was death. So, it was always in my thinking. God has given me a whole new life. It's because I went to Narcotics Anonymous. I would've never been cured of Hepatitis C had I not went to N A.

So, you admit you're an addict. The tiniest spark of light is shining inside you and you fear it's about to go out. It's time to do something different. What you've been doing hasn't been working, right? Embrace that flicker of hope and feel it slowly grow inside you.

Remember, if nothing changes...then, nothing changes.

STEP 1... N A

1. We admitted we were powerless over our addiction; that our lives had become unmanageable:

In this step, we face the reality of our addiction and finally admit our life is out of control. We're preparing ourselves to receive the help we need. We admit we're powerless. We've found a sliver of hope. It's been a very long road to get to this place. You have to understand that for most of my existence, I didn't understand at all. I didn't get it. In my head, I was where many of you reading this are right now. You don't get it right now and that's okay. Really, it's okay. Hopefully, this book will help you find the doorway to the recovery you need so desperately. If you know someone whose life is falling apart, quite possibly, this will open your mind to a deeper level of understanding and maybe, you can help them. Maybe, you don't even realize it, or, you're denying the reality that you have a problem. If anything in this book hits home, trust me, you may need to reassess. You, very well, could be an addict, or, like I mentioned a moment ago, you're reading this because you love someone who's an addict and you don't get it. I remember how lost I used to feel and how I didn't have a clue what I could do about it.

Just know and try to understand. I make no promises and I give no guarantees. There's no advice offered here. I only have suggestions. This information is here for you to choose to embrace, or, to choose to let go.

I think back through the years when so many people had to be literally bewildered by my insanity. I mean, in about every aspect of a normal life, I appeared to have it all together for so many years. So many periods of time that would roll on for years where I'm a family-man. I'm raising children with a wife, working as a cat rat, doing normal things like going out to eat with the family and going on trips and other cool stuff. I'd be doing art shows and book signings with my books, my poetry, posters, and whatever, and you wouldn't have a clue that I was sitting there going insane inside my head, craving cocaine so bad my brain was exploding. Then, out of nowhere, there

I'd go... absolute madness would appear. I can see why my behavior would turn heads and cause whispers, at times.

The life of a drug-addict, through the eyes of someone who's not an addict, has to be shocking, even devastating.

Many addicts, for the longest time, can be turning their world upside down and everyone around them can be in shock, thinking, "What's wrong with that person? That person is nuts. What in the hell is wrong with that person? He had a great job, a family, beautiful home, what the hell's going on with him?"

All this time, the addict thinks all this behavior is normal. Because, after a while, when you exist at the animal level, when you exist in torment, chaos and madness, day in and day out, that insanity begins to feel normal. The street hustle, for an addict in active addiction, is on. You think you get so smooth and slick with your 'addiction survival persona', that you don't realize the only person you're really hustling is yourself. This is sad, sick and very true. In case you're wondering, that addition survival persona is that person you pretend to be in active addiction, so, you can deal with street people and drug-dealers. It's a dangerous world and you have to create this image that you're tough and mean, so, nobody will hassle you or try to rob you.

Drug-addiction doesn't care about gender, race or economic stature. You just don't see or feel any of that when it's right in your face. How can anyone even begin to find hope, when, literally, there is none? How can anyone find faith when the deep, dark hole kills all the light? Conquering the feelings of powerlessness and overcoming the fear of a miserable existence is an almost impossible task. Feeling completely lost, and then, finding one's self is a very long and deep journey.

When you walk in to that first N A meeting, you hurt so bad you don't even realize that new life is possible. Deep down, here's what you really want... you want to figure out how to keep using your drug of choice and all the problems in your life just go away. Unfortunately, it doesn't work that way. I've yet to meet a social crack-head, or, a responsible one. They don't exist. The good news is this. If you keep coming to the meetings, eventually, you'll realize that living clean takes work. It's part of the journey for the newcomer to just want to know how to not use anymore.

Not everyone that uses or drinks is an addict.

But, many are. Some of these same people still destroy any priority list formulated. Some of these same people still self-destruct. Addiction crosses all boundaries. It doesn't care who you are, in life, what your plans are for a bright future, how your life is, or how you want it to be. You can have everything in the world going for you and still at the dismay and absolute confusion from everyone that knows you, you blow it. You start leisurely and innocently drinking or smoking a little weed, you start doing an occasional line of coke at a weekend party and this seemingly unimportant behavior, suddenly turns deadly, or, throws your life into utter chaos.

Many addicts don't start figuring it out until everything's fallen apart. The disease takes a person over and destroys everything in its wake. Sound familiar? It slips in like a thief in the night. It'll grab you from the clutches of all your best intentions, when you least expect it. An occasional party, a few drinks here and there and then, your daily life-schedule will start to waver. Your appointments will suddenly be put on the back-burner. It won't be apparent at first. You never plan to divert from your structured path.

Come on! Get real! This is you we're talking about, right? You never expect drugs or alcohol to be a problem in your life. Deny! Deny! Deny! I mean, you're you, right? This type of thing NEVER happens to you, right? WRONG!

If you ever even question if you're an addict, or not, ask yourself why you would question that. Is your life falling apart around you and you don't know why? You could be caught in a neurotic paradox and not even know it. So, you wonder what that means. I'll tell you what that means. An addict in active addiction is famous for this. I'll use me for an example. My life was falling apart. I literally had chaos everywhere I went and everywhere I looked. Every single time I was caught up in active addiction, I had cops always looking for me. I had dope-dealers looking for me.

I had friends that had let me borrow money that I hadn't paid back. They'd gotten tired of trying to find me. MY family, one by one, backed away for the sake of their own sanity and survival. I owed the bank. My health was falling apart. I had recurring pancreatitis. I had chronic liver disease, with Hepatitis C. You get the picture. There were disasters in every part of my life. In my mind, it was everybody else's fault. I blamed everyone else for all this crap going on in my life.

Here's the neurotic paradox.

Here's the reality of my situation. It was actually no one else's fault. I didn't actually have a hundred different problems and horrible situations going on in my life. I HAD ONE. I had one problem that created all this shit-storm in my life. What was that one problem?
I'm an addict in active addiction. That's the problem.

In other words, if I could figure out how to fix this one problem, that being this monster called active addiction, I believe, one by one, I could work these other problems out. How? Because, things would start to matter, to me, again and I'd focus on resolving them with solutions instead of complicating them with more problems.   In other words, I could change my hedonic calculus. I could face my destroyed self-efficacy and remove my addiction survival persona. I could work to turn that into my recovery survival persona. Somewhere, I lost myself and I needed to open myself up to who I am in the NOW and do what's necessary to embrace who I lost inside, somewhere along the way.
Addiction will change your path in life. Everything you'd planned in life that you wanted to work so hard to make happen will suddenly not be as important. Your life plans won't matter as much. That's not really it! Everything's still important.
It's just that the drugs, including the alcohol, start to matter more and you don't understand why. Here's a big reason why... addicts have a thinking problem. Thinking is a behavior. Our thinking is filled with some very bad behavior.

WHAT'S WRONG WITH ME?

There's a question asked by everyone afflicted with addiction... The following is the disease-model explanation for what happens inside the brain of an addict.

For the brain, the difference between normal rewards and rewards from a drug are like standing next to someone and talking in a normal voice and then, suddenly, for no reason, they scream at you. The brain has to immediately adjust to the overwhelming surges in dopamine and other neurotransmitters by producing less dopamine or by reducing the number of receptors that can receive signals. What happens then, because of that dopamine's impact on the reward circuit of the brain, (sometimes, called the pleasure center) of someone who abuses drugs, can became abnormally low and that person's ability to experience any pleasure is reduced.

Cognitive behavioral interventions are key to a treatment service. The truth is, the desire to use lingers strongly in early recovery. The majority of relapses happen within the first 72 hours. Even without the physical cravings, the addict remembers the rush of that dopamine surge. Their obsession and compulsion takes over inside their thinking. The most ideal recovery plan will allow the addict to pursue a fulfilling life, free of the chains of drugs, including alcohol. A life that will provide natural and real rewards once the previous source of dopamine is no longer available.

Like I said earlier, we have a thinking problem.

Our best thinking gets us into our worst situations.

Read that again.... Our best thinking gets us into our worst situations.

I'm sure many of you ask these questions;

1. How does an addict really stop using?
2. How does an addict live a normal life?
3. Is it possible to find a new and better way to live?
4. Why can't I use and drink occasionally?

   Those are questions that anyone in active addiction or with a loved one fighting addiction, wants answered. There is no worst feeling than to feel lost, confused and hurt over someone in the family, like a friend, or a relative who is completely caught up in active addiction, whose life is in complete and utter chaos, and not have a clue how to fix that. Not have a clue how to make that person stop stealing, start showering, start seeing their children, start working again and most of
all, how to make them stop using and abusing dope, all the time. It's horrible to not have any idea how to change this person's behavior and make them care about life again.

   I'll try to answer those questions, or, at least, help you have a better understanding.

   Also, remember this... most relapses happen within the first 24 to 72 hours. You know why? Because, as an addict begins to sober and clean up, the thinking takes over. The cravings take over. The real feelings that have been suppressed and numbed with the drugs including the alcohol, begin to surface.

   Those feelings and thoughts affect the emotions and it occurs to the addict, who is now beginning to feel everything, it would be easier to just say 'to hell with it' and go get high again. So, those first 72 hours are crucial to an addict's recovery.

Are you done yet?

If you are, here's one proven path to RECOVERY...   Okay.

   Find a detox center, if you need that and go there. Take a few extra pairs of socks and a few T-shirts, Don't forget your insurance card, even if it's state aid. Hopefully, they'll have a bed for you. If they don't, they will soon. Go back that afternoon, then, the next morning. Be persistent. You'll get a bed. While you're in detox, they'll assess you for a treatment center. Here's what a treatment center did for me and this is why I suggest one. It was a course in self-awareness. I realized in treatment that I had no idea who I was. I didn't even know me, at all. So, part of learning about me was realizing I'm a drug addict with a disease called addiction.

For that reason alone, for me, treatment was worth it. It gave me a sense of purpose, a pathway to pursue with a list of goals. I was lost and treatment did help me with a direction and a plan to work with. I must tell you, also, Narcotics Anonymous is in no way connected to any treatment centers. They are two separate entities with a common goal... both helping the next suffering addicts. In Illinois, State insurance will pay for your treatment if you're unable to work. If you're working, you probably have insurance. It's different in every state, so, check it out to be sure. Everybody's situation is different. The day you get out of treatment, 30 days, 60 days, or, however long, go to a meeting and you keep going to those meetings by any means

necessary. Let me say that again... The day you get out of treatment, go to a meeting and listen to the other addicts in the room. Keep going to those meetings. Get to know the people in the meetings. Especially the ones who have multiple years of clean time. Listen to what they say when they share. Many addicts relapse because they don't take going to the meetings seriously. Go to 90 meetings the first 90 days you get out of treatment and then, you decide for yourself.

Also, all those dope-dealers phone numbers and those people in your phone that still use and still drink, lose those numbers. Delete them all! Now, start getting phone numbers of people that go to N A.

I suggest every time you get a number from someone at N A, when you add the number to your contacts, put N A in front of their name. Then, over time, as you collect a whole lot of new N A families, numbers, you'll have them all together, in your contacts.

KEEP YOUR RECOVERY FIRST IN YOUR LIFE... Don't plan your meetings around everything else. Plan everything else around your meetings. We're there for each other. We're your new best friends. You'll learn more as you go and the clarity, oh, my goodness, the beautiful clarity. Best high ever. Who knew?

No matter what happens in your life, don't use and I promise you, your life will start to spiral upward? As long as you don't use any drugs, including booze, your life will continue to get better. Even the bad days will be better.

Do this, get clean for a year.

Commit yourself to one year of clean time and like the members of N A suggest, go to 90 meetings in the first 90 days. Start meeting people at the meetings in recovery. Let's suppose, after a year, a full year, you don't like the clean life. Then, by all means, go back out. Every 11 minutes, someone in America dies from an opioid overdose.

Recovery's not for people who need it. Recovery's for people who want it.

I kept going. I kept getting high. I continued to exist in the chaos of my own insanity. Through all the absolute bullshit, all the many, many times coke, heroin, crystal meth, or whatever would grab me by the
ass and you'd think, okay, he's going back to treatment now for sure. This is it! He's going to get help now, but, nope. Back into the madness I'd go, head-first. Year after miserable year. If you remember, the first time I went to treatment in April of 1983, I ended up there after I overdosed. I was taken by ambulance and was in intensive care in a coma for 3 or 4 days. I don't even know how many days. I just know that's how I ended up in detox and then, in treatment. The next and final time I found recovery was 37 hard, very hard, years later. This time I stumbled into an N A meeting at Sanity with my best friend, Ed.

I think this is how it actually unfolded for me, to finally embrace recovery. I was 37 years older than when I'd first went to treatment. I'd literally been using sporadically forever. Talk about an empty soul. It was around 2010 and I'd just gotten divorced. My liver was shot. Like an insane person, I was drinking rum every night traveling all over Texas, dying really, using my art showings as an excuse to exist in a wasted state of mind and hide all the pain. When I got back to

Illinois a year later, I continued in active addiction. I literally had a broken back, I was in the last stage of cirrhosis with Hepatitis C and no surprise, death was coming fast. What do I do? I lose it. I was existing on massive amounts of pain pills for my back and I felt so ashamed, because I started slipping downtown at 2 or 3 am on my Harley, in my disabled and wasted condition, buying eight-balls of coke from thugs. Then, going home alone, sitting in my bathroom alone, shooting the coke till it was gone, alone. One night, sitting there after doing a hit, I had a sharp pain in my chest. It felt like I was having a heart attack. I probably was, I mean, come on, I was shooting cocaine at my age and drinking rum, but, no matter, at the same time as this, I had a life-changing epiphany. It happened like this. As I was mixing another hit of the coke in the spoon, in the midst of complete depression and sweating like a dog, I accidently looked in the mirror and I saw myself. I looked into my own eyes and I didn't like who I saw at all. I saw how miserable I looked. My matted hair, my white skin and purple lips. Then, I stopped what I was doing and froze. I stopped and really looked into the glass. The questions poured from my brain like a cheap shot of whiskey. "What the fuck is wrong with me? Do I really want to die? Is this how it ends for me? My family will be so ashamed. I'm ashamed. My children, man? I can't do this to my children. I just can't. My liver's shot, I'm dying and here I am shooting coke like I'm thirty. No more." That was it. I guess this is what we call a defining moment. I shot the rest of that coke to get rid of it and get this… I was still having sharp chest pains. It was horrible. Do you see the insanity in that behavior? Sitting here right now, writing this, I see the insanity in that. I have to wonder… how on earth did I sink so low and exist in such despair for so many years. I guess that's why it's important to live in the now. I know one thing.

For me, that was really it. No more. This was me hitting my bottom.

Chapter 20

DO THE WORK OTHERS AREN'T WILLING TO DO
AND YOU'LL GET THE THINGS OTHERS WILL NEVER HAVE.

WHAT IS ADDICTION?

That's a great question. Let's begin there. The National Institute of Drug Abuse (NIDA) defines addiction as a chronic, relapsing brain disease that is characterized by compulsive drug-seeking and use, despite harmful consequences.

1. In the United States, 8–10% of people over the age of 12 are addicted to alcohol or other drugs. That's approximately 22 million people. That number is growing dramatically, even as you read this. 2. (Cigarette smoking is also an addiction that kills people.) Addiction is chronic—but it's also preventable and treatable. When a disease is chronic, that means it's long-lasting. It can't be cured, but it can be managed with treatment. Other examples of chronic diseases include asthma, diabetes, and heart disease. It's critical that treatment simultaneously addresses any co-occurring neurological or psychological disorders that are known to drive vulnerable individuals to experiment with drugs and become addicted in the first place. Otherwise, the best addiction treatment in the world alone is not effective for those with co-occurring illnesses. Addiction is a disease. Respected institutions like the American Medical Association and the American Society of Addiction Medicine define addiction as a disease.
3.   Studies published in top-tier publications like "The New England Journal of Medicine" support the position that addiction is a brain disease.

4.   A disease is a condition that changes the way an organ functions. Addiction does this to the brain, changing the brain on a physiological level. It literally alters the way the brain works, rewiring its fundamental structure. That's why scientists say addiction is a disease. Although there is no cure for addiction, there are many evidence-based treatments that are effective at managing the illness. Like all chronic illnesses, addiction requires ongoing, life-long, management that may include the Narcotics Anonymous 12 step program, therapy, and lifestyle changes.

Duel Issues- Mental Illness and addiction...

In the N A literature it clearly states, we must abstain from all drugs in order to recover. But, there are situations where a doctor may prescribe medicine for mental illness, or, even methadone to wean someone off opiates, etc. Realize that anyone with a mental health issue should be under the care of a mental health professional. Treatment plans can include visits to mental health professionals for the proper care. Any medicines like psychotropic drugs that are prescribed by a doctor and taken correctly shouldn't interfere with a recovering addict's clean time. Anytime, you questions issues of this nature, contact your sponsor.

Hopefully, in time, an addict can stop the use of a maintenance program such as Sub Oxone, methadone, or, the Vivitrol shot and work to live a life in recovery.

Once in recovery from substance use disorder, with the correct treatment plan, it is possible for a person with mental health issues, who's under the care of a doctor, to go on and live a healthy and successful life. Addiction and mental illness are both treatable with professional help and recovery should be the expected outcome of treatment.

Relapse does NOT have to be a part of recovery.

Living life completely free and clean is and should be an addict's ultimate goal.

~<>~

Stormy Monday- sitting on his 2007 Street Glide- Miss Mojo-2015

SOMETHING TO THINK ABOUT... (Please note... The following information is NOT to push anyone away from N A or A A. As we continue to grow in recovery, we hopefully learn to remain teachable. So, consider this part of that education some of us didn't even know we needed. Why not embrace the info and share it, so, we don't continue to spread the misinformation among newcomers.)

Pick a program.

A good sponsor will tell you that. Muddying the messages in meetings does not send a clear message to the newcomers. What does that mean? It means this. A A and N A are not the same program. Suggestion: Stop spreading that false information. A A was created for alcoholics specifically. A A is for alcoholism. Go to an A A meeting and they'll be very clear about that. Hi, I'm whoever and I'm an alcoholic. I have another 24 hours SOBER. That's a good thing. No confusion. A A is a clear-cut 12 step program to aid in the recovery of alcoholism. If you happen to be an alcoholic, it's good to be a friend of Bill W.

338

To recap... Drug-addicts, on the other hand, were being kicked out of A A meetings in southern California back in the early days. So, the addicts knew they had to do something different to try to start saving addicts lives. A small group led by Jimmy K. asked permission from A A to borrow the concept of A A and create a 12 step program with literature specifically for people who suffer from addiction. N A recognizes alcohol as a drug. Study the Traditions and it's very clear. It's either, "Hi, I'm whoever and I'm an alcoholic at A A", or, it's clearly, "Hi, I'm whoever and I'm an addict", at N A.

A lot of treatment centers promote this confusion. It's no one's fault. Fault is irrelevant. As we continue to grow in the program, be it N A or A A, we begin to familiarize ourselves with the specific 12 Traditions which send a clear message to each program.

And a....this is also false information. It's actually not possible to be an addict and a alcoholic. Not if you actually read the literature. It's a simple deduction. Ask yourself... do you have problems drinking too much alcohol, but, you've never used drugs? If so, there's a very good chance Alcoholics Anonymous is for you. On the other hand, if you've used different drugs, drank alcoholic liquors like whiskey, vodka, gin, wine or beer, or, taken way too many pills way too often, snorted coke, smoked meth, or, used opiates, maybe you eat too much all the time or gamble way too much or maybe you consider yourself a sex freak having sex with just about anybody, or, you demand sex all the time from your spouse... well, there's a real good chance Narcotics Anonymous might be your cup of tea. One more thing... It's in the literature. I encourage you to read the literature. If you're abusing alcohol, I suggest you stop by an A A meeting and get yourself the "Big Book". Do yourself a favor and spend some time reading it. If you're abusing drugs, including the alcohol, stop by a Narcotics Anonymous meeting and acquire, "The Basic Text" and spend some time reading it.

"Every day CLEAN for an addict is truly a miracle". No truer words could be spoken. Those words are in the basic Text. Addicts in recovery live each day CLEAN. Alcoholics live one day at a time SOBER.

We don't live clean AND sober. It's one or the other. Saying to others, "Oh, there the same program." No, they're not. It's nothing personal. Don't take it personal, but, it just shows lack of education on the actual differences between the two. Honestly, read the literature. Also, saying, "Oh, it doesn't matter, I go to both." That just promotes the lack of understanding of the differences. I realize we're all on different levels of our recovery knowledge. I know there's so much more I'm looking forward to learning. Just be aware that when someone in the program introduces themselves as clean and sober, what that really means is this. They haven't learned that we're one or the other, yet. In time, if you stay in recovery, hopefully, you'll learn that addicts are learning how to live clean at N A and alcoholics go to A A to learn how to live sober.

If any of this strikes a nerve, or, makes your brain feel defensive because you've been living clean and sober for so many years, don't shoot the messenger. I'm just stating facts.

Read the Basic Text if you love N A, or, read the Big Book if you love A A. If you're not sure, by all means, read them both. Then, if one connects with you, pick that one. I have a final thought on this. I do my own recovery and I help others whenever I can. That's why I've spent several years of my life writing this book. After you read this and if you do make the decision to continue to identify yourself as "clean and sober", or, "I'm an alcoholic and an addict".... that's on you. It doesn't matter to me, or, affect me in any way.

It's your recovery. Do what keeps you clean.

You can be part of the solution or you can be part of the problem. You get to choose.

~<>~

ENABLER

In this chapter I'm going to share with you more very important information about addiction. You may not understand this, then again, hey, maybe you will. Maybe you've lived with an addict that you loved with all your heart, or, as heartbreaking as it is, maybe, one of your children is an addict, or, maybe, a loved one that means the world to you, is an addict. Maybe you have a dear friend, or a child, that's put you through the worst hell ever, for a long time, borrowing, burning you, apologizing over and over, then, burning you again, when all you ever wanted to do was help. Help your friend, help your son or your sweet daughter, clean up and be normal again. Whatever normal is. Worst yet, somewhere, between helping at least a hundred times, not sleeping, worrying, making excuses to cover for your loved ones insanity and chaos, it hits you one morning at about 3 am during another sleepless night... "HELPING'S NOT HELPING."

Trying to help your child or your friend clean-up is, in many ways, pushing that person you love with all your heart, closer and closer to the grave. It's a difficult truth to process, but, it's very true. You're enabling this person to stay wasted, to continue spiraling downward, and to continue on this nightmarish path to certain ruin and death. STOP IT! PLEASE, JUST STOP IT! Don't do that anymore! I know, right now you're thinking, I couldn't possibly understand how much you love that person you're helping. But, I do understand. You can still be empathetic and not allow yourself to be used.

Even more devastating than all of these things, more horrendous than your mind can process or accept, maybe, someone you loved very much with every fiber of your being, your son, your daughter, your wife or your husband, has died because of addiction. Overdosed. Gone forever. I believe you, more than anyone, will understand what I'm about to say... Listen to me... No one and nothing could've stop me from using.

No one. Nobody. Nothing. Until something inside me snapped and I made the conscious decision to make life or death decisions for change, nobody was going to make me stop using. I know it's a part of addiction that none of us really understand or get, but, it's like that for all addicts. So, pay attention to this...Try to understand this. Try to be aware, I'll say it one more time... No one and nothing could've stop me from using.

If you're holding on to guilt, for not saving this person. For not reaching out and giving them money, or, whatever they said they needed. Let go of your guilt. I know it's not easy, but, you have to let it go. It'll eat you like cancer. This disease consumed your loved one. It was out of your hands. There was nothing you could do to change the outcome. So, hold on to the memories and let the guilt go, for your own inner peace. Let me try to explain.

This is from my own personal experience.

Not my job, not my wife who I loved with all my heart, not my children who I worshipped and treasured, not my family who always loved me unconditionally, not my friends who I valued deeply, not overdosing multiple times, not any nasty jail and I was in a whole bunch of nasty jails, not any hell-hole prison and I was in some of the worst of the worst...not near death or bad health, not threats from anyone, nothing, let me repeat, no one and nothing could've stop me from using. Everything and everyone tried to stop me, so, I wouldn't die, but, NO WAY! Dope took me over.

The harsh reality is this... addiction is the most mysterious, most cunning and baffling disease known to man and, unfortunately, very deadly.

So, let's talk about this. You say you have a son, or, a daughter, maybe, it's your cousin, or, your lover, hell, it could be your best friend. Whoever it is, this person has a drinking or using problem. They can't stop drinking, or, using cocaine, or, heroin, or, whatever their drug of choice happens to be. You really love this person and it kills you to see them so messed up all the time. So, out of your deep and sincere love for this person, you help pay their bills, you help buy their groceries, you give them gas money, or, maybe, you're paying their rent, so, they don't lose their home. You reason with yourself. "Oh, I'll help this person for a while and they'll clean up eventually and pay me back." WRONG! WRONG, WRONG!!!

That's not going to happen. I'm just being brutally honest with you before you start spending half your check on this person with absolutely good intentions. Your hearts in the right place. But, what you're doing could kill this person you love so much.

I have a few SUGGESTIONS...

It's okay to set boundaries. It's okay to show compassion and still not give them money.

They will NEVER STOP using as long as you continue to make it possible for them to do so. I know you mean well, but, giving the using addict money for any reason is a deadly mistake. Let me repeat this... helping the addict, till the final breath, because you see your FRIEND, FAMILY MEMBER OR LOVER so messed up and you think by helping, things will get better and they'll want to stop. NO! It doesn't work that way. HELPING AN ADDICT WITH MONEY AND A PLACE, PAYING THEIR BILLS, giving them gas money, etc. It's a path to death. You're enabling the person to continue on the path of active and deadly addiction.

Here's the reality of it.

Once we get consumed by active addiction, all of that stuff like paying bills, rent, lights, etc., doesn't matter. Priorities get lost in the haze. They no longer exist to an addict. The number one and only priority is to get money to buy drugs. So, when the enabler hands over that money for whatever, supposedly for the rent, or, to pay a bill, or, to buy some food, hell, there's a million reasons to give an addict money and there's one serious reason not to.

I assure you they will buy drugs instead. An enabler means well, but, enabling is not good for the addict's recovery.

If the addict survives all the hell, chaos, self-destruction and pain, there will be that final small flicker of light somewhere on that path, inside that body and mind that will flicker and go out. That's the weary soul falling into darkness. Then, the myth of willpower goes right out the window. Only then, when no one and nothings left, in most cases, will, inside the addict's sick mind, getting clean, make more sense than continuing to exist in active addiction.

Just know, INSTEAD, you can always explain to the addict that your love is still there and it will be forever. That won't change. But, you don't know how to help them stay alive and that scares you. You just know giving them money is not helping them while they're in active addiction. So, inside your heart, you believe the answer is to NOT help them get high.

Whatever the answer is, giving them money will NOT help the situation.

Sometimes you have to grab the bull by the horns.

THE DEEPER SOUL...

SPIRITUALITY... Somebody once asked me, "You think the man upstairs is really out there? Do you think Gods really there?"

People come from all walks of life, all with their own personal belief systems. Some get busy in life and never connect. Some simply don't believe. For others, like myself, my mother, my late father and my five sisters, it was never a question. Faith in God, for my family, and many others, has always been the driving force in our lives. Having a Higher Power can mean different things to different people. That's just reality. So, I think your actions and how you answer that question, could very well impact your entire life.

Here's the thing... a lot of addicts, when they hit a bottom, and we've all hit different bottoms at different times, have only a few places left to go, a 12-step meeting, detox, treatment, jail or death. Then, there's an emptiness. The soul died. There's nothing left. Many have no idea what a Higher Power is, nor, do they want to know. Many have no concept of God or, any pre-conceived notions of a God of their understanding. There's no understanding. In time, with recovery, as our spirit comes back to life and things start to matter, spirituality enters the thinking. We start asking questions. We know we need something to hold onto, but, we don't know what it is. We all need a Good Orderly Direction.

After some deep soul-searching and pulling from my own belief system, here's my thinking on this... I've been through a lot of life experiences. Some were very messed up. I'm not unique and I'm not delusional. But, I do have a testimony that may help addicts find recovery. Addicts do a lot of crazy shit in active addiction. We all have our own set of struggles. After a lifetime of surviving, over and over, year after year, with so many battles, I have to believe Gods out there. With so many things going on, so much loss and tragedy I've gone through, all the life-changes in the blink of an eye, I have to believe Gods out there. When I think about the enormous amount of friends and family I've lost, all the personal and serious health trauma I've experienced and lived through, I know God must be out there. All the health issues I've survived like Hepatitis C, chronic liver disease, major spine injuries, multiple surgeries, repeated pancreatitis, multiple divorces, multiple overdoses, alcohol poisoning, terminal illness, heart attacks, all the forks in the road, the misery, the pain, the despair, man, I don't know how I couldn't think God's out there. He's my Higher Power! Hell yes! God's out there!

This is what I believe. Like the story about the one set of footprints in the sand and how the lost soul feels alone and forsaken, because he only sees one set of footsteps in the sand. Most of us already know that's not the lost soul's footprints walking in the sand, silly rabbit. That one set of footprints in the sand is God's footprints, when he's carrying you.

Even in those times, actually, especially in those times, when we don't think he's working in our lives, that's when he's got us most. That's what I believe. We do have free will, but, I believe with all my heart, God is the all-knowing. He knows far more than all of us. In my book, he's the Great Spirit. He's the One God. He's our Creator! Hello, you there? Listen to me, he'll guide you, if, you'll let him, but, you have to steer the car. We've all said it a million times... You can lead a horse to water, but, you can't make him drink it.

You want to feel God? Has God made you mad? Do you feel he's given up on you?

You want to become more spiritual? I have a few suggestions. Try talking to him. Do it while you're alone if you want. Tell him what's on your heart. Ask him for help. Tell him what really needs to happen in your life and ask him for some intervention. Pray to God! I want you to know, as you grow in a 12 step program, like Narcotics Anonymous, your spirituality is growing, too. It's part of the program. It's part of a good, healthy and spiritual life! Many of us are like the walking dead when we first stumble into a meeting. Our souls are gone somewhere else. We're dead inside. Many of us don't understand that at first, but, if we stick it out and stay, if we keep coming back and when we do get a sponsor and begin working the steps, and we keep it a WE program, we'll find that a relationship with the God of our understanding plays an important and major role in improving our spiritual principles. Why not go somewhere alone and pray out loud to the God of your understanding?   Be grateful for everything in your life and remember our Narcotics Anonymous 12th step. It's the perfect step to pay close attention to in your day to day life.

12. Having had a spiritual awakening as the result of these steps, we tried to carry this message to the addict and to practice these principles in all our affairs.

Remember this... God, who is my Higher Power, is not mad at you. He hasn't forsaken you. He's waiting for you to open your heart and talk to him. So, you've prayed to him and you don't think he's answered you? We've all heard it a million times and I believe it's true. God works in mysterious ways. He doesn't follow our plan. We don't control his actions. God does things his way in his own time. In time, with faith, if you're cognizant and cued in, you'll be surprised when you realize that your prayers are, or, were answered.

Have faith in your Higher Power.

Chapter 21

Forgive yourself for not knowing what you didn't know before
you learned it.

SUGGESTIONS...

We're NOT responsible for our disease. But, we ARE responsible for our recovery. Once we make the conscious decision to live in recovery, why not make every effort to feel the joys of a robust recovery. What is a robust recovery, you ask? I would have to say it means getting the most out of living clean along your new path.

The following are Narcotics Anonymous suggestions shared with me, by those with more recovery than me, so, that, along the way, I can now share them with you...

We truly are links on a never-ending chain. Here are some suggestions we pass from addict to recovering addict, in the hopes that recovery will stick and the addict will decide to stay.

1. The best first thing to find recovery is STOP USING.
2. Get a sponsor, you've come to know, and can learn to trust.
3. Recovery is an active change in our ideas and attitudes.
4. Meetings strengthen our recovery with our new-found tools.
5. Involvement with the fellowship is a valuable tool.
6. We share our pain in the meetings with others.
7. We learn that service work will get us out of ourselves.
8. It's helpful to have a sponsor who's worked the steps.
9. Work the steps with your sponsor, in the correct order.
10. We seek solutions, not problems.
11. Pain shared is pain lessened.
12. Thoughts of getting high? You don't have to act on it.
13. There's spiritual growth in helping others.
14. We cannot keep the gift of recovery unless we give it away.

15. No matter what, we don't use. Embrace new-found clarity.
16. Remain in the NO MATTER WHAT CLUB... don't ever use.
17. We learn that RECOVERY is a life-long journey.
18. Being clean and living in recovery, two different things.
19. Carry the message of recovery to the still-suffering addicts.
20. We learn that N A is a spiritual, not religious program.
21. Willpower won't keep us clean. Surrender to a Higher Power.
22. We must abstain from all drugs in order to recover.
23. As we continue to grow, we do our best to remain teachable.
24. We always try to do the next right thing.
25. We try really hard to always be humble.
26. We do our best to live an honest program.
27. The pink cloud feels great. Enjoy it and know it may go away.
28. Good and bad things still happen in recovery. Stay clean.
29. Work the N A program, the N A program will work for you.
30. We do our own inventory.
31. Be vigilant in your recovery.
32. Isolation and complacency can lead to relapse. Be cognizant.
33. Recovery is first in your life. You're no good to anyone using.
34. Plan life around meetings. Don't plan meetings around life.
35. Keep coming back, more will be revealed.

I want to share with you something not often discussed. After you succeed in getting clean, realize living clean is a life-time journey.

Once you get clean you have to figure out how to stay clean, or, what's the point? Right?

Yes, of course, work the N A program, but, what else?

It's equally important to create a new life, so, you can make it easier to NOT USE. Fill your life with positive goals. College, hobbies, a good job, clean friends to spend time with, family, fun activities, bowling, art classes, camping, canoeing and cook-outs, etc., Stay busy in the positive. Don't get lazy in this endeavor. It's vital. This is the path to a robust recovery. Do not isolate.

If you don't create a new life, then, all the factors that led you into the addiction that wreaked havoc on your life will most likely, catch up with you again.

Read the N A literature thoroughly. The 'Basic Text', 6th Edition, is priceless to an addict seeking recovery. The 'Just for Today' has a bit of wisdom for each day of the year. You'll be amazed how often the daily read from the JFT will hit you right between the eyes relative to your particular situation in life. We also have a book, titled, "Living Clean". I enjoy reading chapters in this book often. Also, we have the 'Green & Gold', another really great read. We even have a book about sponsorship.

Also, in the N A program, always respect everyone's anonymity. If you want anyone to know you're in recovery and a member of N A, that's your business, but, NEVER, EVER let anyone outside the program know any other N A members name. What goes on in N A stays in N A. Take me, for example... I want everyone to know I'm in recovery. I own that and sharing that with others actually helps me stay clean. One could say I live RECOVERY OUT LOUD!!!! I own it! That's my personal choice. I want people to see the different and better me and then, have that aha moment when they realize why I was such a mess most of my life. I want to instill in others the possibilities... hey, if I can change my life from the nightmare I survived, so can you, no matter how dire your situation is. This is my RECOVERY OUT LOUD!!!

WHAT TO EXPECT AT AN OPEN N A MEETING...

To begin our open meetings... First, on the business side, at our Group conscience meetings, we vote in our chair people from members who've expressed an interest. They must have at least 3 to 6 months of clean time, based on what the members agree to. These people agree to chair meetings at specific days and times.

It's the chair person's responsibility to: Unlock the door and open the meeting place, Greet the addicts, especially the new ones.

Turn on the lights,

Make coffee,

Hand out correct literature to read,

Chair the meeting,

Count the 7th Tradition cash

And secure the cash, in an envelope, as pre-arranged, for the treasurer, any clean-time tags, give them out to celebrate clean time,

And amount of cash, are recorded in accounting back-up ledger,

Open the floor for sharing,

And finally, keeping the meeting orderly,

Allow 3 to 5 minutes of sharing from each member that wants to share, and, then, close the meeting with announcements.

Huddle and say serenity prayer or 3rd step prayer.

Then, clean the meeting room,

Clean the coffee pots and cups,

Take out garbage, Turn out the lights and finally, Lock the door.

To help you better understand the workings of an N A open meeting... Here's a typical meeting from beginning to end...

To begin... (Usually one hour long) Doors are open, addicts greeted and sitting down. Chair-person introduces self and gives the name of the meeting place, the time and day. Together, led by chair person, we say the Serenity Prayer. After any announcements, addicts read the following, "Who is an addict", "what is the NA program"? "Why are we here", "how it works" and "the 12 Traditions"? Then, we celebrate clean time for those that earn it. It's here that we recognize any newcomers and give them a hug. The reason for this is simple. The newcomer is the most important person in the room. We know how difficult it is to walk into an N A meeting the first time. It takes a lot of courage. So, recovering addicts reflect back when a newcomer is in the room. It reminds each of us how horrible it can be out there in the streets. It's a good reminder for each of us why we're in recovery. Of course, there are meetings all over the world and I'm sure all meetings are a little different, but, the N A program is set in stone. After we celebrate clean time, someone reads the "Just for Today". After that, the chair-person reads a page or so from the Basic Text. Lastly, in honor of the 7th Tradition which states we're fully self-supporting, we pass a basket and collect money from the addicts in the meeting. This is counted by the chair-person and sealed in an envelope. That is recorded in our accounting notebook and the envelope is put away for rent, books, lights, coffee, etc. After the money is collected, the floor is then open for sharing. This is where all the addicts can share what's on their minds or in their hearts. We try to be respectful of the time. This means we suggest no one share longer than 3 to 5 minutes. No cross-talking. This gives more people the opportunity. Some just listen and that's okay, too. Usually, the meetings last one hour. We close the meeting with the 3rd step prayer or serenity prayer. What goes on in the meetings is supposed to stay in the meetings. Addicts must feel comfortable to share insane things they've done with others. So, we keep what's shared in the room.

We have open meetings for everyone, we have closed meetings for members of N A, area meetings for business affairs, we have interesting speaker meetings to share experience, strength and hope, we have group conscience meetings to vent, air our differences and communicate our thoughts and feelings to the group. Always remember this...

Everyone in N A is equal.

Hospitals & Institutions... H & I - H & I is another great way to do service work in the Narcotics Anonymous program. In a group conscience meeting, you let it be known that you'd like to do H & I. WHAT IS H & I?

H & I is another way for recovering addicts to do service work. Usually, the addict should be in recovery for at least 6 months. (Approved by the home group, group conscience & the hospital or institution) Once approved, the recovering addict responsible for scheduling, etc., schedules recovering addicts to chair meetings at hospitals, treatment centers, detox, jails and even prisons. This gives the patients at these facilities an opportunity to get familiar with N A.

This will, hopefully, help them on their path to recovery.

COURAGE...

After soul-searching, you've decided the time has come. It's been hell. You admit you're at the end of your rope. You threw your priorities to the side a long time ago. Life's a mess and it's been that way. The drugs, the sex, the food, or, the gambling, whatever it may be, is destroying every part of your world. A lot of your friends have already overdosed and died from drug-use. The deaths are hitting way too close to home. People are dying all around you. You're scared. It's not easy at all, but, you've finally gotten the courage to go to an N A meeting. Someone told you about a meeting place. You want to check it out. You found out when and where it's happening and you go. It took all your courage you had inside your heart to actually go to that first meeting.

But, the truth is, you're so sick and tired of existing in a state of constant cravings and pain, going to this meeting has to feel better than that. So, you did it. You went in and sat down. People kept coming up and introducing themselves and giving you a hug. I bet you didn't expect that. I know I didn't. That made you feel welcome.

It wasn't quite as awkward. Maybe, you were a little shy at first. No one in the streets had hugged you for a long time, in fact, you've forgotten how long it's been, so, it felt good to get those hugs. The people there surprised you. They were really nice to you and made you feel comfortable. You didn't expect that for some reason, but, it made you feel good about being there. There was fellowship and it felt good to feel that after being alone for so long. It seemed that everyone knew each other. Hmmm. This might be okay.

This is very important information I'm about to share with you. It was told to me by someone at an N A meeting with more clean time than me. So, now, I'm sharing it with you and today, hopefully, you'll find recovery and you'll share this information with the next suffering addicts. That's who we are. We help each other.

You might think it's a place where people are going to confront you, maybe even angrily, and they'll demand you stop using drugs right now and change.

That won't happen. You'll be the most important person at that meeting.

For the newcomer, we suggest you go to 90 meetings in 90 days. When you get to that place of surrender, many will tell you they went to two or three hundred meetings in 90 days. So did I. I was scared to not be at all the meetings for quite some time. I really wanted to stay clean, so, I went to every meeting offered at Sanity, my home group. I went to 2 or 3 meetings a day for the first 32 months of my recovery. It took me that long to feel ok going to 5 or 6 meetings a week. Meetings are very important. It doesn't matter how much clean time you have, meetings will always be important to attend.

Once you go for a while, you'll find more clarity and gain more understanding. Plus, the meetings will grow in you. The fellowship with like-minded people is inspiring.

It does take a lot of courage to walk into that first meeting, but, believe me, it's so worth it. I assure you, you won't be met with any anger or demands. That's simply not how Narcotics Anonymous or the 12-steps works. No demands will be made on you during any meeting: participation in events like camping, fishing, game nights, speaker meetings or whatever are always voluntary... and, remember, sharing is always voluntary. The only thing asked is that you share your first name so that people can identify you during meetings. If you consider yourself an addict, it's okay to say so. It's good to admit it and to own it. You can also choose to go into the meetings, sit quietly and listen.

Many will do that for a while until they feel more comfortable opening up. Then, usually, the flood-gates open. All the pain, hurt, misery and sorrow comes flowing out. We learn that what we say inside those meeting rooms and see inside those meeting rooms is supposed to stay inside those rooms. We ask that no one brings drugs, weapons, or, paraphernalia into our meetings.

There are closed meetings and open meetings. New-comers are encouraged to go to open meetings and to sit and listen to others share their experience, strength and hope. If something is heavy on someone's heart, then, sharing is okay, usually from three to five minutes. Non-addicts may also attend an open N A meeting. They are welcome to observe, listen and show support for the newcomers. Closed meetings are for addicts. Speaker meetings are for guest speakers. A guest speaker will speak for the better part of an hour and are a great source of inspiration and hope for the still suffering addicts.

This will all be done with the help of a sponsor. A sponsor is someone you meet in the meetings that you like and learn to trust enough to share your information. It may take a little time to find the sponsor you really want to work with. It will be someone you have become friends with over time. Regardless of your progress in the 12-steps, there's always someone at an N A meeting that will be willing to help you along the way.

Any concerns or issues can be discussed at a group conscience meeting. Other business will happen at area meetings. There are other factions of N A, also, which can be explored as you continue to grow in the program. We encourage participation and fellowship.

It's important to be aware that we're all equal. Anonymity means we're equal the moment we walk in the door. So, you're a doctor, a nurse, maybe a painter. Not in an NA meeting. Everyone is an addict. Nothing more, nothing less. All equal. Maybe you're a fat guy, or, a skinny chick, a Christian, you might be ugly as a dog, or, tell me no, you could be dumb as a box of rocks... It really doesn't matter.   In the Narcotics Anonymous meeting, we're all addicts. No Senators, Governors, mayors or teachers... no fancy guys, or, penniless vagabonds. There's no separation by name or title. So, you're a

China-man, a Russian, or, a Filipino, hey, you're Mexican, look, there's one of those white guys, or, there's a real pretty girl, or, it could even be a black guy and his wife, might be a Catholic, or, could be Jewish... good news, in a meeting, nobody cares whatsoever. You're an addict. Dude, chick, confused, very confused, it doesn't matter.

In an N A meeting, you're an addict and we're all equal. Never forget that!

Positions are voted in, like Treasurer, chair-people, etc.

Remember, this is a spiritual, not religious program. ~<>~

It's never too late to become what you might have been.

MAINTENANCE...

The following is controversial in the Narcotics Anonymous family. No matter our possible differences, we do agree on one thing... our common goal is to live a life free of the chains of addiction.

First and fore-most, just know I'm very aware we each must do our own recovery. We all have plenty of situations, or, issues, in our own lives. We have no business taking someone else's inventory. It's true that what works for one person may not work for another. Here's why I finally grew to accept that truth. It's a simple reality that slapped me right across the face. Here it is. A A doesn't work for me. I was a dope-shooting junkie. BAM! A A doesn't hit me right. I tried it several times and I couldn't connect to it. However, when I walked into an N A meeting, there was an instant connection that continued to grow. When I started reading the N A literature, that confirmed it. I identified with it. I didn't identify with the A A big book. No one's at fault here. It just wasn't for me. The point is this. If A A doesn't click with me, then, I can only deduce that N A might not click for some either. That's it in a nutshell. So, I'm more open-minded about that than I once was, not that long ago. I consider that growth. Here's the thing. I assure you I've personally tried to get clean and stay clean about every way possible. I've bargained with myself a hundred times and made these idiotic and dumbass deals with myself to try and rationalize my drug-use and abuse. "Okay, I'll only shoot an eight-ball on Friday night." Yeah, right! How about this one? "I'll only buy a gram of crack when I get paid and that's it. Period." It even sounds stupid as I write it, but, at the time, I really meant that. It doesn't work. The whole check and everything of value will be gone. I've been weaned off a severe heroin addiction with methadone a few different times. My mistake the first time, was, I used it for about 4 months after I was clean and then I said, screw it and went back to shooting heroin. So, from that, I learned something. Let the methadone serve its purpose, to wean an addict off opiate addiction. Then, stop using it. Live clean. This is what I grew to believe after my own personal experience.

I was young then and I know first-hand, its difficult getting and staying clean for a younger person. I failed at it, too, so, I get it. But, it can be done.

When I was strung out on China-white at 18 years young, my shooting partner and I would occasionally cop methadone in the streets, on the island of Oahu, to get high on. It would just help us with our physical withdrawals while we waited on our dope, our China-white heroin.

Plus, this is important and where I've personally, grown to. I want you to understand one thing. I always suggest Narcotics Anonymous because in my personal experience, I know it works. One doesn't have to look far at all to see addicts living in recovery all over the world because of N A. So, because of that, I always want addicts to find something that works. However, like I said, as I continue to grow and become more educated about addiction, I'm beginning to realize we really are all different. Maybe N A might not work for you. Even if you're not willing to put in the work to make N A work for you, the bottom line is it still doesn't work for you. So be it. I know A A doesn't work for me and I'm sure that's entirely because I was into drugs and I didn't relate to a program that doesn't recognize drug use. I didn't just drink. I needed more than a program designed for alcoholism. I needed a program designed for addiction. I needed a program that considers alcohol a drug, also. So, I get it and I understand.

Here's the deal. Here's what really matters. If N A doesn't work for you, I pray you find something that does. Whether it be a maintenance program with methadone, sub Oxone, or, whatever. I hope you find something that works in your life. I say if it helps improve your quality of life and helps you stay off the streets, has you developing relationships with your family again, helps you go to work every day and overall, improves your day to day living, do it. I say go for it! If it doesn't affect your finances in a negative way, absolutely, go for it. Let's not let our egos cloud our judgement. Here's what's important. You're trying your best to live a better life. The goal here is to live a meaningful life with purpose and some level of inner-peace. So, do whatever you feel you need to do to make your life and the lives around you better. If you feel clarity in your thinking and a true sense of inner-peace on your journey, it's your journey. But, please, share your experience, strength and hope with the still-suffering addicts. Help others find a better way.

Just be aware that the misuse of a drug to string along the addiction has some very strong personal opinions on the matter. We each have a right to our own opinions and beliefs. Remember, no matter what, continue to do you. Don't let others affect your recovery by their comments, or, judgements.

From my experience, just think about this. No judgement here. It's your recovery. If you're part of a maintenance program and you're taking methadone, etc. for a number of years, in truth, even if the program was free and you know it's actually expensive, but, here's the real cost... you're still chained to a drug. You still have to make your regularly scheduled trips to the methadone clinic and believe me, you won't miss a visit, because, you've learned if you stop going, your withdrawal symptoms are more severe than the initial heroin withdrawal symptoms. If you think about it, if you're still making trips to the methadone clinic for your fix, after 3 months, don't you honestly think you're still strung out and you can soul-search your own situation. Only you can decide if you feel you're really in recovery. Like I said, I make no judgements. I'm only pointing out some reality.

You can rationalize and say at least now you're not in the streets using heroin, but, the truth is you're still chasing a high. How can you not agree? It's still costing money that could be better spent elsewhere. Three hundred dollars or more a month out of your finances to stay in a maintenance program is tragic, in itself. Especially if you have children.

Like I said, the people that will have a problem with my perception of this situation will be someone currently strung out on the methadone, someone swallowing sub Oxone every day, or, someone working at a methadone clinic. The people that will acknowledge that it feels amazing to finally have clarity and really be in recovery will be many of the very people that lived on methadone, or, sub Oxone for a number of years and finally broke free of the chains, weaned themselves down and no longer take any of those drugs. These are the addicts that are, hopefully, working the N A 12 steps with a sponsor, going to meetings and living in recovery. They will speak often of the new-found clarity they feel after finally breaking completely free of all maintenance drugs and all drugs, including booze. These are the addicts who've learned, NO MATTER WHAT, they can't use any drugs, including alcohol, to live a clean life in recovery.

Clearly, our literature speaks of the mentally ill, or, the sick, also. If someone is mentally ill, or, sick, and are being prescribed drugs by a physician and the addict takes these drugs as prescribed, according to the Basic Text, this will not affect clean time.

What we learn as we continue to grow in the program is addicts who finally do stop the maintenance program find a new level of clarity, once they do actually stop using all drugs.

Then, they can truly begin recovery in complete abstinence. Using your drug of choice, or, some substitute will do nothing but complicate life and confuse us, especially if we're pursuing recovery. Substitution and moderation are only counterfeits that attempt to hide the fact we can no longer use successfully. We accept the fact that no amount of dope can satisfy us but it only takes a little to ruin us. With luck, we might make it back to the program, but, sooner or later, our luck runs out and we must come to meetings and work the steps in earnest.

We simply must remain clean.

The progressive nature of our illness allows our sensitivity to drugs in any form to increase, whether we're using or whether we're clean. There is no grace period of 'fun using' for the person who relapses. The longer we've been clean the greater the danger that we'll die trying to get high. The chemicals lose their ability to smother our spirits and make us into pleasure-seeking savages.

It's no longer a pleasure when you have to do it. It's being chained to the prison of the addiction. The substitution of alcohol or some other drug's no longer an option for us because we now know drugs in any form will reactivate our addiction. There's no safe usage for us. The longer we've been clean, the harder it is to get clean again and your life expectancy is less.

The lessons seems to be: when you quit taking the drugs, your life gets better. Sure, life still happens. Sometimes, bad things happen. But, we learn in recovery when bad things do happen, using will only complicate the situation one hundred-fold.

We must remain in the solution. Using puts us right back in the problem.

Q: When a member of Narcotics Anonymous uses Sub Oxone, Methadone, etc., is this considered clean in the N A program? A: It's your recovery, so, talk to your sponsor. Plus, I suggest you soul-search your heart and come to your own conclusions. Be honest with yourself. If you stop using, will you crave it?

EVERYBODY'S DIFFERENT... TRUE.
SO, NARCOTICS ANONYMOUS DOESN'T WORK FOR YOU?
NOW WHAT?

There's so much more to living in recovery than just staying clean. But, hey, if you find something that keeps you clean in your life, I say, good for you. That's what matters. There are lots of 12 step programs out there. N A, A A, C A, Celebrate Recovery and on and on. What really matters is you're staying clean from all mind-altering drugs. Alcohol included, because, in reality, alcohol is a drug. So, if there's something out there that you've found that keeps you clean and your life continues to spiral upward, I'm truly happy for you. Hopefully, you're developing a spiritual relationship with a higher power as well. As long as you continue to live in the solution and are working on resolving the negatives situations and issues from the chaos of your life, when you were using, I'd say, keep doing that. By all means, embrace more meaningful and positive spiritual principles.

Ask yourself these questions and be honest.

Are good morals beginning to be more important?

Do you really try to always do the next right thing?

Are you actually trying to be honest about everything, no matter what?

Is your spirituality becoming more and more important as time passes?

Does your life seem to matter more?

Do you feel happier inside, in the big picture?

Are you carrying a message of hope to the still-suffering addicts?

Are you praying to your Higher Power?

Do you have an attitude of gratitude? Important stuff...

Do you feel more at peace now and feel true gratitude in your heart?

If you're working a good program, helping others, expressing gratitude daily and feeling a sense of serenity, then, you're on a good path. All of this should be a part of your daily life. You deserve to feel happiness inside, right? These are all fair questions to ask yourself if you're working a program to live clean and spiritually fulfilled.

But, if you happen to be at a crossroads and cannot figure out what to do next, I suggest you give N A a sincere shot. Try it, follow all the suggestions and embrace the gratitude as you begin to peel back the dark pages of your past and open your heart to the possibility of a beautiful and more meaningful life.

If it doesn't click with you, that's okay. I hear it from people. "I tried N A. It doesn't work for me. Well, ya know, even if you're an N A Nazi, (meaning someone critical of other addicts perceptions of N A ways and means) you have to admit everybody's different."

Being someone with a few twenty four hours in the program, I always wonder, "What part of the N A program did this person not do?

The N A program does work, but, you have to be willing to put in the work.

360

Recovery doesn't happen by osmosis. I hear that old argument, "But, everybody's different" and I just smile inside. Here we go again. Yes, everybody is different, but, if you're honestly willing to go to any length to live clean, then, no matter how different we are, N A will help you get clean and learn to live clean, but, we say it over and over, you have to work the N A program. Not your program, the N A program. When someone does say N A doesn't work for them, I wonder if they could really be saying … "Look, I know N A works. I'm just not willing to follow the program the way the N A literature teaches. I'm not willing to live one day at time always trying to do the next right thing. I'm not there yet and that's okay. All we can really do, at this point, is pray for this addict to survive and find a way to live clean and attain some level of happiness.

Remember, millions have proven trying to work your own program simply doesn't work.

HARD LESSONS…

It's the paths we choose that lay our ground-work. For many, that's a blueprint to success. It's the pursuit of dreams with the ambition and passion to go for it, letting nothing get in the way that drives us.

Many of us don't even think about any of that, or, realize that in our earlier years. I know I didn't. Maybe you did. Maybe you had a dad or a mom pushing you into college and they had your life all mapped out the way they saw it happening. I didn't have that. Maybe that's a good thing. Maybe it's not. I just know it was off my radar and it most definitely lends credence to the beginning of my ups and downs. No matter, really, on all our winding paths, we all have personal life-lessons.

They shape, form and twist us like clay, into who we become in the years beyond. It's the design of time, it's the great master's plan. Without even thinking about it, when we're young, we all go in different directions.

Think about it. Many of us go through the years of school with an open mind, willing to learn all we can, like walking down a pathway, lined up with fancy stepping stones, just to show us the way. Then, as time passes, this group captures memories and they go on to college. They merge like flowing traffic, into corporate life. The plans for these folks are all business with the possibility of a life-story memory book, instead, getting dusty on some long forgotten shelf. There's no time for fun and games in this particular world. All those wild moments were left back in the younger, more irresponsible college days, in the parties at the frat houses and the sororities. Many others get caught in their own tunnel-vision. They, unfortunately, walk through life, narrow-minded, lost and even confused.

Possibly, they were abused or misused and really just want to find out, finally, who they really are. Maybe the drug life stole who they were at one time. They want to rediscover that person they lost in order to survive, or that person that died in the midst of the unspeakable trauma of their childhood. They may not even realize the suppressed yearning they possess within to peel back the layers to who they are inside. Their spirit's been crushed or taken and they need to reboot. They need to start life over, so to speak. Others move about exploring the endless possibilities, never really settling for the planned events of life. They are the free-spirited gypsy's in the wind. These love children are always on the prowl for the next good high or the last goodbye.

Then, there are some who come out of High School and forge into warrior training for God and country. These are, for whatever reason, the chosen few. These are the ones that believe there is good in the world. There is something good inside us all and they're willing to lay down their lives for the truth that churns and burns within them. Like I said, we all have our own paths. I've learned, through time and on the paths I've traveled, to never judge anyone. Every single human has their own set of particular circumstances.

We all have our own closets filled with strengths and weaknesses, hopes, dreams, humiliations, hurts, pains, griefs, sorrows, losses, joys, wants and needs. Much of this, for an addict, is affected as a result of addiction.

Everyone has their own baggage. Some far more than others. A lot of who we become is a direct result of who we were, what we survived and how well we've adapted, as a result of any trauma and environmental shaping, along the way. No matter... we still create our own path. If you're not happy in your life, change it.

~<>~

Chapter 22

WISDOM

Life amounts to what we put into it. Most everybody figures that out as we get older. Some are just born into the good life. They get the goods handed them. Sweet, easy and squeaky clean! No ifs, ands, or buts. I'm serious, no bullshit, just step up and step off flush like a big dawg.

Mr. Green behind the ears on that shit right there! I've always worked for everything. In my life from the beginning, nobody gave me shit. If it's been like that for you, then, you know where I'm coming from. That's got to be why being grateful is so important to me. That's why being thankful means so much these days.

I always did wonder about something, though. When life is handed to you, I mean on a platter, all simple like, do you get a bucket of shallow with that shit? Ya know, a little slap on the ass and a couple of atta boys. That's some funny shit, man. For real, though, if you've been blessed with no stress, more power to you. Now look, is it just me, or, well, here's the thang, in the streets, when an addict's caught up in the hustle, why is it you got to get drug through nasty-ass mud, slapped like a bitch, beat like a dog, kicked in the face and cut like a log, just for a thug mutt to realize you're desperate. In fact, you might be deeper than any deep they ever knew and they might be you 7 lifetimes ago. Then, you got to pull that reverse crescent and right hook out of your bag of tricks to survive out there. It's not worth it, man. Life has so much more to offer. Wake up to that. As we get older, start living clean, we realize inner- peace matters so much more than knocking out some arrogant prick and his little group of circle-jerk buddies. Life means more. Serenity means more when the stench of disloyalty swims into view. In life, the smarter soul walks away. The smarter soul makes the circle smaller and the bond of the real brothers and sisters even deeper. Especially, when all you really want to do is breathe in the air, touch a sweet and classy woman, search her pretty eyes for a lifetime or two, do a

364

double-check inside your thinking to make sure your souls still there. Maybe, just sit on a beach and run your fingers through the warm, sparkly sand. Let the gratitude wash around you and stare out into the Heavens, making sure you still got a good recovery plan. Making sure that the real priorities are still the ones you can't even see with your naked eyes. Like I said, life sure has a way. Let me give you a little peep inside my thinking. Remember those precious times when you would watch those gorgeous sunsets... and the spirituality of it was precious and so overwhelming you let it wrap around you like a blanket and warm your whole being. Just to be able to sit back and think about that good, deep stuff that pours through your soul in the wee wee hours. See, I'm a thinker, too. To survive in those streets, strung out, hustling hustlers, playing players... deep shit. I sit back, like, well, think about this, some mysterious stranger, in the midst of some serious-ass chess game, like, maybe you, watching the soldiers, the pawns, bishops, rooks, knights, all with their different strategies, smooth plays, tactics, manipulations and pathways. Each in a different playing field, different set of rules, different morals, standards, closet secrets and perceptions of how we think it is as opposed to how it really may be.

Then, we have all the queens making their moves. Mindful of the smooth, careful and sometimes, not so careful, moves coming back. Ever so surely the silent moves come. We're all players, right? Don't lie. Street people know. The seductive, sexy women, so clever, cautiously, calculating four or five moves out. The men, smooth, some clumsy, some with their chests pumped out, nervous their manhood may be challenged. Many, just praying their manhood will be challenged to high-light their prowess. All the Kings of the jungle! The bad boys. You know who you are! Don't you? Well, here's something for you. Even your life could turn on a dime. Shit could crumble around you like fog in the morning, in a blink, so, maybe find some humility along the way in your game, and learn to be humble. Learn to be grateful. I get it. Not so easy. That's a tough row to hoe for a player. It'll change your psyche. But, really, when you're all alone, 4 am, sitting there thinking, imagine leaving the game and finding a real life? Yes! A real life. There's a better life, waiting for you to make it happen. That's all I'm saying. I'm just trying to put a bug in your ear...plant a seed, add some more light to the world. It's getting dark.

So, let's get back to this...Well, since we're on the subject, tell me, what does matter? Trust me on this one. What really matters, for real, matters? I mentioned it earlier. You can't see that important shit with your eyes. It's invisible. It's not street shit. It's not whipping any body's ass, cutting somebodies throat or shooting anybody in the heart and I'll tell you something else, too, it doesn't shine when the lights come on. It's not bullying people, dogging people or taking somebodies shit. That's all street shit. Serenity. Inner-peace. That's where it's at. In this theatre of operation, I know what I'm talking about. I lived it. At the end of the day, the only thing you got is the mirror. It's who you really are inside. What really matters is when the lights are out, or, the stranger needs a dollar. It's when nobodies looking because you're in a room all alone and that mirror's all you got. Take a look in that glass and listen to that little steadfast voice, the one whispering inside your soul, nurturing guidance to your better sense of reasoning. Better listen and friend, you better keep listening. If you're caught up in the drug-life, in the allure of the street lifestyle, you might want to pay attention here...   Time in a cell is depressing as Hell. Did you hear me? Say that with me! Time in a cell is pure hell. It's the definition of misery. If you don't give your freedom more than a second thought, go without it for a while. The taste of free life. We usually don't even give it a second thought. We're talking about potentially priceless moments in your youth taken from you and shoved in a small dark concrete and iron box. It's a deep, deep scar and I don't care who you are or how tough you pretend to be, losing time in your youth, or, any of your time, to prison, is a horrible experience. I know a few seasoned with time, sprinkled with knowledge, flavored with life, types out there. Thinking twelve moves out! It might be you. It could be me. No matter, they're there. They're experienced by the ways of the scarred path, the dark and alone way. They're beaten down to no end. They have the hardened resonance emanating with their mere presence. They're not asking for respect, because the desire within others, to respect them emanates from their very nature, their very presence. Eventually, the misguided nature of puppeteers find their own truth. In time, they will demand their space, their inner space, their self-respect. It's something to think about.

What you just read is me saying to you, no matter what, don't lose your freedom. Think it through. THINK before you act. Instead of the wrong path, that will suck you in and pull you down, why not try to evolve into a meaningful path and be the best version of yourself?

Stay in the light.

SPIRITUAL PRINCIPLES...

Here's the thing. As an addict in active addiction, our morals go right out the window. There's no end to what I would do when my active addiction and my cravings controlled and ravaged my heart, soul, body and mind. Like most addicts, I really have existed at the animal level and not even care that the water and lights were turned off, the rent was due and my entire life was in complete and utter chaos. None of that mattered.

I think deep down these things did matter somewhere inside me, but, feeding my addiction mattered more. I continued to steal, lie, cheat, rob, and whatever was necessary to fulfill my cravings. Jail didn't stop me. Prisons didn't stop me. Hospitals didn't stop me. Nearly dying from overdoses repeatedly didn't stop me. This disease took me over. My spirit died and my ability to make good moral decisions didn't exist. That was my life in active addiction. In recovery I'm able to make wiser and more loving decisions based on principles and ideals that have real value in my life. It's no different for everyone in recovery. We discover that we suffer from a disease, not a moral dilemma. I believe that.

Daily practice of our twelve step program allows us to change from the monsters we were in active addiction to a person guided by our higher power. Working the steps with our sponsors opens the door in our lives to a deeper possibility of spirituality. We've learned from our group experience that those who keep coming to meetings, regularly stay clean. Without honest sharing, we'll use again. It's an honest program. But, the thing is, at first, it's really hard to be honest. Trying to do the next right thing for all the right reasons, is a good beginning. We're so used to manipulating people to get our drugs that being honest will take work and time. Over time, if we keep working the program, we do grow spiritually. Part of growing more spiritual is being as honest as we can, all the time. I mean no matter what, truly honest. Not only with others, but, also, honest with ourselves.

TOOLS...

We play the tape all the way through. We begin to think about consequences! That becomes a huge part of our thinking process in our bag of tools. Not like before when we used, with no thought of consequences, whatsoever. "Let's see, if I do this, this will happen." Consequences matter. With the principles of our recovery, we also try not to judge or moralize one another. There will be times, no matter how long we've been in recovery, even after we've lost the desire to use, when we really feel like using. It just happens. That little voice on our shoulder begins to whisper. "It's okay, go ahead, you can use. Don't worry about it." Those thoughts will cross through your thinking. We want to literally run from our own thoughts. It makes us feel terrible, even lousy. Tools matter.

There's something else I learned in N A and it took time and work, but, it finally clicked. I have to break down all the PROBLEMS I created while using, one by one, and face them more like they're situations. Situations, we discover, do have solutions we can work through. Someone that was clean longer than I, told us that at a meeting and now I'm sharing it with you. To some of you, this seems like common-sense, but, it's not common sense to an addict that's been out there in the streets, hustling and using.

We need to be reminded of where we came from and that it'll be worse if we relapse. This is when we need the program the most. This is when sitting in a meeting and listening to newcomers describe how miserable they feel, how life out there using is just as bad as it always was, is important. We need to hear from the newcomers often. Newcomers are the most important people at any meeting. They're miserable and all of us in recovery, need to see it and be reminded. It's like slapping our disease in the face with reality. Also, in our recovery, having a sponsor is so important. Someone that, through time, you've grown to trust. A sponsor is an important tool to have in recovery. Remember, your sponsor will know a lot of your behaviors while you were using. You'll share those things with that person when you're doing your forth step, so, it's important to find someone and get to know them, before you ask them to be your sponsor.

After I was in recovery for over two and a half years I started realizing something. I would sit in those meetings day after day, never missing. I was actually scared to miss a meeting for over two and a half years. I knew when I was in a meeting, I was safe. I was clean and I was going to stay clean. So, I went every day and I loved the life. I still do. It was pieces of time in between the meetings that worried me.

So, I went to all the meetings I could for over thirty-two months. Then, and only then, was when I backed off from so many meetings. What I've discovered is when I'm having a bad day, everything sucks and life on life's terms is complicated and rough, this is when I need a meeting most. When I'm having a great day, an absolutely amazing, euphoric day, and loving my clean-life, filled with a sense of peace and clarity, that's when the meeting needs me most, sharing my experience, strength and hope. The more we go to meetings the easier it is to be honest with ourselves and others. Things start to really matter to us. People start to matter. Family notices you changing and real friends start coming back around. You become nicer and more polite.

You become more positive and you begin to pray out loud and in front of people. Spiritual principles, man. This is a direct result of working the program. This is a direct result of working the twelve steps with your sponsor. This is a result of you doing service work and enjoying helping others. Bad days still happen, but, you're much better prepared to handle them.

We all hear the stories about working the steps. How working through each step, in the correct order with a sponsor is life-changing. How the notorious fourth step will, most likely, be a notebook filled with your mistakes and character defects. How it will be so difficult to write down, and, along the way, grasp, how truly messed-up, your life has been. When it's in writing and the notebook is a hundred and eighty pages deep and you've spent several months on the fourth step, you'll feel the layers peeling back in your soul. Even though it's been hell, admitting some of these terrible things you've done, it'll take the weight of the messed-up world you created, off your shoulders. Emptying your conscience of your life of dirty deeds, seeking forgiveness and being forgiving to others are major turning points on the road to recovery. The good news is this... this is for everyone, no matter your race, sexual identity, creed, religion, or, lack of religion.

Pain shared is pain lessened.

There must be honest sharing in the meetings. It's very important to attend meetings regularly. Be involved. Do service work. Meet others in recovery who also don't use and start going to different places where people don't use. Of course, practicing new and improved spiritual principles will strengthen your recovery.
Basically, we only have to change one thing... Everything.

The older I get in life, the more I realize how little I know.

Learning to be humble...

The awareness that we're actually recognizing beautiful things in life... That's a dream come true. Those little things that never used to matter begin to matter now. I never used to notice so many things in life. They would just pass me by. That's startling to me now. How could I have missed so much beauty that was all around me? How? The world is filled with so many amazing things. We just have to pause and take it all in. Things like the cloud formations on a beautiful day, or, with the spring rain, how the brown grass begins turning the prettiest shades of green, like new carpet.
The list is endless.
How peaceful to be able to watch the serenity of another sunset. How amazing to watch the whole world light up inside my children's eyes. How beautiful their smiles are! How fulfilling it is to wake up with inner-peace, content and grateful for another awesome day. I love my "Now". The masquerade is over. But, not the party. Life can be the party. Walking through a big park full of gorgeous, colorful, flowering trees on a beautiful day and taking it all in. Standing there with your arms raised to the spacious blue sky like you're hugging the whole wide world.

Feeling the warm and gentle summer breeze as it caresses your face. Strolling down to a sandy beach and finding your own little spot near the waves... feeling those waves as they languish onto the shore, just to wet the white sand and flow slowly back out to the ocean. All these things are spiritual. They move me. They embrace my spirit and surround me with such joy and give me a real sense of peace.

I've never felt that before. Think about it. Don't you want to experience these things, too? You can. It takes work, but, I believe in you.

Close your eyes for a minute. It's okay, seriously, close your eyes. Now, imagine living somewhere like Hawaii for almost two years and not really noticing you're in Hawaii. Think about that! I mean, really! I did that. I actually did that. I lived in the land of paradise where everything is beautiful, everything smells great and looks gorgeous. It's a tropical paradise! I lived in the midst of all that and spent most of my days hugging a toilet, overdosing, nodding, burning all my shirts and my fingers and staying inside. Yes. Staying inside.   Just so I could shoot more dope. Heroin possessed my spirit. Every fragment of me disappeared into an oblivious, lost shell of who I was put in the world to be. I must have overdosed on heroin a dozen times in Hawaii. Just as many times, I would wake up, freezing and soaking wet from an ice-cold shower I'd been thrown into. God always let me pull through. But, I've seen others die while doing the same thing.

Don't forget, along the way. Addiction is a monster! Its voice can whisper the sweetest stuff inside your head and do it, often, all the time, everywhere. One of the things that voice will whisper is this..."you don't need a meeting today. You're fine. You've done this and this and this and this. You should be fine. No need for a meeting." Listen to me, my friend. It's very, very easy to submit to that voice. We're addicts. We're always looking for the easy way. Addiction is patient, very subtle, it's progressive and don't forget, it's incurable. So, stay alert! Stay on point at all times. STAY VIGILENT!

Complacency will lead you right back into active addiction.

It may be a slow, cunning process, but, if you're not aware of the possibility of this happening, I assure you, it will. So, just like it's been told to me, right now, I'm telling you... stay vigilant with your Narcotics Anonymous program... AND STAY CLEAN! Don't use! It's very cunning, so, always be aware. When you feel yourself wanting to slack, when you find yourself missing meetings, isolating, putting off calling your sponsor, these are red flags! Pay attention to these warning signs.

Don't forget that! One final thought to always remember and I feel this is worth repeating. On those days that seem so perfect, life feels beautiful, you feel happy inside and maybe, just maybe, that little voice inside you is whispering, "everything is wonderful, you don't need a meeting today." Well, maybe you don't.

But, I promise you, someone at that meeting isn't having a perfect and happy day, like you, and that person needs to hear from you. That particular person might not have any hope left inside their soul. You sharing your goodness, your joy and your testimony just might be that little flicker of hope that will get them through to a brand new day. You could very well be the only light in their darkness. You could be that one person that saves them, that gives them just enough courage to stay clean for one more day. Then, we have the other side of the coin... some days just don't go right. No matter what you do, things just seem out of whack. You feel a little off center, depressed or unhappy. Maybe you're having some cravings, anxiety, or, someone somewhere said something and it's triggered you. Maybe life just sucks and people don't act right.

On those days, you definitely need a meeting. Mr. HP has a way of sending the exact message you needed to hear at those meetings. Everyone notices it. You'll go into a meeting and there'll be a specific situation going on in your life. Try as you will, you're having a difficult time working through it. It's weighing on you heavy. You've been searching your soul for an answer, but, you can't find anything inside you to hold on to. Then, at the meeting, the 'Just for Today' reading is exactly what you needed to hear. God does that, ya know.

The Deceptive Allure...

Along the way, my feelings became emotions I just kept stuffing deep inside. My interest in everything I did, changed. The people I associated with, changed. Everything that once mattered, didn't anymore. That all seeped in over time. Hard drugs became the only part of any priority list that mattered.

Initially, all an addict wants is to NOT use anymore. Existing with a dead soul isn't anything remotely close to living. It's a very, very dark place to be. It's an empty parking lot on a futile, barren wasteland, standing alone in high wind. It's an empty city by a wind-swept sea with nary a soul that even matters. It's a burned out house in a rundown ghetto and not one body left to help care for any of it. It's the screeching desert on a scorching hot, blistering and miserable day, with the prickly stabs of cactus strewn all along the way. It's walking barefoot through all of that, while you're ripped and shredded flesh burns off your bruised and mangled feet, down to the shattered fragments of your bones. It's those last remaining charred-up bones, lying all along the hot, desert floor, among the prickly cactus.

This is the clutching fingers of eerie death, my friend, gripping you around your dry throat, strangling and choking your struggling breath, from that last little, tiny, remaining flicker of hope left lingering. This is your demise. Like I said, existing with a dead soul is far from living. So much more is reaped by the supple fruits of recovery. Fascinating and incredible things we don't even know, at first. "Just please, DON'T LET ME USE" is our plea, when we first reach for help? It's all that matters at first.

Get to know people in recovery. Reach out. We'll welcome you with open arms and hugs.

The point is, you're making an honest effort to clean up. That in itself is a level of success worth noting.

I don't judge anyone. It's not my place to judge. With the life I've lived, it would be silly for me to point my finger at anyone. But, I've woken to myself. I'm enlightened. Self-actualized as Maslow called it. I have a clarity without drugs, including the alcohol. A clarity that I never had before. The small circle of friends I have now won't stab me in the back. Do yourself a favor. Get away from toxic people. Avoid anyone negative. Smiling faces aren't always your friend. Remember that.

Finding the way...

For me, in that treatment center, in April, 1983, there was a hard-ass recovering heroin addict and Vietnam vet that saw my core issues and took me in. Randy M. became my counselor and my sponsor. He introduced me to myself. Somehow, he pierced through my hardened persona and introduced me to the real me, to this human being, I'd been running from. He showed me this addiction survival persona I carried wasn't really me. It was me having to survive in the madness of the streets. Inside me, was this little boy from my childhood, so filled with self-hate, rage and confusion? I was an empty vessel. I was a confused and angry mess.

Randy helped me realize this beaten down drug-addicted person I'd buried away was actually human. I was actually an okay person with a certain special set of God-given skills and gifts. I'd never let them blossom forth. I'd hidden them away to protect myself.

For the longest time I felt like an alien. I mean after I cleaned up from the drugs and alcohol. All these feelings I'd never felt came rushing in. It was a lot to take in. It didn't feel normal at all. I felt like I was from another planet. But, while I was in treatment, I was tested for IQ level and creativity. My results surprised me and they surprised Randy, too. I'd clearly been on the wrong path.

The bridge to self-awareness...

It made me start to open my eyes. It made me start to believe in myself. It's amazing what the human spirit can accomplish when a person begins to believe in their abilities to achieve goals. Think about it, I was a homeless junkie with nothing. No hope, no belief in myself and no sense of purpose. Spiraling downward into a black hole. I felt lower than a cockroach. Some of you reading this can relate. You're who I'm talking to. I got sick and tired of the bullshit and I decided to do something different. I went back to college. My goal is to be a licensed art therapist. Well, I've painted hundreds of paintings, written several books and blah, blah, blah. Literally too much to talk about.

My accomplishments have spanned many years of my life, even, many times when I was in active addiction. I briefly mentioned some of my accomplishments to help you understand the potential that exist inside of you. Here's what I'm getting at. I came from nothing. I had no belief in myself whatsoever. Are you listening to me? Are you

374

reading this? The change was in me. Just like the change is in you. I, honestly didn't know that at all. I didn't know me at all. For most of my life, I've short-changed myself and I'm just now discovering the depth of that. The truth from my childhood had ripped me apart and made me miserable. But, now, its set me free. I learned that firsthand. These were profound events for me. The emotions poured from me like an endless fountain. I'd been a mess for many years. Clarity can be very emotional as all the feelings and memories from the streets and the past begin to surface. It's like a very hard look in the mirror and it can tear you apart. The cognitive dissonance can be brutal. But, it will also put you back together, if you're willing to go to any length to have a better life and you're honest with yourself. It's not easy, but, if you give it a chance and put in the work, you'll amaze yourself with your accomplishments.

We're all different people put here on earth for different reasons and different purposes. It's not my intention to wave my intellectual wand around, or, scream out on some mountain-top my past and current accomplishments. I shared these things with you because I want you to see what incredible things an addict can achieve. The universe wants us to do well. We just have to decide to do whatever it takes to make good things happen.

Believe me when I tell you, if I were still in active addiction, none of the things I mentioned above would've happened. If I were alive and I doubt that I would be, but, if I were and I was using, you wouldn't be reading this book. I wouldn't have written it. It wouldn't matter to me about any of you. As far as I'd be concerned, you could all go chase headlights. But, you are reading this. I don't feel that way. Most of that hate has left me. In its place is my desire and effort to be a better person.

This is a perfect example of what a person living clean can accomplish and I'm not done yet.

For me, the ambition and drive that wasn't there, grabbed me by the hand and the heart and pulled me toward all the dreams I always wanted to come true.

Once you start believing in yourself, the skies the limit! You literally go from spiraling downward to spiraling up. The moment you make the decision to stop living in the problem and start living in the solution, miracles start happening. Please don't start making excuses why you couldn't possibly do these types of things. I remember when I was using, I could come up with a slew of reasons why I wouldn't be able to do this, or, do that, or, do this, or, do that. You get the picture. Just push all that bullshit by the wayside. You'll be mystified, baffled, amazed and startled at all that you can actually accomplish once you get clean and stay clean. Your life really will begin to spiral upward. It will. It really will.

I went to meetings after treatment, but, not often enough. I still had reservations. It's difficult to be completely honest like this. It's not easy. I mean, I admit after all the shit I went through, and then, treatment, and then, meetings and a sponsor that was meaner than a junk-yard dog, I still relapsed. It took me three years of white-knuckling it to say, "To hell with it," and start shooting dope again. Randy, my sponsor took recovery serious. I wanted to be there, in recovery, like him, but, the truth was, I wasn't ready yet. I hadn't suffered enough. I worked the steps with Randy.

Like I said, I went to meetings for a couple of years and I stayed clean for three years after treatment. But, those reservations... that's a clear sign that a person's not ready for recovery. Then, my grandfather died. He was one of my favorite men on this planet. He was a kind and gentle soul. Papa told me when I was young, that pot wasn't a drug. It was a healing plant. He said the white man made it a drug. It does well for humans if they'll only let it. What Papa told me, many years later was proven to be true? Don't misunderstand this. I'm not in any way condoning the use of marijuana. But, I see all these people with so many diseases and pot changing their lives. I don't think it's intelligent to overlook that. It's something to be aware of.

A lot of things worked together, to put me back out in the streets. After Papa passed away, a brother of mine, Bingo, stopped by my house to tell me how sorry he was that I'd lost my grandfather. He brought with him some heroin, and a rig. He asked if he could do a hit before he left. I said, sure. Then, I proceeded to throw away three years of recovery, as I sat there with Bingo and jumped right back into the drug life. That was nobody's fault but mine. It happens that fast.

A man could blink, be weak for one second and destroy years of recovery. Addiction is a cunning and baffling disease. It will destroy you and laugh right inside your head, as you're dying. It does not discriminate. It crosses all boundaries.

376

One of my major reservations when I first went into recovery was my unwillingness to throw away my syringe and spoon. I carried those around with me, since I was eighteen. I wanted to always be ready to do a hit of dope when I found it. So, I held onto that rig for three years while I was in recovery. Recovery, with reservations, is not recovery. In the eighties, my life reached beyond the insanity level. If this book has made you realize you're an addict, and you're at that place where the hopelessness has taken you over, your life is a mess, your world is in shambles and you can't take it anymore, seek out and find a Narcotics Anonymous meeting. Come with open-mindedness and willingness to go to any length to find and stay in recovery. When the misery of your addiction is greater than your courage to walk in that meeting, you're ready to find a new way to live.

Misery loves company! Here's the best plan! Give yourself 90 days of meetings and stay clean. Remember, no matter what, you cannot use or drink. We actually have a club called the NO MATTER WHAT Club. Join that with us and stick to that plan. NO matter what, don't drink or use. Do that for 90 days and go to a meeting every day. I promise you, in 90 days, you'll be a much better person. You will feel the life breathe back into your soul. You will feel feelings you haven't felt before, because you've been stuffing them away with the drugs and alcohol. You will start to feel hope!

Hope! What a beautiful thing! This will give you the strength to stay the course. This will help you find clarity. This will fill your heart and soul, listening to other drug-addicts share their stories of experience, strength and hope. Keep going to the meetings. You'll soon get in touch with your higher power. Mine is God. I thought he'd left me, but, God never left. He was always there. I'm the one who left. Those streets swallowed me up like a starving dog scraping the last bit of meat off a juicy steak bone. The streets turn quickly and cleverly into full-blown dismal despair. It felt so amazing to leave all that hell, behind. Many never get to. They die. If you don't have a Higher Power, maybe it's time to get to know who yours is. All you have to do is show up and listen. Share when you feel it in your heart to do so. Not until. Remember this, pain shared really is pain lessened. You'll meet people with far more similarities than differences. It may take you a little while to realize that, but, eventually, you'll have an epiphany. It'll be life-changing. That's your spirit coming back to life. Of course, be aware, that many addicts come to meetings because they're court-ordered and a great many of those are just doing time. Most of them have no interest in working the program whatsoever. They just need the chair-person's signature to document they were there for the court system. It doesn't take someone working the program very long to see who those people are. We still show them love. We still give them a hug when they walk in our rooms. Why? Because, we've learned that even though many are faking it, if they keep coming, who knows, they may end up faking it till they make it. What this means is this.

Anyone that keeps coming to our meetings will sit there, day after day or night after night and continually listen to the recovering addicts share their experience, strength and hope. Eventually, this hope will start to sink in. This family environment will start to feel good. This love, this bond, this program will start to make so much more sense than the phony and empty crap going on out in the streets. So, we encourage all to come and just listen. You won't be the first or the last to fake it till you make it.

Addiction is the only prison where the locks are on the inside.

~<>~

Book-signing 2011
Stormy Monday

Chapter 23

NORMIES

Normies! There's a word. I never knew that word existed until I found recovery. Then, after being clean for a while and getting some clarity in my life, I realized how deep that word can travel. For those of you still in the dark, here's what it means. There's a group of people out there that sees an addict in all their chaos, all their self-destruction, gripped in pain and down in misery, and they just don't get it. Many will immediately place an addict into the moral dilemma box. Addiction is not a moral dilemma. Addiction is a thinking disease. Think about it... What normal, everyday human being with a great job, wife, home and all the trimmings, throws all of that away and exist in the streets, like an animal? Homeless and broke. Who does that? That's crazy as hell, right? That's NOT normal and that's sure not a normie.

When I was in High School, I started hanging with the party crowd. I wanted to be "cool", so, I started drinking and eating acid. In my naïve mind, I thought I was just partying in High school like everybody. Whatever everybody in our clique was doing, we all did it. It never, for a second, occurred to me that some people's brains might be wired differently than others. I'm not talking about mental illness. I know a person with mental issues may have a chemical imbalance, or, some wires crossed. This is something else. I'd go to a party with a buddy of mine and everybody would get drunk on Friday night. Then, they'd go home and be at school Monday morning, fresh as a flower. Not me. I could never be satisfied. Friday night was never enough for me. I'd get drunk Friday night and by Monday morning, I'd skip school and still be partying, with no end in sight. I could never understand why I was different from the others, like that. Oh, I had a close friend and he was usually right there with me, getting wasted. It was my brother, Ed. We'd overdo it every time.

Inside my thinking, I thought we were just a little crazier than everybody else. I could never really explain why we'd want to skip school all the time and stay wasted. We started eating acid our junior year. Acid was a big deal in those days. I'm talking 1970. We'd literally live on hits of LSD. We ate it like candy. What happened was a guy I'd met from Chicago was a drug dealer. I actually met him during a drug deal. We did a lot of deals. We started partying a lot and got to a place of 'some trust'. Right at the beginning of our junior year, he fronted me 10,000 hits of Orange Sunshine, for 50 cents a hit. Here I am, 16 years young, selling acid to everybody at school for 2 bucks a hit. I had a whole lot of the High school tripping on acid. I look back at that now with sadness. Anyway, most of these people would buy it and save it for the weekends. Not Ed and me. We'd hallucinate our way through about every day. We just thought we partied harder than everybody else.

Along the way, it got kind 'a weird. People started asking us why we partied so much. Why we skipped school so much? Why we were never home? This behavior carried on after High School when I went in the army. As you know, I was shooting heroin by the time I was 18. The people around me could never understand why my behavior was so chaotic, so insane and so self-destructive. The people I'm talking about would party on a Friday or a Saturday night, go home, spend the rest of the weekend doing family stuff, and then, on Monday morning, they'd go back to work. Those are normies.

The difference is this. An addict's dopamine level spikes dramatically, like someone slammed a door, giving us an immediate euphoria. Then, because of that rapid spike, we chase that euphoria to satisfy the need of our brain. To feed it. To feel that rapid spike of dopamine again. Now, the normie that also did a line of cocaine, same dope and same size line, will get high, but, their dopamine level will rise at a normal rate and they'll feel just as good, just not as rapidly. So, no biggie. Coming down isn't so intense. Someone that doesn't experience this craving could never possibly understand the behavior of an addict in active addiction.

The compulsion to use is almost unexplainable, but, very real. A normies dopamine level rises slowly and the euphoria comes on slower. This is normal. No one knows who an addict will be till the disease rears its ugly head. Normies go about their day and will have a friend who destroys everything in their wake and it's a complete nightmare filled with chaos. A normie sees this happening and, of course, it looks like the person they knew left the building.

The behavior of a using addict defies comprehension. Why on earth would a person sit in a bathroom, alone, for days on end, shooting coke into their arm, every ten minutes, non-stop? Then, do this over and over till they can barely stand and only stop, when passing out from exhaustion is all that's left. That's what addict's will do. I did that, many times, for many years. When an addict is desperately craving a drug and by the way, alcohol is a drug, anyway, when an addict is craving a drug, there are moments of absolute, temporary insanity. At that moment, rational thought goes right out the window. I call it spontaneous madness. I know that's hard to believe, for many.

Normies, understandably so, react differently to the same situation. A few weeks later, these same people can have a few more drinks, turn in early for bed, go to work and not think another thing about it. Then, they can get off work, go through the night and not even think about having a drink, some weed or any other drug. Lots of people can do these things, have an occasional drink, have wine with dinner, smoke a joint, every now and then, and life goes on for them. Many people out there, don't have any interest in using or drinking, whatsoever.

These people can go to a doctor, with pain, be prescribed narcotic pain pills, go home, and take every pill as prescribed by the doctor, never once thinking about those pills in that bottle, sitting, in the cabinet. Let a doctor give that bottle of narcotic pills, Vicodin, or whatever, to a using addict and they would be taken immediately, until they were all gone. Then, the addict will be hell-bent to get some more and do it all over again. The thought will consume the addict into madness until more of the drug is found. The reason I can write this knowing full well how true it is, is because I've lived this. I had a very bad pill addiction for several years. I would work the doctors, non-stop. It's amazing how clever an addict can be when it's necessary. I'd find two or three patients with back injuries or whatever and I'd have them agree to sell me 20 or 30 out of their monthly prescription. They'd usually be prescribed 90 or 180 pills a month. I'd pay them 5 or 6 dollars a pill for the 325 Vicodin. This was over 20 years ago. I would always come up with the money. It was necessary to my addicted thinking.

Chapter 24

If you did whatever it took to get high... Then, you can do whatever it takes to stay clean.

WILLPOWER

One of the major misconceptions a drug-addict will have is the power of self-will. In active addiction, we exist at the animal level so long we become very cunning, very slick, very fast, smooth and manipulative. We get very crafty. All this really bad behavior begins to feel normal. That's called "addiction survival persona." We learn how to lie so good, we start believing the bullshit ourselves, as it rolls out of our mouths. We deal with so much crap in the streets that it becomes second nature.

We exist around so many addicts also struggling at the animal living that, the norm, becomes lost in the haze. We try to control everything around us, losing ourselves in our own sick self-centeredness. We steal from friends and we use whoever we can, as often as we can. The bottom line for an addict is doing whatever we have to do to get our drug of choice. It's a sad truth.

Believe me, if you could look down into the soul of your addict friend, this person you love so much, that has given up everything to chase those damn drugs, what you'd find would shock you. You'd find horrible and deep pain, chaos, self-destruction, depression, madness, insanity, hurt, sorrow and misery. You'd find an empty vessel. The last thing an addict wants to do is all the insanity they do while they're in active addiction. They don't want to hurt their children, their parents, their brothers, sisters, family and friends. That's the last thing they want to look in the mirror and see. The shame within is so profound it's almost indescribable. Some even commit suicide.

We have to develop a thick skin and an iron willpower. We go through life rationalizing to ourselves we have the willpower to stop using drugs anytime we want. Of course, if we're put to the test, we'll fail every time. We have no concept of living in the here and now. All we care about is being high, or, having a way to make money to get high. Addiction slips up and consumes us. We don't see it coming.

Imagine the mind-set of an addict when the entire world's fallen apart and the will to live goes right out the window. By the time an addict truly hits their bottom and gets honest, they're willing to surrender their willpower to a power greater than themselves. Only then

Drugs and alcohol are social party favors to many people. Not to an addict. Drugs are a necessity to an addict. They simply don't have the willpower to stop whenever they want. Many will live in denial and hold on to that myth, as long as they can. That's until their world's fallen apart and their life's spinning out of control. Then, the myth of willpower goes right out the window. Of course, for a very long time, once the addict realizes they can't stop using drugs on their own, they're so filled with shame, they'll try to hide the problem from everyone. Only in their sick mind do they actually believe no one around them knows they're getting wasted all the time. Eventually, if they survive, it all falls apart.

Don't fall prey to the myth of willpower. Realize a drug-addict must surrender their will to a Higher Power to find recovery. I, personally existed for years, lying to myself all the time. Telling myself, "oh, I can quit anytime I want. I just don't want to right now." I'd say this while I was standing in a bucket filled with shit, as long as I could somehow get high from the nasty ordeal. It's nothing new to any addict in active addiction. In fact, it's an ongoing battle within. We rationalize to ourselves and whisper bullshit to ourselves as long as we possibly can. Eventually, of course, all the chaos catches up and life falls around our feet. Even after all that, we still try to get high. Look in the mirror and, at least, be honest with yourself. Willpower doesn't work. We have to surrender and admit defeat to find recovery.

There was no doubt in my mind that I was the one common denominator in all the insanity that followed me everywhere. When I was in a place of complete hopelessness, I had no idea life could be different. No idea!!!

Open-mindedness, willingness and just being honest with yourself is a beginning. Listen to me... our days on this earth are numbered. Give yourself the opportunity to blossom. "Using" for an addict, will never be okay. It will never make your life better. I promise.

Don't you really want to find your true-self?

I want to tell you a story...

It's about something that happened to me a while back. My youngest son, Storm, trains MMA. At this writing in May, 2020, Storm is 17 years young. He lives with me by his own choice and his mother lives not far away and does help with him. Anyway, when Storm was about 14, a 19 year-old bully had stopped by our home and challenged him to a fight. Mistake. Under normal conditions, I wouldn't allow a 19 year old to fight my son, but, Storm trains hard all the time and he wanted to fight the dude. No problem. Well, as expected, the bully was no match for Storm. He beat him up in the street in front of our house. From the fight, he did end up with a black eye. That's no biggie to him. His eye had swollen shut and was several colors of black and purple.

It reminded me about once in Tennessee, years back, when something had happened to me and both my eyes had swollen shut. I was in active addiction at the time. I'd went out and did an all-nighter, drinking whiskey, popping Vicodin, smoking pot and whatever else I could get my hands on. Right before dawn, I thought it would be a great idea to stagger my drunk ass through the projects and go home, so, I could pass out. Long story short, I got jumped by 4 black dudes. The first one stepped out from the corner of an apartment building and had a 2 x 4 in his hands. He took a full swing as he stepped out and hit me across the face with it. I was too drunk to react. They were putting the boots to me and this one dude was doing serious damage on my head and body with this 2 x 4. I was way too drunk to fight, or, I believe, in my head, that I could've whipped all 4 of them. So, I'm getting the shit kicked out of me and this guy with the 2 x 4 was about to let go with another good blast across my face, when, thank God, this old black lady stepped out of her apartment door, I guess she heard us, anyway, she screamed at them, "STOP IT, YOU DAMN FOOLS, YOU GONNA KILL THAT WHITE MAN!" I've never been so glad to hear an old woman scream in my life. He tossed that 2 x 4 to the side and off they went into the night. The sun was just coming up. It would've been a beautiful sunrise, but,   I was busted up something terrible, so, I didn't even pay attention. It was all a blur. I sat down for a while, in a lot of pain. Drunk as hell, all beat up, madder than a hornet that I was so damn drunk I let them get the drop on me. So unlike me. It pissed me off more than anything. I sat there at the corner of that building and I didn't give a shit if they came back. They'd have to give it another shot, I guess. I was already in bad shape. I just about talked myself out of going to the hospital, but, after I'd sat there for a while, it got worse. I forced myself to go, because, I could barely breathe without severe pain, and my head hurt badly. Come to find out, after the x-rays and all, I

was in serious condition.

Truth be told, I know I'm hard-headed and I know I'm stubborn, maybe. Anyway, I had a couple broken ribs, a concussion, plus, my face was black & blue, and swollen big as a watermelon. It's a wonder I didn't lose my teeth, both lips busted wide open. That shit hurt, too. My eyes were swollen shut. I couldn't even see for 4 or 5 days. They damn-near killed me. So, back to the current situation, I'm looking at my son, Storm's black eye, and it's swollen shut, too. Like mine were. I thought I'd better take him to the hospital, just to be safe. We walk into the ER and I'm standing there at the front desk explaining what happened to my son.

All of a sudden, everything changed.

The energy shifted big time. This car pulls right up to the ER door and slams on their brakes. Everybody looked outside, all at the same time. I see these two 18 or 19 year olds, a boy and a girl, in complete panic mode, pulling a kid about the same age out of the car. They were freaking out and then, I saw why. The boy they pulled inside the ER right next to my son and I, was purple. He was blue. He wasn't breathing. He was dead. They announced CODE BLUE and all the nurses and a doctor put the kid on a gurney and pushed him into a room. They were working desperately to bring this boy back to life. My son and I were speechless and frozen in place. This was a lot to take in. I knew my son had never seen anything like this before. I look over and the young man and the young lady that had brought him in were a mess. They were both white as a ghost and crying. Their friend was dead.

They walked over to two seats nearby and sat down. I told my son to stay where he was and I walked over to comfort both of them. They were shook up and lost. They were in shock. I could tell. The young man had such a serious look on his face. At the same time, he had one of those faces that was so filled with life and wonder. They both did. I could tell, under different circumstances, these were two young people I could be friends with. They gave off that vibe of being cool people.

I wanted to help them, to comfort them. I've lost so many friends, through the years, the exact same way, so, I knew their pain, and I wanted to help them. I told them don't give up hope yet. These doctors can perform miracles and their friend was in God's hands. The young man nodded his head and the girl agreed with a nod, also. I said, let's pray to God. I said a short prayer with them. I ask God to help their friend. I looked at both of them and said, "God will decide what happens to him." About ten minutes later, a nurse came out and told them they had saved their friend. I told them to hang in there. "I told you God is a miracle maker! To God goes all the glory." Then, they called my son to get his vitals, so, I left and went in the room with him. When I left, the young man and lady seemed so relieved. They were still sitting there. After they checked my son's vitals, him and I went and sat down in the waiting room, waiting to be seen by the doctor. When we left, they were gone. I prayed for them that night, all three of them.

A few days later, I was asking about the boy that had died. The one they had worked so hard and had succeeded in bringing back to life. Here's what I found out. The young couple that I had comforted were very relieved the hospital had saved their friend. He was doing a lot better and was very lucky to have survived. However, the couple that had so desperately brought him in to the hospital to save him, had went home, and the entire ordeal had drained them both, mentally, physically and emotionally. They went to bed to rest. They both died in their sleep. Overdosed on the same heroin the other boy had taken.

Several years later...

I was at the 2nd annual HOPE FEST. This is an event created by Wendy McCready and friends. I'm one of those friends. The purpose of the HOPE FEST is to raise finances to pay for the Recovery House in Pekin, Illinois. Wendy lost her son, Allen, to a heroin overdose, also. Thankfully, we have now acquired the location for "Alan's House", the new Recovery House in Pekin, Illinois. Saturday, November 23nd, 2019, construction by volunteers began to remodel this home. I, and many others, happen to be on the team with Wendy. There are so many volunteer's working very hard to make Alan's House a positive reality. I created a huge mural in the day room to encourage and inspire others to embrace this home and let it flourish.

So, anyway, I was browsing the vendors at the Hope Fest and I met a beautiful lady named Julie. Her friends call her Jules.

We started talking. She said she knew me from long ago. That she thinks she cut my hair way back then. Very possible, I'm thinking. So, we're talking about doing well for people and things like that. She mentioned she was happily married and how good he was to her. Then, she told me she'd offered haircuts the past few weeks to donate all the proceeds to the Hope Fest for the Recovery house. She said she was doing it in memory of her own son, Cody, whom she'd lost to a heroin overdose. That touched my heart, since, I, too, am a heroin addict, in recovery, and I know how really tough it is to kick a heroin habit. So, my compassion overflowed for the loss of her son. She began to tell me how her life fell completely apart when she lost her son.

She started telling me a story. Jules said her son, Cody, his new girlfriend, Danielle, and another friend, Shane, had been partying. Shane, the friend, overdosed. He literally fell unconscious, then, stopped breathing. They both freaked out and loaded him in a car. Cody drove like crazy to get Shane to the hospital. Jules said the 3 of them made it to the hospital ER, and the doctors and nurses worked diligently to save Shane's life. They succeeded. Shane got another chance at life. Jules went on to tell me, that same boy, Shane, is now serving 29 years in prison for drugs. Jules is trying to help him get a reduced sentence.

Jules then told me after her son, Cody, drove the boy to the hospital, that him and his girlfriend drove back home and went to bed, later that night. She said she asked Cody, over and over, to please be honest and let her know if he'd taken any drugs. He kept saying no. So, he and Danielle went to bed and they went to sleep. They never woke up. Cody and his new girlfriend, Danielle, both died in bed. I ask Jules if she had a pic of her son. She pointed to the top of her display. There he was. Cody. That young man with that serious face, so full of life and wonder. There he was. I thought back to that day. It was him. It was that boy that I had prayed with.

Jule's life was never the same. She went off the deep end, as any mother would that lost her son or daughter. She started drinking and got 3 DUI's. She didn't care. She cursed out the judge. Jules didn't want to live. Not in a world without her son, Cody. She kept drinking and getting into trouble. None of that mattered, anymore, anyway. She ended up in prison. This was the furthest thing from the Jule she'd always been. The professional, so structured, intelligent, caring, and on top of her life-plan. All that was gone now. She sat in prison. She was mad, hurt and angry as hell. All the madness in her head over losing her son, ripped her to shreds and tore her down. Slowly, but surely, she processed the deep levels of pain. It took time to even accept her son, Cody, was gone.

She was stripped down bare to the deepest reservoirs of her soul. Eventually, she let the light begin to seep in again. She made a plan. As time passed, she began to realize Cody would want her to live and be happy. She began to live in that light. She let the light of goodness wash through her and cleanse the pain, bitterness and sorrow from her soul. She decided to do good things in the memory of Cody. That's why her story was brought full circle today by the power of the man upstairs. My friends, there is a power far greater than all of us... a Higher Power that orchestrated all of this. From horrific tragedy blossoms enlightened goodness.

PINK CLOUD...

I will say this. For several months when I first found recovery, I experienced what is called the pink cloud. I'd say a great many recovering addicts fairly new to the program, do. That's when you've been clean for a while and suddenly, being clean feels like the best high you've ever had. Everything is just amazing. Everything feels so perfect. Life is beautiful. What could possibly go wrong! Right? So, we ride that pink cloud thinking this is what recovery is and man, isn't it great. Day after day, you stroll along without a care in the world and you just know, it's because you're in recovery. You see rainbows everywhere and butterflies are all around you. It's amazing! Now, you're clean and you can help everybody in the world, using. You want to be a recovery counselor, because now, you can help every drug-addict in the world. Right? Right!

These are some of the natural feelings we all experience when we first get in recovery. Now that we're clean, we don't understand why everyone we know doesn't jump on our band wagon. We share our new high with everyone. "Hey, people, I'm clean! You should be clean, too!" Sound familiar? We're so proud of ourselves. Well, being proud of our clean time is a good thing. But, in time, we also learn to be humble in our recovery. It's part of our recovery to help the next suffering addicts. But, it's not feasible to go out and save the whole world. We learn that, too, hopefully. The life lessons in recovery are endless. We learn coping skills, also, because, face it, we lose the ability to cope with any and everything, when we're using.   The truth is this. The pink cloud is a great feeling. It does feel absolutely amazing. Ride that cloud for as long as you can. If you get the pink cloud more than once, which is very possible, enjoy the ride. But, know this. Life still happens. Life on life's terms can be harsh and even, brutal. People still die. Friends and family are still in accidents. Friends still use drugs, overdose and go to prison. People still cheat, lie, steal and just don't act right. Life still happens. SOME OF THE TOOLS WE LEARN IN RECOVERY ARE JUST FOR THESE SITUATIONS. You can be rolling along, clean, floating on that pink cloud and BAM... reality hits and some traumatic life situation happens and knocks you right off that big, fluffy pink cloud you've been floating on. Your mom or dad dies, your child runs away, your friend overdoses and dies, your dog gets hit by a car and hey, good things happen, too. You get that new job. Need to celebrate, right? Remember, no matter what, don't use or drink. We learn in recovery to work through and resolve situations and prioritize. We learn to celebrate, still have fun and not use or drink. Yes, it can be done! We don't have to use or drink to have fun. Amazing, right! We learn to make a list of things that need to be done and check them off as we do them. We learn to work through the situations. We learn to call each other. We're taught to play the tape all the way through. We all experience the pink cloud. Just be prepared to deal with life when the cloud goes away. That's why we call it recovery. We learn how to recover from life stuff, while we're clean. We learn how to fix life stuff, to overcome obstacles, help each other and live our clean life, one day at a time.

What comes easy, won't last.
What lasts...won't come easy.

~<>~

The Mondays, from the left, Jackie, blue hat, June, Stormy, Barb (RIP), Markie, Susie, Our sweet Mother in the center. A beautiful memory.

~<>~

If you focus on gratitude... you'll start to attract prosperity and abundance.

Left to right- Oldest son, Jesse- Stormy Monday-youngest son- Storm

PRINCIPLES BEFORE PERSONALITIES...

There's a lot more to recovery than getting clean and going to meetings. All the street persona, ghetto talk and lying should be left at the door. But, for some, it may take time to shed that street skin. One of the first things you'll notice when you start going to meetings is this. There's every imaginable type person under the sun there. Think about it, everybody, rich, poor, male, female, confused, black, white, brown, yellow, purple and green, gets high.

Everybody parties and what happens is the addicts, hopefully, find recovery in a meeting they love to go to... and the addict makes the meetings daily. This meeting becomes that special home group. We meet lawyers, bikers, cops, crooks, dealers, moms, strippers, lawyers and Doctors in the rooms. We meet everybody of every possible job and economic level, in the rooms. What we start to realize when we first start going to meetings is how messed up we really were and still are. I don't mean on the drugs either. I mean our spiritual principles and moral compass are both in the toilet.

Many of us come in red-flag flying, paranoid, scared, and defensive, beat-down and spiritually empty. All hope gone! What we don't realize, or, expect in that first meeting is this. Just about everyone smiles and greets us with a hug. Didn't see that coming! We're all taught that the newcomer is the most important person at every meeting. So, when we first walk in the rooms we're made to feel welcome. All of us remember how it feels to walk in to that first meeting. It's not easy. We make everyone feel welcome because everyone is welcome to our open meetings. We've been dealing with addicts, street people and hustlers, out there in the jungle, so, our level of trust is non-existent. It takes time. But, time is what we have. What we learn in Narcotics Anonymous is the education we didn't even know we needed. As the toolbox begins to fill with all this new found knowledge, we realize we're spending time with a lot of people we don't really know. None of us are perfect. Face it, some of us are assholes by nature. Some of us are kind and gentle people. Some don't care about anyone else. Self-centeredness is at the core of our disease, so, most of us, if not all of us, are used to thinking of no one but ourselves. Now, we're learning how to be better people. We have to realize that we all have different personalities. We're all different in so many ways. We're taught, "Principles before Personalities" soon after we walk in the doors. At first, we've read the room and we know who we'd normally gravitate to and want to be friends with. We all do that. By the same token, we also know who we wouldn't spend a moment with, outside the rooms. There might be one or two we don't like much at all.

But, because we don't know these people, we stay quiet about it and hope in time, this person proves to be a good person. Regardless, he likes her, she likes him, I don't like you and you don't like me. This is that one place where those things need to be set aside. Think about it. Here we are, all together, in a room, sharing somewhat personal things about our lives with one another. If anything, we have addiction in common. Now, we have recovery in common. We also have N A in common.

We want everyone to fellowship, to get to know one another, because, the truth of it is this. We're an N A family. Good, bad, or, indifferent. Any of us could relapse at any time. We have an incurable life-long disease. So, suck it up. When we share, that person you don't think you like might be the very person that says exactly what you need, desperately, to hear, that changes your day in a beautiful way. Realistically, through the years, principles before personalities, becomes more and more prevalent. The reality is this. There are some people we don't want to be around. If you don't want to be around somebody, I suggest you don't be around them. But, never let someone keep you out of an N A meeting. NEVER! We respect each other's recovery by being there to help when and if that addict is suffering. Let me make it clearer. Let's say there's a guy in recovery and I don't care to be around him. We've fellowshipped some and realize our mojo just doesn't click. For me and probably for him, too, it's easier to avoid one another, as long as we don't avoid our meetings. Meeting makers really do make it, but, in order to do so, we have to work the program.

Beyond that, I personally, don't go around people I don't want to be around. I think that's normal human nature. But, if someone I don't care for and maybe they don't care for me either, well, if they come into a meeting I'm at, we show each other respect at the meeting and we help whoever we can, whenever they need it. That's putting principles before personalities. It doesn't mean we're going to breakfast in the morning, or, any morning, but, our recovery comes first. Always. Who knows, down the road, given time and, obviously much needed growth from both of us, we may become good friends. Anything is possible in Narcotics Anonymous.

THE POSSIBILITY OF NOW...

Imagine you wake up tomorrow morning and you're completely clean. Did you process that? I'll say it again. Imagine you wake up in the morning and you're completely CLEAN! No more drugs and no cravings!! YESSSS!!!! CLEAN! NO MORE! DONE!

You have no cravings. Yaaaaah!!!! Not even one. It's really happening... you're starting your new and better life, all over. That

393

pain inside your guts that you'd gotten so used to, it's gone. The constant anxiety is gone. That emptiness you've felt for waaay too long... it's gone, too. It feels like the light that went out inside you, long ago, has turned back on. You feel alive. You feel inspired. You're so happy! You feel amazing.

Out the door you go to begin your day... to begin your new life... The sun is shining...What will you do different? Well...Think about that. Explore that.

What will you do different?

So, do it!

UNDERSTANDING THE N A TAGS...

The following are the tags Narcotics Anonymous uses to celebrate clean time... This means NO DRUGS INCLUDING ALCOHOL. We earn these tags and we're proud of what they represent. We must abstain from all drugs in order to recover.

White Tag- Celebrates the first day clean or back from a relapse.

Orange tag- Celebrates 30 days clean

Green tag- 60 days clean

Red tag- Ninety days clean

Blue tag- Six months clean

Yellow tag- Nine months clean

Reflective white tag- One year clean

Gray tag- Eighteen Months clean

Black tag- 2 or more years clean

Purple tag- Multiple decades Pink tag- Twenty-five years clean. Then, we give coins for each year clean.

Infinity coin is for the recovering addict that lives and died while clean.

CONGRATULATIONS ON YOUR CLEAN TIME! Clean time is a huge deal. It's not easy to live in recovery, completely clean of all drugs, including alcohol. But, I promise YOU the rewards are worth it. The ability to repair family, friends and love relationships. The never-ending process of spiritual growth. The new family of clean addicts that get you, that understand the battle you fight every moment of every day. Better health, improved spiritual principles and living honest. Finding yourself... Yes, the rewards are endless.

GET CLEAN & STAY CLEAN.

Everybody with a year or more of clean time, raise your hands!

JOIN THE NO MATTER WHAT CLUB- NO MATTER WHAT, DON'T DRINK OR USE.

The here and now...

Embrace the here and now. Think long and hard about this. You only get here and now once, so, embrace the sanctity of it. Right now. This moment. Feel it. Touch it, experience it inside your soul. Completely encompass every singular NOW inside your being. You'll be amazed how the senses of the moment become enlightened when your body, mind and spirit are completely in touch with your right now. It actually makes time feel as though it's somehow slowed down. I'm talking about experiencing life clean of all drugs. No booze, no anything that will alter the clean and clear, mind and body. The moment becomes raw and alive. It becomes who you really are inside and it feels great knowing you're in touch with that. There's a precious level of enlightenment we can experience when we stop, pause in life, sit back and take it all in, I mean truly take in all of the moment. That's the top of the mountain in Maslow's hierarchy approach. It's like meditation, or, the attainment of the most enlightened spiritual self in the humanistic theory. It's a meditative state and the deepest and most meaningful soul level. Imagine embracing each moment in time with such monumental importance. True treasures are found in this place. That's reaching into self with very special tools not given to everyone. If you've been chosen to have the intellect and the passion to surround yourself with the reality of the NOW, you would really benefit from not taking that level of consciousness for granted. If you soul-search it, this is a really deep place reserved for deeper souls. With that being said, I still believe, if you stop long enough and allow yourself the moment to soak into your personal time and life, you can feel each moment as it begins to mean more. String those together and it's an incredible series of uncommon events that wash through you like warm sunlight on a beautiful day.

Another thing of value I've learned is this... I don't have to be high or drunk to enjoy life to the fullest. I grew up thinking if I didn't get high or wasted, I'd miss the party. Everybody was getting messed up and I wanted to be part of the cool group. So, I would, like so many others, fall for the peer pressure. In time, I've come to realize in life we have to make and own our decisions. We also have to deal with our own consequences.

Here's another eye-opening point. Just because others are getting drunk or high doesn't mean I have to join in. That's called being responsible. That's called making adult decisions that will directly impact the rest of your life. It may not seem like it at the moment, but, I assure you, everything affects everything. The positive impact from making your own responsible decisions may be an amazing result that will enhance your quality of life in an amazing way, for the rest of your time on earth. We don't see that when we're young. We're far too busy knowing everything already. As we grow older, we begin to realize and admit how little we actually do know. But, that level of wisdom takes time and multiple hard knocks and life experiences to comprehend.

Making a life plan with short and long range goals were the last things on my mind in my latter teen years. I played life off the cuff, dangerously spontaneous with a big old whatever attitude and a whole bunch of fuck-it in my pocket. I had what is commonly known as tunnel vision. I only saw and believed what I wanted to see and believe. No one could tell me shit. I mean how could they? I already knew everything. Well, in true young & dumb and full of cum fashion, I thought I knew it all. I look back now and realize how truly reckless that thinking is. Make a daily written plan and stick to it. You'll have a structured and much happier life, I assure you.

I want to leave you with this...

Have you ever really sat back, alone, and thought about the profound and heavy stuff that's happened in your life? I mean, really sat back and let your past ups and downs play out in detail inside your head. Just given yourself enough solitude to ponder how you got to where you are and realize the roads been really long and bumpy and without the drugs... oh, the possibilities!

See, in our youth, we always know the way. Even when we have no clue, we step up and step out. We find the road that fits. We seek the path of fun and we stumble and fall, anyway. But, that's okay. Along the way, we cry at our misgivings, we laugh at our mistakes and then, of course, we make some more. As we grow older, we discover something we don't even think about. But, it happens. We implement hesitation in our thought process. What this is, is a prelude.

We stop and think about things a moment longer. We think about a mistake we made or that feeling of standing at a crossroad. Maybe, we want, deep down, to do the right thing, but, then, no matter the outcome, we move forward, anyway. It's our deeper self, reaching for the pinnacle of wisdom, but, not quite achieving its humble grace. Wisdom is attainable, my friends, but, not found in youthful passing. Wisdom only finds us with an overwhelming, unbelievable and deeper journey through the tunnel of time. Professor Will B. Experienced, leads the way. Through the years, filled with ups and downs, after spiraling down so far into the world of no hope, hopefully, we grow with lessons into the beauty of life. Like seeds in the bountiful garden. What I've come to realize is this. Emotionally, for many years, I lived on a barren, isolated and empty island all alone. No one can pierce the leather-thick, scorched, animal hide, my soul, had survived to be. I lived in darkness, nurturing my demons. I've come from so much worse. I was a rambling man on the frontier of painful destitution and my down-trodden, forbidden ways I've kept from most of man. I'm a recluse, captured, by the internal dwellings of the soldiers that marched, fruitlessly, within me. I paint, I write, I escape from myself. Does this sound eerily familiar? If you're an addict, I'm sure it does run parallel with your sense of knowing.

I know we all seek our own ship at sea for rescue from madness. I've discovered, when a man or a woman, lives a lifetime of pain and suffering, the wounds around the heart grow deep with the pits and holes that fill with the anguish within. The scars permeate and isolate the stream of long ago dreams, far beyond the seeing-eye. Scars are the Great Spirit's, profound way of reminding us we've experienced a trauma or an event that was so overwhelming it left us marked. The mark only serves as the tattoo while the real and true scar travels through the soul.

Addiction has no remorse and takes no prisoners. We become prisoners of ourselves, of our own thinking. The disease has one goal and that goal is to destroy us. We lock ourselves up with our own battle within and so many of us, I should say, far too many of us, sit back, using, drinking, getting high, and one by one we die while we're telling everyone how much we want to clean up. Promising everyone we've hurt that we're sick of this shit and we are cleaning up really soon.

All the while, life slips through us, across us, past us and by us, and we, many times, miss the glory and miss the purpose, set sail, by our own desires... and we die, alone, in active addiction. How many ways can I tell you drugs kill? They kill you and me. They kill people we love and people we cherish. Drugs kill.

Life is a precious treasure, my friend.

Its arms reach for us in the night and those arms hold us close. We make love to the idea of another day. We caress the thoughts of a better, more profound imagination. We linger at the smiles that light our way, the ones we've lost somewhere, and we trudge onward, honestly wanting our life to be different and better. We want love. We want a happy life with no drugs, no booze, none of it. We want that life so much! We reach for comfort in the arms of someone willing to hug us.

We smile, but inside, we're barely holding on. Helping others, along the way, we discover a sense of purpose we'd lost somewhere. We forget, in our haste, how fragile we really are. Listen to me, my life was a nightmare for many years. If you feel that in your life right now, there is hope.

Your first goal is to get clean and stay clean.

Don't forget that. If I can do this, anyone can do this. That includes you. The only person in your way right now is you. Do something about that. Get outside yourself. Help others. Get busy and stay clean. Your better life is waiting for you.

Today, I fill my life with positive things.

College, family, a small circle of friends, Narcotics Anonymous, MMA with my youngest son and breakfast with my oldest son and daughter. I do things with my children and I stay busy writing and painting. When I can, I get in the wind on my Harley Davidson Street Glide. Nothing beats wind therapy. I work around my house doing things to improve it. Notice I said my house. That's part of living clean. Good things begin to happen. The universe conspires to nudge you on to the right path and works to help keep you there. Things that never mattered before like your credit score, it starts to matter. Unheard of, right, but, true.

I have two awesome dogs now. They are American Bully's, Mr. Bull and his savage son, Mr. Bear. Bull is blue and white. Bear is red and white. They're true beasts.

I'm very close to all my children. Hopefully, we'll do some fishing when the weather allows. I have breakfast often with both my sons, Storm, Jesse, and his girlfriend, Taylor and my daughter, Misty. I'm working to be even closer to all my children and grandchildren. My goodness, I'm blessed with 7 grandchildren thus far. Madi, Blake, Alys, Kiera, Kyndra, Mariah and Aurora! They're all amazing!!! That number will probably get bigger. Love it! This is all new to me, but, it's exciting. Life has meaning. We just had Thanksgiving dinner at Misty's home. It was wonderful. It was a long time coming. I feel very blessed.

Give yourself a chance to live happy.

We carry the message of hope. That's what we do to stay on the path of recovery. So, hold on to this. It's good stuff. Don't let it go and remember, we all keep saying this because it's true... you can't keep recovery unless you give it away. So, be a warrior and don't be afraid to be the best you can be! Live your life completely clean and be grateful for the opportunity to make your life better. Imagine the happiest life possible. Now, make it so.

Here's a recovery plan just for you... (Suggestions)

1. Get clean!
2. Now, stay clean no matter what.
3. Go to lots of N A meetings.
4. Listen to other addicts share.
5. After a few meetings, share your story.
6. Remember this, pain shared is pain lessened.
7. Read the N A literature.
8. Pursue a relationship with a higher power.
9. Get a sponsor. Someone who's worked the steps.
10. Work the N A 12 steps under the guidance of your sponsor.
11. Reach out and fellowship with others in recovery.
12. Remember, different playmates and different playgrounds.
13. Do service work, make coffee, take out the garbage, etc.
14. Help others to stay outside your own head.
15. Call your sponsor when you need to talk.
16. Carry the message of recovery!

How messed up do we have to get before we decide we've had enough?

Monday girls- left- Susie, Jackie, Raina, (ex-wife) Barb (RIP) Barbara Jean (Mother) Markie and June. 2000

LIVING CLEAN IN THE NOW...

It's early on a Friday morning, around five. The sun's just coming up. I love nights like this. What a different world I live in now. I live clean. Spirit intact. Emotions healthier than ever. I feel whole, even human. This is new territory. I've been clean about six years now. It's almost surreal most of the time, these days. I wake up with gratitude seeping from my every pore of my skin.

Once again, I'd worked on a painting all night. Some Enigma filling the air, setting a mystical mood and my spirit slipped focus-deep into a four by five foot blank canvas. I walked right into it hours ago. It's not blank now and I was tired. But, it was a good tired.

The last thing I remember was snuggling my head into my favorite pillow for some deep sleep. Suddenly, it was sometime later, after I'd passed out, that I woke up. My heart felt like a bass drum. It was beating so fast and hard, it startled me. The vibration echoed all the way through my chest. It felt bad. Like, straight out of the blue and straight out of a deep sleep, my soul was being tortured. Crazy, right?

What I feel is real these days. Like I said, I live clean, so, whatever it is, that's what it is. It's just more than I wanted to wake up to and deal with. What I mean is, this shit hit me fast. It came out of nowhere. I got confused for a quick second. The pounding in my chest continued. It reverberated through me and made me reach for air. A feeling of desperation grabbed me. It traveled from the top of my head and shook me into the heels of my feet. Then, it hit me. The realization washed through me like fog on a cool morning. My prison nightmare was back.

It started just like it always does. I'm on three gallery in Menard. The gangs inside the walls can't get along and never will. That's how the ball rolls. Respect maintains the fore-front at all times.

After a while, this war-zone mentality works on your head. It gets in your psyche. It's like a jagged scar in your soul and this shit runs deep for men and women. I started having nightmares after I got out. It's about the same nightmare every time. We're all locked in our cells. The kites have flown and the words out. All the cons have shanks (knives). There's fifty, two-man cells on one side of a gallery and five levels of galleries in a cell house. The doors open and all hell breaks loose.

What a way to wake up. After I did my time, I broke my big toe on my right foot twice, kicking the wall and screaming like a wild man, thinking I was in a bloody riot. That woke me up. My son, Storm, ran into my bedroom one night after I woke him screaming and kicking the wall. I was whooping on somebody in the nightmare. Sometimes, I just need to get away for a while.

A ride on my Harley does it for me. It soothes my soul and lets me start breathing again. It helps me clear my head and get things moving again. I work on these paint projects all the time, too. Plus, I'm always working on writing projects. The voices always lead me back to a good ride with some brothers. Sometimes, I think shit happens to keep us in check. But, on the flip side of the horrible stuff, some memories are priceless.

Anyway, after waking up and regrouping a bit, then, fiddling with that painting for a while, adding some details, I decided to head to St. Louis to spend a weekend with my old prison brother Mingo. On the phone, he said he had a friend that owned a cool, biker spot. He gave me the address and said to meet him there. That sounds like a good plan to me. Sometimes, it's just better to get away for a bit. I packed up my Street Glide and right around sunset, I headed out. Being high on life itself, being free, breathing in the air and the pure clarity of it all, I can honestly say, I was comfortably numb. Down the highway I went. My thoughts began to flow freely as the wind danced through my hair. Under the effervescent moonlit night, a blanket of sparkling, shining stars flashed across the pearly sky. The dancing shadows, rocked on stead-fast and moved in unison inside my head. They formed shapes of free-flowing, erotic and sensual women, like perfectly synchronized, nearly hypnotic, feminine light-trails. The female images of energy masses consumed me. The road in front felt good to my soul.

Fluctuating like a puzzled time-teller between the pediment and stony cracks on the highway, I'd ingeniously wired the sound chambers on my Harley, Miss Mojo. I popped in some Dave Chastain, a bad-ass musician and coincidently a long-time dear friend. Dave was singing "Something for the pain". Perfect for a night ride. His music filled the cool night air and my Harley cut a steady path through the night. Right through that eerily mystical tunnel of trees, the band's powerful, steady beat filled the air. Then, out of nowhere under the cover of darkness on the highway alone, a dark and strange rider approached from the rear.

From moment one, I had him locked in. He passed me and then, mysteriously evaporated. My eyes never left him. I watched that happen. In the blink of an eye, this Nomad among strangers, simply, without hesitation, vanished. I let this soak through me, slowly. After all, this was a road warrior who briefly nodded at me as he passed me. I saw this myself when I looked right at him. Plus, I saw him in the mirror. This man had held on tightly. He intervened, inside my thinking, only long enough to bridge a gap. It was between two biker brothers on the road alone, catching the wind. My mind was leaning into the goings on and I was tripping on this shit. Somewhere, this was on the other side of the fruitcake spectrum. Just dig deep in the Fruit-loop box. I swear I'm not crazy.

The Magistrate of foremost wondering dug deep on this road of thinking. Of course, I'd nod back through the tangled maze of all the miles as I soul-searched inward. Staring, through the aging broken window of time. I'd try my hardest to find that secret path we all want to find so dearly. I was, at best, in some deep thought and clean, completely drug-free, so, I had beautiful clarity.

The jagged road unraveling before me proved to be eye-opening in this darkest of hours with a million stars shining bright to light the way. I rolled through the night air with the warm wind blowing around my bearded face, mentally content with the same determination of a crippled, starving puppy, fighting over that last full-dripping tit on momma's fat, supple belly. I stumbled with stoic demeanor inside my unrestrained, witty head.

My thoughts were unraveling onward like a ball of thread. With the warm night and the slapping wind, the long miles unrolling before me, I was finally at long last, at one with my own broke-in leathers and my own scarred and tortured body, in what's left of my own soul-searching world.

I've finally found a beautiful inner-peace. As I approached the city, I drew invisible lines in my head across the endless path of bright-shining stars. I followed the trails in every direction and gathered my thoughts. They were like broken trinkets in a worn-out bag. I stored them in this priceless beat-up, memory pouch and pushed them all in a seldom used empty hole. The hole was beneath my almost used-up heart.

Well, I don't mind telling you, I lit up pretty big when I pulled into the club parking lot. I rolled in and there's my brother, Mingo, standing near a bunch of over-sized dudes from East St. Louis. "The Bright Light Society", said the bright, flickering sign. Shit! I like this place already. I rode Miss Mojo through the maze of shiny chrome and all those fancy, show-room colors, scattered all over the parking lot. Man, there were nice bikes everywhere. I grinned, as I flashed back through what had been running through my head, over the past several miles. I had to laugh! You know how this shit works! Sometimes your brain plays out some wild trips on those open roads. While that bike's lassoing those miles and the soul settles in for the ride, the head kicks in to overdrive.

Like, just now, playing it out on that long stretch of road. Man, I was soul-searching some heavy shit. With dark flashbacks always eating at me, a road-trip was always the answer to the question. It always will be, for me. Man, I love to explore on my Harley while I run through some timeless memories through the wrinkled pages in my head.

So, my American spirit does welcome the adventure. Negotiating with past demons, I guess. We all do that shit, right? Try to figure out better ways of doing things, then, in the end, when it's all said and done and all the bullshit's swept away and you're actually standing raw and real, so to speak, you realize this head-trip's not about demeanor at all.

This shit's about reality. It's about being real. This is about how, no matter how much bullshit crawls on us, each of us, we're all the same, really, I mean, when it comes to life and what life really is, man, we all find that G-spot in the same ol' soul-searching way. We all ride into the wind in our own particular way. We all seek to be at one with the mystical spirits in the welcome wind.

"That ride was nice. Man, it was just what these old bones needed." Mingo smiled at me, with those old eyes of his and we hugged like the true brothers we still are today. He's mellowed over the years and settled into a pretty good lifestyle. Gone were the wild, hell-raising and drug-dealing days. He'd traded his crazy times in to mentor misguided and confused youth. He helped lost bikers and anybody that reached out, to find their way to a better life. He also spoke at Church's and enjoyed fishing in the big lake by his house.

Sometimes he'd horse-trade a Harley project. Every now and then he'd get lucky and meet a female. Mingo's a good old and true friend. This time we hadn't seen each other for three or four years. Years ago, spending those hard years celling together, running together, made our bond unbreakable. After prison, we hooked up and lived some hard years in the streets, too.

Our brotherhood was one that could only be understood by fellow brothers with similar paths and similar history's. We're true friends for life. Eventually, he dropped his street name and just went by his real name. No more Mingo. He was Chris. For me, inside my head, he was still my brother, Mingo. Inside a part of me, I reckon he'll always be Mingo.

Anyway, we sat back, with some of his homeboys and talked away the night. Truth be told, it was more like an N A meeting than anything else. No one was drinking, smoking dope or partying. We shared stories of our crazy past and talked about how we worked through certain things and we talked about how much we loved life today, clean from all the drugs, including that wicked booze. It feels mighty good to stay away from booze and dope. The entire night was like a big old bowl of warm soup for the soul. That and an endless pot of good coffee and we were good.

They were a good bunch of dudes on similar paths and I felt right at home. Eventually, we made our way to Mingo's crib, crashed and the next day, we rode our Harleys for most of the day. Mingo was a Harley man, too. He had a nice 98 Road King.

We rode most of the next day. Later that Sunday, we cooked up some of the fish he'd caught there by his house. Brother Ming does a lot of fishing these days. He's retired, too, just like me. We're both retired from the street lifestyle. I'm happy to spend time with him. He's still got that warrior spirit. But, now, he channels it to help people on the wrong path. Since I knew him back in the day, I give him mad props for the changes made.

Anyway, we sat back and started reminiscing some more. His Pitbull, Boz, came strutting through. Mingo started showing the big old dog some love, wrestling with him. It reminded me of my two big dogs, back home, Mr. Bull and his son, Mr. Bear. They're all thick and beefy block-head American Bully's. Bull is blue and white and Bear is Red and white.

Mingo made us a couple of cold glasses of sweet tea and since him and I'd cleaned up, years earlier, we sipped our tea and sat back. We spent quite a while talking about our children and grandchildren. Then, we traded ideas on 'helping others' and reminisced a little more about the old days. We talked about how wild we used to be. We sure had some crazy times and it's only by the grace of the man upstairs that we both survived those days. 99% of the people we ran with back in the old days are all gone now. Dust in the wind... May God bless them all.

That afternoon, after a beautiful weekend, I left Mingo's house in St. Louis and headed back to my home outside of Peoria, Illinois. The ride back was peaceful. Complete serenity. I settled into my seat and enjoyed every minute. I'm so at peace inside my soul these days. My recovery has given me such a fulfilling sense of gratitude. I feel that inside me the moment my eyes open every single day. I feel like a whole person that I'd never met before and I continue to be very grateful. The kicker... I really like this new person. I've learned to like me. I've learned that I do have value and I do have meaningful purpose. When someone doesn't have those things for so many years and then, through work and time, trial and error and an education in N A that we don't even realize we need, these things develop inside the psyche of a human being and become far more important than the idea of a path of chaos and self-destruction.

For these very reasons, I don't toy with the idea of one more party or one more high, anymore. I've been down that road too many times in my past and you know what, it's a no-win every single time. Something else I've discovered living clean is this. Everything's not always perfect in life and I can't fix everybody. But, it can damn sure be a lot better than losing everything and existing in emptiness with nothing.

We addicts help whoever actually reaches out for help. That's what we do. If we can, we'll help. That's what we all do who actually live in recovery. We share a message of hope. Mainly because we've all felt what existing with no hope feels like. One of the most meaningful phrases I've learned at an N A meeting is this... You can't keep it unless you give it away. The wisdom in that statement exceeds the norm in human understanding. Let me get this straight. Let's break it down. We've been given something, but, the only way we can keep it... is to give it away. Wow!!! What is this something we're giving away, so, we can keep it? *This something* is Hope. We're sharing the message of recovery. Basically, this is the entire reason I wrote this book. To share the message of hope. To let suffering addicts know we do recover. When we decide working to live clean makes more sense than existing spiritually dead in emptiness, we reach out for help.

Do you have it in you to live clean? Do you have it in you to put in the work to change your life? To work hard to be more honest and really try to do the next right thing in your day to day life? Hey, it's not easy to change and it's sure not easy to live clean every single day, but, I promise you, if you stick to your guns every minute of every day, no matter what, I promise you, it's worth it. Are you willing to be honest with yourself? Only you know the answer to that.

Any of us in recovery can share the tools with you to clean up and change. Hit those meetings and meet some people in recovery for fellowship. We can fill your head with countless catchy N A phrases, free for the taking, many of which I've tucked inside these pages, but, you, *you* are the only person that's responsible for the work you have to put into changing your life.

These words are for you, the addict... The addict that's made a complete mess of your life and you've finally arrived at that place, we all know and pray that deep down really exists. I'm talking about that place of surrender, where you've had it, you're sick and tired of being sick and tired, and you're done. I mean you're really done. Many don't survive to embrace that opportunity to be done. To change and find inner-peace. Way too many die. Gone forever. Gone. Dust in the wind. It all comes down to this... It's time for you to make a conscious decision that has the power to change your world. No more misery, no more pain, no more emptiness and no more pity-pot. *Make yourself change.* Do it! No more procrastination. The bottom line is a simple well-known fact. It's time right now for your new beginning. What you've been doing has never worked. It never will. You know that better than we do. It's time to live clean and open your mind to another way of doing things. If nothing changes...nothing changes. The other choice is dismal. You'll die, more sooner than later, without ever really living.

Now, my suggestion is to make a plan and embrace the possibility of a better life.

Why not go for it!

THE END...
Of a meaningless life

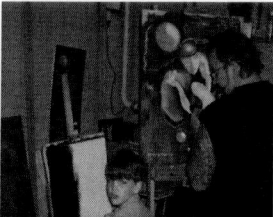

My six incredible children...many moons ago... (From the top... Misty, Jesse Miles, Sunni, Breezi and Storm... (RIP to our son, Elijah Blu, gone, but, never forgotten.

RESOURCE REFERENCES (RR) USED IN "ADDICTION-One Man's Road to Recovery"

I, Stormy Lee Monday, author of, "ADDICTION-One Man's Road To Recovery" thank Narcotics Anonymous World Service Office (N A), The National Institute of Drug Abuse (NIDA) & The New England Journal of Medicine for the following RESOURCE REFERENCES... (RR) Also, please note... Some of the things in the recovery portion of this book, "ADDICTION-One Man's Road to Recovery", are shared in and out of meetings among other addicts around the world to aid in any and all suffering addict's recovery. Some of the Narcotics Anonymous ideology in the Basic Text is also shared within these pages by this author, "Stormy Monday", who is also an addict in recovery. This will, hopefully, help other suffering addicts, their family and friends, also find recovery, and understand better the disease of addiction. To God, my Higher Power, goes all the glory. Signed, Stormy Monday (Recovering addict/ author/ artist)

Pages

298- Are you in Denial?- N A ideology RR
300- Recovery begins with Surrender - N A ideology RR
302- A Journey through Narcotics Anonymous? - N A ideology RR
303- The birth of Narcotics Anonymous (N A history N A.org.) RR
307- Work those 12 Steps - Basic Text RR
308- Sponsor/ Toolbox- N A ideology
311- Step 1 in Narcotics Anonymous- N A literature RR
319- What is Addiction? New England Journal of medicine RR
320- Duel Issues- N A Basic text-RR
321- Pick a Program- N A Traditions RR
323- Enabler- N A ideology RR
326- Spirituality- N A ideology RR
329- Suggestions for recovery- N A ideology RR
331- What to Expect at an open Narcotics Anonymous meeting- N A.org RR
333- Hospitals & institutions- N A- RR 337- Maintenance- ?
341- Narcotics Anonymous doesn't work for you-?
347- Spiritual principles- N A ideology RR
352- Complacency- N A ideology RR
359- What is a normie?- N A ideology RR
368- What is a pink cloud? N A ideology RR
373- Understanding the N A tags- N A- RR

All images except 1 by Stormy Monday
Edited by Stormy Monday
6 x 9 Book formatting by Stormy Monday
Front cover design by Stormy Monday
Back cover design by Stormy Monday
Poetry by Stormy Monday
Written by Stormy Monday
A very special thank you to BookBaby Publishing!

Friends and family living it up on the beach in Florida. Life is good!

(A few of the friends & fans around the world)

IN YOUR OWN WORDS.......

I'm in Russia and own a gallery in New York, Stormy, I really love your work! You have a very distinct recognizable style. I'll email you more info on American flat, and how we can make a really great collaboration happen. I would love that. Thank you, Marina S R...

I met Stormy in Chicago on a movie set. Stormy, I love your amazing art. It looks perfect in the movie trailer, "Blood Money, The Movie". Stormy Monday Art, and Stormy Monday, will be in that movie. We're shopping the movie trailer, now, in the spring, 2019. Filming is in Chicago. Don't miss it! Sincerely, Louis, Producer/ writer

Stormy, I came into connection with you, through a dear, mutual friend of ours, Tami Le, in Tennessee. Her stories of you are amazing.

Stormy, you, alone, having been the inspiration that opened her eyes, giving her the courage and strength she needed to move forward with her life and away from a small southern town. You're a true inspiration to people everywhere, all over the World. The best always, Tracy R...

I remember it well. It doesn't matter where or when we met, brother. But, it was way back on North Street. Early- seventies. We've been solid as a rock ever since. Hard-core, die-hard, bad-ass motherfuckers we were. Still are, too! Whenever, wherever we were, we were having fun, I'm absolutely sure of that. Doing shit most people are scared to do and then, we'd do it again! The road goes on forever and the party never ends. I love and respect you, man! See you in the next World. Believe it brother! Much LH&R, Jim

I'm in Florida. You are one of a kind, Stormy Monday!! In all of your paintings & writings, you express your heart, soul, & mind. You go so deep into yourself to express the BEST talent that I've ever seen or heard of before from any one man! Everything from you is an inspiration to someone out there in this world, whom can relate to

412

you in all aspects of life. Don't ever quit what you're doing. I've loved you always and for a very long time! We met long ago and I'm proud that I know you. Such great memories. Love always, Kimmi Sue W E...

♥ Stormy Monday. We met in Chicago, both auditioning for "America's next Great Artist", on Bravo TV. You're amazing in so many ways. We almost made the show, my friend. Best always. Dara N B/ artist...

On the serious side, I've been, both publishing and reading the many stories of Stormy Monday for a great many years. He'll take you down many unfamiliar roads, but, he'll always leave you knowing and thinking about all the places you've been. He's an excellent writer.
Thanks for your writing, Storm. Biker Bob B/ publisher...

I don't think you'd want our whole story!! We were crazy nuts in those days!! We dated back then and I loved riding on your Harley. I do remember going for lots of long rides on your bike. One day we were riding and you didn't realize your Harley was leaking oil pretty bad. My back was covered in oil. That was real pretty and now, it's a great memory!!! No big deal. We always had so much fun!!! Great times, Donna D P...

I'll never forget this. You walked up to me at a bar and told me I had beautiful eyes, even though I was wearing a tight mini skirt! I thought that was classy. Plus, your eyes. Elizabeth L

Oklahoma here, how on earth do I thank you when thank you isn't enough. I purchased your book, "Soul Seeds", today. As I headed for an appointment, I grabbed it, then, I began reading it, when I first sat down in the waiting room. Before I'd reached the end of page fourteen something inside that book had stirred the insides of my soul. Your words moved me beyond my own understanding. I cannot describe the peace that flowed inside me. It was your words in the book. I know this. I will read this book, many, many times. It will be on the head-board of my bed forever. Love, Teresa K...
Stormy, you're an amazing person, not only are you a gifted artist, but, you're so giving. You have a heart of gold. You walked into my

restaurant as a guy painting a mural on my wall, and you left as a member of my family. You're a brand name and I'll always be able to say, "I have an original Stormy Monday." I wish you nothing but the best of luck and good fortune in everything you do. Sincerely, Andrew S/ business owner...

Stormy, Wow, oh, wow ... I'm really digging your art and writing, Stormy. Always. Kathy Jean... Model

I'm way south in Florida... I want an Original Stormy Monday. "Mountain Home." I'm a huge fan. Creative genius, that's you. Much respect, Denny J H/ architect...

I met Stormy Monday way back, when I was just a little girl... You and my dad, Scott L. Shore (R.I.P.) were best friends and roommates. There was a broken crayon box, incident & we both know how that happened. I was staying the weekend with my dad. I remember, you guys lived at the end of a dead-end street. You were the only white people that lived on the street and nobody messed with you or my dad. Everyone else on the street was black. I was sitting in the floor coloring in my coloring book, and BAM! You beat the shit out of some guy in the living room that ripped you off, I think. Somehow, during the fight, you broke my crayons and they were all over. You did say you were sorry to me, after you kicked his butt, and then, you kicked him out of the house. Crazy that after all these years, I still remember that... I LOVE YOU! You're my favorite artist ever and ever's a long, long time. Tiffany S...

We met at an Alice Cooper concert at the barn in 1971. We were both tripping on acid. You were so high, you couldn't figure out how to get in the Barn to watch the concert. I was so high I ran out of the place freaked out. I was also tripping my ass off. We both stood in the parking lot hallucinating like two wild-men. That's how we met. We were high as hell! After that, we started hanging out like brothers. I remember many times sitting around that big cable spool table, listening to Kiss and smoking dope with about five or six hot foxes. Let's see, Gina, Vanessa, Darla, Crystal and Carol and there was, Billy and Rebel and so many others. We were in the living room at you and Billy's party house. That was 2202 North Street in Peoria,

Illinois. We all scattered like wild dogs after you got busted and went to prison for being the wildest man in the bunch. Must have been around 1974. Crazy times for sure! Btw, everybody I just mentioned, is dead because of drugs, except you, me and Vanessa. Much love brother, Edward A M...

Everyone indulge in this genius author, poet and artist's work. See for yourself how great Stormy Monday's art, poems and books are and even buy some beautiful artwork for your home and/or office! Read his books! We've been friends since the days we studied martial arts together, back, all through the late 70's and eighties. He's thoroughly dangerous when necessary and talented beyond understanding! Much love and respect, Dennis J/ martial artist, musician/ drummer...

Awesome! I didn't know you could rap. I was watching the video, "The World of Stormy Monday." You're doing all the vocals in the music tracks, all through the video, and you wrote all the lyrics. Wow! I had no idea. Sounds beyond great and then watching you paint that mural, and then, all the books. You're unbelievable! Sincerely, Chris C...

I'm in London, Stormy. I love your art. Very classy man. Endless talent! Tanya Artist M/ world-class artist...

I'm in Corpus Christi... I miss your face.... I love you, you're my Stormy Lee Monday.... ♥ you know exactly where we met. You're always in my heart. Always! Ashley N B/ artist...

So, you're quite the famous man in the USA, Mr. Stormy Lee Monday! Best wishes from the UK. We love you over here, too! Much admiration, Ann F/ world-class artist...

I met Stormy when he saved my life. Thank you from my heart. (Nuff said :) I'm forever grateful to you. I owe you my life. Whatever you want or need for the rest of my life. Jason M...

I hope you don't mind that I tell everyone about your amazing art! Stormy Monday Art! Also, you're an amazing human! You help so many people all the time and you don't even talk about it. I love and respect you. Lynette/ huge fan

Hi, I'm in Miami, Florida. Your art is gorgeous, Stormy. I love, love I your work! You're so kind, wise and amazing. Forever, Linda M/ CEO

Stormy, you have beautiful sayings and art! I love your words. You make me think all the time. I love that you can write things that mean
a lot to me, inside. I'm always looking for your writing. You're writing matters the most to me! Sincerely, Debra M/ homemaker

Stormy, I love your fabulous paintings... I'll have to get a print of that "Angel Watching" and 'Heart Implosion'...and I'd love to have the original 'Angel Watching'. Honestly, the work your Higher Power allows you to create is mind-blowing. We met long ago and you know how. I'm grateful we survived those streets. Many we knew didn't. Susan B/ old friend...

I'm in Indiana... Rocking it, as always Stormster! I love your work. Your art has a very free, unsolicited flow to it. Masterful Escapism at its finest... Keep up the amazing work, my brotha. No boundaries for you! Keep' em coming, Mr. Storm :) David M/ air-brush artist...

Stormy, New York here, I'm a huge fan of all you do and have been for a long time, I love your art and writing. New York is calling, Mr. Monday! Always, G Yvonne D/ CEO/ owner...

Hello from New York... Amazing work, Stormy!!! You're truly a genius. Your art, Wow! It takes my breath away. I can stare at one of your paintings all day. I actually own a few. Ellen R C...

Hi from New Mexico. I knew you were good Stormy, but, your art and words are a lot more amazing than I realized. My Brother, we met long ago and far away, out in those wild streets. We've been brother's ever since. Much LH&R, Larry E...biker/ retired Cat

Loving you in Arkansas... I Love your work, Stormy! Your art is amazing! I love you, Stormy. You're truly a genius! This is art weekend here and there you are on my wall with the Masters of the world. Sincerely, Tamshaw C/ art collector

Wow, great work, Stormy! Your art and writing, WOW! Genius! YOU! Gillie S...
Stormy, your art and writing are both amazing! I can tell you're in a very high place of connection. How incredibly gorgeous! Your work is so creative ... so beautiful! Lisa Z/ Enlightened fan

Stormy, amazing art work! You're a real renaissance man! Always, Stephane Z...
 LA here. Fabulous art work! Fabulous man! My favorite artist in the whole world! Darla M/ huge fan

Enjoying life in Virginia... AMAZING!!!!! LOVE, LOVE, LOVE! Stormy, you're a creative genius! Wow! You are. With love, Eva C/ friend and fan.
 Louisiana loves you, Stormy. Lovely and colorful! That's Stormy Monday
 Art! Some of the best art on this planet! Cornelia B G/ huge fan.

You're an amazing artist, Stormy. I live in Vegas, but, we've known each other since we were young. North-enders in P-town! You go, Stormy Monday! I know where you came from and there's nothing stopping you. Keep on painting and writing! I wish you the very, very best, always. You'll conquer the world with all your talent! I know a genius artist and his name is Stormy Monday. Sincerely, Leslie S/ friend and fan.
I saw your show in Austin, Texas... Stormy Monday, you're a world-class artist. A class-act! I feel very blessed to have met you. Michelle P/ art fan

Serene in Philadelphia... Stormy, you have the Attitude of Gratitude. That makes you great. Your art is pure genius. You're a Renaissance man! Gregory L'E

I have your art in Dubai... Stormy Monday Art... Excellent artist! One of the very best in the world. Bahia A/ huge fan of Stormy Monday

Your art & writing are amazing! I want one of your Originals and love your poetry. Misty D...

Fairbanks, Alaska... Great Work. Stormy, I'm very impressed. I love your style! It's so original. Even if you didn't sign your work, I'd know it was yours. That's amazing to me. I tell everyone I know about you. With love, Donna S...

Some of your art pieces are very Dali-esque. I'm a HUGE fan of abstract art and after visiting the Dali Museum in St. Pete, Florida, several times throughout my childhood, I now realize how truly gifted you are. I love everything about your art. You're very unique. You and your art are very unique. Much respect to you, Tracy R...

I love your art. Stormy, I want the 'Weeping Willow tree', painting, Mr. Master artist. Lori L...

New York, New York... I would love to go to a gallery showing of your work, Stormy. You have so many everywhere. Please let me know when and where you have showings, so I can attend. Everyone talks about your art and how incredible it is. Respect. Cara H H/ your number one fan

Huge fan in Florida... Stormy, you always have profound words of wisdom... you're a genuine genius. You really are. Why didn't you run for President? I'd vote for you right now!! Plus, you're so hot and sexy. Dawn A...

Your wisdom and humanity always shine from you, Stormy. You have a very humble and kind message for everyone. You're so inspirational for all that read your words. Amy W B...

Cynthia M in Florida... Stormy, you're so beautiful, inside and out. I'm so lucky to call you friend. We met a whole lifetime ago. I still love you and all you do for everyone. You help so many in life and never say a word about it. That makes you special. Friend and fan

418

Ohio here... Stormy, when you leave this world you'll leave a legacy to your children. You've become an actual legend in our time. I've watched this happen. No one can change all the good you've put in this world. You have no idea how many people's lives you influence, literally inspiring people all around the world all the time. You don't get to see that. A genuine shining star is what you are! I've actually felt the atmosphere in a room change when you entered. I've seen this first-hand. I've seen women melt in your hands like ice-cream. It doesn't surprise me. You're literally so much more than people know. You've known homelessness and you've survived being both helpless and hopeless. You've been there. You write the most beautiful poetry, you're an amazing actor, an incredible muralist, and, an awe-inspiring master painter. You know how to capture and mesh elusive colors like no one I've seen. Your talents are real and raw. They come directly from your heart, mind, body, and soul. You're kind and gentle, too, but, within you lies a fierce warrior. Your books are also amazing. Your words flow from some secret place deep in the soul. I'm honored to call you my friend. Gina Petitpas, world traveler, poet, artist.

Brother in Chicago... We met in the 70's. Packing heat, crazy as hell, bad motherfuckers. We partied, Storm, hard. I love you like a brother. Think about where we came from, brother, straight ghetto and look at you now. Fuckin' gifted genius, man. Stormy Monday, my brother to the end. Your talent is off the chart. God bless you, man. Much
LH&R Johnny Aprile/ brother   (RIP brother Johnny)

Stormy Monday, I've said it before and I'll say it again... you're an amazing person. Your gifts are far beyond understanding for many people. God has touched you, my friend. Greg W/ musician/ friend/ fan
Brother Storm, You're, by far, the best writer I know. The way you put words together is a thing of beauty. I read everything you write. I love your art, too. You're a true genius among us. Love and respect,
Flat Top/ Preacher/ musician/ Safety advocate

BOOKS WRITTEN BY STORMY MONDAY

ADDICTION * One Man's ROAD TO RECOVERY
THE SECRET PATH
SOUL SEEDS
UNDER A BLUE MORNING SKY
THE JOURNEY
AN IMAGE PRESSED IN TIME
STORMY MONDAY ART Collector's Edition
BikerSpot magazine/ eYe of the Storm/ Monthly stories
Muralist
Gallery showings Nationwide
Art/ mural Commissions

Contact DEEP SOUL PUBLISHING @ 309-643-3452, for bookings, questions, books, art showing schedules, art commissions, murals, dances in the rain, laughing for no apparent reason, pondering the mystery of time, sharing philosophical ideas on premonitions, walking down a white, sandy beach, deep spiritual conversations, or, anything ridiculously relating to Stormy Monday Art. Stormyleemonday@yahoo.com. More Stormy Monday Art, stories, poetry and photos on Facebook. "Thank you" to Narcotics Anonymous and the NA literature for the Resource References. Also, thank you for an education I didn't even know I needed. © Copyright 2015

**This book is for the next suffering
addicts... and all who love them.**

The Invisible Me ...

Think about the invisible me....
The *me* you never got to know.
Hold me close inside your thinking, like welcome warmth on
a cold, winter's day.
Reach inside and embrace the traces I've so carefully left,
Tucked quietly away.
You'll find me somewhere inside those barren, dark, empty, corners.
For you, I left them whispering, "Find me, find me, find me". More than
empty words and hollow thoughts, I promise you'll find there.
Search deep through those cluttered areas and forgotten closets for folded
and worn-out papers, telling stories like an old friend.
Stacked long ago in aging, weary boxes
are faded and crumpled images, like memories, lying in wait, waving?
Waiting in earnest, just to say hello.
Memories pressed among the paper...
I left them so carefully, yet, randomly...
For you... Lisa

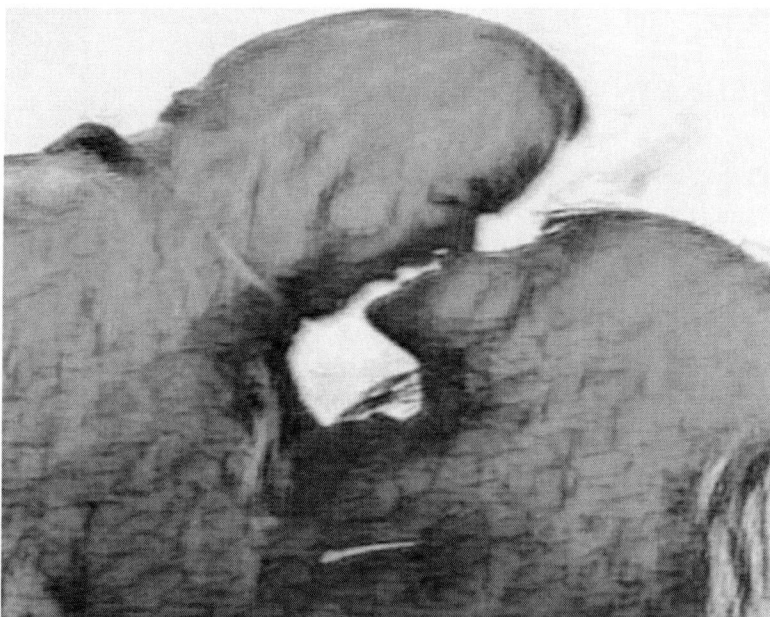

STORMY LEE MONDAY- BIO

Writing, painting, drawing and helping others... That's Stormy Monday. His art, writings, poetry, murals and drawings are who he is. His creativity, since childhood, has been an integral part of his life. He was tagged the "Poet Prophet" in the sixties and for good reason. His award-winning verses are stories that unfold from memories, rich in wisdom, deep with lessons in life and strewn with tales of long-lost loves. His timeless art perfectly captures Monday's tilted view of the World. Stormy Monday art can be found in homes, galleries, churches and offices, around the globe. He's painted and sold his art on beaches from Florida to California, the Gulf Shores, throughout Tennessee, Missouri, Texas, New Mexico, Arizona, Colorado, Illinois, and all through the Midwest, South and Southwest. Monday's also a well-known muralist. He has murals all over the Midwest and the southwest. His style is singular. On canvas, Monday speaks his own language. His work is uniquely original, hypnotic, mysterious and breath-taking. It'll leave you transfixed, captured and spellbound. He paints in all mediums, whether alive with vivid color, or, eye-catching, black and white. His art slips in and out, flowing and rhythmic, moving from abstract to surrealistic, across the realm of one canvas.

His finished works are both profound and poetic. His subliminal themes envelop you in vivid color and leave you screaming for more.

Monday's also an award-winning author. His books include the number 12, Publisher's Best Seller, "The Secret Path" and his first book, "The Journey", also, "An Image Pressed in Time" and "Soul Seeds". "The Secret Path" and "Souls Seeds" can be bought in bookstores, online stores and signed copies can be found at all his shows. Currently, Monday just completed his newest book, "ADDICTION-One Man's Road to Recovery". It will be released in the spring, 2020. This is a must-read. This book gives hope to the still-suffering addicts. Monday's also working on his next book, an erotic fictional story titled, "Under a Blue Morning Sky." He's also creating a coffee-table edition of his most popular Art, titled, "INSIDE THE EYE". The ART of STORMY MONDAY.

From the summer of 2013 till the spring of 2019, Monday also wrote a monthly story for "BikerSpot Magazine", titled, "eye of the Storm". Several of his art pieces will be in an upcoming movie, titled, "Blood Money, The movie". Filming is in Chicago. The trailer is completed and is being shopped now. Stormy Monday is managed exclusively by "Deep Soul Talent". He produces his own showings and is also a member of 22VA Art Group. Currently, Monday's a student at ICC, pursuing a degree in Applied Sciences. He's also a graduate of the DACT program and maintained a 4.0 GPA. He's consistently on the President's Honor List and was also inducted into The National Honor Society.

I remember how dismal life felt inside my soul when I was using and strung out. I'll never forget that. At that time in our lives it's almost impossible to care enough about anything to even want to change for the better. Life is hard when you lose everything. Just hold on to the information in this book and don't let go. Honestly, make yourself reach out for help. Make yourself push through all the darkness, self-pity and misery. If you don't give up and you really reach deep inside your heart, you can work your way out of how bad your life is going right now. It can get better. DON'T LOSE HOPE! It is true... WE DO RECOVER... (With work). Believe me, if I can crawl out of the dark hell I was existing in, you can crawl out, too. I'm talking to you. The universe wants you to live clean. It's waiting for you to want it, too. Reach inside yourself and find the strength to find help. WE REALLY DO RECOVER, but, it doesn't happen with osmosis. Be honest with yourself & willing enough to go to any means necessary to get clean and stay clean. It's inside you.

ILLINOIS HELPLINE
For Opioids and other substances
833-2FINDHELP
HelplineIL.org
NATIONAL ADDICTION HOTLINE
855-828-4583
STOP LIVING IN THE PROBLEM & GET IN THE SOLUTION.

When you're spending life addicted, like the last remaining coin in a lonely traders money bag and emptiness fills your longing heart, life is empty and lonely. The barren halls of weariness press hard against you. That's your time flying away with desperate cries for your once hopeful dreams. Those dreams are now gone and your dying soul screams, "There must be more... there must be more!"

Maybe, just maybe, drugs have taken you away. Taken you away from yourself. You have an absence of self. Your longing soul is crying and pleading for a better life. The one that waits for you, even now. Maybe, the happy life you long for is in another place, in a different world, in a different way. There are stepping stones, like flat, broken rocks, strewn in long weeds and faded grass, waiting for you to take a different path that'll lead you to your happier and more fulfilling life. We all know you want it, but, your soul must reach out in tears, pleading that you want it. Surrender. Take one step at a time, and you'll embrace the sunrise of a new life, once again. Your path is waiting. Do you feel it call your name?

These passing days of chaos and self-destruction are like stones skipping across a calm and mirrored lake. They disappear to never be seen again.

I hope when you think of me
You smile
As you remember

Profound...prolific...prophetic... Do you own a Monday?
A "STORMY MONDAY"!

424